Social
Metacognition

FRONTIERS OF SOCIAL PSYCHOLOGY

Series Editors:
Arie W. Kruglanski, *University of Maryland at College Park*
Joseph P. Forgas, University of New South Wales

Frontiers of Social Psychology is a series of domain-specific handbooks. Each volume provides readers with an overview of the most recent theoretical, methodological, and practical developments in a substantive area of social psychology, in greater depth than is possible in general social psychology handbooks. The editors and contributors are all internationally renowned scholars whose work is at the cutting edge of research.

Scholarly, yet accessible, the volumes in the *Frontiers* series are an essential resource for senior undergraduates, postgraduates, researchers, and practitioners and are suitable as texts in advanced courses in specific subareas of social psychology.

Published Titles

Negotiation Theory and Research, Thompson
Close Relationships, Noller & Feeney
Evolution and Social Psychology, Schaller, Simpson & Kenrick
Social Psychology and the Unconscious, Bargh
Affect in Social Thinking and Behavior, Forgas
The Science of Social Influence, Pratkanis
Social Communication, Fiedler
The Self, Sedikides & Spencer
Personality and Social Behavior, Rhodewalt
Attitudes and Attitude Change, Crano & Prislin
Social Cognition, Strack & Förster
Social Psychology of Consumer Behavior, Wänke
Social Motivation, Dunning
Intergroup Conflicts and their Resolution, Bar-Tal
Goal-directed Behavior, Aarts & Elliot
Social Metacognition, Briñol & DeMarree
Social Judgment and Decision Making, Krueger

Forthcoming Titles

Explorations in Political Psychology, Krosnick & Chiang
Group Processes, Levine
Behavioral Economics, Stapel & Zeelenberg

For continually updated information about published and forthcoming titles in the *Frontiers of Social Psychology* series, please visit: **www.psypress.com/frontiers**

Social
Metacognition

Edited by
Pablo Briñol and
Kenneth G. DeMarree

Psychology Press
Taylor & Francis Group

New York London

Psychology Press
Taylor & Francis Group
711 Third Avenue
New York, NY 10017

Psychology Press
Taylor & Francis Group
27 Church Road
Hove, East Sussex BN3 2FA

© 2012 by Taylor & Francis Group, LLC
Psychology Press is an imprint of Taylor & Francis Group, an Informa business

Printed in the United States of America on acid-free paper
10 9 8 7 6 5 4 3 2 1

International Standard Book Number: 978-1-84872-884-4 (Hardback)

Library of Congress Cataloging-in-Publication Data

Social metacognition / editors, Pablo Briñol and Kenneth G. DeMarree.
    p. cm. -- (Frontiers of social psychology)
  Includes bibliographical references and index.
  ISBN 978-1-84872-884-4 (alk. paper)
  1. Metacognition. 2. Social psychology. I. Briñol, Pablo. II. DeMarree, Kenneth G.

BF311.S646 2012
302--dc22
                                            2011015590

Visit the Taylor & Francis Web site at
http://www.taylorandfrancis.com

and the Psychology Press Web site at
http://www.psypress.com

Contents

SECTION III   EXPERIENTIAL METACOGNITION

SECTION IV   INTERPERSONAL METACOGNITION

Preface

Metacognition refers to thinking about our own thinking. Metacognition has assumed a prominent role in social judgment because people's thoughts about their own thoughts can magnify, attenuate, or even reverse the impact of primary cognition. The present volume presents the most advanced research areas in social psychology, where the role of metacognition has been studied. Specifically, the chapters of this book address important topics in social psychology and are organized into four substantive content areas: "Attitudes and Decision Making," "Self and Identity," "Experiential Metacognition," and "Interpersonal Metacognition." Each section consists of several chapters summarizing recent work on critical topics, such as attitude strength, persuasion, bias correction, self-regulation, subjective feelings, embodiment, and prejudice, among others. This book also emphasizes interpersonal aspects of metacognition as they play an essential role in close relationships and group, consumer, and clinical interactions. Thus, this book offers an up-to-date description of the social psychological literature employing metacognitive concepts.

We would like to thank a number of people who have been critical in making this volume not only possible, but also an exciting adventure. First, and foremost, we thank all the authors contributing to this book. Each chapter is written by a recognized expert on the respective topic. Thanks to the authors, this volume offers a state-of-the art view of the many ways in which metacognition has been examined by social psychologists. It was a pleasure and honor to work with this selection of outstanding authors. Indeed, they produced chapters that are very informative, educational, and fun to read.

We are very grateful to Richard Petty for his invaluable mentoring and for his support and comments on this project. His mentoring has inspired and delighted us through the years, and he has served as a stimulating and admired role model. Thanks also to Michael Serra for his helpful feedback on the introductory chapter.

We would like to extend our sincere appreciation to the editors of the *Frontiers* series, Arie Kruglanski and Joe Forgas, who kindly invited us to edit this volume and provided valuable feedback on the configuration of this book. Furthermore, we would like to thank Stephanie Drew and Paul Dukes, our editorial team at Psychology Press, for their helpful motivation and efficiency. We also want to thank Julio Briñol for letting us use his wonderful art for the cover of this book. Finally, we also wish to thank Bea and Amanda for their welcome company, patience, and support during the time we worked on this project.

This project has been supported in part by the Spanish MEC project number PSI2008-01909 to the first editor and by NSF award number 0847834.

Pablo Briñol and Kenneth G. DeMarree

About the Editors

Pablo Briñol received his PhD from the Universidad Autónoma de Madrid, where he currently serves as associate professor. He is also a regular visiting scholar at Ohio State University. Dr. Briñol has published several books and book chapters in the domain of attitudes and persuasion. His research has appeared in top journals of the field, including *Psychological Bulletin, Advances in Experimental Social Psychology, Journal of Personality and Social Psychology,* and *Psychological Science.*

Kenneth DeMarree received his BA from the University of Rochester and his PhD in social psychology from Ohio State University. His research has been published in the field's top journals, including *Journal of Personality and Social Psychology, Personality and Social Psychology Review,* and others.

Contributors

Anja Achtziger
Department of Psychology
University of Konstanz
Konstanz, Germany

Pablo Briñol
Facultad de Psicología
Universidad Autónoma de Madrid
Madrid, Spain
and
Department of Psychology
Ohio State University
Columbus, Ohio

Jessica F. Cantlon
Department of Brain and Cognitive
 Science
University of Rochester
Rochester, New York

Gerald L. Clore
Department of Psychology
University of Virginia
Charlottesville, Virginia

Taya R. Cohen
Organizational Behavior and Theory
Tepper School of Business
Carnegie Mellon University
Pittsburgh, Pennsylvania

Kenneth G. DeMarree
Department of Psychology
Texas Tech University
Lubbock, Texas

Stéphanie Demoulin
Faculté de Psychologie et des Sciences
 de l'Education
Université catholique de Louvain
Louvain-la-Neuve, Belgium

David Dunning
Department of Psychology
Cornell University
Ithaca, New York

Bridgid Finn
Department of Psychology
Washington University
St. Louis, Missouri

Teresa Garcia-Marques
ISPA—Instituto Universitário
Lisbon, Portugal

Peter M. Gollwitzer
Department of Psychology
New York University
New York, New York
and
University of Konstanz
Konstanz, Germany

Allyson L. Holbrook
Survey Research Laboratory
University of Illiniois at Chicago
Chicago, Illinois

Jeffrey R. Huntsinger
Department of Psychology
Loyola University Chicago
Chicago, Illinois

Nate Kornell
Department of Psychology
Williams College
Williamstown, Massachusetts

Kristjen B. Lundberg
Department of Psychology
University of North Carolina
Chapel Hill, North Carolina

Sarah E. Martiny
Empirical Educational Research
University of Konstanz
Konstanz, Germany

Kimberly Rios Morrison
Department of Psychology
University of Chicago
Chicago, Illinois

Gabriele Oettingen
Department of Psychology
New York University
New York, New York
and
University of Hamburg
Hamburg, Germany

Richard E. Petty
Department of Psychology
Ohio State University
Columbus, Ohio

Michael Ross
Department of Psychology
University of Waterloo
Waterloo, Ontario, Canada

Derek D. Rucker
Kellogg School of Management
Northwestern University
Evanston, Illinois

Lawrence J. Sanna
Department of Psychology
University of Michigan
Ann Arbor, Michigan

Emily Schryer
Department of Psychology
University of Waterloo
Waterloo, Ontario, Canada

Pedro P. Silva
ISPA—Instituto Universitário
Lisbon, Portugal

Lisa K. Son
Department of Psychology
Barnard College
New York, New York

Leigh Thompson
Kellogg School of Management
Northwestern University
Evanston, Illinois

Zakary L. Tormala
Graduate School of Business
Stanford University
Stanford, California

Penny S. Visser
Department of Psychology
University of Chicago
Chicago, Illinois

Jacquie D. Vorauer
Department of Psychology
University of Manitoba
Winnipeg, Manitoba, Canada

Benjamin C. Wagner
Department of Psychology
Ohio State University
Columbus, Ohio

Duane T. Wegener
Department of Psychology
Ohio State University
Columbus, Ohio

Adrian Wells
Department of Clinical Psychology
University of Manchester
Manchester, United Kingdom

Vincent Y. Yzerbyt
Faculté de Psychologie et des Sciences
    de l'Education
Université catholique de Louvain
Louvain-la-Neuve, Belgium

1

Social Metacognition
Thinking About Thinking in Social Psychology

PABLO BRIÑOL and KENNETH G. DEMARREE

INTRODUCTION

*M*etacognition is thinking about thinking. Specifically, metacognition refers to a person's thoughts about his or her own thoughts or thought processes. One useful way to think about metacognition is to distinguish between primary and secondary cognition. Primary thoughts are those that occur at a direct level of cognition and involve our initial associations of an object with some attribute, such as "that car is beige" or "I like tennis." These thoughts are often called "object level" thoughts (Nelson & Narens, 1990).

In addition to primary thoughts, people can also generate other thoughts that occur at a second, metacognitive level that involve reflections on the first-level thoughts (e.g., "Is that car really beige or is it tan?" "I am not sure how much I like that car."). As noted recently by Petty, Briñol, Tormala, and Wegener (2007), metacognition has assumed a prominent role in social judgment because secondary thoughts can magnify, attenuate, or even reverse the impact of first-order cognition. Metacognitive thoughts can also produce changes in thought, feeling, and behavior and thus are critical for a complete understanding of human behavior (e.g., Metcalfe & Finn, 2008).

The present volume focuses on topics within social psychology, where metacognition has been examined in some depth. The main goal of the volume is to present several of the most important and advanced research areas in social psychology where the role of metacognition has been studied. This book is organized into four substantive content areas: attitudes and decision making, self and identity, experiential, and interpersonal. Before addressing these four areas and

1

the chapters contained within each, we begin by discussing some general issues of interest regarding social metacognition.

Dimensions of Metacognitive Judgment

Metacognition refers to a wide range of a person's mental activity. As such, there are many dimensions on which metacognitive thoughts can vary. For example, Petty and colleagues (2007) suggested that people can think about their thoughts in terms of a variety of dimensions such as valence, number, target, origin, evaluation, and confidence. These dimensions are useful to classify the judgments people make about their thoughts. For example, Wagner, Briñol, and Petty (Chapter 3, this volume) describe how these dimensions can serve to organize thoughts in response to persuasion. There are other ways in which metacognitions can vary, and we briefly mention some of the most frequently used dimensions in this section.

Dunlosky and Metcalfe (2009) propose that metacognition can be divided into three primary facets: metacognitive knowledge, monitoring, and control. Metacognitive knowledge refers to people's beliefs about thinking (e.g., "An easy way to remember names is to associate a person's name with a salient physical feature."). Metacognitive monitoring refers to evaluating one's own thoughts with respect to some thought standard (e.g., "My mood might be leading me to be overly positive about this candidate's policies."). Metacognitive control refers to the regulation of one's own thinking (e.g., "Because my mood might be biasing my thinking, I might want to be less positive in my judgment." See Wegener, Silva, Petty, & Garcia-Marques, Chapter 5, this volume). Some of the chapters in this book refer to this classification of metacognitions (e.g., Achtziger, Martiny, Oettingen, Gollwitzer, Chapter 7, this volume).

Metacognitive thoughts can also vary in the referent thought. This might seem somewhat obvious because the chapters in this volume deal with a range of different primary thoughts (e.g., about one's group members, attitudes, stereotypes, etc.). However, these referent thoughts can vary in systematic and interesting ways. For example, a person could think about a specific primary thought (e.g., "I like the proposed tax policy.") or about a specific thought process (e.g., the reasoning process used to form the judgment of the tax policy). In these examples, the primary thoughts are relatively concrete in nature (in this case, a specific judgment or the thought processes that produced it), but it is worth noting that people can also have metacognitive thoughts about their thoughts or thought processes in general. Metacognitive knowledge about more general thinking often constitutes a person's *lay theories* about his or her own thinking (e.g., moods can affect thinking). In addition, it is possible that a metacognitive thought could, itself, be further reflected upon (e.g., "I do not want my reasoning processes to be affected by my mood."). Several chapters in this volume address issues of tertiary metacognition (e.g., DeMarree & Morrison, Chapter 6; Wagner et al., Chapter 3; Wells, Chapter 17—all this volume; see also Nelson & Narens, 1990).

One other way in which metacognitive thoughts can vary is the degree to which metacognitions are reflective versus reflexive. Some metacognitions are relatively effortfully and intentionally generated, such as when a person is engaged in very careful decision making (e.g., a person will have a lot of thoughts about the issue and might carefully and consciously consider the validity of each thought; Petty, Briñol, & Tormala, 2002). Other metacognitions are reflexive, and at the extremely low end of this continuum are metacognitive experiences and inferences such as the ease with which a thought is generated or retrieved (Schwarz et al., 1991). Furthermore, the impact of metacognitive thoughts (i.e., the impact they exert on final judgment or behavior) can also be relatively reflective versus reflexive, and this is conceptually orthogonal to the degree to which the metacognition itself was thoughtfully generated. This distinction is addressed in several chapters of this volume (e.g., Briñol, Petty, & Wagner, Chapter 12; Son, Kornell, Finn, & Cantlon, Chapter 9; Wegener, Silva, Petty, & Garcia-Marques, Chapter 5—all this volume).

It should be clear at this point that metacognitive thoughts vary in a number of interesting dimensions, including also the degree to which they are accurate or grounded in reality (e.g., Dunning, Chapter 4; Schryer & Ross, Chapter 8—both in this volume). A central premise of this book is that this variety of metacognitive processes can provide profound insight into human behavior and thought. Before describing the specific contributions in this volume, we next address several definitional issues regarding social metacognition and then briefly describe the historical antecedents of social metacognition.

Thinking About Our Own Thoughts Versus Thinking About the Thoughts of Others

Although there are multiple definitions of metacognition (see Dunlosky & Metcalfe, 2009), we understand metacognition as thinking about one's own thinking. As noted, this definition involves the distinction between primary and secondary cognition. The chapters in this volume refer to this general distinction. However, some authors have conceived metacognition more broadly as people's thoughts about their own and *others'* mental states (e.g., Jost, Kruglanski, & Nelson, 1998; Wright 2002). According to this expansionist approach, any thought about a thought (one's own or those of another person) would qualify as metacognition.

Although this is an interesting perspective (e.g., related to the theory of mind) and a substantive area in its own right, we define metacognition as thinking about one's own thinking. One of the main reasons for focusing the definition on one's own (vs. others') thoughts is that metacognitive processes that lead to changes in the impact of a primary thought (e.g., relying more or less on that thought) are more likely to occur if the primary thought is in one's own head. For example, the degree of confidence a perceiver has in a target person's thought (e.g., "I'm *sure* that Bart likes Butterfinger candy.") cannot directly affect the extent to which the target's behavior follows from that thought. However, it is worth noting that what a person thinks about others' thoughts can influence how the person thinks about his or her own thoughts and own behavior. For example, Rucker, Petty, and Briñol (2008) found that the confidence people have in their own evaluations of products (a metacognitive dimension) is affected by whether they think that other consumers have thought in a biased or an objective manner about the same products.

The distinction between thinking about one's own rather than others' thoughts is an important one that has generated a growing debate spanning several intellectual disciplines. The debate revolves around the extent to which thinking about one's own mind and thinking about another person's mind are really two different, separable phenomena, and whether one develops (both evolutionarily and across the life span) as a result of the other. That is, do we know our own minds because we evolved the ability to think about others' minds, or vice versa (Son et al., Chapter 9, this volume; see also Carruthers, 2009)?

Social Aspects of Social Metacognition

The prefix "social" is used in many ways within social psychology, often with different meanings (e.g., McGuire, 1999, for a review). For example, one can use social to label thoughts that deal with social objects (e.g., perceptions of other people or relationships). Social can also be used to label thoughts that are originated or shared by members of a society, thoughts that are communicated to other people, and thoughts that contribute to maintaining the status quo (e.g., system justification, stereotypes, etc.).

Another interesting usage of social is for imputing an emergent, transcendental quality to thoughts such that they have an existence outside individual heads, as in language structures, institutions, or bureaucracies that transcend the individual. Any given thought does not have to possess all these meanings to be considered social. Thus, because a thought is widely shared does not imply that it is communicable deliberatively. For example, although cultural truisms are accepted by most people in a society, they might not be communicated to others and may operate without even entering awareness (e.g., McGuire & Papageorgis, 1961).

Following these uses of social to refer to primary cognition, one could refer to social metacognition in similar ways. For example, thoughts about a primary cognition of social content would be considered an example of social metacognition. That is, social metacognition can refer to thoughts about social thoughts. Many of the chapters in this volume deal with social metacognition from this point of view because they relate to what people think about their social thoughts (e.g., Yzerbyt & Demoulin, Chapter 13, this volume). For example, attitudes about other people can vary in their metacognitive properties (such as confidence or perceived ambivalence; Visser & Holbrook, Chapter 2, this volume). In this way, social metacognition is no different from metacognition as studied by cognitive and developmental psychologists, except as it provides a broader and richer set of topics to which one can apply metacognitive concepts.

Also as noted for primary cognition, social can be also used to label thoughts that originate from or are shared by members of a specified society or to refer to thoughts that contribute to maintain the current social status quo. From this perspective, thoughts about thoughts that refer to social categories can be considered social metacognition. There are many examples of this use of social metacognition through the chapters of this book. For example, Huntsinger and Clore (Chapter 11) show that positive affect serves as a "go" signal (treated at the level of secondary cognition) that can increase the reliance on stereotypes (treated as primary cognitions). Similarly, Briñol and colleagues describe in Chapter 12 how bodily responses produce confidence (treated as secondary cognitions) that can validate stereotypical thoughts. Furthermore, social metacognition depends on cultural views about how our mind works. For example, many of the theories people have about how their own thoughts are affected by others are based on culturally based naïve theories.

Social can be also used to label secondary thoughts that are shared with or communicable to other people. For example, in the chapter on close relationships, Jacquie Vorauer (Chapter 14) examines the secondary cognitions people have regarding the extent to which their primary thoughts (e.g., about fears of rejection) are being concealed from, detected by, and shared with significant others. Thus, people can think about their thoughts in order to decide whether, how, and why to share them with others. Furthermore, these decisions about sharing thoughts can help (or hurt) groups and organization in their functioning and other dimensions (Thompson & Cohen, Chapter 15). Examples such as this go beyond much of the research on metacognition as studied previously in other domains, providing an illustration of how important it is to consider interpersonal aspects of metacognition.

Finally, we noted that one of the most intriguing uses of social to refer to primary cognition is the idea that social thoughts can include shared social realities (e.g., as in language structures, institutions, or bureaucracies that transcend the individual). One could wonder to what extent it is possible for metacognition to be understood at a similar level of analysis. If shared cognitions can be considered primary thoughts in certain social contexts, then people (and groups) could further think about those shared thoughts.

In addition to translating the common uses of the term "social" from primary cognition to secondary cognition, there are other potential ways in which thinking about thinking can be considered social. For example, metacognitions can be the object or the target of social influence. Obviously, there is ample evidence within social psychology that reveals that primary cognitions (e.g., thoughts, feelings, attitudes, beliefs, intentions, etc.) can be changed by persuasion and social influence. Several chapters in this book reveal that secondary cognitions are also malleable through social influence. The work on persuasion through self-validation (Briñol et al., Chapter 12; Wagner et al., Chapter 3—both in this volume) clearly illustrates that people's assessments of the validity of their thoughts can be modified through changes in the source, message, recipient, and context of persuasion. For example, Petty et al. (2002) gave participants false feedback about the extent to which other people shared similar thoughts to the ones participants listed in response to a persuasive proposal, and they found that this affected persuasion by influencing thought confidence.

Research on attitude confidence (i.e., the extent to which people are sure of the validity of their opinions; see Visser & Holbrook, Chapter 2, this volume) also reveals how metacognitions can change as a function of different forms of social influence (see also Rucker & Tormala, Chapter 16, this volume). Perhaps the clearest illustration of this category comes from this book's final chapter on metacognitive therapy by Adrian Wells: A number of techniques are described to deliberatively induce changes in people's thoughts about their own thoughts.

Are Metacognitive Thoughts Consequential or Merely an Epiphenomenon?

One of the most critical questions that one can ask about metacognition is whether secondary cognitions are influential in guiding behavior or are merely epiphenomenal. That is, to what extent does metacognition plays a role in the organization, functioning, and impact of thought? Of course, one can also question whether *any* thought plays a role in guiding behavior (e.g., Baumeister, Masicampo, & Vohs, 2011; Wegner, 2002) or whether people have introspective access to their thoughts and thought processes in the first place (Wilson, 2002).

True "direct access" forms of introspection have been criticized because understanding one's thoughts likely requires some degree of interpretation from the person (e.g., to translate from the language of thought to something that is verbally expressible). Carruthers (2009) has even taken an extreme position by arguing that people do not know what they think. According to his view, introspection does not exist (i.e., it is a mere illusion) and people confabulate whenever they express their thoughts. Although the degree of interpretation is likely to vary along a continuum (see Petty & Briñol, 2009), there are many cases demonstrating the usefulness of introspective reports for examining primary cognition. For example, the thoughts that people report having in response to a persuasive appeal consistently predict their subsequent judgments and behavior (e.g., Petty et al., 2002; Petty, Ostrom, & Brock, 1981).

Not surprisingly, similar questions about people's access to and the impact of secondary cognitions have also been raised. Fortunately, reports based on introspection of secondary cognition often provide insight into metacognitive processes and are useful in predicting people's judgments and behavior. For example, early work on metacognition in the cognitive psychology literature indicated that people's perceptions that they would be able to recognize an answer from a list of available options predicted their actual recognition (e.g., Hart, 1965). Furthermore, metacognitive processes, such as students' perceptions that they "know" enough information for a test (over and above students' actual knowledge of the material) were found to regulate their behavior (e.g., by discontinuing studying to take a test on the target material; Flavell, Friedrichs, & Hoyt, 1970). Across chapters, this volume offers a variety of cutting-edge illustrations of how powerful and consequential metacognition can be in affecting human judgment and behavior.

Although reports of secondary cognitions are useful in understanding metacognition, we do not mean to imply that it is necessary for people to evaluate their metacognition explicitly in order to observe its effects. For example, research has revealed that thought confidence can be consequential even when researchers do not explicitly measure it (e.g., in studies that manipulate variables known to affect confidence without measuring confidence directly; for a review, see Briñol & Petty, 2009a). In other words, the notion that people might not always be aware of their metacognition does not necessitate that such metacognitions are less impactful or any less metacognitive in nature. Indeed, metacognitions, like primary cognitions, can sometimes stem from factors that are difficult or even impossible to verbalize consciously (just as the basis of the primary cognition cannot be verbalized; see

Wagner et al., Chapter 3, this volume). In sum, people are capable of reporting metacognitive judgments, and these reports map onto predictable and important outcomes; however, people do not *need* to reflect consciously on their metacognitions or even be aware of the origins of their metacognitive judgments for them to have an impact (see Briñol & Petty, 2009b, for a discussion).

Historical Antecedents in the Study of Social Metacognition

Metacognition itself became the object of systematic investigation in the late 1960s and early 1970s. As nicely described by Dunlosky and Metcalfe (2009) in their historical review and as illustrated by the preceding examples, the initial work on metacognition is deeply rooted in the study of human memory. Indeed, cognitive psychologists have long been interested in people's perceptions and theories of their own memory. For example, Jacoby proposes that memory does not operate like a "file drawer," but instead is often the product of metacognitive inferences based on cognitive experiences (e.g., Jacoby, Kelley, & Dywan, 1989). One example is the feeling of familiarity, which is often taken to indicate that something is known or remembered (Jacoby, Kelley, Brown, & Jasechko, 1989). In combination with transitory cognitive experiences, judgments of memory are also influenced by people's lay theories of memory, such as people's beliefs about the type of information they are more or less likely to recall (Costermans, Lories, & Ansay, 1992; Strack & Förster, 1998).

Of course, people's lay theories of memory are not always accurate. For example, perceived familiarity can stem from factors that are unrelated to a person's actual familiarity with the information in question (e.g., Reder & Ritter, 1992). Similarly, people's theories of their own memory can sometimes lead them astray. In many cases, people are overconfident about their memory ability, believing that they can or will remember things that they ultimately forget.

In addition to memory, considerable research attention has been devoted to understanding people's judgments of their own knowledge (e.g., Koriat, 1993) and learning (e.g., Dunlosky & Nelson, 1994). Research indicates that although such judgments can be based on the actual presence or absence of information in memory, they are also influenced by additional factors such as the ease with which information comes to mind, regardless of the appropriateness of these factors as cues (e.g., Serra & Metcalfe, 2009). In fact, there is a long history of research in the cognitive domain focusing on the subjective experience of memory or, more specifically, on the feeling of cognitive fluency with which information can be retrieved from memory (e.g., Benjamin & Bjork, 1996; Metcalfe, 2009; Nelson & Narens, 1990).

A relevant area that has served as a bridge between the traditional study of metacognition by cognitive psychologists and social metacognition can be found in the work on eyewitness confidence by social psychologists such as Gary Wells, Michael Leippe, and Donna Eisenstadt. In this context, judgmental confidence (a metacognition expressed by an eyewitness) is a compelling argument to convince police investigators, prosecutors, and juries of the validity of eyewitness testimony (e.g., Wells & Loftus, 1984). It makes intuitive sense to believe eyewitnesses who are certain of their judgments. However, as it is the case with other judgments, certainty is often overly high and not well calibrated to the accuracy of eyewitness testimony (e.g., Leippe, Wells, & Ostrom, 1978; see also Dunning, Chapter 4, this volume).

There are several possible reasons for overconfidence. For example, people often have the lay belief that they are good at face recognition (e.g., Wells, Olson, & Charman, 2002). Other social psychological processes, such as postdecisional dissonance reduction (lineup identification is an irreversible decision), mood regulation (uncertainty feels bad), and impression-management concerns (confidence is a desirable quality) can further lend insight into eyewitness overconfidence (for a review, see Eisenstadt & Leippe, 2010). Furthermore, eyewitness confidence can be a product of social influence (Wells & Bradfield, 1998; see also Rucker & Tormala, Chapter 16, this volume). In sum, social psychological principles are relevant for understanding both the intrapsychic processes (e.g., dissonance) and the interpersonal processes (e.g., social consensus) that affect metacognitive confidence in this influential domain.

Within social psychology, one of the earliest and most influential demonstrations that people's thoughts about their thoughts can be consequential came from research on what is called the *ease of retrieval* paradigm. In the original study on this topic, Schwarz and colleagues (1991) asked participants to list either six examples of their own assertiveness (which was easy) or twelve examples (which was difficult). Interestingly, people who had to retrieve fewer examples viewed themselves as *more* assertive, despite having fewer examples on which to base this judgment. Schwarz and colleagues reasoned that people considered the ease with which the thoughts could be retrieved from memory and inferred that if retrieval was easy, many more examples were likely to be available. As described by Sanna and Lundberg (Chapter 10, this volume), the experience of ease can operate through a simple metacognitive inference about primary thoughts (e.g., heuristic inferences of availability of primary thoughts) and by processes of secondary appraisals of primary thoughts (i.e., by validating primary thoughts), depending on the circumstances (see also Briñol et al., Chapter 12, this volume).

Another contribution that highlights the importance of metacognition within social psychology comes from the research on attitude strength (Petty & Krosnick, 1995). Strong attitudes are defined as those that are durable (persistent and resistant) and impactful (influencing judgments and behavior). As described in the chapter by Visser and Holbrook (Chapter 2, this volume), metacognitive perceptions related to one's attitudes, including attitude certainty and attitude importance, predict strength outcomes. For example, attitudes held with greater certainty are more resistant to change, stable over time, and more predictive of behavior than attitudes about which there is doubt (see also Rucker & Tormala, Chapter 16, this volume).

Finally, 1998 marked the full-scale arrival of metacognition to social psychology, with the publication of an edited volume on metacognition (Yzerbyt, Lories, & Dardenne, 1998) and a special issue of the *Personality and Social Psychology Review* (*PSPR*) on social metacognition (Mischel, 1998). In their edited book, Yzerbyt and colleagues combined classic topics in metacognition (e.g., feelings of knowing, theories about memory) with work that focused on topics of particular interest for social psychologists, such as research on stereotyping, and work on corrections from unwanted social influences (see, for example, Mussweiler & Neumann, 2000; Wegener & Petty, 1997; Wilson, Gilbert, & Wheatley, 1998).

The special issue of *PSPR* served to introduce the idea of metacognition definitively to many social psychologists. In fact, only 2 years later, another volume edited by social psychologists appeared summarizing the work on metacognition (Bless & Forgas, 2000), particularly as it relates to subjective experiences, such as ease of retrieval (e.g., Skurnik, Schwarz, & Winkielman, 2000). Since then, metacognition has been an important theme within social psychology—one that is constantly present in mainstream social psychology journals, books, and conferences. The present volume summarizes much of the work on social metacognition done in recent decades, providing an up-to-date picture of this area of research.

THE CHAPTERS IN THIS BOOK

After introducing some of the basic concepts related to social metacognition, we now turn our attention more directly to the contents of this book. As noted, we have divided it into four substantive sections: "Attitudes and Decision Making," "Self and Identity," "Experiential Metacognition," and "Interpersonal Metacognition." Each section consists of several chapters, each of which examines a specific set of issues within the larger topic. Although we have referred to the chapters in the previous sections, the next section introduces them around these four core topics and provides a brief overview of the contents of this volume.

Attitudes, Social Judgment, and Decision Making

Research on attitudes and decision making has played a central role in establishing the importance of metacognition in social psychology. The first section of this book highlights several areas of particular importance. In Chapter 2, Visser and Holbrook systematically review research on attitude strength and discuss how metacognitive variables, such as attitude certainty and importance, can predict whether attitudes translate into behavior and thought, resist change, and are stable over time. In their chapter, attitudes are the primary cognitions (e.g., "I like Sara.") for which people have a number of secondary cognitions (e.g., "I am sure of my evaluation of Sara," "My attitude toward Sara is mixed," or "I think my evaluation of Sara could resist an attack.").

In Chapter 3, Wagner, Briñol, and Petty review multiple dimensions of metacognitive judgments, including perceptions of number, purpose, and validity of thoughts. They then discuss how these dimensions provide unique insight into whether, how, or when people will be persuaded. In this chapter, thoughts in response to persuasive proposals are the primary cognition and the perceptions of those thoughts in terms of these dimensions are the secondary cognitions. Furthermore, Wagner and colleagues introduce the possibility that people can think about their metacognitions in what it could be labeled as the third level of cognition, or meta-metacognition.

These two chapters reveal that metacognitive dimensions such as confidence are consequential. However, confidence judgments in the social domain seldom refer to the accuracy of judgments. That is, in social psychological research it is not common to use the objective criteria of accuracy as people's thoughts often relate to judgments or actions involving other people, groups, political views, preferences, and so forth. For example, it is difficult to determine whether one's confidence in an attitude toward a significant other or toward a brand is accurate in any objective sense. In relative contrast, David Dunning (Chapter 4) focuses on how people assess the quality of their judgments. In this chapter, metacognitive confidence typically refers to the estimation of how likely it is for an answer (e.g., a judgment or a decision) to be correct, and criteria for accuracy are typically available. Dunning reviews research indicating that people tend to have unrealistically high levels of metacognitive confidence in their judgments and describes many interesting factors that produce this overconfidence (for a rare example of underconfidence, see Koriat, Sheffer, & Ma'ayan, 2002).

Whereas Dunning ends with some important suggestions for debiasing judgments of confidence, Wegener, Silva, Petty, and Garcia-Marques (Chapter 5) discuss debiasing more generally. This chapter focuses on the desire to be accurate in one's attitudes and judgments, discussing the many metacognitive processes used to detect and correct for biases in judgment. In this chapter, people's attitudes and judgments are the primary cognition and people's perceptions of the extent to which those judgments are accurate or biased constitute the secondary cognition of interest. The operations in which people engage to deal with perceived biases (e.g., thought suppression, subtraction, correction, recomputation, adjustment, control, and so forth) are also metacognitive in nature, because they involve a secondary cognition operating on a primary cognition. An interesting feature of this chapter is the distinction between amount of thinking and level of thinking. That is, thoughts that produce a bias and thoughts that identify and correct for a perceived bias can vary in depth of thought. Thus, extent of elaboration is relevant at the primary level of cognition (e.g., biased elaboration based on low vs. high amounts of thinking) and also at the secondary level of cognition (e.g., relatively low vs. high thoughtful correction processes).

Self and Identity

The study of the self and identity is a major research area within social psychology, and it serves as an important bridge to other areas of psychology (e.g., clinical and developmental psychology). The self is inherently metacognitive in nature, as self-awareness necessitates awareness of one's own mental states (James, 1890/1950) and self-regulation involves monitoring and controlling one's thoughts, feelings, and behavior (Baumeister, 1998). The chapters in this section examine several important ways that metacognitive processes have provided insight into the self.

In Chapter 6, DeMarree and Rios Morrison discuss metacognitive concepts relating to the self-concept and self-evaluation. They begin by noting that some self-conceptions are more consequential and more stable than others (i.e., self-conceptions vary in strength), and they discuss metacognitive features of self-conceptions (e.g., certainty, importance, clarity) that predict these outcomes. Further, people's lay theories about their self-conceptions and abilities also have consequences in predicting these outcomes and others (e.g., the structure of self-conceptions). In this chapter, a person's self-conceptions are the primary cognition, whereas perceptions of or beliefs about these self-conceptions are the secondary cognitions. One unique issue that DeMarree and Rios Morrison discuss is how a person's cultural context can affect metacognition. Finally, these authors discuss the role that metacognition plays in responding to threats to one's self-conceptions.

Although responding to self-threats is a form of self-regulation, people have a wide range of goals beyond simply keeping a positive and certain view of the self, and these goals often play a central role in individuals' psychological functioning. Achtziger, Martiny, Oettingen, and Gollwitzer (Chapter 7) discuss how metacognitive principles can be important for understanding a wide range of goal pursuits. They note that a person's metacognition is relevant in determining which goals to pursue and how to pursue these goals, and in monitoring the success of one's ongoing goal pursuit. These authors note that implementation intentions, a self-control strategy that seeks to bind a specific goal-relevant behavior to an appropriate context, are not only useful in dealing with temptations and external reality (e.g., "If I see a hostile player talking to me, I will look in another direction."), but also in dealing with people's own thoughts (e.g., "If I notice that I feel anger against another player, I will think about scoring instead of lashing out.").

Schryer and Ross (Chapter 8) examine people's perceptions of themselves across time. They focus on how people's lay theories, including theories of stability (e.g., "I'm the same person I've always been.") and change (e.g., "Going to college increased my intelligence.") can shape people's recollections of earlier mental states (e.g., "This led me to estimate lower intelligence in high school."). Sometimes people's lay theories are accurate and sometimes they are inaccurate (e.g., in terms of presence, direction, or magnitude of perceived change). Regardless of the extent to which they are grounded in reality, these lay theories are also used in predicting future mental states, which in turn has consequences for people's current behavior. Thus, this chapter provides an interesting contribution by extending the focus of metacognition from the thoughts people have about current (primary) thoughts to the thoughts they have about past and future (primary) thoughts.

The section on the self closes with a chapter by Son, Kornell, Finn, and Cantlon (Chapter 9). This comprehensive chapter examines how research on evolutionary and life-span development can lend insights into the origins and nature of metacognition. Among the issues discussed in this chapter are how (or whether) awareness of one's own mental states (i.e., metacognition) is related to one's knowledge about others' mental states, whether consciousness or language is necessary for metacognition, and whether nonhuman animals can engage in metacognition. The construct of metamemory, or knowledge about one's knowledge, provides the unifying theme of this chapter. Among other interesting features, Son and colleagues' contribution is unique because they combine research in social, cognitive, developmental, and animal psychology in addressing some of the fundamental questions about metacognition.

Experiential Metacognition

As noted, one of the earliest and most influential demonstrations that people's thoughts about their thoughts can be consequential came from research using the *ease of retrieval* paradigm (Schwarz et al., 1991). Schwarz and colleagues reasoned that people might consider the ease with which thoughts can be retrieved from memory and, in testing this idea, found that people viewed themselves as more assertive after retrieving few (easy to generate) rather than many (difficult to generate) examples of their past assertive behavior.

As nicely reviewed by Sanna and Lundberg (Chapter 10), numerous studies across many domains of judgment now document that the ease with which information is processed or retrieved from memory can trump the actual content of the information in determining social judgments. In this chapter, the thoughts that come to mind (e.g., memories of previous assertive behaviors) are the primary cognition and the inferences resulting from ease with which those thoughts come to mind are the secondary cognition under examination. This chapter describes a large number of paradigms by which ease and fluency can affect social judgment. Sanna and Lundberg note that although traditional interpretation of the classic ease of retrieval effect has relied on a heuristic approach (ease indicates that more congruent thoughts are available), more recent accounts argue that other mechanisms are also possible (e.g., ease indicates that the current thoughts are valid) under specific circumstances.

The metacognitive experience of ease is but one "feeling" that can affect a person's thought use. In Chapter 11, Huntsinger and Clore describe emerging research indicating that affective reactions can exert an impact on the extent to which people rely on their thoughts. For example, when people are happy (vs. sad), they tend to rely more on their accessible cognitions, regardless of the nature of those primary cognitions. In this inspirational chapter, a wide range of thoughts (e.g., stereotypes, attitudes) take the role of primary cognitions and affect signals whether these primary cognitions can be trusted or not (i.e., affect affects secondary cognition). According to Huntsinger and Clore, positive affect confers value to accessible primary cognitions, which regulate the extent to which people rely on those thoughts. In their formulation, positive affect serves as a "go signal" that encourages the use of mental content, whereas negative affect serves as a "stop signal" that discourages use of primary cognitions.

In the final chapter of this section, Briñol, Petty, and Wagner (Chapter 12) shift focus to subjective experiences provided by a person's physical body. In their chapter, they argue that bodily experiences, such as a person's posture, gestures, and movements, can influence the confidence a person has in his or her own thoughts. As with the other chapters in this section, any thoughts that people have (e.g., in response to a persuasive message, about themselves, or about others) are the primary cognition of interest; a person's confidence in these thoughts (resulting from the person's body) is the secondary cognition. Using the self-validation framework, which states that a person's thoughts are used to the extent that they are seen as valid, Briñol and colleagues explain how other variables, such as ease or emotions, can affect social judgment through a single psychological mechanism of metacognitive nature.

Interpersonal Metacognition

As described previously, there are many ways in which social metacognition is "social." The final section of this book includes examples where the primary cognitions are clearly social (e.g., about one's feelings for another person) and occur in a social context (e.g., a group, an influence situation). This section begins with Yzerbyt and Demoulin (Chapter 13) describing metacognition as it relates to stereotyping and prejudice. In the first part of the chapter, people's stereotypes are the primary cognition of interest, whereas judgments of the appropriateness, justifiability, or validity of those stereotypes are the secondary cognitions of interest. In addition to describing the consequences of these metacognitive appraisals, Yzerbyt and Demoulin discuss how naïve theories (e.g., about perceived entitativity or essentialism of an outgroup) influence individuals' confidence in their own stereotypic beliefs. The second part of the chapter focuses on metastereotypes, or social targets' thoughts about social perceivers' (i.e., *other* people's) stereotypic beliefs. Importantly, this section discusses some of the consequences of people's metastereotypes, which then involve people thinking about their own thoughts.

In Chapter 14, Jacquie Vorauer analyzes the social psychological literature in close relationships from a metacognitive perspective. In this chapter, thoughts about the self as a partner, thoughts about the other person as a partner, and thoughts about the self–other relationship (e.g., fears of rejection) are the content of primary cognitions. Accompanying these primary cognitions are secondary cognitions, such as perceptions about the extent to which these thoughts are apparent to one's partner (e.g., thought transparency) and shared by one's partner. Throughout this engaging chapter, Vorauer emphasizes the role of egocentric biases in close relationships. This bias refers to the extent to which people perceive their own thoughts to be relevant and use them in judging a partner's thoughts and feelings. This bias then affects communication between partners and, ultimately, relationship satisfaction and intimacy. Importantly, people in close relationships differ in their motivation and ability to detect and correct for egocentric biases, and these mental activities involve metacognitive processes.

People think about their thoughts not only with regard to their significant others, but also with respect to the groups and organizations to which they belong. In Chapter 15, Thompson and Cohen examine how team members think about the way their own group processes information. The idea that groups, like individual people, can think about their own thought processes is at the core of a variety of interesting phenomena, including transactive memory, shared mental models, distributed cognition, and knowledge sharing. For example, people think about the extent to which their thoughts (primary cognition) are similar to those of other group members (secondary cognition), which in turn affects people's willingness to share these thoughts with others.

This chapter offers a clear and complete description of these and other important aspects of thinking about thinking, focusing on whether and when metacognitive processes can help or hurt teams. For example, when brainstorming in groups, people generate ideas (primary cognition) that come to mind relatively easily.

People enjoy that feeling of ease (secondary cognition) and, in this particular context, will often think that if thoughts come to mind with ease then the group must be useful in stimulating ideas, even though this is not always necessarily the case. Another important topic discussed in this chapter has to do with the perceptions that a person has about his or her group identity (primary cognition) and the extent to which these perceptions are held with importance, commitment, superiority, deference, or happiness (secondary cognitions).

Taken together, the first three chapters of this section examine how people deal with thoughts that transcend the self (e.g., thoughts about self–other relationships) and how they judge (and perceive that others judge) those thoughts. The three chapters provide a stimulating description of how a variety of metacognitions can play a critical role in the final impact of those thoughts (e.g., whether people end up sharing those thoughts with others or not).

In the next chapter, Rucker and Tormala (Chapter 16) examine similar issues in the domain of consumer interactions. For example, these authors describe models of knowledge in consumer interaction, such as the persuasion knowledge model. According to this model, consumers have knowledge about the agent of persuasion, knowledge about the target of persuasion, and knowledge about the interaction between them, and they use all this knowledge to change or evaluate their strategy in the influence situation. Rucker and Tormala also describe research examining how people perceive the outcomes of social influence (i.e., resistance or change in the targeted attitudes), making further inferences about the resulting attitudes. These metacognitive perceptions can then strengthen or weaken a person's resultant attitudes (e.g., "I just resisted a strong argument, so I'm *sure* my opinion is correct."). In this case, both the process (i.e., observations about one's thought processes) and the outcome (i.e., shifts in attitude certainty) are metacognitive in nature.

In the final chapter in the volume, Wells (Chapter 17) examines social influence in the therapeutic context. What is unique about Wells's metacognitive model of psychological disorder is that the maladaptive thought patterns that lead to disorder do not always stem from primary cognitions (e.g., "I think everything is threatening."), but instead from secondary cognitions (e.g., lay theories about one's need to focus on negative thoughts). Because of the focus on secondary cognition as a key cause of suffering, Wells's metacognitive therapy directly targets these metacognitions. That is, the therapist focuses on changing secondary cognition.

According to this view, two people can have the same primary thought (e.g., "I am worthless") but have different reactions (secondary cognitions) to such a belief. As Wells nicely illustrates, one person might dismiss negative thoughts as being overly self-critical whereas another might spend days analyzing why he or she is a failure. In addition to describing systematically the role of metacognition in the etiology and maintenance of psychological problems, the chapter provides examples of protocols that can be useful in assessing the metacognitions underlying mental disorders, as well as illustrations of the interventions designed to change them. Among other techniques, Wells recommends shifting people from assessing their primary thoughts to assessing their metacognition and separating the self from the content of the thoughts.

CONCLUSION

The present volume offers an up-to-date description of the social psychological literature employing metacognitive concepts. In addition to the work described in this book, a number of emerging lines of research also lend support to the importance of considering metacognitive factors in social behavior. Among others, this includes work on metacognitive regulation as a reaction to stereotype threat (Johns & Schmader, 2010) and work on how mood changes as a function of thought motion and speed (Pronin & Jacobs, 2008). Rather than employing metacognitive concepts to understand new phenomena, emerging research on metacognition is reaping the benefits of advances in psychological measurement, including using implicit measures (e.g., Petty, Briñol, & DeMarree, 2007) and brain imaging techniques (e.g., Fleming et al., 2010). Thus, although there is a lot of exciting research that already establishes the merit of considering metacognition to understand human social behavior and thought, much more is to come.

We hope that the current volume serves as a comprehensive review to readers interested in social metacognition. Psychologists' understanding of a wide range of topics can be increased with a consideration of metacognitive processes. It is worth noting that, in many cases, the metacognitive *processes* are similar, despite differences in the specific research topic. For example, the metacognitive assessment that a thought or judgment can be trusted as a valid basis for action can be initiated by factors such as the (actual or perceived) informational basis of the mental content, the ease with which the mental content is processed, a person's mood and bodily state, and a number of motivational factors.

Further, these assessments that a thought can be trusted can be useful in understanding the impact of thoughts or judgments in a large range of contexts as illustrated by the chapters of this book. This is a critical point because, by appreciating and understanding findings on topics outside our own specializations, we can often gain insight into the topics that are most central to our own interests. The processes that fall under the umbrella of social metacognition offer a great deal of explanatory breadth and, as such, are amenable to this sort of application.

REFERENCES

Baumeister, R. F. (1998). The self. In D. T. Gilbert, S. T. Fiske, & G. Lindzey (Eds.), *The handbook of social psychology* (4th ed., Vol. 1, pp. 680–740). New York, NY: Oxford University Press.

Baumeister, R. F., Masicampo, E. J., & Vohs, K. D. (2011). Do conscious thoughts cause behavior? *Annual Review of Psychology, 62*, 331–361.

Benjamin, A. S., & Bjork, R. A. (1996). Retrieval fluency as a metacognitive index. In L. M. Reder (Ed.), *Implicit memory and metacognition* (pp. 309–338). Hillsdale, NJ: Lawrence Erlbaum Associates.

Bless, H., & Forgas, J. P. (Eds.) (2000). *The message within: The role of subjective experience in social cognition and behavior.* Philadelphia, PA: Psychology Press.

Briñol, P., & Petty, R. E. (2009a). Persuasion: Insights from the self-validation hypothesis. In M. P. Zanna (Ed.), *Advances in experimental social psychology, 41,* (pp. 69–118). New York, NY: Academic Press.

Briñol, P., & Petty, R. E. (2009b). Source factors in persuasion: A self-validation approach. *European Review of Social Psychology, 20*, 49–96.

Carruthers, P. (2009). How we know our own minds: The relationship between mind-reading and metacognition. *Behavioral and Brain Sciences, 32*, 121–138.

Costermans, J., Lories, G., & Ansay, C. (1992). Confidence level and feeling of knowing in question answering: The weight of inferential processes. *Journal of Experimental Psychology: Learning, Memory, and Cognition, 18*, 142–150.

Dunlosky, J., & Metcalfe, J. (2009). *Metacognition.* Thousand Oaks, CA: Sage.

Dunlosky, J., & Nelson, T. O. (1994). Does the sensitivity of judgments of learning (JOLs) to the effects of various study activities depend on when the JOLs occur? *Journal of Memory and Language, 33*, 545–565.

Eisenstadt, D. & Leippe, M. R. (2010). Social influences on eyewitness confidence: The social psychology of memory self-certainty. In R. M. Arkin, K. C. Oleson, & P. J. Carroll (Eds.), *The uncertain self: A handbook of perspectives from social and personality psychology* (pp. 36–61). New York, NY: Psychology Press.

Flavell, J. H., Friedrichs, A. G., & Hoyt, J. D. (1970). Developmental changes in memorization processes. *Cognitive Psychology, 1*, 324–340.

Fleming, S. T., Weil, R. S., Nagy, Z., Dolan, R. J., & Rees, G. (2010). Relating introspective accuracy to individual differences in the brain structure. *Science, 329*, 1541–1543.

Hart, J. T. (1965). Memory and the feeling-of-knowing experience. *Journal of Educational Psychology, 56*, 208–216.

Jacoby, L. L., Kelley, C., Brown, J., & Jasechko, J. (1989). Becoming famous overnight: Limits on the ability to avoid unconscious influences of the past. *Journal of Personality and Social Psychology, 56*, 326–338.

Jacoby, L. L., Kelley, C. M., & Dywan, J. (1989). Memory attributions. In H. L. Roediger & F. I. M. Craik (Eds.), *Varieties of memory and consciousness: Essays in honor of Endel Tulving* (pp. 391–422). Hillsdale, NJ: Lawrence Erlbaum Associates.

James, W. (1890/1950). *The principles of psychology.* New York, NY: Dover.

Johns, M., & Schmader, T. (2010). Meta-cognitive regulation as a reaction to the uncertainty of stereotype threat. In R. M. Arkin, K. C. Oleson, & P. J. Carroll (Eds.), *The uncertain self: A handbook of perspectives from social and personality psychology* (pp. 176–192). New York, NY: Psychology Press.

Jost, J. T., Kruglanski, A. W., & Nelson, T. O. (1998). Social metacognition: An expansionist review. *Personality and Social Psychology Review, 2*, 137–154.

Koriat, A. (1993). How do we know that we know? The accessibility model of the feeling of knowing. *Psychological Review, 100*, 609–639.

Koriat, A., Sheffer, L., & Ma'ayan, H. (2002). Comparing objective and subjective learning curves: Judgments of learning exhibit increased underconfidence with practice. *Journal of Experimental Psychology: General, 131*, 147–162.

Leippe, M. R., Wells, G. L., & Ostrom, T. M. (1978). Crime seriousness as a determinant of accuracy in eyewitness identification. *Journal of Applied Psychology, 63*, 345–351.

McGuire, W. J. (1999). *Constructing social psychology: Creative and critical processes.* Cambridge, UK: Cambridge University Press.

McGuire, W. J., & Papageorgis, D. (1961). The relative efficiency of various types of prior belief-defense in producing immunity against persuasion. *Journal of Abnormal and Social Psychology, 62*, 327–337.

Metcalfe, J. (2009). Metacognitive judgments and control of study. *Current Directions in Psychological Science, 18*, 159–163.

Metcalfe, J., & Finn, B. (2008). Evidence that judgments of learning are causally related to study choice. *Psychonomic Bulletin and Review, 15*, 174–179.

Mischel, W. (1998). Metacognition at the hyphen of social-cognitive psychology. *Personality and Social Psychology Review, 2*, 84–86.

Mussweiler, T., & Neumann, R. (2000). Sources of mental contamination: Comparing the effects of self-generated versus externally provided primes. *Journal of Experimental Social Psychology, 36,* 194–206.

Nelson, T. O., & Narens, L. (1990). Metamemory: A theoretical framework and new findings. In G. H. Bower (Ed.), *The psychology of learning and motivation: Advances in research and theory* (Vol. 26, pp. 125–173). San Diego, CA: Academic Press.

Petty, R. E., & Briñol, P. (2009). Introspection and interpretation: Dichotomy or continuum? *Behavioral and Brain Sciences, 32,* 157–158.

Petty, R. E., Briñol, P., & DeMarree, K. G. (2007). The meta-cognitive model (MCM) of attitudes: Implications for attitude measurement, change, and strength. *Social Cognition, 25,* 657–686.

Petty, R. E., Briñol, P., & Tormala, Z. L. (2002). Thought confidence as a determinant of persuasion: The self-validation hypothesis. *Journal of Personality and Social Psychology, 82,* 722–741.

Petty, R. E., Briñol, P., Tormala, Z. L., & Wegener, D. T. (2007). The role of meta-cognition in social judgment. In E. T. Higgins & A. W. Kruglanski (Eds.), *Social psychology: Handbook of basic principles* (2nd ed., pp. 254–284). New York, NY: Guilford.

Petty, R. E., & Krosnick, J. A. (1995) (Eds.). *Attitude strength: Antecedents and consequences.* Mahwah, NJ: Lawrence Erlbaum Associates.

Petty, R. E., Ostrom, T. M. & Brock, T. C. (1981) (Eds.). *Cognitive responses in persuasion.* Hillsdale, NJ: Lawrence Erlbaum Associates.

Pronin, E., & Jacobs, E. (2008). Thought speed, mood, and the experience of mental motion. *Perspectives on Psychological Science, 3,* 461–485.

Reder, L. M., & Ritter, F. E. (1992). What determines initial feeling of knowing? Familiarity with question terms, not with the answer. *Journal of Experimental Psychology: Learning, Memory, and Cognition, 18,* 435–451.

Rucker, D. D., Petty, R. E., & Briñol, P. (2008). What's in a frame anyway? A meta-cognitive analysis of the impact of one versus two sided message framing on attitude certainty. *Journal of Consumer Psychology, 18,* 137–149.

Schwarz, N., Bless, H., Strack, F., Klumpp, G., Rittenauer-Schatka, H., & Simons, A. (1991). Ease of retrieval as information: Another look at the availability heuristic. *Journal of Personality and Social Psychology, 61,* 195–202.

Serra, M. J., & Metcalfe, J. (2009). Effective implementation of metacognition. In D. J. Hacker, J. Dunlosky, & A. C. Graesser (Eds.), *Handbook of metacognition in education* (pp. 278–298). New York, NY: Routledge.

Skurnik, I., Schwarz, N., & Winkielman, P. (2000). Drawing inferences from feelings: The role of naive beliefs. In H. Bless & J. P. Forgas (Eds.), *The message within: The role of subjective experience in social cognition and behavior* (pp. 162–175). Philadelphia, PA: Psychology Press.

Strack, F., & Förster, J. (1998). Self-reflection and recognition: The role of metacognitive knowledge in the attribution of recollective experience. *Personality and Social Psychology Review, 2,* 111–123.

Wegener, D. T., & Petty, R. E. (1997). The flexible correction model: The role of naive theories of bias in bias correction. In M. P. Zanna (Ed.), *Advances in experimental social psychology* (Vol. 29, pp. 141–208). San Diego, CA: Academic Press.

Wegner, D. M. (2002). *The illusion of conscious will.* Cambridge, MA: Bradford.

Wells, G. L., & Bradfield, A. L. (1998). "Good, you identified the suspect": Feedback to eyewitnesses distorts their reports of the witnessing experience. *Journal of Applied Psychology, 83,* 360–376.

Wells, G. L., & Loftus, E. F. (Eds.). (1984). *Eyewitness testimony: Psychological perspectives.* New York, NY: Cambridge.

Wells, G. L., Olson, E. A., & Charman, S. D. (2002). The confidence of eyewitnesses in their identifications from lineups. *Current Directions in Psychological Science, 11,* 151–154.

Wilson, T. D. (2002). *Strangers to ourselves: Discovering the adaptive unconscious.* Cambridge, MA: Belknap.

Wilson, T. D., Gilbert, D. T., & Wheatley, T. P. (1998). Protecting our minds: The role of lay beliefs. In V. Y. Yzerbyt, G. Lories, & B. Dardenne (Eds.), *Metacognition: Cognitive and social dimensions* (pp. 171–201). New York, NY: Sage.

Wright, P. (2002). Marketplace metacognition and social intelligence. *Journal of Consumer Research, 28,* 677–682.

Yzerbyt, V. Y., Lories, G., & Dardenne, B. (1998). *Metacognition: Cognitive and social dimensions.* New York, NY: Sage.

Section *I*

Attitudes and Decision Making

2

Metacognitive Determinants
of Attitude Strength

PENNY S. VISSER and ALLYSON L. HOLBROOK

INTRODUCTION

*P*sychologists have long recognized that attitudes—our summary evaluations of the people, places, and things in our environment—can be tremendously powerful. Attitudes direct our attention away from some objects and toward others, they color our interpretation of stimuli, they bias the thoughts we generate, and they shape what we later recall about an event. And attitudes motivate and guide our actions, leading us to approach some objects and avoid others. Indeed, a large literature documents the many diverse ways that attitudes influence our perceptions, cognitions, and behavior, profoundly shaping virtually all aspects of social behavior (for a review, see Albarracin, Johnson, & Zanna, 2005).

Equally clear from this literature, though, is that attitudes do not always do so. In fact, although some attitudes exert a powerful impact on thinking and on behavior, others are largely inconsequential. Similarly, whereas some attitudes are very firm—resistant to even the strongest challenges and persistent over long spans of time—other attitudes are highly malleable, yielding easily to persuasive attempts and fluctuating greatly over time. The term "attitude strength" is used to capture this distinction.

The distinction between strong and weak attitudes has been the focus of sustained scholarly attention for more than two decades. Of particular interest has been the identification of specific features of strong attitudes that differentiate them from weak attitudes, and a large literature now exists that does precisely this (for reviews, see Petty & Krosnick, 1995; Visser, Bizer, & Krosnick, 2006).

Interestingly, many of these strength-related attitude features involve subjective judgments about one's attitude. These include judgments about the validity and correctness of one's attitude, for example, and judgments about how important the attitude is to the self. Indeed, to a very large degree, the impact of an attitude on thought and behavior depends on metacognitions of this sort. Attitudes that are deemed personally important, for example, are more predictive of behavior than are attitudes judged to be less important (e.g., Budd, 1986). They are also more resistant to change (e.g., Fine, 1957; Gorn, 1975), and they influence information processing more powerfully than do attitudes deemed less important (e.g., Holbrook, Berent, Krosnick, Visser, & Boninger, 2005). As these examples illustrate, knowing an individual's attitude toward a particular object is not always sufficient for predicting his or her cognitive and behavioral responses to the object. Doing so also requires a clear understanding of the individual's thoughts and judgments *about* his or her attitude.

Thus, the study of metacognition, or "thinking about thinking," has a rich tradition within the attitude literature. Within this domain, attitudes are conceptualized as the primary level cognition—the object about which additional thoughts are generated. Strength-related judgments about the attitude (e.g., how much importance one ascribes to the attitude, how certain one feels about the validity of one's attitude) are secondary level cognitions.

In this chapter, we examine the role of metacognition in regulating the impact and durability of an attitude. We begin by reviewing a number of strength-related attitude features, distinguishing between those that are exclusively metacognitive (involving subjective judgments for which no objective indicators exist) and those that reflect objective properties of the attitude that give rise to related metacognitive judgments. We review the evidence regarding the relative impact of objective and metacognitive indicators of attitude strength. We then review the antecedents and consequences of these metacognitive variables, and we conclude by identifying directions for future research.

ATTITUDES AND ATTITUDE STRENGTH

An attitude is a general, relatively enduring evaluation of an object. Attitudes are *evaluative* in that they reflect the degree of positivity or negativity that a person feels toward an object. Attitudes are *general* in that they capture an individual's overall, global evaluation of an object. Attitudes are *enduring* in that they are represented in long-term memory and remain at least somewhat stable over time. Finally, attitudes are specific to particular objects, unlike diffuse evaluative reactions like moods or general dispositions.

As we alluded before, not all attitudes are created equal. Some attitudes are strong and durable, whereas others are weak and malleable. More specifically, strong attitudes are those that (1) resist change in the face of challenges, (2) persist over long spans of time, (3) guide information processing, and (4) motivate and direct behavior (Krosnick & Petty, 1995). In recent decades, a high priority within the attitude literature has been to clarify the determinants of attitude strength.

Strength-Related Attitude Features

These efforts have been very fruitful. Attitude researchers have identified a number of factors that differentiate the strong from the weak. These include

- *Certainty*—the degree to which people are sure that their attitudes are valid and correct
- *Knowledge*—the amount of information people have stored in memory about the attitude object
- *Importance*—the degree to which people care about and attach psychological significance to an attitude
- *Elaboration*—the amount of thought that has been devoted to the attitude object
- *Accessibility*—how quickly and easily the attitude comes to mind when the attitude object is encountered
- *Ambivalence*—the degree to which people simultaneously experience both positive and negative reactions to an attitude object
- A handful of others

In separate programs of research, each of these attitude features has been shown to relate to one or more of the four defining properties of strong attitudes (for a review, see Petty & Krosnick, 1995).

Subjective Versus Objective Indicators of Attitude Strength

Some of these strength-related features are inherently subjective, involving individuals' judgments about their own attitudes (e.g., importance, certainty). Other features reflect objective aspects of the attitude itself (e.g., the volume of attitude-relevant knowledge supporting the attitude, the evaluative consistency versus inconsistency of that information). Even in the case of these objective indicators, however, subjective or metacognitive parallels exist. For example, in addition to the actual amount of information that people have stored in memory, they very often render judgments about their knowledge base, perceiving themselves to be highly knowledgeable about some attitude objects and less knowledgeable about others. Similarly, in addition to the actual copresence of positivity and negativity toward an attitude object that characterizes ambivalence, people very often perceive some attitudes to be conflicted or evaluatively mixed and other attitudes to be unambiguously positive or negative.

This raises interesting questions about the relative contributions of subjective and objective strength-related attitude features. One perspective suggests that objective attitude properties regulate the strength and durability of an attitude but that subjective judgments do not (e.g., Bassili, 1996). According to this perspective, judgments about one's attitudes, such as certainty and importance, are not meaningful or consequential in their own right, but are instead fleeting assessments constructed on the spot, derived from any number of psychological or situational factors but quite independent of the actual strength of the attitude (e.g., Bassili, 1996; Haddock, Rothman, Reber, & Schwarz, 1999; Haddock, Rothman, & Schwarz, 1996).

In fact, however, a wealth of evidence challenges this perspective. As we review in more detail in subsequent sections, metacognitions have indeed been shown to shape the impact of attitudes on thought and behavior powerfully (e.g., Holbrook et al., 2005; Petty, Briñol, & DeMarree, 2007; Visser, Krosnick, & Simmons, 2003). Similarly, metacognitive attitude properties regulate attitude change, differentiating attitudes that are firm and those that are flexible (e.g., Fine, 1957; Gorn, 1975; Tormala & Petty, 2007). Further, different metacognitive properties have been shown to influence thought and behavior in distinct ways and to arise from disparate antecedents (for a review, see Visser, Bizer, & Krosnick, 2006).

In one investigation in the political context, for example, the importance that people attached to their policy attitudes (but not the certainty with which they held those attitudes) predicted whether they turned out to vote on election day, whereas certainty (but not importance) predicted the degree to which people found a nonpreferred presidential candidate acceptable (Visser et al., 2003). Importance and certainty sometimes had interactive effects: Both were positively related to attitude-expressive behavior, for example, but the combination of high importance and high certainty was associated with particularly high levels of such behavior.

As we review in greater detail later in the chapter, metacognitive attitude properties appear to have at least partially distinct origins as well. After a spate of intense news media attention to global warming, for example, Americans came to attach more importance to their attitudes on that issue, but they did not come to hold their attitudes with greater certainty (Visser et al., 2003). Attending closely to the news media has been shown to increase the amount of knowledge that underlies a particular policy preference (but not the importance attached to the policy preference), whereas perceiving a connection between the policy and one's core values leads people to attach greater importance to the policy preference (but not feel more knowledgeable about it; Visser, Krosnick, & Norris, 2011).

ANTECEDENTS AND CONSEQUENCES OF METACOGNITIVE ATTITUDE PROPERTIES

As we have seen, people's subjective judgments about their attitudes can be tremendously consequential. But how do people arrive at these judgments and precisely how do the judgments influence thought and behavior? We next review the available evidence about the antecedents and consequences of the most prominent metacognitive attitude properties.

CERTAINTY

Attitude certainty refers to the amount of confidence a person attaches to an attitude. It has usually been measured by asking people how certain or how confident they are about their attitudes or how sure they are that their attitudes are valid, accurate, or correct (see Gross, Holtz, & Miller, 1995).

Antecedents

A number of contributors to attitude certainty have been identified. Interestingly, in many cases, these factors appear to regulate attitude certainty through metacognitive processes.

Direct Experience   Attitudes that are based on direct experience with an attitude object tend to be held with greater certainty than are attitudes based on indirect experience with an object, such as learning about the object from secondhand reports (e.g., Fazio & Zanna, 1978a; Wu & Shaffer, 1987).

Actual and Perceived Attitude-Relevant Knowledge   Direct experience with an attitude object may increase attitude certainty because such experiences convey more information about the object than do indirect reports. Attitudes that are based on a great deal of information tend to be held with greater certainty than those based on little information (e.g., Smith, Fabrigar, MacDougal, & Wiesenthal, 2008). Importantly, the effect of knowledge volume on attitude certainty is mediated by subjective perceptions of knowledge: Those who actually possess more attitude-relevant knowledge perceive themselves to be more knowledgeable than those who possess relatively little information, and it is this perception that leads them to feel more certain about their attitudes (Smith et al., 2008).

Knowledge Structure   Independently of knowledge volume, attitude certainty is also influenced by the complexity of one's knowledge base, or the number of distinct dimensions that underlie a set of stored information (Fabrigar, Petty, Smith, & Crites, 2006). For example, global attitudes toward a department store are held with greater certainty when individuals possess knowledge about several distinct departments within the store than when individuals possess information about only one department within the store, even when the total amount of knowledge is equivalent (Fabrigar et al., 2006).

Actual and Perceived Prior Elaboration   Attitudes that are based on extensive cognitive elaboration are also held with greater certainty (Smith et al., 2008). Like attitude-relevant knowledge, elaboration leads to greater attitude certainty, at least in part through its impact on metacognitive appraisals. That is, elaboration causes people to perceive themselves as more knowledgeable about an attitude object and to perceive themselves to have thought carefully about it; each of these subjective judgments renders people more certain of their attitudes (Smith et al., 2008). Indeed, recent evidence suggests that simply perceiving oneself to have thought carefully about one's attitude (independently of the actual amount of elaboration) is sufficient to increase the certainty of the attitude (Barden & Petty, 2008).

Attitude Accessibility   Manipulations of the ease with which an attitude can be retrieved from memory have been shown to influence attitude certainty. It is well established, for example, that repeatedly expressing one's attitude renders the attitude more cognitively accessible (e.g., Powell & Fazio, 1984), and repeated attitude expression also increases the certainty with which individuals hold their attitudes (e.g., Holland, Verplanken, & van Knippenberg, 2003; Petrocelli, Tormala, & Rucker, 2007).

Accessibility of Attitude-Supportive Information   The subjective experience of ease or difficulty in generating attitude-relevant information can also influence attitude certainty (Haddock et al., 1996, 1999; Wänke, Bless, & Biller, 1996). In one study, for example, attitude certainty was higher among participants who had been induced to generate a few arguments in support of their attitudes (which participants found relatively easy to do) than among participants who were induced to generate many arguments in favor of their attitude (a task that participants experienced as difficult; Haddock et al., 1999). In addition, the ease or difficulty of retrieving attitude-supportive information can affect the apparent validity of that information, further contributing to increases or decreases in attitude certainty (Tormala, Petty, & Briñol, 2002).

The subjective experience of successfully defending one's attitude against attack can also influence attitude certainty (e.g., Tormala, Clarkson, & Petty, 2006; Tormala & Petty, 2002, 2004). For example, the experience of handily defending one's attitude against a strong challenge leaves people feeling more certain that their attitudes are valid (Tormala & Petty, 2002). On the other hand, even when people have successfully resisted persuasion, the perception that they have not done an especially good job of defending their attitudes can result in people feeling less certain about those attitudes (Tormala et al., 2006).

Finally, when persuasion efforts successfully bring about attitude change, people hold their newly formed attitudes with greater certainty when they were persuaded despite their best efforts to resist (Rucker & Petty, 2004). That is, people who tried to counterargue a persuasive message ended up being more certain of their new attitudes relative to people who were not explicitly trying to resist persuasion.

Consensus   Attitudinal consensus can also affect the certainty with which individuals hold their attitudes. To the extent that others share one's attitude, the attitude tends to be held with greater certainty (e.g., Festinger, 1954; Petrocelli et al., 2007; Visser & Mirabile, 2004).

Online Versus Memory-Based Attitude Formation   Another determinant of attitude certainty is whether the attitude was formed through an online process (whereby individuals continually update their attitudes as new information is received) or through a memory-based process (whereby individuals construct their attitudes on the basis of the information they have stored in memory). Attitudes formed through an online process tend to be held with greater certainty than those formed through a memory-based process (Bizer, Tormala, Rucker, & Petty, 2006).

The mechanism of this effect is not well understood, but Bizer and colleagues (2006) offered several possibilities. It may be that people who form their attitudes online perceive themselves to have devoted more cognitive effort to arriving at the appropriate attitude, which would increase attitude certainty (Barden & Petty, 2008). Further, people who form their attitudes online may perceive themselves to have based their attitudes on a more complete set of information, increasing attitude certainty (Smith et al., 2008). Finally, attitudes formed through online processes may be perceived to be easier to report than memory-based attitudes. This subjective experience of retrieval ease may cause people to feel more certain of their attitudes (e.g., Haddock et al., 1999).

Consequences

Attitudes held with certainty tend to exhibit the defining qualities of strong attitudes. That is, relative to attitudes held with less certainty, they tend to exhibit greater resistance to change (e.g., Bassili, 1996; Krosnick & Abelson, 1992; Petrocelli et al., 2007; Tormala & Petty, 2002), greater stability over time (e.g., Bassili, 1996), increased attitude–behavior correspondence (e.g., Berger & Mitchell, 1989; Fazio & Zanna, 1978b; Rucker & Petty, 2004; Tormala & Petty, 2002; Visser et al., 2003), and more pronounced influence on other judgments (e.g., Marks & Miller, 1985; Visser et al., 2003).

In addition to these core indices of attitude strength, certainty has been linked to a number of other consequences. For example, presumably because feelings of certainty signal to individuals that they have all of the information they need to justify their attitude, certainty tends to be associated negatively with the processing of relevant information (e.g., Edwards, 2003; Tiedens & Linton, 2001; Weary & Jacobson, 1997).

This effect is not inevitable, however. It is fairly well established that people tend to process more deeply messages that are framed in ways that match rather than mismatch their own characteristics, presumably because such messages appear personally relevant (e.g., Wheeler, Petty, & Bizer, 2005). Recent evidence suggests that when messages are explicitly framed in terms of confidence, they are processed more carefully by individuals who feel quite confident relative to those experiencing doubt (Tormala, Rucker, & Seger, 2008). Thus, there may be at least some circumstances under which attitude certainty may increase rather than decrease information processing.

IMPORTANCE

Attitude importance refers to the amount of psychological significance a person ascribes to an attitude (see Boninger, Krosnick, Berent, & Fabrigar, 1995). Because this construct is, by definition, a perception of an attitude, it has typically been measured by asking a person to indicate how personally important an object is to him or her or the extent to which he or she personally cares about the object (see Boninger, Krosnick, Berent, & Fabrigar, 1995).[1]

Antecedents

Three primary antecedents of attitude importance have been identified: self-interest, value relevance, and social identification.

Self-Interest   First, attitude importance is often driven by the perception that an attitude object is linked to one's material self-interest (e.g., Boninger, Krosnick, & Berent, 1995). That is, people attach importance to an attitude when they feel that their rights, privileges, outcomes, or lifestyle could be directly affected by an attitude or attitude object.

Value Relevance   An attitude may also be personally important because an individual views the attitude object as relevant to his or her basic social or personal values or because of the individual's abstract beliefs about proper modes of conduct or desired end-states (Boninger, Krosnick, & Berent, 1995).

Social Identification   Attitudes can become personally important because of an individual's identification with particular reference groups or individuals (Boninger, Krosnick, & Berent, 1995). For example, even if an attitude object does not impinge on one's own material self-interest, the attitude may be deemed personally important if it is perceived to be relevant to the material interests of a reference group or individual.

Other Potential Antecedents   In addition to these primary causes of attitude importance, other potential antecedents have also been identified. For example, Festinger (1957) suggested that one way people can reduce the negative state of dissonance is to decrease the perceived importance attached to one or more of the relevant cognitions. Indeed, there is evidence that people will trivialize inconsistent cognitions to reduce dissonance when trivialization is the first or easiest mode of dissonance reduction available to them (e.g., Simon, Greenberg, & Brehm, 1995). This suggests that the importance that people attach to particular attitudes may depend in part on the consonance of those attitudes with other cognitive elements.

Consequences

Like other strength-related attitude features, attitude importance has been shown to regulate resistance to attitude change (e.g., Fine, 1957; Gorn, 1975) and persistence over time (e.g., Krosnick, 1988a). Importance has also been shown to increase the impact of an attitude on thought (e.g., Howard-Pitney, Borgida, & Omoto, 1986; Krosnick, Boninger, Chuang, Berent, & Carnots, 1993) and behavior (e.g., Krosnick, 1988b; Visser et al., 2003). In addition, a host of more specific consequences of attitude importance have been identified, clarifying the nature of attitude importance.

Attitude Expression   People who attach personal importance to a particular attitude are more likely than those who attach less importance to the attitude to discuss their views and in other ways express their attitude publicly. For example, people who attach importance to an attitude are more likely to write a letter to a public official or attend a public forum to express their views on the issue (Visser et al., 2003, 2011). People who attach importance to a particular attitude are also more likely to try to persuade others to adopt their position (Visser et al., 2003).

Information Seeking   People who ascribe importance to an attitude appear to be especially motivated to acquire additional attitude-relevant information (e.g., Krosnick et al., 1993). Further, when given an opportunity to actively select information that would enable them to use their attitudes in a subsequent judgment, people who attached importance to those attitudes were especially likely to do so (Berent & Krosnick, 1993; Visser et al., 2003). Similarly, when given the opportunity to learn about a set of fictitious political candidates by reading statements they made on various issues, people sought more information on issues that they regarded as personally important than on issues about which they cared less deeply (Holbrook et al., 2005).

Information Processing   People who ascribe personal importance to an attitude also attend more closely to attitude-relevant information and process it more deeply (e.g., Holbrook et al., 2005). For example, rather than attending equally to the vast array of information to which they are exposed in the course of watching a presidential debate, people seem to focus selectively on information relevant to their important attitudes at the expense of information about less important attitudes (Holbrook et al., 2005).

Attitude Accessibility   Because people think more often and more deeply about their important than their unimportant attitudes (and because they express those attitudes more frequently), attitude importance also leads to heightened attitude accessibility (Bizer & Krosnick, 2001). Thus, the personal importance of an attitude object partially determines the speed and ease with which an individual's attitude comes to mind when he or she encounters the attitude object.

Interestingly, because of its impact on attitude accessibility, attitude importance has also been shown to moderate the relation between implicit and explicit attitude measures. Across two different attitude objects, as attitude importance increased, the relation between implicit and explicit measures of the same attitude object also increased (Karpinski, Steinman, & Hilton, 2005).

Affective Reactions   Attaching importance to an attitude also has affective consequences. For example, when confronted with a counterattitudinal persuasive message, individuals high in attitude importance tend to experience more intense negative affect (Zuwerink & Devine, 1996). Furthermore, negative affect has been shown to mediate partially the relation between attitude importance and resistance to attitude change, suggesting that attitude importance confers resistance to persuasion, in part, through affective processes.

PERCEIVED KNOWLEDGE

Perceived knowledge refers to an individual's subjective sense of the amount of knowledge he or she has stored in memory about an object. It is typically assessed through self-reports of attitude-relevant knowledge (e.g., Davidson, Yantis, Norwood, & Montano, 1985; Wood, 1982).

Antecedents

Objective Knowledge   It is tempting to assume that perceived knowledge is largely a function of the amount of information one actually possesses about an attitude object. In fact, however, subjective and objective knowledge are only weakly associated (e.g., Krosnick et al., 1993; Radecki & Jaccard, 1995), suggesting that objective knowledge is not the only cause of perceived knowledge. In fact, the existing evidence suggests that the relation between objective and perceived knowledge is rather complex.

It is clear, for example, that acquiring new knowledge can increase perceptions of knowledgeability, particularly when the new information is complex (i.e., relevant to distinct dimensions of the attitude object) and evaluatively consistency (Fabrigar, et al., 2006; Smith et al., 2008). But acquiring new knowledge does not inevitably increase perceived knowledge. In fact, acquiring unusual new information can actually reduce perceived knowledge (Kruger & Dunning, 1999; Rucker, Lee, & Briñol, 2010). Further, perceived knowledge can be influenced by the amount of information learned about a different topic. Gaining a large amount of information about an unrelated attitude object can reduce the degree to which individuals feel knowledgeable about a target attitude object (Tormala & Petty, 2007).

Elaboration   Perceived knowledge can also be influenced by variables independently of objective knowledge. For example, inducing people to think deeply about an attitude object can increase perceived knowledge about the object, even controlling for objective amounts of knowledge (Smith et al., 2008).

Context   The context can also influence perceived knowledge. For example, perceptions of other people's knowledgeability about an attitude object is associated with one's own perceived knowledge: People who rate their peers as knowledgeable also tend to rate themselves as more knowledgeable, even controlling for objective knowledge (Radecki & Jaccard, 1995). As we have already seen, knowledge about other issues can influence perceived knowledge about a target issue (Tormala & Petty, 2007). Gaining information about an unrelated issue can yield a contrast effect whereby perceived knowledge about a target issue is reduced.

Importance   Other variables may directly influence both objective and perceived knowledge. For example, attitude importance has been shown to influence objective and perceived knowledge, such that greater importance leads to the acquisition of actual knowledge (Holbrook et al., 2005) and greater perceived knowledge (Radecki and Jaccard, 1995).

Consequences

Attitudes perceived to be supported by a large store of knowledge have many of the consequences for behavior and cognition that are associated with attitude strength more generally. For example, several studies have shown that perceived knowledge is positively associated with the likelihood of acting in attitude-congruent ways (e.g., Ahmed, 1993; Visser, 1998) and expressing one's views publicly (e.g., Holbrook & Krosnick, 2005).

Exposure to Information   Perceived knowledge may also guide other behaviors, such as choosing to acquire additional information about the issue. For example, Radecki and Jaccard (1995) found that people low in perceived knowledge about an issue sought out more information about that issue than people high in perceived knowledge. Holbrook and Krosnick (2005) also found that people low in perceived knowledge sought out information about that issue, but only among respondents for whom the issue was personally important.

Resistance to Persuasion   Evidence regarding resistance to attitude change has been mixed. Some findings suggest that feeling knowledgeable about an attitude renders people less susceptible to change in response to attitude-relevant information (e.g., Visser, 1998) or introspection (e.g., Wilson, Kraft, & Dunn, 1989), but other investigations have failed to detect a relation between perceived knowledge and susceptibility to attitude change (e.g., Holbrook & Krosnick, 2005).

Overconfidence   Perceived knowledge can sometimes lead to overconfidence, with implications for other behaviors. For example, participants high in perceived knowledge about an issue are more likely to guess the answers to difficult questions about the issue rather than admit ignorance (Bradley, 1981). They are more likely to engage in risky behavior, perhaps because they believe their knowledgeability will allow them to avoid the potential risks (Jaccard, Dodge, & Guilamo-Ramos, 2005).

Hostile Media Phenomenon   Perceived knowledge may also be associated with perceptions of attitude-relevant stimuli, such as media coverage of the issue. For example, Vallone, Ross, and Lepper (1985) found that participants who perceived themselves to be more knowledgeable were more likely to perceive specific news stories as biased against their own opinions. However, several researchers have found that perceived knowledge was unassociated with more general perceptions of bias in media coverage of the issue (e.g., Holbrook & Krosnick, 2005; Visser, 1998).

Certainty   Finally, perceived knowledge about an attitude object may also influence other subjective judgments, such as attitude certainty. For example, Smith and his colleagues (2008) found that perceived knowledge fully mediated the effect of objective knowledge on attitude certainty. Perceived knowledge also partly mediated the effect of elaboration on certainty.

SUBJECTIVE AMBIVALENCE

Ambivalence refers to the degree to which a person has both favorable and unfavorable reactions to an object (see Thompson, Zanna, & Griffin, 1995). Subjective ambivalence refers specifically to the degree to which individuals perceive their attitudes to be evaluatively mixed. For example, to assess subjective ambivalence, Priester and Petty (1996) asked participants to report the extent to which they felt conflicted, indecisive, and mixed reactions toward an object.

Antecedents

Conflicting Evaluative Reactions   Not surprisingly, a strong predictor of subjective ambivalence is the copresence of positive and negative reactions toward an object. A number of different formulae have been suggested for combining independent indices of positivity and negativity to capture the subjective experience of ambivalence (see Priester & Petty, 1996; Thompson et al., 1995, for reviews). Although these formulae are based on slightly different assumptions about how the conflicting reactions influence ambivalence, they are typically highly correlated, and they are fairly strong predictors of subjective ambivalence (e.g., Preister & Petty, 1996; Thompson et al., 1995). Subjective ambivalence is especially strong when an individual's positive and negative reactions to an attitude object are both highly accessible and for people who are high in the preference for consistency (Newby-Clark, McGregor, & Zanna, 2002).

Interestingly, however, a number of studies have demonstrated that the copresence of positivity and negativity toward an attitude object is far from a perfect predictor of subjective ambivalence. For example, Thompson et al. (1995) measured positive reactions, negative reactions, and subjective ambivalence toward an object and used various calculations of ambivalence to predict subjective ambivalence. The relations between subjective ambivalence and the various combinations of positivity and negativity were moderate in size, with correlations ranging from .21 to .40.

Priester and Petty (1996) made similar comparisons, in this case manipulating rather than measuring people's positive and negative reactions to an attitude object. They, too, found that the copresence of positivity and negativity was only moderately associated with subjective ambivalence, with correlations ranging from .36 to .52. This evidence suggests that a substantial amount of variance in the subjective experience of ambivalence is attributable to other factors, and a growing body of evidence has begun to identify some of these antecedents.

Interpersonal Attitude Conflict   Although traditionally conceptualized as intrapsychic evaluative tension, recent evidence suggests that the subjective experience of ambivalence can also arise from *interpersonal* evaluative tension (Priester & Petty, 2001). That is, even when their own reactions to an object are unambiguously positive or negative, people can nonetheless experience ambivalence if important others hold views that are discrepant from their own. Conversely, attitude discrepancies with a disliked other reduce subjective ambivalence (Priester & Petty, 2001). Thus, ambivalence can arise from social as well as intrapsychic evaluative conflict.

Anticipated Conflicting Reactions

Another contributor to subjective ambivalence is the anticipation of conflicting reactions to an attitude object. For example, people with predominantly favorable reactions to a consumer product can nonetheless experience some degree of ambivalence if they anticipate that there may be negative information about the product of which they are unaware (Priester, Petty, & Park, 2007).

Doubt About Attitude Bases   When people are motivated to think carefully about an attitude object and perceive themselves to have based their attitudes on the source of a message rather than on the substance of the arguments presented, they experience greater ambivalence (Tormala & DeSensi, 2008). This may be due to the anticipation of conflicting reactions: Because their attitudes were not based on substantive information about the attitude object, they may anticipate that conflicting information that they have failed to take into consideration may exist.

Implementational Mind-Set   In the study of goal pursuit, researchers have long differentiated between deliberative and implementational mind-sets (e.g., Gollwitzer, 1990; Gollwitzer & Bayer, 1999). People tend to adopt a deliberative mind-set initially, objectively considering the various courses of action available to them. Eventually, though, they typically transition to an implementational mind-set, which discourages continued consideration of alternative courses of action and encourages a selective, goal-congruent analysis of information. These mind-sets have been shown to influence subjective ambivalence: As people transition into an implementational mind-set, they experience less subjective ambivalence, even toward objects that are unrelated to their current goal pursuit (Henderson, de Liver, & Gollwitzer, 2008).

Consequences

A large literature confirms that, subjectively, ambivalent attitudes tend to exhibit many of the defining qualities of weak attitudes. Relative to unconflicted attitudes, they are less predictive of behavior (e.g., Armitage & Conner, 2000; Conner et al., 2002), less stable over time (e.g., Armitage & Conner, 2000), less resistant to persuasion (e.g., Armitage & Conner, 2000; Visser & Mirabile, 2004), and less accessible in memory (e.g., Bargh, Chaiken, Govender, & Pratto, 1992; Krosnick, 1989).

Subjective ambivalence has also been shown to regulate information processing. Specifically, some research has shown that ambivalence increases the depth with which individuals process attitude-relevant information, presumably in an effort to resolve the experience of evaluative conflict (e.g., Maio, Bell, & Esses, 1996). But more recent work has demonstrated that ambivalence can increase *or* decrease the depth of information processing, depending on whether people anticipate that the information is likely to reduce ambivalence (Clark, Wegener, & Fabrigar, 2008). Specifically, subjective ambivalence has been shown to increase the depth with which participants process proattitudinal persuasive messages, but decrease the depth with which counterattitudinal messages are processed. Further, the impact of ambivalence on information processing appears to be driven by perceptions of the likely impact of the information on people's levels of ambivalence.

Objective Versus Metacognitive Indices of Ambivalence   Our focus in this chapter has been on the subjective experience of ambivalence, which, as we noted earlier, is partly a function of objective ambivalence. It is worth noting that at least one set of studies has directly examined the impact of subjective ambivalence on various attitude effects while statistically controlling for the impact of objective ambivalence (Holbrook & Krosnick, 2005). This investigation demonstrated that subjective ambivalence strongly predicts a wide range of outcomes, above and beyond an objective index of ambivalence. In fact, subjective ambivalence predicted some outcomes that objective ambivalence did not predict.

For example, across two different attitude objects, subjective and objective ambivalence each accounted for unique variance in resistance to attitude change. But only subjective ambivalence predicted unique variance in people's interest in receiving additional information about the target attitudes, and only subjective ambivalence predicted unique variance in the frequency with which people actively selected attitude-relevant information when given a choice of information to receive. In both cases, greater subjective ambivalence was related to less interest in attitude-relevant information, presumably because the information was not perceived to be likely to reduce ambivalence. Also, subjective ambivalence (but not objective ambivalence) uniquely regulated the impact of particular policy discrepancies on candidate preferences. Individuals who were relatively unconflicted about the issue were more likely to use that issue as a basis for evaluating the candidate than those who experienced more conflict.

REMAINING ISSUES AND DIRECTIONS FOR FUTURE RESEARCH

A wealth of evidence attests to the critical role of metacognition in regulating the impact of attitudes on thought and behavior. Yet, much remains to be learned. We conclude by considering some of the remaining challenges and opportunities for future research.

Clarifying Causal Relations

Great strides have been made in recent years in documenting the causal mechanisms through which many of the strength-related metacognitions operate, but more work remains to be done in this area. Continued efforts to clarify the particular cognitive, affective, and behavioral processes by which these judgments exert their influence will further refine our understanding of attitudes and their effects.

Of course, efforts to elucidate the causal processes by which strength-related attitude features exert their influence will be particularly compelling if they incorporate experimental manipulations of the various factors. Although a growing body of research in this area has employed such manipulations, much of the existing evidence is correlational. Greater reliance on experimental designs will be important in future efforts to clarify the causal processes by which facets of attitude strength operate.

Almost certainly, the causal pathways through which these various metacognitive judgments exert their effects are partially overlapping. Indeed, as we have already seen, metacognitive judgments of one type (e.g., perceived knowledge) sometimes serve as antecedents of others (e.g., attitude certainty). Thus, a careful delineation of the causal mechanism by which these metacognitive judgments operate is likely to yield a more integrated understanding of the broad umbrella of strength-related attitude processes.

Work of this sort may also consolidate apparently disparate effects. Because much of the research on attitude strength has involved examinations of individual strength-related features in isolation, there may be overlap among strength-related features that has gone undetected. It may be, for example, that effects attributed to one feature are in fact driven by another factor with which it is correlated. It may be possible, then, to account more parsimoniously for the workings of strength-related attitude features.

Interactions Among Metacognitive Factors

Another fruitful direction for future research involves greater attention to the ways that various strength-related attitude features interact to produce cognitive and behavioral outcomes. For example, attitude importance and attitude certainty have both been shown to predict attitude-congruent behavior, but the combination of high importance and high certainty has been found to produce especially pronounced increases in attitude-expressive behaviors (Visser et al., 2003). Further work of this sort is likely to yield additional insights regarding the conditional effects of the various strength-related features on thought and behavior.

More importantly, elucidating interactions among strength-related features may change our conceptualizations of particular features. Recently, for example, Clarkson, Tormala, and Rucker (2008) have demonstrated that the impact of attitude certainty on resistance to attitude change depends on the degree of ambivalence. In a series of studies, they found that to the extent that people are not conflicted about an attitude object, certainty reduces susceptibility to attitude change, consistent with a great deal of past research. But to the extent that people hold ambivalent attitudes toward the object, certainty increases susceptibility to attitude change. On the basis of these data, Clarkson and colleagues have advocated a new conceptualization of attitude certainty: Rather than invariably strengthening an attitude, they propose, attitude certainty may amplify the dominant effect of the attitude on thought and behavior.

This provocative investigation illustrates the potential value of systematically documenting the interactive effects of various strength-related attitude features. Doing so may clarify the conceptual nature and psychological workings of these features, further refining our understanding of attitudes and attitude strength.

Dimensionality of Metacognitive Attitude Judgments

Attitude certainty has typically been conceptualized as a unitary construct, but recent evidence suggests instead that, in fact, it can be meaningfully decomposed into two distinct factors: attitude clarity and attitude correctness (Petrocelli et al., 2007). Whereas the former refers to the subjective sense of knowing precisely what one's attitude is toward a given object, the latter refers to the subjective sense of confidence in the validity of one's attitude. Although these metacognitive judgments tend to be correlated, they have been shown to load onto separate factors in both exploratory and confirmatory factor analyses. More critically, they have at least some unique antecedents and each explains unique variance in resistance to attitude change. This suggests that there is utility in distinguishing between these two facets of attitude certainty.

It is possible that other strength-related attitude features are also multidimensional. For example, attitude importance has typically been considered a unitary construct that arises from three potential antecedents (self-interest, social identification, and value relevance) and that sets into motion an array of cognitive, affective, and behavioral outcomes. But it may be worth entertaining the possibility that attitude importance is instead a multidimensional construct. That is, the precise nature of attitude importance and the particular consequences that it produces may depend on the specific antecedent that gave rise to it. Attitude importance driven by value relevance may be conceptually distinct from attitude importance due to a link between an attitude object and one's material interests. Both may be distinct from attitude importance that results from identification with a reference group or individuals. Each of these facets of attitude importance may elicit somewhat different motivations: to protect the attitude that expresses one's core values unwaveringly, to strive to hold the objectively correct attitude toward the object that impinges on one's self-interest, and to remain in step with important others with regard to the attitudes that they deem important.

CONCLUSION

In 1935, Gordon Allport famously described the attitude as "the most distinctive and indispensable concept in contemporary American social psychology" (p. 198). According to Allport, attitudes powerfully shape virtually all aspects of social thought and behavior.

With the benefit of 75 years of sustained scholarship on the attitude construct, we now recognize that Allport was telling only half of the story. Attitudes often do exert a profound impact on thought and behavior, but they do so only when they are strong. As we have seen, whether an attitude is strong or weak depends to a substantial degree on a set of metacognitive judgments about the attitude: how confident one is that the attitude is correct, how much personal importance is ascribed to the attitude, how much knowledge the attitude is perceived to be based on, and how conflicted one feels about the attitude object. To predict a person's cognitive and behavioral responses to an object accurately, therefore, it is essential to know not only his or her attitude toward the object, but also a broad set of metacognitive judgments about the attitude.

NOTE

1. Although conceptualized as a metacognitive judgment about the importance of one's attitude toward an object, most scholars have measured the personal importance of the object per se, on the presumption that the latter is a more straightforward judgment for individuals to render and is in practice interchangeable with the former (see Boninger, Krosnick, Berent, & Fabrigar, 1995). Indeed, reports of the importance of the attitude *object* have been found to be extremely strongly correlated with reports

of the importance of the attitude itself. For example, in one set of studies across a variety of attitude objects, the median correlation between the two constructs was .94 after correcting for random and systematic measurement error (Fabrigar & Krosnick, 1993). Nonetheless, other scholars have advocated distinguishing between the two, pointing to evidence that perceiving an *object* as important tends to inspire objective processing of object-relevant information, whereas perceiving a particular attitude toward the object as important (i.e., deeming it important to evaluate the object favorably) can inspire biased processing (see Petty, Briñol, Tormala, & Wegener, 2007).

REFERENCES

Ahmed, S. A. (1993). The effect of moderating variables on the attitude behavior relation. *International Journal of Public Opinion Research, 5,* 78–85.

Albarracin, D., Johnson, B. T., & Zanna, M. P. (Eds.) (2005). *The handbook of attitudes.* Mahwah, NJ: Lawrence Erlbaum Associates.

Allport, G. W. (1935). Attitudes. In C. Murchison (Ed.), *Handbook of social psychology* (pp. 789–844). Worcester, MA: Clark University Press.

Armitage, C. J., & Conner, M. (2000). Attitudinal ambivalence: A test of three key hypotheses. *Personality and Social Psychology Bulletin, 26,* 1421–1432.

Barden, J., & Petty, R. E. (2008). The mere perception of elaboration creates attitude certainty: Exploring the thoughtfulness heuristic. *Journal of Personality and Social Psychology, 95,* 489–509.

Bargh, J., Chaiken, S., Govender, R., & Pratto, F. (1992). The generality of the automatic attitude activation effect. *Journal of Personality & Social Psychology, 62,* 893–912.

Bassili, J. N. (1996). Meta-judgmental versus operative indexes of psychological attributes: The case of measures of attitude strength. *Journal of Personality and Social Psychology, 71,* 637–653.

Berent, M. K., & Krosnick, J. A. (1993). Attitude importance and selective exposure to attitude-relevant information. Unpublished manuscript, Ohio State University, Columbus, OH.

Berger, I. E., & Mitchell, A. A. (1989). The effect of advertising on attitude accessibility, attitude confidence, and the attitude–behavior relationship. *Journal of Consumer Research, 16*(3), 269–279.

Bizer, G. Y., & Krosnick, J. A. (2001). Exploring the structure of strength-related attitude features: The relation between attitude importance and attitude accessibility. *Journal of Personality and Social Psychology, 81,* 566–586.

Bizer, G. Y., Tormala, Z., Rucker, D. D., & Petty, R. E. (2006). Memory-based versus online processing: Implications for attitude strength. *Journal of Experimental Social Psychology, 42*(5), 646–653.

Boninger, D. S., Krosnick, J. A., & Berent, M. K. (1995). Origins of attitude importance: Self-interest, social identification, and value relevance. *Journal of Personality and Social Psychology, 68,* 61–80.

Boninger, D. S., Krosnick, J. A., Berent, M. K., & Fabrigar, L. R. (1995). The causes and consequences of attitude importance. In R. E. Petty & J. A. Krosnick (Eds.), *Attitude strength: Antecedents and consequences* (pp. 159–190). Mahwah, NJ: Lawrence Erlbaum Associates.

Bradley, J. V. (1981). Overconfidence in ignorant experts. *Bulletin of Psychonomic Society, 17*(2), 82–84.

Budd, R. J. (1986). Predicting cigarette use: The need to incorporate measures of salience in the theory of reasoned action. *Journal of Applied Social Psychology, 16,* 633–685.

Clark, J. K., Wegener, D. T., & Fabrigar, L. R. (2008). Attitudinal ambivalence and message-based persuasion: Motivated processing of proattitudinal information and avoidance of counterattitudinal information. *Personality and Social Psychology Bulletin, 34,* 565–577.

Clarkson, J. J., Tormala, Z. L., & Rucker, D. D. (2008). A new look at the consequences of attitude certainty: The amplification hypothesis. *Journal of Personality and Social Psychology, 95,* 810–825.

Conner, M., Sparks, P., Povey, R., James, R., Shepherd, R., & Armitage, C. J. (2002). Moderator effects of attitudinal ambivalence on attitude–behavior relationships. *European Journal of Social Psychology, 32,* 705–718.

Davidson, A. R., Yantis, S., Norwood, M., & Montano, D. E. (1985). Amount of information about the attitude object and attitude–behavior consistency. *Journal of Personality and Social Psychology, 49,* 1184–1198.

Edwards, J. A. (2003). The interactive effects of processing preference and motivation on information processing: Causal uncertainty and the MBTI in a persuasion context. *Journal of Research in Personality, 37,* 89–99.

Fabrigar, L. R., & Krosnick, J. A. (1993). What motivates issue public membership: Personal importance or national importance? Unpublished manuscript, the Ohio State University.

Fabrigar, L. R., Petty, R. E., Smith, S. M., & Crites, S. L., Jr. (2006). Understanding knowledge effects on attitude-behavior consistency: The role of relevance, complexity and amount of knowledge. *Journal of Personality and Social Psychology, 90,* 556–577.

Fazio, R. H., & Zanna, M. P. (1978a). On the predictive validity of attitudes: The roles of direct experience and confidence. *Journal of Personality, 46,* 228–243.

Fazio, R. H., & Zanna, M. P. (1978b). Attitudinal qualities relating to the strength of the attitude–behavior relationship. *Journal of Experimental Social Psychology, 14,* 398–408.

Festinger, L. (1954). A theory of social comparison processes. *Human Relations, 7,* 117–140.

Festinger, L. (1957). *A theory of cognitive dissonance.* Stanford, CA: Stanford University Press.

Fine, B. J. (1957). Conclusion-drawing, communicator credibility, and anxiety as factors in opinion change. *Journal of Abnormal and Social Psychology, 5,* 369–374.

Gollwitzer, P. M. (1990). Action phases and mind-sets. In E. T. Higgins & R. M. Sorrentino (Eds.), *The handbook of motivation and cognition: Foundations of social behavior* (Vol. 2, pp. 53–92). New York, NY: Guilford Press.

Gollwitzer, P. M., & Bayer, U. (1999). Deliberative versus implemental mindsets in the control of action. In S. Chaiken & Y. Trope (Eds.), *Dual-process theories in social psychology* (pp. 403–422). New York, NY: Guilford.

Gorn, G. J. (1975). The effects of personal involvement, communication discrepancy, and source prestige on reactions to communications on separatism. *Canadian Journal of Behavioral Science, 7,* 369–386.

Gross, S. R., Holtz, R., & Miller, N. (1995). Attitude certainty. In R. E. Petty & J. A. Krosnick (Eds.), *Attitude strength: Antecedents and consequences* (pp. 215–246). Mahwah, NJ: Lawrence Erlbaum Associates.

Haddock, G., Rothman, A. J., Reber, R., & Schwarz, N. (1999). Forming judgments of attitude certainty, intensity, and importance: The role of subjective experiences. *Personality and Social Psychology Bulletin, 25,* 771–782.

Haddock, G., Rothman, A. J., & Schwarz, N. (1996). Are (some) reports of attitude strength context dependent? *Canadian Journal of Behavioral Science, 28,* 313–316.

Henderson, M. D., de Liver, Y., & Gollwitzer, P. M. (2008). The effects of an implemental mindset on attitude strength. *Journal of Personality and Social Psychology, 94,* 396–411.

Holbrook, A. L., Berent, M. K., Krosnick, J. A., Visser, P. S., & Boninger, D. (2005). Attitude importance and the accumulation of attitude-relevant knowledge in memory. *Journal of Personality and Social Psychology, 88,* 749–769.

Holbrook, A. L., & Krosnick, J. A. (2005). Operative versus meta-psychological measures of ambivalence: Differentiating the consequences of perceived intra-psychic conflict and real intrapsychic conflict. In S. C. Craig & M. D. Martinez (Eds.), *Ambivalence and the structure of political opinion*. New York, NY: Palgrave Macmillan.

Holland, R. W., Verplanken, B., & van Knippenberg, A. (2003). From repetition to conviction: Attitude accessibility as a determinant of attitude certainty. *Journal of Experimental Social Psychology, 39*, 594–601.

Howard-Pitney, B., Borgida, E., & Omoto, A. M. (1986). Personal involvement: An examination of processing differences. *Social Cognition, 4*, 39–57.

Jaccard, J., Dodge, T. and Guilamo-Ramos, V. (2005). Meta-cognition, risk behavior and risk outcomes: The role of perceived intelligence and perceived knowledge. *Health Psychology, 24*, 161–170.

Karpinski, A., Steinman, R. B., & Hilton, J. L. (2005). Attitude importance as a moderator of the relationship between implicit and explicit attitude measures. *Personality & Social Psychology Bulletin, 31*, 949–962.

Krosnick, J. A. (1988a). Attitude importance and attitude change. *Journal of Experimental Social Psychology, 24*, 240–255.

Krosnick, J. A. (1988b). The role of attitude importance in social evaluations: A study of policy preferences, presidential candidate evaluations, and voting behavior. *Journal of Personality and Social Psychology, 55*, 196–210.

Krosnick, J. A. (1989). Attitude importance and attitude accessibility. *Personality and Social Psychology Bulletin, 15*, 297–308.

Krosnick, J. A., & Abelson, R. P. (1992). The case for measuring attitude strength in surveys. In J. Tanur (Ed.), *Questions about survey questions* (pp. 177–203). New York, NY: Russell Sage.

Krosnick, J. A., Boninger, D. S., Chuang, Y. C., Berent, M. K., & Carnot, C. G. (1993). Attitude strength: One construct or many related constructs? *Journal of Personality and Social Psychology, 66*, 1132–1151.

Krosnick, J. A., & Petty, R. E. (1995). Attitude strength: An overview. In R. E. Petty & J. A. Krosnick (Eds.), *Attitude strength: Antecedents and consequences* (pp. 1–24). Mahwah, NJ: Lawrence Erlbaum Associates.

Kruger, J., & Dunning, D. (1999). Unskilled and unaware of it: How difficulties in recognizing one's own incompetence lead to inflated self-assessments. *Journal of Personality and Social Psychology, 77*, 1121–1134.

Maio, G. R., Bell, D. W., & Esses, V. M. (1996). Ambivalence and persuasion: The processing of messages about immigrant groups. *Journal of Experimental Social Psychology, 32*, 513–536.

Marks, G., & Miller, N. (1985). The effects of certainty on consensus judgments. *Personality and Social Psychology Bulletin, 11*, 165–177.

Newby-Clark, I. R., McGregor, I., & Zanna, M. P. (2002). Thinking and caring about cognitive inconsistency: When and for whom does attitudinal ambivalence feel uncomfortable? *Journal of Personality and Social Psychology, 82*, 157–166.

Petrocelli, J. V., Tormala, Z. L., & Rucker, D. D. (2007). Unpacking attitude certainty: Attitude clarity and attitude correctness. *Journal of Personality and Social Psychology, 92*, 30–41.

Petty, R. E., Briñol, P., & DeMarree, K. G. (2007). The meta-cognitive model (MCM) of attitudes: Implications for attitude measurement, change, and strength. *Social Cognition, 25*, 657–686.

Petty, R. E., Briñol, P., Tormala, Z. L., & Wegener, D. T. (2007). The role of meta-cognition in social judgment. In A. W. Kruglanski & E. T. Higgins (Eds.), *Social psychology: Handbook of basic principles* (2nd ed., pp. 254–284). New York, NY: Guilford Press.

Petty, R. E., & Krosnick, J. A. (1995). *Attitude strength: Antecedents and consequences.* Mahwah, NJ: Lawrence Erlbaum Associates.

Powell, M. C., & Fazio, R. H. (1984). Attitude accessibility as a function of repeated attitudinal expression. *Personality and Social Psychology Bulletin, 10,* 139–148.

Priester, J. R., & Petty, R. E. (1996). The gradual threshold model of ambivalence: Relating the positive and negative bases of attitudes to subjective ambivalence. *Journal of Personality and Social Psychology, 71,* 431–449.

Priester, J. R., & Petty, R. E. (2001). Extending the bases of subjective attitudinal ambivalence: Interpersonal and intrapersonal antecedents of evaluative tension. *Journal of Personality and Social Psychology, 80,* 19–34.

Priester, J. R., Petty. R. E., & Park, K. (2007). Whence univalent ambivalence: From the anticipation of conflicting reactions. *Journal of Consumer Research, 34,* 11–21.

Radecki, C. M., and Jaccard, J. (1995). Perceptions of knowledge, actual knowledge and information search behavior. *Journal of Experimental Social Psychology, 31,* 107–138.

Rucker, D., Lee, A. Y., & Briñol, P. (2010). Learning more yet knowing less: The effects of information acquisition on subjective knowledge and information processing. Unpublished manuscript. Northwestern University.

Rucker, D. D., & Petty, R. E. (2004). When resistance is futile: Consequences of failed counterarguing for attitude certainty. *Journal of Personality and Social Psychology, 86,* 219–235.

Simon, L., Greenberg, J., & Brehm, J. (1995). Trivialization: The forgotten mode of dissonance reduction. *Journal of Experimental Social Psychology, 68*(2), 247–260.

Smith, S. M., Fabrigar, L. R., MacDougall, B. L., & Wiesenthal, N. L. (2008). The role of amount cognitive elaboration, and structural consistency of attitude-relevant knowledge in the formation of attitude certainty. *European Journal of Social Psychology, 38,* 280–295.

Thompson, M. T., Zanna, M. P., & Griffin, D. W. (1995). Let's not be indifferent about (attitudinal) ambivalence. In R. E. Petty & J. A. Krosnick (Eds.), *Attitude strength: Antecedents and consequences* (pp. 361–386). Mahwah, NJ: Lawrence Erlbaum Associates.

Tiedens, L. Z., & Linton, S. (2001). Judgment under emotional certainty and uncertainty: The effects of specific emotions on information processing. *Journal of Personality and Social Psychology, 81,* 973–988.

Tormala, Z. L., Clarkson, J. J., & Petty, R. E. (2006). Resisting persuasion by the skin of one's teeth: The hidden success of resisted persuasive messages. *Journal of Personality and Social Psychology, 91,* 423–435.

Tormala, Z. L., & DeSensi, V. L. (2008). The perceived informational basis of attitudes: Implications for subjective ambivalence. *Personality and Social Psychology Bulletin, 34,* 275–287.

Tormala, Z. L., & Petty, R. E. (2002). What doesn't kill me makes me stronger: The effects of resisting persuasion on attitude certainty. *Journal of Personality and Social Psychology, 83,* 1298–1313.

Tormala, Z. L., & Petty, R. E. (2004). Resisting persuasion and attitude certainty: A metacognitive analysis. In E. S. Knowles & J. A. Linn (Eds.), *Resistance and persuasion* (pp. 65–82). Mahwah, NJ: Lawrence Erlbaum Associates.

Tormala, Z. L., & Petty, R. E. (2007). Contextual contrast and perceived knowledge: Exploring the implications for persuasion. *Journal of Experimental Social Psychology, 43,* 17–30.

Tormala, Z. L., Petty, R. E., & Briñol, P. (2002). Ease of retrieval effects in persuasion: A self-validation analysis. *Personality and Social Psychology Bulletin, 28,* 1700–1712.

Tormala, Z. L., Rucker, D. D., & Seger, C. R. (2008). When increased confidence yields increased thought: A confidence-matching hypothesis. *Journal of Experimental Social Psychology, 44,* 141–147.

Vallone, R. P., Ross, L. and Lepper, M. R. (1985). The hostile media phenomenon: Biased perception and perceptions of media bias in coverage of the Beirut massacre. *Journal of Personality and Social Psychology, 49,* 577–585.

Visser, P. S. (1998). Testing the common-factors model of attitude strength. PhD dissertation. The Ohio State University.

Visser, P. S., Bizer, G., & Krosnick, J. A. (2006). Exploring the latent structure of strength-related attitude attributes. In M. Zanna (Ed.), *Advances in experimental social psychology* (Vol. 38, pp. 1–67). San Diego, CA: Academic Press.

Visser. P. S., Krosnick, J. A., & Norris, C. M. (2011). Challenging the common-factor model of strength-related attitude attributes: Contrasting the antecedents and consequences of attitude importance and attitude-relevant knowledge. In J. A. Krosnick & I. A. Chiang (Eds.), *Explorations in political psychology.* New York, NY: Psychology Press.

Visser, P. S., Krosnick, J. A., & Simmons, J. P. (2003). Distinguishing the cognitive and behavioral consequences of attitude importance and certainty: A new approach to testing the common-factor hypothesis. *Journal of Experimental Social Psychology, 39,* 118–141.

Visser, P. S., & Mirabile, R. R. (2004). Attitudes in the social context: The impact of social network composition on individual-level attitude strength. *Journal of Personality and Social Psychology, 87,* 779–795.

Wänke, M., Bless, H., & Biller, B. (1996). Subjective experience versus content of information in the construction of attitude judgments. *Personality and Social Psychology Bulletin, 22,* 1105–1113.

Weary, G., & Jacobson, J. A. (1997). Causal uncertainty beliefs and diagnostic information seeking. *Journal of Personality and Social Psychology, 73,* 839–848.

Wheeler, S. C., Petty, R. E., & Bizer, G. Y. (2005). Self-schema matching and attitude change: Situational and dispositional determinants of message elaboration. *Journal of Consumer Research, 31,* 787–797.

Wilson, T. D., Kraft, D., and Dunn, D. S. (1989). The disruptive effects of explaining attitudes: The moderating effect of knowledge about the attitude object. *Journal of Experimental Social Psychology, 25,* 379–400.

Wood, W. (1982). Retrieval of attitude-relevant information from memory: Effects on susceptibility to persuasion and on intrinsic motivation. *Journal of Personality and Social Psychology, 42,* 798–810.

Wu, C., & Shaffer, D. R. (1987). Susceptibility to persuasive appeals as a function of source credibility and prior experience with the attitude object. *Journal of Personality and Social Psychology, 52,* 677–688.

Zuwerink, J. R., & Devine, P. G. (1996). Attitude importance and resistance to persuasion: It's not just the thought that counts. *Journal of Personality and Social Psychology, 70,* 931–944.

3

Dimensions of Metacognitive Judgment
Implications for Attitude Change

BENJAMIN C. WAGNER, PABLO BRIÑOL,
and RICHARD E. PETTY

INTRODUCTION

*J*ust as people can evaluate social and physical objects, so too can they evaluate their own thoughts and thought processes. The human capacity for self-reflection has long been recognized by philosophers and psychologists alike (James, 1890/1983). In recent decades, researchers have examined how people's judgments about their own thoughts and feelings can impact the attitudes and behaviors that they ultimately exhibit. Critically, this process of thinking about one's own thinking—namely, *metacognition*—involves a distinction between *primary* and *secondary cognition*. Primary cognition involves the immediate associations between attitude objects and traits, whereas secondary cognition refers to the reflective judgments that are made about primary cognitions.

In this chapter, we will delineate the multiple dimensions on which people can evaluate their primary cognitions and will also consider the consequences of these evaluations in terms of attitude change. Some of the same categories that have traditionally proven effective for classifying primary thoughts can also be used to describe metacognitive thoughts (Petty, Briñol, Tormala, & Wegener, 2007). In this chapter, we organized metacognitive thoughts in terms of the perception of the (a) valence, (b) number, (c) target, (d) origin, (e) confidence, and (f) summary evaluation of primary cognition. After a general description of these dimensions of thinking about thinking, the second section of this chapter provides a description of how each of these categories can be consequential for attitudes and persuasion. In the final part of the chapter, we examine the possibility that, just as we think about our primary cognitions, we can also have higher order (e.g., third level) metacognitions (i.e., cognitions about metacognitions), with further implications for attitude change.

DIMENSIONS OF THOUGHTS IN RESPONSE TO PERSUASION

Over the past 50 years, researchers have developed numerous theories of persuasion (see Eagly & Chaiken, 1993; Petty & Briñol, 2010). One of the earliest assumptions was that effective influence required a sequence of steps leading to absorption of the content of a message (e.g., exposure, attention, comprehension, learning, retention; see McGuire, 1985). However, the available research evidence shows that message learning can occur in the absence of attitude change and that attitudes can change without learning the specific information in the communication (Petty & Cacioppo, 1981).

Cognitive response theory (Greenwald, 1968; Petty, Ostrom, & Brock, 1981) was developed explicitly to account for the low correlation between message learning and persuasion observed in many studies, and for the processes responsible for yielding to messages. In contrast to the traditional learning view, the cognitive response approach contended that persuasion depends on the extent to which individuals articulate and rehearse their own idiosyncratic thoughts about the information presented. According to this framework, appeals that elicit issue-relevant thoughts that are primarily favorable toward a particular recommendation produce agreement, whereas appeals that elicit unfavorable thoughts toward the recommendation are ineffective in achieving attitude change—regardless of message learning. The extent to which a thought was favorable (or unfavorable) toward the position advocated by the persuasive proposal was termed *valence* and served as a chief determinant of persuasion.

In addition to the *valence* of a recipient's thoughts, a second feature of thoughts that is important for persuasion is the *number* of thoughts that the person generates. Number is important in two ways. First, the greater the number of positive or negative thoughts a person generates, the greater the extent of attitude change or resistance that is expected. Second, attitudes that are based on a relatively high number of thoughts are generally more persistent over time, more resistant to change, and more likely to produce attitude-consistent behavior than are attitudes based on a relatively low number of thoughts (Petty, Haugtvedt, & Smith, 1995).

The thoughts that people generate can vary on several dimensions in addition to valence and number. In the attitude-change literature, thoughts generated in response to a persuasive message are also classified according to their target (i.e., subject) and their origin (i.e., their original source). We describe these categories in detail in the next section. Importantly, thoughts can be coded according to these categories by external judges as well as by the participants who generated the thoughts. To the extent that people evaluate their own thoughts using these categories, they are forming metacognitive judgments.

In addition to valence, number, target, and origin, a few other dimensions of metacognitive judgment warrant discussion. Specifically, these include thought confidence and a dimension that is best characterized as thought evaluation.

Thought *confidence* refers to assessments of the validity or correctness of one's thoughts, and thought confidence—also known as thought certainty—is perhaps the most thoroughly studied of all of the metacognitive dimensions (Briñol & Petty, 2009). The *evaluation* dimension of metacognition involves people's judgments about whether they like or dislike a particular thought (regardless of whether it is perceived to be positive or negative, valid or invalid).

In the next section, we describe how each of these six dimensions of metacognition is relevant for attitudes and persuasion. Then, we describe research exploring the notion that people can have metacognitions about their own metacognitions. Finally, we discuss the impact of persuasion on attitude structure, paying special attention to the possibility that people can store metacognitive judgments in memory and that these metacognitive judgments can impact downstream information-processing, judgment and behavior.

THE IMPACT OF METACOGNITIVE JUDGMENTS ON PERSUASION

Perceived Valence of Primary Thoughts

We have already noted that according to the cognitive response theory of attitude change (Greenwald, 1968; Petty et al., 1981), persuasion occurs not so much because people learned message arguments or source cues, but rather because they cognitively responded to them with either favorable or unfavorable thoughts. Thus, a person might learn an argument but resist it by counterarguing, or not learn an argument but succumb to it because of a favorable thought that was generated. In essence, the cognitive response approach to persuasion holds that virtually all attitude change is ultimately self-persuasion in that even external messages are influential primarily because of the idiosyncratic favorable or unfavorable thoughts that people have in response to the messages (Petty & Cacioppo, 1981). The cognitive response approach provides a useful framework for understanding persuasion when people are motivated and able to think about a message (Petty & Cacioppo, 1986).[1]

Notably, the original formation of the cognitive response approach assumed that the person would perceive a thought to be favorable when the thought was actually favorable toward the proposal, whereas an unfavorable thought would be perceived as a counterargument. This assumption is largely correct, as suggested by the high correlation between the ratings of favorability from external coders and the ratings of favorability from the participants that generated the thoughts (see Cacioppo, Harkins, & Petty, 1981). In some cases, though, a person might believe that his or her thought is favorable toward the position advocated in the message at the same time that an external coder could rate this thought as being unfavorable (or vice versa). For instance, a person who enjoys a challenge might say to himself, "This argument is hard to understand." The person who generated this thought could label it as "favorable," whereas an external coder who does not know that individual could label it as "unfavorable." Future research should explore the potential causes—and effects—of the divergence between self- and other-rated thought valences. As has been the case with other discrepancies between objective and subjective judgments, it is likely that the message recipient's own perception of valences is more important in determining persuasion than the perception of others is.

Perceived Number of Primary Thoughts

As noted, according to the cognitive response model, an appeal that elicits issue-relevant thoughts that are (or are perceived to be) favorable toward a particular recommendation produce agreement, whereas an appeal that elicits thoughts that are (or are perceived to be) unfavorable toward the recommendation is ineffective in achieving attitude change. In addition to affecting persuasion by influencing the *valence* (favorable or unfavorable) of thoughts that came to mind, early work on the cognitive response approach also emphasized how persuasion could be affected when variables influenced the *number* of thoughts of a particular valence that were generated. For example, if a person would normally be counterarguing a proposal, introducing some distraction would disrupt these negative thoughts, thereby producing more persuasion than if no distraction were present (Osterhouse & Brock, 1970). However, if a person would normally be thinking favorable thoughts, distraction has the opposite effect (Petty, Wells, & Brock, 1976).

The actual number of thoughts that people generate has to do with the primary level of cognition. From the point of view of metacognition, what matters is the subjective perception of the number of thoughts that the person has generated. One way that people can make metacognitive judgments about number of thoughts involves the ease with which thoughts come to mind. Specifically, people can use the ease with which they generate thoughts as a cue indicating the prevalence of such thoughts, with greater ease indicating greater availability (Tversky & Kahneman, 1973). Interestingly, in some cases the implications of ease of retrieval are at odds with the implications of the actual number of thoughts one has generated. For instance, in the classic study on ease, Schwarz and colleagues (1991) demonstrated that people experience difficulty in generating a high number of aggressive behaviors that they have performed, whereas they find it relatively easy to name just a few examples of aggressive behavior. As such, people judge themselves to be more aggressive when listing only a few behaviors than when listing many, reflecting the use of ease of retrieval as a heuristic cue indicating prevalence or probability (Tversky & Kahneman, 1973; for a more thorough discussion of ease, see Sanna & Lundberg, Chapter 10, this volume).

In the context of persuasion, people infer that the easier it is to generate information in favor of a position (e.g., one's own assertiveness), the more supportive information there must be. Conversely, having difficulty in generating such information would be associated with perceptions that there is little support available for that particular position. These inferences about the availability of information could then impact persuasion. This interpretation provides an excellent illustration of how the perceived number of thoughts (availability) rather than the actual number of thoughts matters for the influence of ease on attitude change. Although this heuristic explanation makes sense when people have limited ability to think and when the ease is salient before judgment (Kuhnen, 2010), more recent work has suggested that when people are engaged in thoughtful judgments, ease affects attitudes by affecting thought confidence (Tormala, Falces, Briñol, & Petty, 2007; Tormala, Petty, & Briñol, 2002). Although this *self-validation* interpretation is described in more detail in the section on confidence, for now it is sufficient to note that it allows us to understand the effects of ease under high-thinking conditions and the explanation is not based on perceptions of the number of thoughts, but rather on the perceptions of the validity of the thoughts.

In closing this section, it is important to note that although perceptions regarding the number of thoughts that a person has generated can influence attitude change, so too can perceptions of the amount of elaboration that the person has performed influence *attitude strength*, which refers to the extent to which an attitude is durable and impactful (Krosnick & Petty, 1995). In one relevant study, Barden and Petty (2008) asked undergraduate participants to generate thoughts about the adoption of wireless Internet (WiFi) networks at their university. After participants listed their thoughts, they were randomly assigned to receive bogus feedback indicating that they had, on average, listed fewer (i.e., low-thought condition) or more (i.e., high-thought condition) thoughts than their peers.

Of course, no differences in actual number of thoughts listed were observed between the two feedback groups. Nonetheless, participants who were told that they had listed fewer thoughts than their peers perceived that they had thought less about the topic than did participants who were told that they had listed more thoughts than their peers. Additionally, these perceptions of amount of thinking influenced attitude confidence, with greater perceived thinking predicting greater attitude certainty. Perhaps most notably, these effects were independent of the actual amount of thinking that participants engaged in, demonstrating that metacognitive perceptions involving extent of thinking are consequential for attitude strength (see also Rucker, Petty, & Briñol, 2008).

Perceived Target of Primary Thoughts

The target dimension refers to what the person perceives the thought to be about. Possible targets for primary cognitions involve the self, other people, and groups, as well as any number of physical objects or abstract ideas that a person can consider. For example, in the context of persuasion a person might wonder: Does the thought refer to the message (i.e., "This argument is very convincing!"), the source (i.e., "The speaker is very attractive!"), or to something else (i.e., "This room is very hot!")? Thus, *target* refers to the referent of a thought. In fact, thoughts can be about anything. However, what matters for the purposes of metacognitive judgment is not what the thought is actually about, but rather the person's judgment about the thought's referent. Because human judgment is subjective and is beset by several biases and distortions (Griffin & Ross, 1991), it is perhaps unsurprising that judgments about the referent of one's thoughts can be shaped by factors that are irrelevant to the thoughts' actual referents.

Research on attitude change has examined the possibility of classifying thoughts in response to persuasive proposals as a function of perceived target. For example, Chaiken and Maheswaran (1994) presented participants with a message about a consumer product. This message ostensibly originated from a high- or low-credibility source. After processing the message and reporting their attitudes toward the product, participants were given 3 minutes to list the thoughts that they had during the experiment. Later, these thoughts were coded by independent raters for the thoughts' target and valence. Findings demonstrated that thoughts about the source and thoughts about the product's attributes exerted independent effects on participants' attitudes toward the product. Thus, we can see that the target of a person's thoughts is an important determinant of persuasion. Although in this particular research thoughts were coded by external judges, it is common for research in persuasion to have participants code their own thoughts as well (e.g., Rucker, Briñol, & Petty, 2010), and similar findings would be expected in such a case.

Perceived Origin of Primary Thoughts

The origin of thoughts refers to the perceived source of a particular primary cognition. People can ask themselves questions such as "Where did this thought come from?" and "Did I think of this myself, or did I hear somebody else say it?" Additionally, people may ask themselves whether their thoughts originate in their emotions or from their knowledge and beliefs. Critically, a number of consequences can flow from individuals' judgments about the origin (or origins) of their thoughts. For example, people are more satisfied with their lives when they attribute their positive thoughts to internal characteristics than when they attribute these same positive thoughts to external factors (e.g., weather, a soundproof room; Schwarz & Clore, 1983). Additionally, people who are able to attribute negative physiological arousal stemming from cognitive dissonance to external factors (e.g., the inges-tion of a pill) are less likely to attempt to resolve the underlying dissonance than are individuals who cannot attribute their negative arousal to the effects of a pill (Zanna & Cooper, 1974; see also Schachter & Singer, 1962).[2]

The social psychological literature is rich in these kinds of examples. One con-text in which metacognitive judgments about thought origins seems to be particu-larly consequential has to do with eyewitness memory. One notable controversy in this domain involves cases in which people "recover" memories about past episodes of abuse. Specifically, some have argued (e.g., Loftus & Ketcham, 1994) that indi-viduals who claim to have uncovered repressed memories of traumatic episodes are, in fact, "recalling" events that they previously imagined or that somebody else described to them. Underlying these effects, presumably, are errors in *source monitoring*, a process whereby individuals misjudge the origins of a particular thought or memory (see Johnson, 2006). As we can see, thoughts that are initially generated by other people can, in some cases, be mistaken for thoughts generated by the self or for memories of events that the self has actually experienced. Once (mis)attributed to the self, the thoughts can have greater impact than they would have if they were attributed to external origins.

The perceptions of the origin of thoughts can be also consequential for per-suasion. In a recent line of work, Briñol, Petty, Gascó, and Horcajo (2009) asked participants to generate positive or negative thoughts regarding their bodies. Then, participants were led to believe that their thoughts originated externally (i.e., they arose from societal views) or internally (i.e., they arose from the self). Specifically, thoughts about the body were said to emerge from the "particular views of their culture through socialization" (external origin) or to emerge "from deep down inside of the self." The results revealed that the direction of the thoughts that participants had generated had a greater impact on reported body satisfaction when the origin of the thoughts was perceived to be the self than when it was perceived to be an external source. As a result, perceiving positive thoughts as coming from the self (vs. others) made people feel better about their body image, but perceiving negative thoughts as coming from the self produced the opposite effect.

In another study in this line of research, we replicated these findings for attitudes toward fast food. Specifically, after thinking about the benefits or costs of eating fast food, participants were led to believe that food-related thoughts were learned from others (external source) or were innate (internal source). As expected, the direction of the thoughts (positive or negative) had a greater impact on attitudes and behavioral intentions regarding eating fast food when people perceived the self (vs. others) as the source of the thoughts. Importantly, these findings were moderated by a number of variables, including self-esteem. Having the perception that thoughts are generated internally only led to a greater influence of thoughts on attitudes among participants with high self-esteem. Moreover, like the ease of retrieval effect described earlier, these effects are assumed to be mediated by thought confidence.

A final way that people can make judgments about the origin of their thoughts involves making judgments about their thoughts' basis. Relevant to illustrating this notion is the *tripartite model* of attitude structure, according to which attitudes are based on (a) affect or feelings; (b) cognitions, or beliefs and knowledge; and (c) behaviors or actions (Breckler, 1984; Zanna & Rempel, 1988). Importantly, the primary basis of one's attitude can have important implications for attitude change. For example, it is generally more effective to change attitudes that are based on emotion with emotional strategies rather than with more cognitive or rational ones (Edwards, 1990; Fabrigar & Petty, 1999).

But although it is sometimes easy for a person to categorize his or her thoughts as being mostly affective or cognitive, this need not be the case. That is, people's beliefs about the basis of their attitudes on a particular subject do not always correspond with the more objective basis of their attitudes (See, Petty, & Fabrigar, 2008). And just as the basis of the attitude object can have important implications for attitude change, so too can the perception of those bases. For instance, See, Petty, and Fabrigar (2008) showed that both the actual and the perceived bases of one's attitude on a particular topic can predict the extent to which people are persuaded by messages that are framed in terms of these bases. Specifically, messages that match (real or perceived) attitudinal bases lead to greater persuasion than do messages that do not match attitudinal bases (for reviews on matching and persuasion, see Briñol & Petty, 2006; Petty, Wheeler, & Bizer, 2000).

Confidence in Primary Thoughts

One of the most essential dimensions of metacognitive thought consists of the degree of *confidence* people place in their thoughts, ranging from extreme certainty to extreme doubt about their thoughts' validity. Thus, two people might have the *same* thought, but one person might have considerably greater confidence in that thought than the other, and the greater confidence in the thought is, the greater its impact on judgment will be. This idea is referred to as the *self-validation hypothesis* (Petty, Briñol, & Tormala, 2002). The key notion is that generating thoughts is not sufficient for them to have an impact on judgments. Rather, one must also have confidence in them. The self-validation hypothesis makes a number of straightforward predictions. First, it suggests that just as assessing attitude confidence has been very useful in determining which attitudes guide behavior (e.g., Fazio & Zanna, 1978), so too would assessing thought confidence be useful in determining which thoughts generated in response to a persuasive communication predict attitudes. In line with this reasoning, Petty and colleagues (2002) found that attitude–thought correlations increased as self-reported thought confidence increased.

Furthermore, direct manipulations of thought confidence can have a similar impact. In one study, for instance, following exposure to a message containing strong or weak arguments in favor of a new university exam policy and a typical thought listing task, Petty and colleagues (2002) asked the college student recipients to think about situations in which they had felt confidence or doubt in their thinking. Those who articulated past instances of confidence became more certain of the validity of their recently generated thoughts than did those who reflected upon instances of doubt. High thought confidence led to greater persuasion when recipients' thoughts were largely favorable, but high thought confidence led to less persuasion when recipients' thoughts were largely unfavorable. Thus, confidence (vs. doubt) increased the impact of thought valence on attitudes.

According to the self-validation hypothesis, anything that enhances confidence in thoughts will increase the impact of valenced thoughts on attitudes and anything that enhances doubt will reduce the impact of valenced thoughts. Thus, if people are generating favorable thoughts about themselves or a new proposal, they will be more persuaded if they are nodding their heads or are feeling happy, affirmed, or powerful because these variables instill confidence in the favorable thoughts and lead people to use them more than if they are shaking their heads or are feeling sad, not affirmed, or powerless (see Briñol & Petty, 2009, for a review). However, if people are generating unfavorable thoughts (e.g., because message arguments are weak), then these same variables (e.g., nodding one's head or feeling powerful) will lead to *less* persuasion because people will have confidence in their unfavorable thoughts and will use these thoughts in forming their judgments.

As noted earlier, people also consider their thoughts to be more valid when they are generated with ease rather than difficulty (see also Briñol, Petty, & Wagner, Chapter 12, this volume). Thus, diverse self-validation variables can interact with the direction of people's thoughts to influence judgments. Although we have only discussed self-validation processes in reference to recipient variables so far, self-validation can involve other types of variables as well. As reviewed by Briñol and

Petty (2009), the self-validation framework provides a novel way to understand the effects of source variables (e.g., credibility, similarity), message variables (e.g., matching, repetition), and context variables (social consensus). In each case, this recently discovered mechanism has pointed to new effects and a new understanding of established effects.

In closing, it is important to specify when attitudes are likely to change through self-validation processes. Two critical variables to consider are *timing* and *elaboration*. First, when confidence inductions follow information processing, then confidence is likely to operate via the metacognitive process outlined previously because, if a sense of confidence *precedes* thought generation, the thoughts are not a plausible cause of the confidence. Second, this metacognitive role for confidence is more likely to arise when people are thinking a great deal than when people are not thinking very much because metacognition requires cognitive effort beyond primary cognition. Thus, the self-validation effects described in this section were more apparent in high-thinking situations (e.g., situations fostering high personal relevance; Petty & Cacioppo, 1979) or individuals (e.g., individuals high in need for cognition; Cacioppo & Petty, 1982) and when the validating variable followed thought generation, rather than preceded it. Of course, confidence can play other roles under different circumstances (e.g., affecting the extent of thinking; see Briñol, DeMarree, & Petty, 2010, for a review), but here we have chosen to highlight its metacognitive role.

Evaluation of Primary Thoughts

Lastly, the *evaluation* dimension of metacognition involves people's judgments about the desirability of a particular thought. That is, people can have attitudes toward their own thoughts. People can evaluate whether they like their thoughts or not and to what extent they consider their thoughts to be desirable or appropriate. If people like their own thoughts, then these thoughts are especially likely to affect downstream judgments and behaviors. If people do not like their own thoughts, they might be less influential.

One way in which people can evaluate whether they like their thoughts is by considering how they feel about them, how the thoughts make them feel, and how they felt at the time of thought generation. For instance, if a person feels happy about his thoughts, he is likely to use those thoughts in forming attitudes. Likewise, happiness that is unrelated to one's primary cognitions can lead individuals to rely more on these cognitions in forming summary judgments (e.g., Briñol, Petty, & Barden, 2007; see also Huntsinger & Clore, Chapter 11, this volume). However, emotions can lead to somewhat paradoxical effects, depending upon the appraisals of the emotions that are highlighted. For instance, consider the case of anger. Anger is an unpleasant emotion that is associated with a high degree of confidence (Tiedens & Linton, 2001). If an individual is feeling angry and is focusing on his or her level of confidence, then anger should be able to validate his or her thoughts and lead to corresponding attitudes and judgments. If another individual is feeling angry but is focusing on the unpleasantness associated with that emotion, then he or she may feel bad about his or her primary cognitions, leading to attitudes and judgments that are relatively less affected by the direction of these cognitions

(Briñol, Petty, Stavraki, Wagner, & Díaz, 2010; see also Briñol, Petty, & Wagner, Chapter 12, this volume).

Importantly, the impact of anger on judgment as a function of self-validation or invalidation highlights the distinction between liking one's thoughts and having confidence in one's thoughts. Focusing on the valence of their emotions may lead people to like or dislike their thoughts, whereas focusing on the confidence associated with their emotions may lead people to feel confident or doubtful in their thoughts. In most cases, people like the thoughts they consider valid and dislike the thoughts they consider invalid. However, liking and confidence are not always overlapping constructs. It is possible to like a thought without having much confidence in it: "I like to think that I am great at sports, although I am uncertain that this is really true." Similarly, it is possible to dislike a thought a great deal while having utmost confidence in that thought: "I hate to be right, but I am sure my friend cannot survive that automobile accident."

Just as there are situational factors that can influence whether people like their thoughts (e.g., transitory affect), so there are also individual differences in evaluation of thinking. People vary in the extent to which they enjoy effortful thinking (Cacioppo & Petty, 1982), and this variation predicts the likelihood that people will think carefully across situations and topics (for a recent review on need for cognition, see Petty, Briñol, Loersch, & McCaslin, 2009). Thus, we can see that people's metacognitive judgments about whether thinking is good and enjoyable are related to the amount that they think about any given topic. If people evaluate thinking as fun, they are more apt to think carefully when presented with the opportunity to do so; if people dislike thinking, they are relatively unlikely to engage in effortful processing of a particular message (Cacioppo, Petty, & Morris, 1983).

PERCEPTIONS OF SECONDARY THOUGHTS

So far, we have differentiated between thoughts that occur at the primary level of cognition and thoughts about those thoughts, or secondary cognition. Briñol, Rucker, Tormala, and Petty (2004) suggested that it is necessary to distinguish further between two qualitatively different aspects of metacognitive, secondary thoughts. The first is the *nature of the belief itself*—what does a person believe about the content, the amount, or the origin of his or her thoughts? As we have described, these judgments are consequential for attitude change and need not be grounded in reality. A second aspect of a person's metacognitions is a *value judgment of the secondary belief.* Specifically, people may believe that it is either appropriate or inappropriate to think about their own thoughts in one way or another. In other words, just as people think about their thoughts, people can also have thoughts about their metacognitions. In some ways, these thoughts about metacognitions could be considered to occur at the meta meta level, and the same dimensions that are useful to understanding regular metacognition might be relevant for understanding this third level of cognition.

Some initial evidence suggests that what people think about their secondary cognitions can have implications for attitude change. For example, as we have seen, people generally construe ease in retrieving thoughts as evidence that these thoughts are valid or that these thoughts indicate that the target of these thoughts is especially prevalent or likely. However, people need not perceive metacognitive ease in such positive terms. That is, if people's naïve theories regarding the meaning of ease could vary (or even be changed), then they could form different judgments based on their experiences of ease. In a study investigating this point, Briñol, Petty, and Tormala (2006) asked participants to generate either two or 10 arguments in favor of a counterattitudinal proposal. Additionally, half of participants were told that ease of retrieval in generating thoughts reflected thoughts that were low in complexity and that, in fact, intelligent people often experience more difficulty in generating thoughts than do unintelligent people, given that intelligent people have more neuronal connections, the operation of which can be taxing. The remaining participants were provided opposite information, which reflected the perhaps default association of ease with confidence and validity.

Consistent with expectations, Briñol, Petty, and Tormala (2006) found the traditional ease-of-retrieval effect only among participants who received the "ease is good" instruction. That is, these participants were more confident in their thoughts when these thoughts were relatively easy to generate, meaning that participants listing two arguments (i.e., easy task) reported more favorable attitudes than did participants listing 10 arguments (i.e., difficult task). Among participants who were instructed that "ease is bad," an opposite effect emerged. Specifically, this group reported more favorable attitudes when listing 10 arguments than when listing two arguments. Thus, people's interpretation of the *meaning* of metacognitive ease is critical in determining downstream judgments.

This research by Briñol, Petty, and Tormala (2006) reveals that interpretations regarding the meaning of a variety of metacognitive experiences can impact downstream judgment.[3] For instance, people generally associate perceptual fluency with familiarity and perceptual difficulty with unfamiliarity or novelty (e.g., Jacoby, Kelley, Brown, & Jasechko, 1989). However, this naïve theory linking fluency with familiarity is malleable; when induced through a training procedure to associate fluency with unfamiliarity (and difficulty with familiarity), the "typical" effect of fluency on familiarity judgments can be reversed (Unkelbach, 2006). In addition to affecting familiarity judgments, the metacognitive experience of ease (or fluency) can increase positive evaluations of attitude objects (Zajonc, 1968). In the context of goal pursuit, however, metacognitive ease (relative to difficulty) is associated with less favorable evaluations of goal means. That is, because the instrumentality of a behavior (or means) for goal fulfillment positively correlates with the effortfulness of that behavior (or means), people show more positive evaluations of goal means when these means are associated with metacognitive difficulty than when they are associated with metacognitive ease (Labroo & Kim, 2009).

Metacognitive interpretations regarding the meaning of regulatory depletion for attitude certainty can also vary, thereby producing different attitude certainty judgments. In one set of studies, Wen, Rucker, Tormala, and Clarkson (2010, Experiments 1 and 2) showed that people typically associate cognitive depletion with having thought a great deal about a particular subject. Because thinking a lot about a topic—or believing that one has thought a lot about a topic (see Barden & Petty, 2008)—is associated with increased attitude certainty, people who feel depleted while thinking about a topic report greater certainty in their attitudes for that topic (Wen et al., 2010). However, when induced to associate depletion with uncertainty and nondepletion with certainty (Wen et al., 2010, Experiment 3), this pattern was reversed, such that participants who were feeling depleted reported less attitude certainty than did participants who were not feeling depleted. Thus, we can see that people's judgments regarding the meaning of their metacognitive experiences can impact other, downstream judgments. What is more, people's judgments regarding the meaning of their metacognitive experiences are malleable, indicating that people who are having similar metacognitive experiences may show very different ultimate judgments as a function of their lay theories linking these experiences with meaning (see also Job, Dweck, & Walton, 2010).

THE IMPACT OF ATTITUDE CHANGE ON ATTITUDE REPRESENTATION

Insights From the Metacognitive Model

The studies described in the previous sections illustrate that metacognitive judgments can change attitudes and attitude strength. In this section we examine how being persuaded can impact attitude structure. According to the metacognitive model (MCM) of attitude structure (Petty & Briñol, 2006; Petty, Briñol, & DeMarree, 2007), attitudes consist of evaluative associations (positive and negative), and the evaluative associations are linked to validity tags that can be represented in various ways, (e.g., confidence/doubt). Essentially, the MCM argues that people attach validity tags to object-association links, storing the entire set of associations in long-term memory. Thus, persuasion can entail the development and metacognitive validation of novel object-association links *as well as* the metacognitive invalidation of existing object-association links.

To illustrate, consider the case of a former smoker. This person may have both positive and negative evaluations of cigarette smoking stored in memory, but may tag the latter as "true" or "valid" while tagging the former as "false" or "invalid." In this case, the person would be endorsing the stored association between "smoking" and "bad" and rejecting the stored association between "smoking" and "good." As such, the person would not acknowledge any explicit conflict with respect to his or her true attitude toward smoking. That is, the former smoker would likely state that he or she had a very negative attitude toward cigarette smoking that was held unambivalently (Petty & Briñol, 2009).

In this situation, explicit attitude measures would show that this individual had been persuaded from a pro- to an antismoking position. However, implicit measures would detect the presence of (rejected) evaluations that conflict with explicitly endorsed evaluations. This is because validity tags are more distantly related to the attitude object than are evaluations of that object, meaning that validity tags are generally less likely to be activated—or are likely to be activated less strongly—than are evaluative associations, assuming that the starting point is activation of the attitude object itself. In cases in which a high amount of cognitive resources are available—as in the case of explicit measures about which respondents can deliberate—both the object evaluations and the validity tags are activated, meaning that responses reflect the validity information that people have stored regarding the object-evaluation association.

In cases where cognitive resources are constrained, however—as often happens when people respond to implicit measures, particularly those involving speeded responses—people's responses to attitude objects tend to reflect largely the influence of their automatic evaluative associations and not the influence of validity tags (for a related argument, see Fazio & Olson, 2003.) Thus, the MCM of attitude structure provides an explanation of why, in some cases, explicit and implicit attitude measures yield discordant attitude estimates.

Interestingly, the continued presence of rejected evaluative associations following attitude change can have important implications for attitude strength and information processing. For instance, storing both positive and negative evaluative associations for the same attitude object—even when only one set of these evaluative associations is explicitly endorsed—can produce a state of *implicit attitudinal ambivalence* (Petty & Briñol, 2009). That is, people with both positive and negative evaluative associations toward an attitude object show more ambivalence toward that object on implicit measures than do people who have more univalent evaluative associations (Petty, Tormala, Briñol, & Jarvis, 2006, Experiment 2), despite the fact that the two groups report similar (and low) levels of ambivalence on explicit measures. Further, individuals possessing implicit attitudinal ambivalence report more discomfort with respect to the attitude object (Rydell, McConnell, & Mackie, 2008) and engage in more extensive processing of information related to the attitude object (Petty et al., 2006, Experiments 3 and 4), presumably reflecting an ambivalence-reduction strategy (Briñol, Petty, & Wheeler, 2006; for a recent review on implicit ambivalence, see Petty, Briñol, & Johnson, 2011).

SUMMARY AND CONCLUSIONS

Thoughts generated in response to a persuasive proposal are typically classified into a number of categories by judges or by the people who generated the thoughts, themselves: valence (e.g., "Is the thought favorable or unfavorable toward the proposal?"), number (e.g., "Are there many or few thoughts?"), target (e.g., "What is the thought about?"), and origin (e.g., "From where does the thought come?"). Just as coding thoughts for these dimensions has provided a very fruitful approach for understanding some of the psychological processes that underlie attitude formation and change, coding metacognitions along these same dimensions has also been important for the study of persuasion.

In addition to these aspects of secondary cognitions, two additional dimensions are uniquely metacognitive and were covered in our review: one's *evaluation* of a thought, and one's *confidence* in that thought. Whether people like their thoughts and whether these thoughts are held with confidence are consequential in terms of the impact of these thoughts on attitudes. The precise distinctions among these dimensions are somewhat arbitrary and overlapping, but they serve as a practical way to organize the growing literature on metacognition and persuasion. By using this framework to organize the chapter, we do not imply that a particular study was originally designed to assess just one of the specific dimensions. In fact, due to the overlap among dimensions, some of the studies described under one dimension could plausibly be discussed as relating to a different dimension. For example, the research examining whether people think that their thoughts come from the self or from others has been discussed under the *origin* dimension, but it could plausibly fit under the *confidence* dimension because origin influences confidence.

In this chapter, we highlighted the idea that not only does what a person thinks about his or her thoughts matter for persuasion, but it is also important to consider the judgments people make regarding the meaning of these secondary cognitions. Our research has shown that whether ease of retrieval impacts judgments depends on whether people consider that metacognition to be something good or bad (Briñol, Petty et al., 2006). Similar to the work on self-validation processes showing that confidence applies to whatever is in people's minds, we argue that the dimensions outlined in this chapter (including confidence) can be applied not only to assess primary cognitions but also to assess secondary cognitions.

In our final section, we described how being persuaded can change the structure of individuals' attitudes, paying particular attention to the metacognitive validity tags that people attach to their object-evaluation associations. Thus, attitude change can involve not only the creation (and validation) of novel object-evaluation links but also the invalidation of existing object-evaluation links. Importantly, these metacognitive validity tags are stored in memory as part of the overall attitudinal representation, influencing downstream consequences such as information processing of attitude-relevant information and scrutiny of attitude-relevant persuasive communications.

Across each of the sections in this review, we noted that people's metacognitive judgments about their own thoughts, beliefs, and attitudes can be inconsistent with more objective indicators of these same dimensions. As an example, people may believe that an attitude's basis is affective (e.g., feelings) when, in reality, the attitude is based in cognition (e.g., knowledge, beliefs; see See, Petty, & Fabrigar, 2008). Also, people can attribute thoughts to themselves when, in fact, these thoughts originated in others (Briñol et al., 2009; Johnson, 2006; Loftus & Ketcham, 1994). Finally, people's beliefs about the extent to which they have thought about an attitude object or issue are sometimes unrelated to the true extent to which they have thought about that object or issue (Barden & Petty, 2008).

These discrepancies likely arise because people often are unaware of—or unable to verbalize—the true origins and nature of their thoughts, judgments, and behaviors (Nisbett & Wilson, 1977). In fact, when they are asked to consider the basis for their attitudes, people can focus on information that is irrelevant to their attitudes' basis, leading them to use their attitudes less in guiding subsequent behavior (Wilson, Dunn, Bybee, Hyman, & Rotondo, 1984; Wilson et al., 1993). Of course, speculating on the basis of one's attitude need not disrupt the influence of that attitude on behavior; presumably, if individuals contemplate the *actual* basis for their attitudes (e.g., based on high thought), these attitudes can become more, not less, predictive of behavior (e.g., Petty, Haugtvedt, & Smith, 1995).

NOTES

1. When people are unmotivated or unable to think carefully about a message, attitudes are influenced less by message-relevant cognitive responses than by thoughts about simple cues (e.g., "If an expert says it, it must be correct.") or by simple associations to the message that can occur with little if any thinking (Petty & Cacioppo, 1986). Under low-thinking conditions, metacognitive processes are less likely to operate (see Briñol & Petty, 2009).
2. Another case in which judgments regarding the origin of one's thoughts can impact attitudes involves evaluative conditioning. Specifically, Jones, Fazio, and Olson (2009) demonstrated that the affective reactions elicited by valenced unconditioned stimuli (i.e., positively and negatively valenced images) are spontaneously attributed to conditioned stimuli (i.e., novel, neutral objects in close temperospatial contiguity with the unconditioned stimuli) under certain circumstances (i.e., when the conditioned stimulus is particularly salient), thereby leading the conditioned stimuli to "take on" the valence of the unconditioned stimuli. Essentially, such effects reflect the judgment that the origin of one's positive or negative affective reactions is the conditioned stimulus rather than the unconditioned stimuli. It is important to note that this account is based on a relatively low-thought process, unlike most of the metacognitive processes described in this chapter. That is, according to Jones and colleagues, evaluative conditioning relies on a relatively simple misattribution inference similar to the self-perception and heuristic processes that do not require extensive thinking to operate. As noted, metacognitive processes require relatively more elaboration.
3. People can trust (and like) their metacognitions for reasons other than their naïve theories about their secondary thoughts. For example, consistent with the idea that power can validate thoughts (Briñol et al., 2007) regardless of their nature, recent research has shown that high-power individuals are more likely to use their metacognitive experiences of ease (Weick & Guinote, 2008).

REFERENCES

Barden, J., & Petty, R. E. (2008). The mere perception of elaboration creates attitude certainty: Exploring the thoughtfulness heuristic. *Journal of Personality and Social Psychology, 95,* 489–509.

Breckler, S. J. (1984). Empirical validation of affect, behavior, and cognition as distinct components of attitude. *Journal of Personality and Social Psychology, 47,* 1191–1205.

Briñol, P., DeMarree, K. G., & Petty, R. E. (2010). Processes by which confidence (vs. doubt) influences the self. In R. M. Arkin, K. C. Oleson, & P. J. Carroll (Eds.), *Handbook of the uncertain self* (pp. 13–35). New York, NY: Psychology Press.

Briñol, P., & Petty, R. E. (2006). Fundamental processes leading to attitude change: Implications for cancer prevention communications. *Journal of Communication, 56,* S81–S104.

Briñol, P., & Petty, R. E. (2009). Persuasion: Insights from the self-validation hypothesis. In M. P. Zanna (Ed.), *Advances in Experimental Social Psychology* (Vol. 41, pp. 69–118). New York, NY: Elsevier.

Briñol, P., Petty, R. E., & Barden, J. (2007). Happiness versus sadness as a determinant of thought confidence in persuasion: A self-validation analysis. *Journal of Personality and Social Psychology, 93,* 711–727.

Briñol, P., Petty, R. E., Gascó, M., & Horcajo, J. (2009). *Perceived origin of thoughts: A self-validation perspective.* Unpublished manuscript.

Briñol, P., Petty, R. E., Stavraki, M., Wagner, B. C., & Díaz, D. (2010). *Anger: A self-validation analysis*. Unpublished manuscript.

Briñol, P., Petty, R. E., & Tormala, Z. L. (2006). The malleable meaning of subjective ease. *Psychological Science, 17,* 200–206.

Briñol, P., Petty, R. E., & Wheeler, S. C. (2006). Discrepancies between explicit and implicit self-concepts: Consequences for information processing. *Journal of Personality and Social Psychology, 91,* 154–170.

Briñol, P., Rucker, D. D., Tormala, Z. L., & Petty, R. E. (2004). Individual differences in resistance to persuasion: The role of beliefs and meta-beliefs. In E. S. Knowles & J. A. Linn (Eds.), *Resistance and persuasion* (pp. 83–104). Mahwah, NJ: Lawrence Erlbaum Associates.

Cacioppo, J. T., Harkins, S. G., & Petty, R. E. (1981). The nature of attitudes and cognitive responses and their relationships to behavior. In R. Petty, T. Ostrom, & T. Brock (Eds.), *Cognitive responses in persuasion* (pp. 31–54). Hillsdale, NJ: Lawrence Erlbaum Associates.

Cacioppo, J. T., & Petty, R. E. (1982). The need for cognition. *Journal of Personality and Social Psychology, 42,* 116–131.

Cacioppo, J. T., Petty, R. E., & Morris, K. (1983). Effects of need for cognition on message evaluation, argument recall, and persuasion. *Journal of Personality and Social Psychology, 45,* 805–818.

Chaiken, S., & Maheswaran, D. (1994). Heuristic processing can bias systematic processing: Effects of source credibility, argument ambiguity, and task importance on attitude judgment. *Journal of Personality and Social Psychology, 66,* 460–473.

Eagly A. H., & Chaiken, S. (1993). *The psychology of attitudes.* Fort Worth, TX: Harcourt, Brace, Jovanovich.

Edwards, K. (1990). The interplay of affect and cognition in attitude formation and change. *Journal of Personality and Social Psychology, 59,* 202–216.

Fabrigar, L. R., & Petty, R. E. (1999). The role of affective and cognitive bases of attitudes in susceptibility to affectively and cognitively based persuasion. *Personality and Social Psychology Bulletin, 25,* 363–381.

Fazio, R. H., & Olson, M. A. (2003). Implicit measures in social cognition research: Their meaning and use. *Annual Review of Psychology, 54,* 297–327.

Fazio, R. H., & Zanna, M. P. (1978). On the predictive validity of attitudes: The roles of direct experience and confidence. *Journal of Personality, 46,* 228–243.

Greenwald, A. G. (1968). Cognitive learning, cognitive response to persuasion, and attitude change. In A. Greenwald, T. Brock, & T. Ostrom (Eds.), *Psychological foundations of attitudes.* New York, NY: Academic Press.

Griffin, D. W., & Ross, L. (1991). Subjective construal, social inference, and human misunderstanding. In M. Zanna (Ed.), *Advances in experimental social psychology* (Vol. 24, pp. 319–359). San Diego, CA: Academic Press.

Jacoby, L. L., Kelley, C., Brown, J., & Jasechko, J. (1989). Becoming famous overnight: Limits on the ability to avoid unconscious influences of the past. *Journal of Personality and Social Psychology, 56,* 326–338.

James, W. (1890/1983). *The principles of psychology.* Cambridge, MA: Harvard University Press.

Job, V., Dweck, C. S., & Walton, G. M. (2010). Ego depletion—Is it all in your head? Implicit theories about willpower affect self-regulation. *Psychological Science, 21,* 1686–1693.

Johnson, M. K. (2006). Memory and reality. *American Psychologist, 61,* 760–771.

Jones, C. R., Fazio, R. H., & Olson, M. A. (2009). Implicit misattribution as a mechanism underlying evaluative conditioning. *Journal of Personality and Social Psychology, 96,* 933–948.

Krosnick, J. A., & Petty, R. E. (1995). Attitude strength: An overview. In R. E. Petty and J. A. Krosnick (Eds.), *Attitude strength: Antecedents and consequences* (pp. 1–24). Hillsdale, NJ: Lawrence Erlbaum Associates.

Kuhnen, U. (2010). Manipulation checks as manipulation: Another look at the ease-of-retrieval heuristic. *Personality and Social Psychology Bulletin, 36,* 47–58.

Labroo, A. A., & Kim, S. (2009). The "instrumentality" heuristic: Why metacognitive difficulty is desirable during goal pursuit. *Psychological Science, 20,* 127–134.

Loftus, E. F., & Ketcham, K. (1994). *The myth of repressed memory.* New York, NY: St. Martin's Press.

McGuire, W. J. (1985). Attitudes and attitude change. In G. Lindzey & E. Aronson (Eds.), *Handbook of social psychology* (3rd ed., Vol. 2, pp. 233–346). New York, NY: Random House.

Nisbett, R., & Wilson, T. (1977). Telling more than we can know: Verbal reports on mental processes. *Psychological Review, 84,* 231–259.

Osterhouse, R. A., & Brock, T. C. (1970). Distraction increases yielding to propaganda by inhibiting counterarguing. *Journal of Personality and Social Psychology, 15,* 344–358.

Petty, R. E., & Briñol, P. (2006). A meta-cognitive approach to "implicit" and "explicit" evaluations: Comment on Gawronski and Bodenhausen (2006). *Psychological Bulletin, 132,* 740–744.

Petty, R. E., & Briñol, P. (2009). Implicit ambivalence: A meta-cognitive approach. In R. E. Petty, R. H. Fazio, & P. Briñol (Eds.). *Attitudes: Insights from the new implicit measures* (pp. 119–164). New York, NY: Psychology Press.

Petty, R. E. & Briñol, P. (2010). Attitude change. In R. F. Baumeister & E. J. Finkel (Eds.), *Advanced social psychology: The state of the science* (pp. 217–259). Oxford, England: Oxford University Press.

Petty, R. E., Briñol, P., & DeMarree, K. G. (2007). The meta-cognitive model (MCM) of attitudes: Implications for attitude measurement, change, and strength. *Social Cognition, 25,* 657–686.

Petty, R. E., Briñol, P., & Johnson, I. (2011). Implicit ambivalence. In B. Gawronski, & F. Strack (Eds.), *Cognitive consistency: A unifying concept in social psychology.* New York, NY: Guilford Press.

Petty, R. E., Briñol, P., Loersch, C., & McCaslin, M. J. (2009). The need for cognition. In M. R. Leary & R. H. Hoyle (Eds.), *Handbook of individual differences in social behavior* (pp. 318–329). New York, NY: Guilford Press.

Petty, R. E., Briñol, P., & Tormala, Z. L. (2002). Thought confidence as a determinant of persuasion: The self-validation hypothesis. *Journal of Personality and Social Psychology, 82,* 722–741.

Petty, R. E., Briñol, P., Tormala, Z. L., & Wegener, D. T. (2007). The role of metacognition in social judgment. In A. W. Kruglanski & E. T. Higgins (Eds.), *Social psychology: Handbook of basic principles* (2nd ed., pp. 254–284). New York, NY: Guilford Press.

Petty, R. E., & Cacioppo, J. T. (1979). Issue involvement can increase or decrease persuasion by enhancing message-relevant cognitive responses. *Journal of Personality and Social Psychology, 37,* 1915–1926.

Petty, R. E., & Cacioppo, J. T. (1981). *Attitudes and persuasion: Classics and contemporary approaches.* Dubuque, IA: Win. C. Brown.

Petty, R. E., & Cacioppo, J. T. (1986). *Communication and persuasion: Central and peripheral routes to attitude change.* New York, NY: Springer-Verlag.

Petty, R. E., Haugtvedt, C. P., & Smith, S. M. (1995). Elaboration as a determinant of attitude strength: Creating attitudes that are persistent, resistant, and predictive of behavior. In R. E. Petty and J. A. Krosnick (Eds.), *Attitude strength: Antecedents and consequences* (pp. 93–130). Hillsdale, NJ: Lawrence Erlbaum Associates.

Petty, R. E., Ostrom, T. M., & Brock, T. C. (Eds.). (1981). *Cognitive responses in persuasion.* Hillsdale, NJ: Lawrence Erlbaum Associates.

Petty, R. E., Tormala, Z. L., Briñol, P., & Jarvis, W. B. G. (2006). Implicit ambivalence from attitude change: An exploration of the PAST model. *Journal of Personality and Social Psychology, 90,* 21–41.

Petty, R. E., Wells, G. L., & Brock, T. C. (1976). Distraction can enhance or reduce yielding to propaganda: Thought disruption versus effort justification. *Journal of Personality and Social Psychology, 34,* 874–884.

Petty, R. E., Wheeler, S. C., & Bizer, G. (2000). Matching effects in persuasion: An elaboration likelihood analysis (pp. 133–162). In G. Maio & J. Olson (Eds.), *Why we evaluate: Functions of attitudes.* Mahwah, NJ: Lawrence Erlbaum Associates.

Rucker, D. D., Briñol, P., & Petty, R. E. (2010). Metacognition: Methods to assess primary and secondary cognition. In K. C. Klauer, C. Stahl, & A. Voss (Eds.), *Handbook of cognitive methods in social psychology.* New York, NY: Guildford Press.

Rucker, D. D., Petty, R. E., & Briñol, P. (2008). What's in a frame anyway? A meta-cognitive analysis of the impact of one- versus two-sided message framing on attitude certainty. *Journal of Consumer Psychology, 18,* 137–149.

Rydell, R. J., McConnell, A. R., & Mackie, D. M. (2008). Consequences of discrepant explicit and implicit attitudes: Cognitive dissonance and increased information processing. *Journal of Experimental Social Psychology, 44,* 1526–1532

Schachter, S., & Singer, J. E. (1962) Cognitive, social, and physiological determinants of emotional state. *Psychological Review, 69,* 379–399.

Schwarz, N., Bless, H., Strack, F., Klumpp, G., Rittenauer-Schatka, H., & Simons, A. (1991). Ease of retrieval as information: Another look at the availability heuristic. *Journal of Personality and Social Psychology, 61,* 195–202.

Schwarz, N., & Clore, G. L. (1983). Mood, misattribution, and judgments of well-being: Informative and directive functions of affective states. *Journal of Personality and Social Psychology, 45,* 513–523.

See, Y. H. M., Petty, R. E., & Fabrigar, L. R. (2008). Affective and cognitive meta-bases of attitudes: Unique effects on information interest and persuasion. *Journal of Personality and Social Psychology, 94,* 938–955.

Tiedens, L. Z., & Linton, S. (2001). Judgment under emotional certainty and uncertainty: The effects of specific emotions on information processing. *Journal of Personality and Social Psychology, 81,* 973–988.

Tormala, Z. L., Falces, C., Briñol, P., & Petty, R. E. (2007). Ease of retrieval effects in social judgment: The role of unrequested cognitions. *Journal of Personality and Social Psychology, 93,* 143–157.

Tormala, Z. L., Petty, R. E., & Briñol, P. (2002). Ease of retrieval effects in persuasion: A self-validation analysis. *Personality and Social Psychology Bulletin, 28,* 1700–1712.

Tversky, A., & Kahneman, D. (1973). Availability: A heuristic for judging frequency and probability. *Cognitive Psychology, 5,* 207–232.

Unkelbach, C. (2006). The learned interpretation of cognitive fluency. *Psychological Science, 17,* 339–345.

Weick, M., & Guinote, A. (2008). When subjective experiences matter: Power increases reliance on the ease of retrieval. *Journal of Personality and Social Psychology, 94,* 956–970.

Wen, E. W., Rucker, D. D., Tormala, Z., & Clarkson, J. (2010). The effects of regulatory depletion on attitude certainty. *Journal of Marketing Research, 47,* 531–541.

Wilson, T. D., Dunn, D. S., Bybee, J. A., Hyman, D. B., & Rotondo, J. A. (1984). Effects of analyzing reasons on attitude–behavior consistency. *Journal of Personality and Social Psychology, 47,* 5–16.

Wilson, T. D., Lisle, D. J., Schooler, J. W., Hodges, H. D., Klaaren, K. J., & LaFleur, S. J. (1993). Introspecting about reasons can reduce post-choice satisfaction. *Personality and Social Psychology Bulletin, 19,* 331–339.

Zajonc, R. B. (1968) Attitudinal effects of mere exposure. *Journal of Personality and Social Psychology, 9,* 1–27.

Zanna, M. P., & Cooper J. (1974). Dissonance and the pill: An attribution approach to studying the arousal properties of dissonance. *Journal of Personality and Social Psychology, 29,* 703–709.

Zanna, M. P., & Rempel, J. K. (1988). Attitudes: A new look at an old concept. In D. Bar-Tal & A. W. Kruglanski (Eds.), *The social psychology of attitudes* (pp. 315–334). New York, NY: Cambridge University Press.

4

Confidence Considered
Assessing the Quality of Decisions and Performance

DAVID DUNNING

INTRODUCTION

A day in the life is filled with many decisions. After waking up in the morning, one has to decide what to eat, what to drink, what to wear, what to do after breakfast, what to buy, what to read, what to say, what movie to rent, which food to buy to lose weight, and what gift to buy a friend, among many examples. A lifetime, as well, is defined by major decisions, even if people confront those decisions only once. People's prospects in life are substantially shaped by where they decide to go to school, the career to pursue, what car to buy, which house to live in, what person to marry—if at all—and what city in which to make a home, just to name a few significant decisions that most people face during their journey through life.

This chapter focuses on how people assess the quality of the judgments they reach and decisions they make. Obviously, the specific judgments people reach are important, but often it is second-order, metacognitive assessments that make all the difference. One central metacognitive assessment people make is the confidence they imbue in their judgments. People are likely to act decisively on the judgments in which they are the most certain. On the other hand, they are more likely to act tentatively, wait until more information is in, consult others, or make contingency plans "just in case" when reaching judgments of which they are unsure.

Thus, in this chapter, I focus on these assessments of confidence—these judgments about judgments—and explore how they are constructed. In the judgment and decision-making literature within psychology, there is nearly a half century of research examining how people come to be confident or unconfident in their conclusions, as well as whether that confidence is appropriate given the objective quality of those conclusions (for reviews, see Lichtenstein, Fischhoff, & Phillips, 1982; Moore & Healy, 2008). Specifically, I review work on three core issues about confidence. First, I discuss general findings about whether people reach appropriate levels of confidence in their judgments and actions. Second, I explore the inputs people use to decide whether they should be confident or not—and discuss whether those inputs are appropriate or misleading. I end by discussing ways to improve the quality of people's confidence estimates, to nudge people toward having more insight into the true likelihood that their decisions are well- or ill-founded ones.

However, I must mention that I will discuss confidence for events at two different levels of analysis. The first level focuses on individual judgments. If I have to judge whether the Amazon or the Nile is the longer river, or whether Company A's or B's stock is the best one to buy, or whether it is healthy for me to eat eggs, I can assess just how confident I should be about the conclusion I reach. Psychological research has long examined confidence in such individual decisions across a wide variety of tasks, including whether one has brought to mind an accurate memory, answered a general knowledge question correctly, made the right medical diagnosis, or ventured a correct prediction about how events will unfold in some foreign country—just to name a few examples (see Lichtenstein et al., 1982; Moore & Healy, 2008).

But intertwined with that literature is a similar one looking at assessments about an aggregate set of decisions. That second level I would term the *performance* level, in which people must string a few or many decisions together to complete some complicated or multifaceted task. Completing a course exam, composing a sonnet, and leading a workgroup through a significant project all involve making a number of individual decisions that ultimately add up to some summary level of achievement or failure. Often, the ultimate decisions people make are based on the conviction people have that they have performed well. A student quits studying, for example, when he or she thinks an adequate job of memorizing the relevant class material has been done (Metcalfe, 2009). Thus, in the chapter, I will weave together lessons from the literatures on individual decisions and aggregate performances because they reach similar conclusions about the processes underlying confidence and the suitability of that confidence.

THE APPROPRIATENESS OF CONFIDENCE ASSESSMENTS

The two literatures, for example, reach very similar conclusions about the appropriateness of the people's typical confidence assessments. To put the headline a little too bluntly, confidence estimates tend to reveal a rather imperfect metacognitive insight into whether an individual's decisions are accurate and performances competent. To be sure, confidence and accuracy do relate (Dunning, 2005; Dunning, Heath, & Suls, 2004; Lichtenstein et al., 1982; Moore & Healy, 2008), but the main conclusion from over 40 years of research suggests that certainty and accuracy are often dissociated. This evidence comes in two forms.

Lack of Discrimination

In the first form, if one tracks whether increases in confidence are related to equivalent increases in accuracy, one finds that increases in the former far outpace increases in the latter. In short, the correlation between confidence and accuracy is far from perfect, and people show faulty *discrimination,* which is the skill at distinguishing judgments in which they are right versus those in which they are wrong (Dunning, 2005; Dunning et al., 2004; Lichtenstein et al., 1982).

This fact has been demonstrated repeatedly in studies in which people report the subjective probability that their judgments or decisions are correct ones. Rises in confidence tend not to be matched by commensurate gains in accuracy. For example, people may be asked whether Europe or North America has a greater population or whether Arsenal or Manchester United will win the big soccer fixture coming up; then, they will be asked the chance that their judgment is right.[1] In these specific cases, confidence can range from 50-50 (*I am as likely to be wrong as I am right*) to 100% (*I am absolutely certain that I am right*). Researchers then compare these subjective probabilities to the actual rate of accuracy attained. For example, when people express 70% confidence in their judgments, are they actually right 70% of the time?

Work shows that people at low levels of confidence (e.g., people state they are just guessing) are roughly accurate about their accuracy, in that they achieve chance levels of performance. However, as their confidence marches toward 100%, their accuracy goes up, but hardly at the same rate. In fact, at 100% confidence, people are typically wrong in 15%–30% of their judgments. They concede no error, and are willing to bet money on their certainty, but they make errors roughly one out of every five times (Fischhoff, Slovic, & Lichtenstein, 1977). Similar error rates have been observed, for example, in people trying to predict how their peers will behave (Dunning, Griffin, Milojkovic, & Ross, 1990) and people predicting their own future behavior (Vallone, Griffin, Lin, & Ross, 1990). A similar lack of correlation is seen in estimates of performance (Dunning, 2005; Dunning et al., 2004).

A Bias Toward Overconfidence

The lack of correlation noted previously implies the second dissociation between confidence and accuracy. If one looks at confidence and accuracy overall, one sees that people on average overestimate the overall likelihood that their decisions will prove correct, a phenomenon known as the *overconfidence effect* (Lichtenstein et al., 1982). Hundreds of studies focusing on confidence in individual decisions have shown that the odds people give that their choices will prove right are often significantly higher than actual rates of accuracy. In essence, people achieve accuracy at a far lower rate than they anticipate.

Overconfidence is also robustly evident in people's assessments of the level of their performances (for reviews, see Dunning, 2005; Dunning et al., 2004). Students typically think their work in school deserves a letter grade higher than what their peers—and teachers—believe they deserve (Falchikov & Goldfinch, 2000). Lawyers overrate the quality of their preparation, overestimating the likelihood that they will win a case they are about to try (Loftus & Wagenaar, 1988). Stock traders tend to be overly optimistic that they have picked the right stocks in which to invest (Odean, 1998). Entrepreneurs overeagerly make decisions to start new businesses, leading to excess failure in the business place (Koellinger, Minniti, & Schade, 2007). Surgical trainees overestimate the accuracy of the medical diagnoses they reach after looking at x-rays of possible fractures (Oksam, Kingma, & Klasen, 2000). Collegiate debate teams overestimate how many tournament matches they have won (Ehrlinger, Johnson, Banner, Dunning, & Kruger, 2008).

However, I hasten to note that a lack of discrimination need not necessarily be correlated with a bias toward overconfidence. It is possible for someone to provide confidence estimates that excel at discrimination yet display much overconfidence, and vice versa. For example, consider a person who takes three math tests and believes she scored 40% on the first, 60% on the second, and 80% on the third, but who actually scored 20%, 40%, and 60%, respectively. Her perceptions of her performance are perfectly correlated with reality (an objective gain in 20% in each test is associated with a 20% rise in perception), but she is not precisely unbiased in her overall level of performance, consistently displaying 20 percentile points of bias in an optimistic direction. Thus, distinguishing between discrimination and bias is essential, for they are influenced by different psychological dynamics. The circumstances that improve or degrade discrimination are not the same as those that shape bias—an issue to be returned to later.

In addition, one should avoid overconfidence about overconfidence. Overconfidence is not inevitable. Whether it arises or the degree to which it arises depends on the context and particular judgment or performance at hand (Erev, Wallstein, & Budescu, 1994; Klayman, Soll, Gonzalez-Vallejo, & Barlas, 1999; Moore & Healy, 2008). If a task or judgment is very easy, for example, people are more likely to be underconfident in their responses rather than overconfident (Lichtenstein et al., 1982). But, if there has been a phenomenon in the judgment and decision-making literature that has been easy to find and hard to get rid of, it is the phenomenon of overconfidence—with prospects of inspiring even more empirical research (and potential woe in the real world) in the decades to come.

INPUTS INTO CONFIDENCE

How does overconfidence arise? To answer this question is tantamount to asking how people reach their confidence estimates in general. What inputs do people use to determine whether they should be certain or hesitant? What are the sources of their confidence and doubt?

In all, there are three categories of inputs that people consult to determine whether they should be confident versus unsure. The first category consists of *informational* inputs—pieces of information relevant to the specific decision at hand that people bring to mind as they choose a course of action. For example, if a person is deciding whether Philadelphia, Pennsylvania, or Madrid, Spain, lies further north on the globe, that person is likely to draw upon several pieces of information to work toward a conclusion (e.g., Madrid seems arid, Philadelphia has those chilly winters) and to decide whether that conclusion seems right or iffy. The second category consists of *experiential* inputs, which focus on the experiences people have as they execute the task of reaching a decision, such as whether the decision comes quickly or only after effort.

The final category consists of *background* inputs—broad overarching notions that people might consult to judge whether they should be confident in their conclusions. In the Philadelphia versus Madrid example, a person might have a general hunch that he or she is good at answering trivia questions or good at geography—and thus use those notions to adjust confidence higher or lower. In a sense, a background input is like an informational one, in that it is an explicit thought or belief that people can consult to assess the perceptiveness of their choices, but background inputs apply more broadly to a class of decisions (e.g., whether I am good at geography), not just to a specific judgment (e.g., whether Philadelphia lies farther north than Madrid).

What do we know about each category of metacognitive inputs? Do people weigh them appropriately? Do people exploit all the inputs they have in order to achieve accurate metacognitive perceptions about the quality of their judgments and actions? Or are these inputs exactly the reasons why people show so much overconfidence in their judgments and performances? Let us consider each type of input in turn.

Informational Inputs

People base their decisions on whether they can come up with reasons that favor one course of action over its alternative. Their confidence in a decision is based on just how strongly that information favors the course of action they reach (Hoch, 1985; Koriat, Lichtenstein, & Fischhoff, 1980). For example, suppose a person were deciding whether to buy a company's stock. To the extent that there are many favorable pieces of news about that company (e.g., they just came out with a popular new product or the management team just won an award for sound business practices) and only a few, if any, reasons to be cautious, that person should buy the stock and rest easy with confidence. Thus, it is not a surprise that people rest their confidence on the number and quality of reasons they can cite for versus against the conclusions they reach. To a great extent, this is a rational and appropriate strategy. One should express more confidence about decisions that have a lot of supporting evidence and less confidence about decisions that have little. In thinking about reasons for confidence, however, people possess three habits that cause them to misuse this potentially valuable approach.

Succumbing to Confirmation Bias   The first habit is that people fall prey to *confirmation bias*. Of the options considered, one option often becomes a favorite in the decision process for any number of reasons, such as that it is highlighted by someone else, or seems initially more likely, or constitutes the conclusion that person finds the most congenial (e.g., Russo, Meloy, & Medvec, 1998). Once in place, people rest their confidence mainly on reasons that support this focal option, giving short shrift to any rationale favoring alternatives.

For example, as college seniors begin their job interviews for life after college, they tend to be overly optimistic in their prospects, overestimating the chance that they will obtain high-paying jobs. For the most part, their confidence rises as a function of the number of reasons they can think of for why they will get an attractive job. However, if one intervenes by asking them to consider reasons they might not get such a job, they become much more calibrated in their judgments (Hoch, 1985). This has led researchers to propose that the best thing people can do to avoid overconfidence is to "consider the opposite" explicitly—to consider ways in which their favored or most likely judgment may be wrong (Koriat et al., 1980; Lord, Lepper, & Preston, 1984).

Confirmation bias in informational search may also explain the common finding in the overconfidence literature that people become more certain, but no more accurate, as they are fed more and more information. Clinical psychologists fed more information about a client's case become more confident in their predictions about that client, without any gains in accuracy (Oskamp, 1965). Participants become more overconfident in their predictions about baseball or football team performance as they are given more information about the team (Peterson & Pitz, 1988; Tsai, Klayman, & Hastie, 2008). People also become more confident, but no more accurate, about how well they know their acquaintances the longer they have known them (Gill, Swann, & Silvera, 1998; Swann & Gill, 1997).

Ignoring the Weight Appropriate to Given Information

Another problem is that people also focus on the *strength* of the information they have in hand but neglect the *weight* they should give to that information (Griffin & Tversky, 1992). By strength, I refer to the degree to which information suggests one conclusion over the other. For example, if Jerry tells me that Chip has broken his arm, I would likely guess that Chip will lose the tennis match he is playing this afternoon. Weight refers to the extent that information is reliable or valid. That is, information can appear to favor one alternative decisively over the other, but if its credibility is weak, it should be given less weight. For example, if Jerry is a frequent liar, I should discount his rather strong piece of information about Chip.

Research findings show that people pay substantial attention to the strength of the evidence, but inappropriately overlook issues of weight. MBA students pick stocks, for example, based on how strongly the evidence suggests that a stock is a good one, without paying adequate attention to whether the source of that information is credible (Nelson, Bloomfield, Hales, & Libby, 2001). Investors pour money into mutual funds that have had a recent spurt of profitability, ignoring the fact that short-term gains are not reliable indicators of long-term results. In this way, weak mutual funds (and the suboptimal returns their investors make) are allowed to survive (Harless & Peterson, 1998).

Neglecting the Limits of One's Knowledge

Finally, people neglect the limits of their knowledge (Caputo & Dunning, 2005; Dunning, Johnson, Ehrlinger, & Kruger, 2003; Kruger & Dunning, 1999). When key information is missing or unknowable, people often fail to take this into account—a phenomenon known as *omission neglect* (Sanbonmatsu, Kardes, & Herr, 1992). In a sense, missing information should make people more cautious in their judgments because missing information can take on any value and point a decision in any direction (Yamagishi

& Hill, 1983). But several studies have shown that, in the face of missing information, people make judgments that are just as extreme, if not more extreme, and that are held with just as much confidence, if not more (Sanbonmatsu, Kardes, Houghton, Ho, & Posavac, 2003; Sanbonmatsu, Kardes, & Sansone, 1991).

For example, if asked to judge a quality of a bicycle, people will ignore the fact that important information is missing from its description, such as the bicycle's weight and the strength of its frame, as though that information matters not one whit (Sanbonmatsu et al., 1992). There are some limits to this neglect. If missing information is explicitly pointed out or if people are given complete information for other similar decisions, people will lower their confidence in the face of missing information (Sanbonmatsu et al., 1992). In addition, people with a good deal of expertise will spontaneously give weight to what is missing (Sanbonmatsu et al., 1992, 2003).

Summary   Thus, when it comes to informational inputs, it appears that people take the reasonable step of considering the strength of evidence for one choice over its alternatives in assessing their confidence. However, their deliberation over these inputs typically contains some flaws. They give most weight to information that supports their likely conclusion, fail to consider adequately the weight they should give to information due to its lack of reliability, and neglect to consider information they do not have. The net effect of these habits is to exacerbate any overconfidence in decisions and judgment they ultimately reach. Thus, people's consideration of informational inputs, although proper, can lead to improper results.

Experiential Inputs

Confidence, however, is based not merely on informational inputs but also on the *process* by which people reach their decisions. People base their certainty, in part, on what they experience as they go from confronting the question to providing the answer, such as the ease with which they reach the destination of a conclusion or have experiences that they equate with getting to the right answer. In all, research points to three types of experiential inputs that people use to form their confidence.

Stimulus Familiarity   People are more confident in their decisions to the extent that they feel they stand on familiar ground. For example, if I ask you, gentle reader, about your expertise in *individualized hygienics,* you would probably deny any knowledge about such an alien topic. But, instead, if I ask you about your skill at *personal hygiene* (which refers to the same thing), you might switch to claim some know-how on the subject. Much research shows that people base their confidence on whether the terms included in questions and answers (i.e., the stimuli in front of them) feel familiar (Glenberg, Wilkinson, & Epstein, 1982; Koriat, 2008b).

Like informational inputs, stimulus familiarity seems a reasonable input to use to gauge competence. I am likely to answer questions better about English (a language I know something about) than I am about German (of which I have some familiarity) and, in turn, about Swahili (of which I know nothing). And, to be sure, familiarity can be a valuable input about expertise. However, people use familiarity as an input even when it is independent of their chances of reaching the right answer.

A person's familiarity with the stimulus can be influenced by incidental experiences that have nothing to do with their ability to provide a right answer. Ask people the sum of 45 + 56 and, subsequently, they become more confident that they can give the answer to 45 × 56 (Reder & Ritter, 1992). Ask experimental participants who the prime minister of Canada is, and they are more confident if they have just been exposed, in an offhand and irrelevant way, to the words *prime* and *minister* (Schwartz & Metcalfe, 1992). Familiarity can also be raised by mere repetition of the terms used in questions. Ask people several questions about China, and they become more confident that they can subsequently answer any question about that country; presumably, their knowledge of it has an enhanced feel of familiarity (Arkes, Boehm, & Xu, 1991).

Decision Fluency   People also base their confidence on how quickly or *fluently* they reach an answer (Costermans, Lories, & Ansay, 1992; Koriat, 2008a; Robinson, Johnson, & Herndon, 1997; Schwarz, 2004). If an answer comes quickly, they are confident. If the answer comes only after a slow, effortful, conscious, and time-intensive process, they are less confident. Processing effort is often misattributed to the difficulty of the task itself. For example, asking students to read a recipe in a small and unfamiliar font makes them less confident that any particular individual could successfully cook the dish being described (Song & Schwarz, 2008). Making an answer come to mind more easily makes people more confident in that answer, regardless of whether the answer coming to mind is right or wrong. As an example, Kelley and Lindsay (1993) nudged people to answer general knowledge questions more quickly (such as "What was the last name of Buffalo Bill?") by quickly exposing participants to plausible answers (such as the right one, *Cody*, and wrong ones, such as *Hickock*). Participants answered more quickly after such exposure, and that quickness led to more confidence, irrespective of accuracy.

Other circumstances can ramp up decision fluency in a way that has an effect on confidence but not on judgment quality. Repetition inflates confidence due to fluency. To the extent that people answer the same question over and over, they become quicker and more confident in their response, although the response itself obviously does not gain in accuracy in the retelling (Wells, Ferguson, & Lindsay, 1981; Zaragoza & Mitchell, 1996). Information overload about a topic can also lead to fluency in judgment, and thus confidence, because a person has so much information to draw on to come to a quick and easy answer—one that arises, unfortunately, without any commensurate increase in accuracy (Gill et al., 1998).

Decision Consistency   People's confidence is also shaped by how systematically or consistently they reach their judgments. Errors come in many shapes and sizes and are not necessarily produced by the same process. People can make haphazard reasoning errors due to sloppiness or inattention, but they can also make errors that are *rational*. By "rational," I mean that people have some underlying rule or algorithm that leads to the answers they provide. The term comes from educational psychology, where there is research showing that the errors that primary school students make when they tackle math are far from haphazard. Usually, their errors are systematic, in that the student is rigorously applying a set of rules that inadvertently contain some flaw, omission, or misunderstandings, leading to answers that are always incorrect in exactly the same way (Ben-Zeev, 1995, 1998).

Thus, people can approach tasks in a very exacting and methodical way, but the method they are using may contain some defect that steers them away from the correct solution. They might select the wrong information, or combine it with other information in the wrong way, or give it the wrong weight. But, with a rule or algorithm, people might be left with a feeling of confidence for several reasons. First, habitually following an algorithm might make a decision feel more fluent (Kelley & Lindsay, 1993; Metcalfe, 1998), leading people toward more confidence. Following an algorithm may also blind people to alternative ways of thinking, and much research shows that taking an alternative view reduces inappropriate confidence (e.g., Koehler, 1991; Lord et al., 1984). Finally, consistent and analytical thought is much prized in contemporary Western culture and may simply be seen as the superior way to approach many tasks in life (Lehman, Lempert, & Nisbett, 1988).

In recent work, we have shown that the more systematic or rational people are in their approach to judgment, the more confident—and overconfident—they prove to be. In one study, we examined how people approached Wason selection tasks—a logical reasoning task that few people complete accurately without training. We discovered that the more consistently participants approached these tasks (i.e., they tended to come to the same solution, whether right or wrong), the better they thought they had performed, regardless of the truth. To the extent that participants appeared to approach the task in a haphazard and ad hoc way, they were less confident in their performance (Williams & Dunning, 2010).

Most telling was an examination of participants who solved every problem in exactly the same way, showing 100% consistency in their solutions. Most of these participants were always right in their solutions, but some were consistently wrong. When we compared the perceptions of those who were consistently right versus consistently wrong, we found that both groups were equally confident in their responses and overall performance. In short, following a consistent rule conferred confidence, regardless of whether that rule led down the right or wrong path (Williams & Dunning, 2010).

Summary   People base their confidence on the experiences they have as they tackle judgments and decisions. To the extent that their experience shows signs they associate with good judgment (the stimulus is familiar, the decision comes easily, and they have some consistent rule to follow), they will be more confident in their choices. To the reader, relying on these experiential inputs may seem unsurprising. They may also seem sensible, in that these experiences may actually be associated with real accuracy. This is an intuition to which I will return later, but for now it is important to note that such experiences might be connected to accuracy as well as to other incidental circumstances that have nothing to do with accuracy whatsoever.

Background Inputs

So far, we have been focusing on the concrete experiences people have with the task or judgment at hand. Basing metacognitive assessments of judgment quality on these inputs could be termed a *bottom-up* strategy: One monitors the moment-to-moment experience with the task and infers quality from that. But, can metacognitive estimates also be *top-down*—that is, shaped by general theories people have about themselves and the task?

Our work suggests that metacognitive assessments of decision and performance carry a significant top-down component, in that confidence is very much influenced by preconceived notions people have about their skill and expertise. If Larry already thinks he is a terrific artist, then that painting he finished yesterday is pretty good. If Ned thinks he is not a good cook, then the soufflé is not that tasty. In essence, what a top-down approach to quality assessment means is that a good chunk of the assessment has already been arrived at before people are even aware of the task they will ultimately confront.

Preconceived Self-Beliefs of Competence   We have shown that metacognitive assessments of performance are significantly guided by preexisting self-views. People's perceptions of their achievement on a logical reasoning task are more tightly correlated, depending on the measure, with preexisting beliefs they hold about their logical reasoning competence than with their actual performance (Ehrlinger & Dunning, 2003). Similarly, Kroner and Biermann (2007) found that people's confidence in their performance on a spelling test, a reasoning test, and a quiz on the psychology of perception were all importantly influenced by general views of their academic ability, creativity, and problem-solving skills. In perhaps the most striking demonstration, Bradley (1981) asked college students to answer pointedly impossible questions, such as specifying the boiling point of mercury. Students who had rated their expertise as high were more likely to answer these questions and then to stick to those answers even though they performed at chance levels.

Altering self-views also prompts people to change perceptions about their performance, suggesting that people, indeed, look to these preexisting self-views to inform their metacognitive judgments. In one study, we gave all our participants the exact same test of analytical reasoning, but altered which self-view we said was relevant to it. Roughly half of participants were told that the test focused on abstract reasoning ability, a skill our participants tended to rate rather highly in themselves. The remainder were told that the test measured computer programming skills, an expertise our participant pool tended to deny having. Despite the fact that participants all completed the exact same test and achieved equivalent scores, participants predicted that they had posted a higher score on the test when it was described as about abstract reasoning as opposed to computer programming skills (Ehrlinger & Dunning, 2003).

This reliance on top-down beliefs may explain one curious, but reliable, counterexample to overconfidence in the psychological literature. It has been shown that as people practice a memory test, they become less, not more, confident in their performance and, ultimately, end up underestimating how much they remember—an *underconfidence with practice effect* (Koriat, Sheffer, & Ma'ayan, 2002). This underconfidence seems to arise because people predominantly base their performance estimate on how well they have done with previous versions of a memory test; indeed, their performance estimates correlate with previous performances more than they do with performance on the test being asked about. And, when it comes to remembering their previous performance, people are likely to remember the specific items they got wrong, which leads them to lower their confidence, while the confidence they imbue in the items they got right remains unchanged (Finn & Metcalfe, 2007, 2008). In short, people base their metacognitive estimates of performance on previous experience—ironically making those estimates less accurate about their current performance.

Relation of Background Inputs to Bottom-Up Experiences   These initial demonstrations of the use of top-down self-views in assessments of performance left us with two mysteries. The first was the exact psychological mechanism that links preconceived self-notions to estimates of performance. Were people, for example, anchoring their performance estimates on some general notion of their expertise, or was some other process involved? The second mystery was why bottom-up experiences did not "crowd out" the impact of top-down self-views. After having a concrete and vivid experience with the task, why did people still refer to some abstract ideas about themselves to inform their assessments?

We now believe, with data, that the solution to these two mysteries is intertwined. Bottom-up experiences should not crowd out top-down influences. Instead, they are the very vehicle by which top-down views influence performance estimates. Top-down self-beliefs set up an array of expectations that guide bottom-up experiences with a task. For those holding favorable views of their skills, relative to those without such self-views, they perceive the elements of the task to be more familiar and the process toward an answer more fluent and thus have more confidence in the judgments they make.

We have put this idea to the test in several studies. In one, we asked participants to complete a social reasoning task, asking them after each question to describe their bottom-up experiences (e.g., whether they knew the answer immediately, whether they had to go back and forth between multiple answers, whether they thought they were guessing). We then examined the correlations between preexisting self-views on social intelligence, bottom-up experiences, and assessments of performance. We found that self-views were once again linked to performance assessments, but that this link was, at least partially, explained by differences in how participants described their bottom-up experiences (Critcher & Dunning, 2009).

In a follow-up study, we reran the abstract reasoning versus computer programming experiment described earlier, but this time we introduced the label for the test either before or after participants had taken the test. If top-down self-views influence performance assessments because they alter people's bottom-up experiences, then the impact of self-view information should be more evident if participants were informed of the relevant self-view *before* rather than after they took the test and had bottom-up experiences with it. That is, indeed, exactly what we found (Critcher & Dunning, 2009).

CORRECTING CONFIDENCE ASSESSMENTS

In all, people have a large range of inputs they can call upon to inform their confidence estimates. But this large variety of inputs leaves a puzzle. It would seem that all of the inputs listed previously have some validity to them, so why are people so pervasively overconfident? And why is confidence so imperfectly tethered to accuracy?

One answer to this question is to point out that there is some relation of confidence to accuracy, so the inputs that people rely on to assess their confidence do contain some validity. But those assessments of confidence also contain some error, sometimes substantive, for three reasons. First, these inputs are only imperfect indicators of decision accuracy. Background beliefs of competence, for example, are only mildly correlated with actual performance (Dunning, 2005; Dunning et al., 2004; Mabe & West, 1982), so it is very easy to give them too much weight in assessing the quality of one's decisions and performance. Second, these inputs can be influenced by factors that have nothing to do with accuracy, such as stimulus familiarity influenced by incidental recent experiences, repetition, and information overload, as discussed before. Finally, people often neglect inputs that could lead to more accurate judgments, as described earlier, such as information about an option they are not likely to choose.

Thus, people's assessments of confidence, although they contain some validity, could be improved. Could people somehow be trained to provide confidence estimates that more closely track the accuracy and quality of their judgments and performances? Could they be educated about how to avoid overconfidence? In other corners of psychology, researchers have talked about nudging people toward correcting imperfections at the level of the judgments they make—that is, among the decisions they reach and the actions they choose (Wegener & Petty, 1997). But what about imperfection at the second-order, metacognitive level? When it comes to judgments about judgments (i.e., the confidence people place in those judgments), can people learn to become unbiased as well?

Before talking about improvement in the metacognitive assessment of judgment and performance, it is important to recall that imperfection in confidence estimates can be revealed in two separate ways. One is that they show lack of discrimination between correct and incorrect judgments. The second is through a bias toward overconfidence. Past research has shown that improving discrimination does little to reduce bias and that reducing bias does little to enhance discrimination. Ultimately, there may not be a one-size-fits-all procedure for reducing mistaken confidence in decisions and performance.

Toward More Discrimination

The type of training that improves discrimination may not be the type that reduces overall bias. In fact, this is what Stone and Opel (2000) found in their attempts to debias misguided confidence. In one condition, Stone and Opel trained participants about what features to look for when placing paintings in different historical eras of art. Relative to a control group, this instruction prompted participants to show more discrimination in their confidence ratings. They were much more likely to be right when they were highly confident than when they were uncertain. This instruction, however, did not reduce an overall overconfidence bias. In fact, participants were significantly more overconfident overall in the group that received instruction.

In effect, this finding should not come as a surprise, in that it is anticipated by many studies indicating that experts often show more discrimination than novices in their confidence assessments (see Dunning, 2005, for a review) but fail to show any less overconfidence. Experts in foreign exchange rates are more accurate but no less overconfident in their predictions of future currency trends (Önkal, Yates, Şimga-Mugan, & Öztin, 2003). In predictions about the 2006 World Cup in soccer, knowledgeable individuals were better at predicting game scores, but they still proved even more overconfident in their judgments than novice participants were (Andersson, Memmert, & Popowicz, 2009).

Toward Less Overconfidence

All the preceding steps are more likely to aid discrimination than to reduce bias in metacognitive assessments. That is, giving proper weight to such metacognitive inputs as information, fluency, and background knowledge would likely help people gain more appropriate signals of when their judgment is likely to be correct versus incorrect. However, it may not necessarily aid people in getting rid of overall levels of unrealistic confidence. Why is this? In a Zen-like manner, I can make the assertion that people will suffer overconfidence even if they are not, in general, overconfident people. That is, even if people give appropriate weight to the information and experiences they have in making their decisions, they will nonetheless show some overconfidence in the judgments they reach and the actions they choose.

How to Attain Overconfidence Without Overconfidence   How can this "overconfidence without overconfidence" phenomenon arise? Perhaps the best way to explain it is to think of a metaphor. Imagine an auction in which people have gathered to bid for a variety of items. Consider the first item to be a painting by a well-known artist. Imagine that potential bidders, on average, show no bias in how much they value that painting. Across the people gathered, the average value assigned to the painting equals exactly its true value. At the individual level, however, people will value the painting differently. Some will value it much more highly than others—and more highly than the painting is really worth. Others will value the painting less highly, underestimating its true value.

Now let us have the auction proceed until the bid is exactly at the painting's true value and, at this point, split the assembled into two groups: those who decide to bid further and those who decide not to. What is likely to be true of the group that bids? It contains a number of people who overestimate the value of the painting—a phenomenon known as the winner's curse (Thaler, 1988). In other words, they are overconfident that the correct decision is to bid. What is likely to be true of the opposite group? They underestimate the value of the painting and thus are overconfident that withdrawing from the auction is the correct decision to make. That is, although people at the auction show no bias in their valuation of the painting overall, people ultimately sort themselves into decisions for which they will show overconfidence.

In a sense, making decisions is much like this auction example. Even if people, on average, can assess what the proper course of action is in an unbiased way, they will end up being overconfident in the specific decisions they choose to make. Think of a stock trader who must make many decisions about what to buy in the stock market who is, on average, unbiased in his evaluations of stocks. Whatever information he has, some part will point toward a right answer and some will point to an over- or undervaluation of a particular stock. If the information leads the stock trader to overvalue that particular stock, he will buy it with too much confidence. If the information leads him to undervalue it, he will pass, again with too much confidence. What is true for the stock picker is true of all of us. Even if, on average, our evaluation of which action to take across many decisions is unbiased, we will still show overconfidence in the decisions we ultimately make.

Performance Feedback   Thus, reducing the bias component of overconfidence requires another type of training: showing people that the objective accuracy they achieve never justifies the outsized levels of confidence they inevitably express. In 1980, Lichtenstein and Fischhoff did just that. They asked students to answer 200 general knowledge questions and, for each question to gauge the likelihood that their answer was right. They then presented participants with a report describing how well their accuracy matched their performance. Participants were shown, for example, their rate of accuracy for judgments made with 50% confidence, 60% confidence,…all the way to 100% confidence. Participants duly noted that their confidence tended to be too high, and in a follow-up session answering a new set of 200 questions, their overconfidence evaporated. Other researchers have shown similar results (Benson & Önkal, 1992; Stone & Opel, 2000), but have also shown that this procedure does nothing to improve discrimination.

CONCLUDING REMARKS

In sum, although people make a thousand decisions during the course of their lives, it appears that the typical person has much work to do to improve his or her metacognitive assessments of the quality of those decisions. People have many inputs to gauge their confidence—that is, to assess whether their choices are right or wrong—but they can develop smarter habits to use those inputs better, as well as to look for inputs they often neglect. A day in the life is filled up with many decisions, but people should be wary and make sure those decisions are not made with misplaced confidence.

ACKNOWLEDGMENT

The writing of this chapter was supported financially by National Science Foundation Grant 0745806.

NOTE

1. This method of assessing confidence is only one of several that have been used to assess confidence in decisions and performance. Although these different methods all converge to show that people are typically overconfident, each method at times produces patterns of overconfidence that seemingly contradict those found via different methods (Erev et al., 1994; Moore & Healy, 2008). It is beyond the scope of this chapter to discuss these apparent, often technical contradictions. Thus, we focus on methods involving assessments of subjective probability for individual decisions and summary evaluations for appraisals of performance, which tend to reveal compatible patterns.

REFERENCES

Andersson, P., Memmert, D., & Popowicz, E. (2009). Forecasting outcomes of the World Cup 2006 in football: Performance and confidence of bettors and laypeople. *Psychology of Sport and Exercise, 10,* 116–123.

Arkes, H. R., Boehm, L. E., & Xu, G. (1991). Determinants of judged validity. *Journal of Experimental Social Psychology, 27,* 576–605.

Benson, P. G., & D. Önkal (1992). The effects of feedback and training on the performance of probability forecasters. *International Journal of Forecasting, 8,* 559–573.

Ben-Zeev, T. (1995). The nature and origin of rational errors in arithmetic thinking: Induction from examples and prior knowledge. *Cognitive Science, 19,* 341–376.

Ben-Zeev, T. (1998). Rational errors and the mathematical mind. *Review of General Psychology, 2,* 366–383.

Bradley, M. J. (1981). Overconfidence in ignorant experts. *Bulletin of the Psychonomic Society, 17,* 82–84.

Caputo, D. D., & Dunning, D. (2005). What you don't know: The role played by errors of omission in imperfect self-assessments. *Journal of Experimental Social Psychology, 41,* 488–505.

Costermans, J., Lories, G., & Ansay, C. (1992). Confidence level and feeling of knowing in question answering: The weight of inferential processes. *Journal of Experimental Psychology: Learning, Memory, and Cognition, 18,* 142–150.

Critcher, C. R., & Dunning, D. (2009). How chronic self-views influence (and mislead) self-evaluations of performance: Self-views shape bottom-up experiences with the task. *Journal of Personality and Social Psychology, 97,* 931–945.

Dunning, D. (2005). *Self-insight: Roadblocks and detours on the path to knowing thyself.* New York, NY: Psychology Press.

Dunning, D., Griffin, D. W., Milojkovic, J. H., & Ross, L. (1990). The overconfidence effect in social prediction. *Journal of Personality and Social Psychology, 58,* 568–592.

Dunning, D., Heath, C., & Suls, J. M. (2004). Flawed self-assessment: Implications for health, education, and the workplace. *Psychological Science in the Public Interest, 5,* 69–106.

Dunning, D., Johnson, K., Ehrlinger, J., & Kruger, J. (2003). Why people fail to recognize their own incompetence. *Current Directions in Psychological Science, 12,* 83–86.

Ehrlinger, J., & Dunning, D. (2003). How chronic self-views influence (and potentially mislead) assessments of performance. *Journal of Personality and Social Psychology, 84,* 5–17.

Ehrlinger, J., Johnson, K., Banner, M., Dunning, D., & Kruger, J. (2008). Why the unskilled are unaware: Further explorations of (lack of) self-insight among the incompetent. *Organizational Behavior and Human Decision Processes, 105,* 98–121.

Erev, I., Wallstein T. S., & Budescu D. V. (1994). Simultaneous overconfidence and under-confidence—The role of error in judgment processes. *Psychological Review, 101,* 519–527

Falchikov, N., & Goldfinch, J. (2000). Student peer assessment in higher education: A meta-analysis comparing peer and teacher marks. *Review of Educational Research, 70,* 287–322.

Finn, B., & Metcalfe, J. (2007). The role of memory for past test in the underconfidence with practice effect. *Journal of Experimental Psychology: Learning Memory and Cognition, 33,* 238–244.

Finn, B., & Metcalfe, J. (2008). Judgments of learning are influenced by memory for past test. *Journal of Memory and Language, 58,* 19–34.

Fischhoff, B., Slovic, P., & Lichtenstein, S. (1977). Knowing with certainty: The appropriate-ness of extreme confidence. *Journal of Experimental Psychology: Human Perception and Performance, 3,* 552–564.

Gill, M. J., Swann, W. B., Jr., & Silvera, D. H. (1998). On the genesis of confidence. *Journal of Personality and Social Psychology, 75,* 1101–1114.

Glenberg, A. M., Wilkinson, A., & Epstein, W. (1982). The illusion of knowing: Failure in the self-assessment of comprehension. *Memory & Cognition, 10,* 597–602.

Griffin, D., & Tversky, A. (1992). The weighing of evidence and the determinants of confi-dence. *Cognitive Psychology, 24,* 411–435.

Harless, D. W., & Peterson, S. P. (1998). Investor behavior and the persistence of poorly performing mutual funds. *Journal of Economic Behavior and Organization, 37,* 257–276.

Hoch, S. J. (1985). Counterfactual reasoning and accuracy in predicting personal events. *Journal of Experimental Psychology: Learning, Memory, and Cognition, 11,* 719–731.

Kelley, C. M., & Lindsay, D. S. (1993). Remembering mistaken for knowing—Ease of retrieval as a basis for confidence in answers to general knowledge questions. *Journal of Memory and Language, 32,* 1–24.

Klayman, J., Soll, J., Gonzalez-Vallejo, C., & Barlas, S. (1999). Overconfidence: It depends on how, what, and whom you ask. *Organizational Behavior and Human Decision Processes, 79,* 216–247.

Koehler, D. J. (1991). Explanation, imagination, and confidence in judgment. *Psychological Bulletin, 110,* 499–519.

Koellinger, P., Minniti, M., & Schade, C. (2007). "I think I can, I think I can…": A study of entrepreneurial behavior. *Journal of Economic Psychology, 28,* 502–527.

Koriat, A. (2008a). Subjective confidence in one's answers: The consensuality prin-ciple. *Journal of Experimental Psychology: Learning, Memory, and Cognition, 34,* 945–959.

Koriat, A. (2008b). When confidence in a choice is independent of which choice is made. *Psychonomic Bulletin & Review, 15,* 997–1001.

Koriat, A., Lichtenstein, S., & Fischhoff, B. (1980). Reasons for confidence. *Journal of Experimental Psychology: Human Learning and Memory, 6,* 107–118.

Koriat, A., Sheffer, L., & Ma'ayan, H. (2002). Comparing objective and subjective learn-ing curves: Judgments of learning exhibit increased underconfidence with practice. *Journal of Experimental Psychology: General, 131,* 147–162.

Kroner, S., & Biermann, A. (2007). The relationship between confidence and self-concept—Towards a model of response confidence. *Intelligence, 35,* 580–590.

Kruger, J., & Dunning, D. (1999). Unskilled and unaware of it: How difficulties in recogniz-ing one's own incompetence lead to inflated self-assessments. *Journal of Personality and Social Psychology, 77,* 1121–1134.

Lehman, D. R., Lempert, R. O., & Nisbett, R. E. (1988). The effects of graduate training on reasoning: Formal discipline and thinking about everyday-life events. *American Psychologist, 43,* 431–442.

Lichtenstein, S., & Fischhoff, B. (1980). Training for calibration. *Organizational Behavior and Human Performance, 26,* 149–171.

Lichtenstein, S., Fischhoff, B., & Phillips, L. D. (1982). Calibration of probabilities: The state of the art to 1980. In D. Kahneman, P. Slovic, & A. Tversky (Eds.), *Judgment under uncertainty: Heuristics and biases.* Cambridge, UK: Cambridge University Press.

Loftus, E. F., & Wagenaar, W. A. (1988). Lawyers' predictions of success. *Jurimetrics Journal, 29,* 437–453.

Lord, C. G., Lepper, M. R., & Preston, E. (1984). Considering the opposite: A corrective strategy for social judgment. *Journal of Personality and Social Psychology, 47,* 1231–1243.

Mabe, P. A., III, & West, S. G. (1982). Validity of self-evaluation of ability: A review and meta-analysis. *Journal of Applied Psychology, 67,* 280–286.

Metcalfe, J. (1998). Cognitive optimism: Self-deception or memory-based processing heuristics. *Personality and Social Psychology Review, 2,* 100–110.

Metcalfe, J. (2009). Metacognitive judgments and control of study. *Current Directions in Psychological Science, 18,* 164–168.

Moore, D. A., & Healy, P. J. (2008). The trouble with overconfidence. *Psychological Review, 115,* 502–517.

Nelson, M. W., Bloomfield, R., Hales, J. W., & Libby, R. (2001). The effect of information strength and weight on behavior in financial markets. *Organizational Behavior & Human Decision Processes, 86,* 168–196.

Odean, T. (1998). Volume, volatility, price, and profit when all traders are above average. *Journal of Finance, 8,* 1887–1934.

Oksam, J., Kingma, J., & Klasen, H. J. (2000). Clinicians' recognition of 10 different types of distal radial fractures. *Perceptual and Motor Skills, 91,* 917–924.

Önkal, D., Yates, J. F., Şımga-Mugan, C., & Öztin, S. (2003). Professional vs. amateur judgment accuracy: The case of foreign exchange rates. *Organizational Behavior and Human Decision Processes, 91,* 169–185.

Oskamp, S. (1965). Overconfidence in case-study judgments. *Journal of Clinical Psychology, 29,* 261–265.

Peterson, D. K., & Pitz, G. F. (1988). Confidence, uncertainty, and the use of information. *Journal of Experimental Psychology: Learning, Memory, and Cognition, 14,* 85–92.

Reder, L. M., & Ritter, F. E. (1992). What determines initial feeling of knowing? Familiarity with question terms, not with the answer. *Journal of Experimental Psychology: Learning, Memory, and Cognition, 13,* 435–451.

Robinson, M. D., Johnson, J. T., & Herndon, F. (1997). Reaction time and assessments of cognitive effort as predictors of eyewitness memory accuracy and confidence. *Journal of Applied Psychology, 82,* 416–425.

Russo, J. E., Meloy, M. G., & Medvec, V. H. (1998). The distortion of product information during brand choice. *Journal of Marketing Research, 35,* 438–452.

Sanbonmatsu, D. M., Kardes, F. R., & Herr, P. (1992). The role of prior knowledge and missing information in multi-attribute evaluation. *Organizational Behavior and Human Decision Processes, 51,* 76–91.

Sanbonmatsu, D. M., Kardes, F. R., Houghton, D. C., Ho, E. A., & Posavac, S. S. (2003). Overestimating the importance of the given information in multiattribute judgment. *Journal of Consumer Psychology, 13,* 289–300.

Sanbonmatsu, D. M., Kardes, F. R., & Sansone, C. (1991). Remembering less and inferring more: The effects of time of judgment on inferences about unknown attributes. *Journal of Personality and Social Psychology, 61,* 546–554.

Schwartz, B. L., & Metcalfe, J. (1992). Cue familiarity but not target retrievability enhances feeling-of-knowing judgments. *Journal of Experimental Psychology: Learning, Memory, and Cognition, 18,* 1074–1083.

Schwarz, N. (2004). Metacognitive experiences in consumer judgment and decision making. *Journal of Consumer Psychology, 14,* 332–348.

Song, H., & Schwarz, N. (2008). If it's hard to read, it's hard to do: Processing fluency affects effort prediction and motivation. *Psychological Science, 19,* 986–988.

Stone, E. R., & Opel, R. B. (2000). Training to improve calibration and discrimination: The effects of performance and environmental feedback. *Organizational Behavior and Human Decision Processes, 83,* 282–309.

Swann, W. B., Jr., & Gill, M. J. (1997). Confidence and accuracy in person perception: Do we know what we think we know about our relationship partners? *Journal of Personality and Social Psychology, 73,* 747–757.

Thaler, R. H. (1988). The winner's curse. *Journal of Economic Perspectives, 2,* 191–202.

Tsai, C., Klayman, J., & Hastie, R. (2008). Effects of amount of information on judgment accuracy and confidence. *Organizational Behavior and Human Decision Processes, 107,* 97–105

Vallone, R. P., Griffin, D. W., Lin, S., & Ross, L. (1990). Overconfident prediction of future actions and outcomes by self and others. *Journal of Personality and Social Psychology, 58,* 582–592.

Wegener, D. T., & Petty, R. E. (1997). The flexible correction model: The role of naïve theories of bias in bias correction. In M. P. Zanna (Ed.), *Advances in experimental social psychology* (Vol. 29, pp. 141–208). Mahwah, NJ: Lawrence Erlbaum Associates.

Wells, G. L., Ferguson, T. J., & Lindsay, R. C. L. (1981). The tractability of eyewitness confidence and its implications for triers of fact. *Journal of Applied Psychology 66,* 688–696.

Williams, E., & Dunning, D. (2010). *From formulae to faith: Systematic approaches to decision-making underlie mistaken confidence in self-performance.* Manuscript under review, University of Florida.

Yamagishi, T., & Hill, C. T. (1983). Initial information versus missing information as explanations of the set-size effect. *Journal of Personality and Social Psychology, 44,* 942–951.

Zaragoza, M. S., & Mitchell, K. J. (1996). Repeated exposure to suggestion and the creation of false memories. *Psychological Science, 7,* 294–300.

5

The Metacognition of Bias Regulation

DUANE T. WEGENER, PEDRO P. SILVA, RICHARD E. PETTY, and TERESA GARCIA-MARQUES

INTRODUCTION

*P*eople want to be—or at least to believe that they are—accurate or otherwise appropriate in their perceptions of the social world. They want to form optimal impressions of people, buy products they will continue to like, and support political candidates or policies that they can defend to others. Yet, many personal and contextual factors can get in the way of forming the ideal opinion. Friends might pressure people to support certain views. Celebrities might advocate subpar products, or comparisons of target people or objects with contextual stimuli might create assimilation toward or contrast away from the contextual stimuli. How do people cope with these threats to forming accurate or otherwise reasonable opinions and perceptions?

There are many ways that people can try to remove or avoid bias. Though they represent a wide variety of specific processes, the methods of bias regulation we discuss are related in that they involve the potential for metacognition. That is, they likely include thoughts about one's thoughts or thought processes. Petty, Briñol, Tormala, and Wegener (2007) described six types of metacognitive thoughts (i.e., target, origin, valence, amount, evaluation, and confidence). The first four types of metacognitions parallel dimensions along which primary cognitions have been classified (see Cacioppo, Harkins, & Petty, 1981). That is, judges have coded whether the primary thoughts address one object or another (target); whether the thoughts are a person's own or repeat what the person has seen or heard from others (origin); whether the thought reflects something positive, negative, or neutral about the object (valence); and how many thoughts the person has about the object (amount).

Of course, people can also have their own perceptions about what the target of the thought might be, whether the thought is original to them, whether the thought reflects something positive or negative about the object, and about how many thoughts they have about the object. In addition, people can also have perceptions about whether it is desirable or undesirable to have a particular thought (evaluation) and can perceive a thought as having different levels of validity (confidence).

The different types of metacognitions can be correlated. For example, a thought whose origin is perceived as the self might be evaluated more favorably or held with more confidence than a thought attributed to an unknown other. In part because of these relations, many of the dimensions of metacognition might predict the likelihood of attempts to control bias. From the standpoint of theories of bias control (e.g., Strack, 1992; Wegener & Petty, 1997; Wilson & Brekke, 1994), however, the driving force in many attempts at bias control is perception of an influence as being unwanted, undesirable, or inappropriate. This seems closest to the metacognition of evaluation, where certain thoughts (those perceived as affected by a particular bias) are evaluated negatively.

Thoughts or perceptions might be viewed as unwanted or inappropriate for many (often metacognitive) reasons. Thoughts might be evaluated negatively if they are attributed to an unintended target, stem from an external source (not originating from the self), represent a valence that is not valued, are based on an insufficient (or otherwise unjustifiable) amount of thinking, or fail to produce an acceptable level of confidence. In a very general way, these reasons might be captured by saying that thoughts and thought processes are viewed as inappropriate or unwanted when they do not serve the perceiver's judgment goals (Wegener & Petty, 1997). Perhaps the most common judgment goal is to arrive at a "correct" or "accurate" view of the target (cf. Petty & Cacioppo, 1986). Of course, other goals and motivations are also possible, such as viewing oneself positively (e.g., Kunda, 1990; McCaslin, Petty, & Wegener, 2010), upholding procedural justice (e.g., Fleming, Wegener, & Petty, 1999), or avoiding prejudice (e.g., Fazio, Jackson, Dunton, & Williams, 1995; Plant & Devine, 1998).

BIAS CORRECTION PROCESSES

Three types of bias regulation are discussed: *subtraction* of reactions to contextual stimuli, *theory-based correction,* and *suppression* of thoughts or reactions.

Subtraction of Reactions to Contexts

Much of the early research on bias correction focused on *partialling* or *subtraction* of reactions that are viewed as responses to the context rather than to the target. Thus, these theories provide a crucial role for metacognitions concerning the target of the primary thought or reaction. For example, a person might think that a primary cognition (e.g., a positive thought such as "it makes me happy") is really about the context (e.g., weather) rather than the target (e.g., a politician). If so, the person might have the secondary cognition that it would not be appropriate to use the thought in judging the target. Or, even if the thought is believed to be about the target, if people believe it was provoked by the good weather rather than the target, the person would presumably want to eliminate its influence on the judgment. This type of reasoning is central to many studies inspired by the set–reset model (Martin, Seta, & Crelia, 1990) and the inclusion–exclusion model (Schwarz & Bless, 1992).

Research examining the set–reset model often begins with blatant priming of responses consistent with one of two possible interpretations of an ambiguous target. When research participants are relatively unmotivated or unable to think carefully about the target, the overlap in reactions to the context and to the target is said to result in *setting*—a default treatment of reactions to both the target and context as if they were all reactions to the target. This creates assimilation to the blatant prime (Martin et al., 1990). However, when motivation and ability to think are sufficiently high, the set–reset approach suggests that social perceivers question whether their reactions are due to the context and will *reset* (i.e., partial out reactions attributed to the context). Social perceivers can be confused over which reactions belong to the context rather than the target. Thus, resetting can result in overcorrection when some real reactions to the target are mistakenly attributed to the context and are subtracted (partialled out). This overcorrection then takes the form of contrast (i.e., judgments of the target that are even less like the context than if the context were not present; Martin et al., 1990).[1]

Similarly to the set–reset approach, the inclusion–exclusion model has treated *inclusion* of information in one's representation of the target as the default mental operation and *exclusion* of the information as requiring greater cognitive effort (Schwarz & Bless, 1992). Research inspired by this model typically begins with a target that represents either a superordinate category (where a specific member can be included in or excluded from the category) or a subordinate member (or subset) of a category (where characteristics of the category can be ascribed to or excluded from the representation of the member).

In each case, inclusion leads to assimilation of the target to the context. This occurs when a target category (such as a social group) is assimilated to a contextual member of the group (e.g., Bodenhausen, Schwarz, Bless, & Wänke, 1995; Coats & Smith, 1999) or when a target person is assimilated to a contextual category membership (Fiske & Neuberg, 1990). Exclusion can reduce the assimilation (if the excluded information is subtracted from the target representation) or can lead to contrast (if oversubtraction occurs or if the excluded material is used as an extreme standard of comparison; Schwarz & Bless, 1992). The standard of comparison could directly influence perceptions of the target (Helson, 1964; Sherif & Hovland, 1961) or could redefine the response scale anchors (Ostrom & Upshaw, 1968).

Similarly to the set–reset approach, inclusion versus exclusion of information (and the primary reaction associated with that information) is determined, in part, by the secondary cognition of whether the information is appropriate for inclusion in the target representation. If the information is perceived as appropriate, it is included; if it is perceived as inappropriate, it is excluded. Information can be perceived as inappropriate (and be excluded) if it seems unrepresentative of the target (e.g., because of lack of context and target feature overlap; Herr, Sherman, & Fazio, 1983). Exclusion of reactions is also expected when participants realize that previously encountered stimuli (e.g., primes) other than the target might have created the reactions (Strack, Schwarz, Bless, Kübler, & Wänke, 1993) or that conversational norms, such as norms against redundancy, suggest that use of the reactions is inappropriate (Schwarz, Strack, & Mai, 1991).

Attempts to partial or subtract perceptions could include a variety of metacognitive assessments (i.e., secondary cognitions). Social perceivers could identify the likely sources of thoughts and reactions and assess whether they are informative about the target as currently construed. In order to subtract the thought or reaction, there would likely have to be some cognitive mechanism for setting the thought aside and instead focusing on the thoughts and reactions to be included (e.g., tagging some thoughts as more valid or relevant for the judgment than others). One question of interest is how aware of these mechanisms people would be. The same types of assessments and outcomes could be accomplished by relatively simple cognitive processes that code whether a reaction to a target matches previous reactions to a context and disregards or gives lower weight to those reactions when judging the target.

In the subtraction research conducted thus far, direct measurements of metacognitive mechanisms have not been taken. Yet, a variety of measures might be possible. For example, in order to set aside a particular reaction, some type of monitoring of that reaction might have to take place (similar to the thought-suppression mechanisms discussed later or to those postulated by self-validation theory; Petty, Briñol, & Tormala, 2002). If so, then the thought or reaction to be set aside might become highly accessible in memory as the monitoring occurs and have an impact despite a labeling of incorrectness. Similarly, subtraction (partialling) studies have not directly measured perceptions of appropriateness of reactions or attributions of the reactions to the target or to the contextual stimuli (which should be proximal causes of resetting or exclusion in many settings). Therefore, although many of the judgment outcomes from this research are quite consistent with metacognitive mechanisms, future research incorporating more direct assessment of these metacognitions could help to assess how much explicit forms of metacognition come into play.

Theory-Based Correction

Another view of the metacognitive activity involved in bias correction relies on people's perceptions of the biases at work (see Strack, 1992; Wegener, Dunn, & Tokusato, 2001; and Wegener & Petty, 1997, for comparisons of theory-based correction with the subtraction or partialling approaches). That is, beyond the primary cognitions (that may be relatively biased or accurate), there may also be secondary cognitions that represent perceptions of whether or to what extent the primary cognitions are biased (that may themselves be relatively accurate or inaccurate). Use of these perceptions of bias may also be determined by other secondary cognitions reflecting perceptions of whether the primary cognitions or their use is unwanted or inappropriate.

For some time, researchers have noted that people might realize the potential for bias and make efforts to overcome that bias (e.g., Higgins, Rholes, & Jones, 1977; Thompson, Fong, & Rosenhan, 1981; Wyer & Budesheim, 1987). Early on, researchers attending to lay theories about biases focused on the inaccuracy of those theories and on the inadequate adjustments people made when using the theories (e.g., Nisbett & Wilson, 1977; Wilson & Brekke, 1994).

Despite the potential inaccuracy of lay beliefs about bias, however, social perceivers sometimes use such perceptions. In fact, the flexible correction model (FCM; Petty & Wegener, 1993; Wegener & Petty, 1995, 1997) is based on social perceivers' use of naïve theories of bias. FCM research has shown that people correct in different directions when they hold opposite theories of the direction of the bias (e.g., Wegener & Petty, 1995; Wegener, Petty, & Dunn, 1998). People correct for perceived biases even if there is no real bias (e.g., Petty, Wegener, & White, 1998; Wegener & Petty, 1995). Corrections for perceived rather than actual bias also mean that people sometimes correct primarily for one perceived bias (the most salient bias or the one for which clear beliefs exist), even if other biases are at work (Sczesny & Kühnen, 2004). Perhaps most interestingly, a correction for perceived bias can sometimes lead to creation of the opposite bias. For example, corrections for perceived negativity toward an unattractive or dislikable source can lead that source to be more persuasive than an attractive or likable source (Kang & Herr, 2006; Petty et al., 1998).

Research on theory-based correction addresses a broad set of domains, ranging from attribution (Gawronski, 2004) to impression formation (e.g., Lambert, Khan, Lickel, & Fricke, 1997; Wegener, Clark, & Petty, 2006) to persuasion (Kang & Herr, 2006, Petty et al., 1998) to courtroom judgments (Fleming et al., 1999), and a range of potential biases, including context effects (Petty & Wegener, 1993; Stapel, Martin, & Schwarz, 1998), mood and emotion (Ottati & Isbell, 1996), and stereotypes (Lepore & Brown, 2002). Recent work also demonstrates corrections for broad individual differences such as supposed tendencies to over- or underestimate (McCaslin et al., 2010).

Metacognitive activity is generally considered to be more likely when motivation and ability to think are high (Petty et al., 2007). Consistent with this idea, a number of studies of theory-based correction have manipulated or measured motivation or ability to think, and theory-based correction was more likely with high levels of thinking (e.g., DeSteno, Petty, Wegener, & Rucker, 2000; Isbell & Wyer, 1999; Ottati & Isbell, 1996; Petty, DeMarree, Briñol, Horcajo, & Strathman, 2008; Sczesny & Kühnen, 2004). This does not mean that theory-based correction would always require high levels of thinking, however. If particular biases are faced repeatedly and the same corrections become a commonplace occurrence, the corrections might become routine and less effortful (see Wegener & Petty, 1997; cf. Maddux, Barden, Brewer, & Petty, 2005). Also, some biases might be so salient or obvious that people might engage in a knee-jerk correction without much additional consideration of the target. Such corrections might play a role in the sleeper effect in persuasion (see Priester, Wegener, Petty, & Fabrigar, 1999, for discussion).

On a related note, the general nature of the bias might influence the likelihood of theory-based correction. For example, more thoughtful biases might seem more justified and less "biased" than less thoughtful biases. This could be because of the biased perceptions becoming more integrated with related knowledge and because of the judgments seeming to provide an accurate reflection of the (thoroughly processed) available information. When this occurs, the person is likely to be less motivated to engage in correction and the bias would be harder to eradicate if correction is attempted (Petty & Wegener, 1993; Wegener et al., 2006; see also Schul & Burnstein, 1985). Taken together, then, we are suggesting that one can engage in different levels of elaboration of primary cognitions (e.g., producing biases that were formed in relatively thoughtful or nonthoughtful ways) and also of secondary cognitions (e.g., producing relatively thoughtful or nonthoughtful theory-based corrections).

Significant research supports the possibility of theory-based corrections, but much work remains to be done. For example, much of the research has identified perceptions of bias in one set of participants and corrections that are directionally consistent in another set of participants (e.g., Sczesny & Kühnen, 2004; Wegener et al., 1998). Future research should seek to provide more direct evidence of the links between individuals' perceptions of bias and their corrections when the potential for bias becomes salient (as in Wegener & Petty, 1995). Future research would also benefit from attempts to address the metacognitive mechanisms that might come into play when people identify potential biases. People might often use accessible or salient theories (beliefs) about bias to search for biases, but there could also be other cues to potential bias. For instance, noticing that one's perceptions of a target have changed might alert one that bias is possible, or noticing that there is a factor in the situation that matches the valence of one's current view might prompt one to consider whether that factor produced the reaction (see Wegener et al., 2001, for additional discussion).

Thought Suppression

A third potential strategy for regulating bias is to try to keep the offending thought out of consciousness (i.e., to suppress it). An interesting aspect of suppression attempts is that they are often ineffective and have ironic consequences (such as later thinking more about the very thought one initially tried to suppress—a *rebound* effect; Wegner, Schneider, Carter, & White, 1987). Similar ironic effects of suppression attempts have been replicated in a wide variety of settings (see Wenzlaff & Wegner, 2000), including situations where suppression was spontaneous (not instructed by the experimenter; Macrae, Bodenhausen, & Milne, 1998). Similarly to other bias-regulation research, suppression has received particular attention in stereotyping (e.g., Macrae, Bodenhausen, Milne, & Jetten, 1994) and impression formation (e.g., Newman, Duff, Hedberg, & Blistein, 1996). In parallel with the previous bias regulation processes, the primary cognitions could be stereotype consistent or consistent with a primed concept; however, the secondary perception that the cognition is unwanted might lead to attempts to suppress the primary cognition.

Consistent with metacognition occurring more when motivation and ability to think are high, suppression attempts demand resources (Macrae, Bodenhausen, Milne, & Wheeler, 1996), and the instigation of suppression depends on motivation (Wyer, 2007). For example, after a specific stereotype is suppressed, judgments are more consistent with a stereotype when later confronting a race-unspecified target (where motivation to keep suppressing should be minimal) than when facing a race-specified target from the same group (where motivation to suppress should remain; Wyer, Sherman, & Stroessner, 2000). Suppression is also influenced by practice. People who suppress more often can avoid the ironic effects of suppression even when capacity to think is depleted, which might reflect greater availability of replacement thoughts (Monteith, Spicer, & Tooman, 1998). More practiced individuals might also be less likely to have the unwanted thoughts come to mind in the first place (e.g., Fazio et al., 1995; Lepore & Brown, 1997).

Several accounts of suppression-based rebound effects have been offered. Wegner's (1994) theory of ironic processes in mental control has guided the majority of the research. According to this theory, two search processes are instigated with suppression attempts. An operating (controlled) process searches for internal (memory) and external (environmental) content that differs from the thought(s) one is trying to suppress. Also, an automatic monitoring process searches for failures in suppression (intrusions). This monitoring process is expected to activate conscious operating processes if the undesirable thought begins to intrude.

Because the monitoring process has to keep track of unwanted thoughts, it has to keep them with some level of activation, even if below the level of consciousness. This ironically leads the thoughts into a state of hyperaccessibility (Wegner & Erber, 1992), which may then result in its resurgence as soon as control operations are relaxed (Macrae et al., 1994) or cognitive resources are constrained. Hyperaccessibility can be even greater when there are environmental distractions during suppression because cognitive demands favor the monitoring process and simultaneously interfere with the conscious operating process (see Wegner & Wenzlaff, 1996). Macrae et al. (1994) demonstrated that rebound effects can occur even after a successful initial suppression with the relaxing of the motivation to suppress. In addition, these authors attributed the hyperaccessibility of suppressed thoughts to repetitive priming promoted by the monitoring process.

Förster and Liberman (2004) presented an alternative motivational explanation (see also Martin, Tesser, & McIntosh, 1993). Their motivational inference model assumes that specific metacognitive inferences about underlying motivation, drawn from difficulty in suppression, underlie postsuppression rebound. That is, failures during suppression, as well as the difficulty felt in it, lead to inferences of motivation to use the suppressed thought and consequently increase its "motivation-related accessibility." However, if the difficulty in suppression is not attributed to this motivational drive, rebound effects can be eliminated (Förster & Liberman, 2001).

Rebound effects have also been understood as a consequence of self-regulatory depletion (e.g., Gailliot, Plant, Butz, & Baumeister, 2007; Gordijn, Hindriks, Koomen, Dijksterhuis, & van Knippenberg, 2004). This explanation assumes that people have a limited resource for self-regulation and that suppression is depleting and dependent on the availability of self-regulatory resources. Gordijn et al. (2004) supported this view by showing that the initial suppression of one stereotype increased later use of a totally different stereotype. Thus, in this approach, rebound effects occur because the construct happens to be accessible at a time when regulatory resources have been depleted (by the previous suppression). If other heuristics or simplifying knowledge structures are more applicable to the later activity, then their use would also be enhanced by the regulatory depletion associated with suppression.

A depletion-based explanation could also lead to an alternative account of rebound. That is, the felt depletion could be perceived as greater processing of information that could lead to a reduction in bias control strategies (Wan, Rucker, Tormala, & Clarkson, 2010). This type of attributional explanation also suggests that it might not be actual depletion at work, but rather perceptions of being depleted (Clarkson, Hirt, Jia, & Alexander, 2010).

COMPARING THE TYPES OF BIAS REGULATION

Although subtraction, theory-based correction, and suppression represent independent streams of thought about bias regulation, it seems likely that attempts at bias regulation often involve elements of more than one of these. For example, Yzerbyt, Corneille, Dumont, and Hahn (2001) argued that correction of dispositional inferences, although traditionally associated with other forms of bias control, may also spontaneously involve suppression. It could also be that the proposed operating process in thought suppression might include subtraction of the unwanted thoughts or corrections of judgments or behaviors.

In some cases, one "intended" means of bias regulation might be replaced by another. For example, although there is a lot of evidence that attempts to suppress thoughts can make the thoughts subsequently more accessible, many studies of thought suppression allow for other types of correction in the "suppression" phases of the research. The same goes for postsuppression bias regulation. As described earlier, Wyer et al. (2000) showed that stereotype suppression resulted in application of stereotype-consistent concepts to a race-unspecified target, but not to a target from the stereotyped group. It could be that people resuppressed the primed concepts when encountering the later target from the stereotyped group.

However, it also seems plausible that participants with sufficient cognitive resources were either subtracting thoughts about the target that were attributed to the stereotype or were using a theory of stereotype-consistent biases to correct their judgments. When participants in the Wyer et al. (2000) research encountered the race-unspecified target, they might have been less likely to realize that their perceptions of the target could be biased by the earlier suppression episode, thereby allowing the bias to influence their ratings (see Monteith, Sherman, & Devine, 1998; Sczesny & Kühnen, 2004; Wegener & Petty, 1997).

In addition to suppression, subtraction, and theory-based correction potentially co-occurring (or one process operating instead of another), the processes could also be sequential. Perceptions of unsuccessful use of one process might lead social perceivers to try one of the other processes. For example, if attempting to suppress but having difficulty (lots of intrusions), the person might try to subtract reactions due to those intrusions or to correct for their perceived influence on judgments. Similarly, if a person is having trouble identifying particular thoughts to subtract, she or he might engage in an overall theory-based correction, or if the person has no trustworthy theory of the direction or magnitude of a bias, the person might try to suppress thoughts that seem associated with the biasing factor.

Future research would do well to document more directly the role of each of the corrective metacognitions in influencing target judgments. Assessment of a wider variety of the processes in any one study would facilitate documentation of the possible co-occurrence or sequential implementation of the processes. This might also require some theoretical development to determine how, exactly, to measure some of the key constructs.

For instance, would subtraction (partialling) result in weaker cognitive relations between the target and thoughts/reactions that were subtracted from it? Or would attribution of some thoughts or reactions to a contextual stimulus primarily create closer cognitive associations between the contextual stimulus and those thoughts? Would direct measures of perceptions of reactions as coming from the target or context predict which reactions are subtracted from the target and which inform the target judgment? When a reaction is attributed to a context rather than a target, is the subtraction guided by or somehow combined with theory-based corrections (that might help to determine whether subtraction per se is necessary based on the type of bias the reaction would be expected to create)?

For example, a person might decide how many and what types of thoughts to subtract by consulting a naïve theory of bias. When people become concerned about biases, what determines whether they use subtraction, theory-based correction, suppression, or some combination? Research on such questions would help to create a more integrated view of correction-related metacognition.

Suppression and Correction

A couple of studies have attempted to instigate suppression of the biasing variables or correction according to the perceived bias (Silva, Garcia-Marques, & Wegener, 2010; Yzerbyt et al., 2001). Yzerbyt et al. (2001) proposed that correcting for dispositional influences might spontaneously trigger suppression processes in addition to consideration of situational constraints. Suppression of dispositional inferences would open the door for subsequent rebound effects when participants confront another scenario allowing for dispositional inferences (see also Geeraert, Yzerbyt, Corneille, & Wigboldus, 2004).

Consistent with this assumption, Yzerbyt et al. (2001) found increased dispositional inferences about a subsequent speaker who freely expressed an opinion after previously encountering a speaker forced to express a similar opinion (compared with previously encountering a speaker who also freely expressed the opinion). Moreover, this effect was greater for participants who later reported trying harder to suppress dispositional inferences during the first video. This design assumes that the forced expression makes the expressed opinion seem biased, requiring correction or suppression of the dispositional inference.

In a subsequent study where suppression instructions were contrasted with instructions to "focus on the situation" surrounding the attitude expression continuously, rebound effects only occurred with suppression instructions. These results could suggest that spontaneous suppression of dispositional inferences led to rebound. However, this study might not represent a pure comparison of suppression with correction because directing people to think about the situation might not result only in correction for perceived dispositional bias (just as instructing people to focus on arguments in a persuasive message might not lead them to correct primarily for perceived biases related to the message source).

In a persuasion setting, Silva et al. (2010) directly asked participants to control the biasing effects of an attractive/unattractive source of a persuasive message either by suppressing thoughts about the source or by correcting for the possible influence of the source's characteristics. Those asked to keep the source of the message out of consciousness were ironically more influenced by source attractiveness in a subsequent, ostensibly unrelated persuasive context. However, those instructed to attend to the source characteristics but to ensure that judgments were not influenced by them revealed no subsequent ironic consequences. Thus, suppression and (theory-based) correction seem to be conceptually distinct bias regulation strategies (because they can have different consequences, at least in some settings).

There is, however, room for different mechanisms to bring about ironic effects even without attempts to suppress. For example, inadvertent repetitive priming of the biasing variable might occur with subtraction or theory-based correction (Strack & Mussweiler, 2001). If so, then subsequent ironic effects (including hyperaccessibility) might occur (cf. Macrae et al., 1994). In addition, as noted by Monteith, Sherman, et al. (1998), if many of the studies previously described as involving "thought control processes" actually reflect "response control processes," then at least some rebound effects may have involved subtraction or theory-based correction.

Also, although at least some of the effects of correction or suppression are not dependent on depletion of mental resources (Geeraert & Yzerbyt, 2007), the self-regulation involved in subtraction or correction might sometimes be depleting enough to promote ironic effects. This might be especially likely when people are engaging in a novel correction or are facing a bias that is salient and difficult to overcome. Future research should investigate these possibilities and clarify whether nonsuppression processes can create ironic effects (and, if so, when).

Correction and Recomputation

Though it has not received a great deal of direct attention in bias correction research, it would be ideal for a person to be able to "set aside" a bias and instead use available "unbiased" information to compute judgments (i.e., to *discount* certain pieces of information and use other pieces of information; Schwarz & Clore, 1983). Strack and Mussweiler (2001) conducted a series of studies to compare *adjustment* of responses (generally consistent with theory-based corrections) with what they called *recomputation* (i.e., setting aside biased information to base judgments on remaining information). These researchers provided research participants with stereotype-consistent individuating information so that recomputation would lead to more stereotypic judgments but adjustment (correction for the stereotype) would lead to less stereotypic judgments.

When participants received little individuating information (i.e., little "unbiased" information to use for judgments), an instruction asking people not to be influenced by group membership led to less stereotypic ratings (consistent with theory-based correction or subtraction). However, when participants received a large amount of individuating information, the same instruction led to an increase rather than a decrease in stereotypic ratings (consistent with recomputation).

When sufficient individuating information is available, Dove, Wegener, and Petty (2001, 2003) argued that people would engage in recomputation when it seemed feasible, but would use theory-based correction when recomputation was difficult. They provided research participants with a list of job applicants in which graduates from the participants' own university had higher starting salaries than graduates of a rival university. When target information was re-presented after a correction instruction (not to be biased by university affiliation) but just prior to judgment, recomputation occurred (larger difference in salaries favoring participants' own university). However, when information was not available after the instruction to avoid bias, judgments reflected theory-based corrections (shifts away from favoring one's own university). In a second study, when participants received a conditional correction instruction (when asked to correct if they perceived anything biasing them; see Stapel et al., 1998), both the recomputation and theory-based correction patterns were more pronounced for people high in need for cognition (Cacioppo & Petty, 1982).

ADDITIONAL CONCEPTUAL DISTINCTIONS

It should be clear that not all metacognition feeds into bias correction per se. For example, one can perceive a given thought as valid or invalid without perceiving bias in the thought or attempting to correct for a bias (as specified by the self-validation hypothesis; Petty et al., 2002). It is also important to note that not all bias regulation requires metacognition and that, on a related note, bias regulation can occur at different levels of elaboration. Therefore, one of the direct challenges for future research is to specify how, exactly, each means of bias control can be documented. For some types of bias correction, those means are reasonably apparent, but for others, such data are generally lacking.

Relations With Context Effect Theories

Assessing when metacognitive judgmental correction has occurred is made all the more difficult by models that predict similar judgmental outcomes without referring to bias correction per se. Many studies of bias correction demonstrate a judgmental bias in one condition (e.g., assimilation to a context or impact on judgments by a message source) with less of that bias or even the opposite bias (i.e., contrast from a context or antisource reactions) in another condition. These results are consistent with corrections, but alternative models can produce similar results. For example, theories of assimilation and contrast suggest that contexts produce assimilation when perceivers attempt to interpret the qualities of the target or when they test a hypothesis that the target is similar to the context; however, the same contexts can produce contrast if the perceivers engage in comparisons between the context and target or test hypotheses that the context and target are different (e.g., Mussweiler & Damisch, 2008; Stapel & Koomen, 2001).

These theories, however, do not propose that the comparison or dissimilarity testing has anything to do with attempts to regulate context-induced biases. That is, contrast effects need not result from correction. Thus, in at least some settings, one must be cautious about interpreting judgment results alone as due to bias correction. Even in traditional bias control theories, some of the proposed mechanisms are clearly metacognitive, whereas others are not. For example, if extreme exemplars are excluded from a category and used as standards of comparison (Schwarz & Bless, 1992), this could occur with mechanisms that do not rely on attempts at bias correction per se.

Seeking Correctness and Avoiding Incorrectness (Bias)

One way to compare bias control with other mental activities is to distinguish between seeking correctness and avoiding incorrectness. Wegener and Petty (2001) noted that this distinction captures differences between the elaboration likelihood model (ELM; Petty & Cacioppo, 1986) and the FCM (Wegener & Petty, 1997). The ELM begins with social perceivers seeking correct assessments of targets, whereas the FCM begins with the goal of avoiding biases. According to Wegener and Petty (2001), when the issue of bias is not salient, the default orientation is for seeking correctness, but as the potential for bias becomes more salient, people become more oriented toward identifying and avoiding bias.

These two theoretical frameworks highlight some distinctions that are less salient in other theories. For example, the ELM includes both thoughtful and nonthoughtful processes focused on seeking correctness (such as scrutinizing the merits of the arguments in a persuasive message versus merely counting the number of arguments; Petty & Cacioppo, 1984). The outcomes of a more thoughtful correctness-seeking process can sometimes overcome or change the judgments that would have resulted from less thoughtful correctness-seeking processes; however, this need not reflect attempts to avoid bias associated with the nonthoughtful processes.

If, for example, perceivers believe that the thoughts coming from argument scrutiny are more valid, reliable, or relevant to the merit of the advocacy, they could receive greater weight in judgment than the thoughts coming from counting the number of arguments, which might be perceived as less valid, reliable, or relevant (Petty, 1994). Yet, a resulting decrease in use of the nonthoughtful (perceived as unreliable) output need not reflect perceptions of bias or attempts at bias correction (see also impression formation theories in which group membership can be processed as an attribute of the target; Fiske & Neuberg, 1990; cf. Brewer & Feinstein, 1999).

These distinctions may also be important for social psychological models that specify general "reflexive" or "impulsive" as opposed to more "reflective" modes of thinking (e.g., Lieberman, 2003; Pryor, Reeder, Yeadon, & Hesson-McInnis, 2004; Strack & Deutsch, 2004) or for similar dual-system views of judgment and decision making (e.g., Evans, 2006; Hammond, 1996; Stanovich, 1999). In these approaches, more deliberative, analytic, reflective processes are sometimes described as capable of "correcting" the output of less deliberative, more heuristic, impulsive processes. Yet, as in the ELM example, many such effects need not rely on bias correction per se so much as they rely on validity-based metacognitions or other perceptions that one type of reaction is more reliable or "correct" than another.

This is not to say that perceptions of validity can play no role in bias correction. Surely there are times when people attempt to correct for "biases" that come from invalid or "incorrect" information. However, there should also be times when people are unlikely to use information perceived as invalid or to give such information reduced weight in judgments without any perception that the information would create biases that must be overcome. Thus, from the standpoint of bias regulation, it is important to specify how, exactly, one might document that a particular type of bias correction process is at work as opposed to alternative processes that might regulate judgment outcomes through different means.

Can Metacognitive Bias Regulation Be Automatic?

We noted earlier that some bias regulation has been described as automatic (e.g., Glaser and Banaji, 1999; Maddux et al., 2005). We also noted that bias correction can become routine with practice, even if the correction started as a thoughtful, resource-intensive process (Wegener & Petty, 1997). But if thoughtful, metacognitive corrections become routine (perhaps to the point of becoming automatic), are they still metacognitive and are they still the same process?

This depends, in part, on one's definition of process (see Wegener & Carlston, 2005). The field has not really addressed whether an initially resource-intensive process that becomes more efficient (especially to the point of automaticity) is still the same process. If the same mental operations are performed, though in a speedy, less resource-intensive way, one might be inclined to characterize the process as the same. For example, when a desire to correct for prejudice initially occurs, people likely need to be vigilant of the sources and situations in which they might show bias and then effortfully correct their judgments in these settings (Devine & Monteith, 1999). With repeated practice, however, the assessment of possible bias and the correction for it could occur very quickly and out of conscious awareness (e.g., Maddux et al., 2005). Thus, from this standpoint, quick assessments of one's thoughts could be metacognitive even if those same assessments had previously taken more cognitive effort.

On the other hand, many markers of process differences (e.g., different moderators, different consequences) might be affected when once-thoughtful processes become more efficient. From this standpoint, it could be useful to view routinization of a thoughtful process as a separate process (with different moderators, different cognitive mechanisms for implementation, and possibly different consequences—for immediate or delayed thinking or behavior). For example, there might be situations in which more thoughtful corrections produce outcome judgments that resist change more than similar judgments produced by less thoughtful corrections. As in many circumstances, lack of difference in the judgment outcome can be rather uninformative regarding process sameness, but observed differences (e.g., in resistance of a judgment) can provide reasonable evidence of process differences (of at least quantitative differences in processes and often of qualitative differences as well; see Wegener & Carlston, 2005; Wegener & Claypool, 1999).

In the end, however, the important point may not be whether practiced (automatic) metacognition is or is not still called metacognition or considered a qualitatively different process. The important point is whether a particular perspective on metacognition and bias regulation does a good job of accounting for people's judgments and behaviors. Invariably, this calls for some "lumping" of similar processes together and some "splitting" of some processes from one another (see Petty, Wheeler, & Bizer, 1999). We look forward to research and theory on bias regulation that more directly addresses the similarities and differences among subtraction, theory-based correction, and suppression (as well as other related processes, such as recomputation). Such comparisons would also likely aid in determining whether less thoughtful (even automatic) efforts at bias regulation represent routinized versions of the prominent metacognitive corrections or different types of processes altogether.

NOTE

1. Subtle and blatant primes have different effects. With a blatant prime, low levels of thinking tend to show the assimilation effect, whereas high levels of thinking enhance the likelihood of correction (see also DeSteno et al., 2000). However, more subtle primes can bias thoughts without being identified as biasing, so high levels of thinking lead to assimilation (see Petty et al., 2008).

REFERENCES

Bodenhausen, G. V., Schwarz, N., Bless, H., & Wänke, M. (1995). Effects of atypical exemplars on racial beliefs: Enlightened racism or generalized appraisals? *Journal of Experimental Psychology, 31,* 48–63.

Brewer, M. B., & Feinstein, A. S. H. (1999). Dual processes in the cognitive representation of persons and social categories. In S. Chaiken & Y. Trope (Eds.), *Dual process theories in social psychology* (pp. 255–270). New York, NY: Guilford Press.

Cacioppo, J. T., Harkins, S. G., & Petty, R. E. (1981). The nature of attitudes and cognitive responses and their relationships to behavior. In R. Petty, T. Ostrom, & T. Brock (Eds.), *Cognitive responses in persuasion* (pp. 31–54). Hillsdale, NJ: Lawrence Erlbaum Associates.

Cacioppo, J. T., & Petty, R. E. (1982). The need for cognition. *Journal of Personality and Social Psychology, 42,* 116–131.

Clarkson, J., Hirt, E., Jia, L., & Alexander, M. (2010). When perception is more than reality: The effects of perceived versus actual resource depletion on self-regulatory behavior. *Journal of Personality and Social Psychology, 98,* 29–46.

Coats, S., & Smith, E. R. (1999). Perceptions of gender subtypes: Sensitivity to recent exemplar activation and in-group/out-group differences. *Personality and Social Psychology Bulletin, 25,* 515–526.

DeSteno, D., Petty, R. E., Wegener, D. T., & Rucker, D. D. (2000). Beyond valence in the perception of likelihood: The role of emotion specificity. *Journal of Personality and Social Psychology, 78,* 397–416.

Devine, P. G., & Monteith, M. J. (1999). Automaticity and control in stereotyping. In S. Chaiken & Y. Trope (Eds.), *Dual process theories in social psychology* (pp. 339–360). New York, NY: Guilford Press.

Dove, N., Wegener, D. T., & Petty, R. E. (2001, February). *Information availability and bias correction strategies*. Paper presented at the annual meeting of the Society for Personality and Social Psychology, San Antonio, TX.

Dove, N., Wegener, D. T., & Petty, R. E. (2003, February). *Information availability, need for cognition, and bias correction strategies*. Paper presented at the annual meeting of the Society for Personality and Social Psychology, Universal City, CA.

Evans, J. St. B. T. (2006). The heuristic-analytic theory of reasoning: Extension and evaluation. *Psychonomic Bulletin and Review, 13*, 378–395.

Fazio, R. H., Jackson, J. R., Dunton, B. C., & Williams, C. J. (1995). Variability in automatic activation as an unobtrusive measure of racial attitudes: A bona fide pipeline? *Journal of Personality and Social Psychology, 69*, 1013–1027.

Fiske, S. T., & Neuberg, S. L. (1990). A continuum of impression formation, from category based to individuating processes: Influences and motivation on attention and interpretation. In M. P. Zanna (Ed.), *Advances in experimental social psychology* (Vol. 22, pp. 1–74). New York, NY: Academic Press.

Fleming, M., Wegener, D. T., & Petty, R. E. (1999). Procedural and legal motivations to correct for perceived judicial biases. *Journal of Experimental Social Psychology, 35*, 186–203.

Förster, J., & Liberman, N. (2001). The role of attribution of motivation in producing post-suppressional rebound. *Journal of Personality and Social Psychology, 81*, 377–390.

Förster, J., & Liberman, N. (2004). A motivational model of post-suppressional rebound. *European Review of Social Psychology, 15*, 1–32.

Gailliott, M., Plant, E. A., Butz, D., & Baumeister, R. (2007). Increasing self-regulatory strength can reduce the depleting effect of suppressing stereotypes. *Personality and Social Psychology Bulletin, 33*, 281–294.

Gawronski, B. (2004). Theory-based bias correction in dispositional inference: The fundamental attribution error is dead, long live the correspondence bias. *European Review of Social Psychology, 15*, 183–217.

Geeraert, N., & Yzerbyt, V. Y. (2007). How fatiguing is dispositional suppression? Disentangling the effects of procedural rebound and ego-depletion. *European Journal of Social Psychology, 37*, 216–230.

Geeraert, N., Yzerbyt, V. Y., Corneille, O., & Wigboldus, D. (2004). The return of dispositionalism: On the linguistic consequences of dispositional suppression. *Journal of Experimental Social Psychology, 400*, 264–272.

Glaser, J., & Banaji, M. R. (1999). When fair is foul and foul is fair: Reverse priming in automatic evaluation. *Journal of Personality and Social Psychology, 77*, 669–687.

Gordijn, E., Hindriks, I., Koomen, W., Dijksterhuis, A., & van Knippenberg, A. (2004). Consequences of stereotype suppression and internal suppression motivation: A self-regulation approach. *Personality and Social Psychology Bulletin, 30*, 212–224.

Hammond, K. R. (1996). *Human judgment and social policy*. New York, NY: Oxford University Press.

Helson, H. (1964). *Adaptation-level theory: An experimental and systematic approach to behavior.* New York, NY: Harper & Row.

Herr, P. M., Sherman, S. J., & Fazio, R. H. (1983). On the consequences of priming: Assimilation and contrast effects. *Journal of Experimental Social Psychology, 19*, 323–340.

Higgins, E. T., Rholes, W. S., & Jones, C. R. (1977). Category accessibility and impression formation. *Journal of Experimental Social Psychology, 13*, 141–154.

Isbell, L. M., & Wyer, R. S., Jr. (1999). Correcting for mood-induced bias in the evaluation of political candidates: The roles of intrinsic and extrinsic motivation. *Personality and Social Psychology Bulletin, 25*, 237–249.

Kang, Y.-S., & Herr, P. M. (2006). Beauty and the beholder: Toward an integrative model of communication source effects. *Journal of Consumer Research, 33,* 123–130.

Kunda, Z. (1990). The case for motivated reasoning. *Psychological Bulletin, 108,* 480–498.

Lambert, A. J., Khan, S. R., Lickel, B. A., & Fricke, K. (1997). Mood and the correction of positive versus negative stereotypes. *Journal of Personality and Social Psychology, 72,* 1002–1016.

Lepore, L., & Brown, R. (1997). Category and stereotype activation: Is prejudice inevitable? *Journal of Personality and Social Psychology, 72,* 275–287.

Lepore, L., & Brown, R. (2002). The role of awareness: Divergent automatic stereotype activation and implicit judgment correction. *Social Cognition, 20,* 321–351.

Lieberman, M. D. (2003). Reflective and reflexive judgment processes: A social cognitive neuroscience approach. In J. P. Forgas, K. R. Williams, & W. von Hippel (Eds.), *Social judgments: Implicit and explicit processes* (pp. 44–67). New York, NY: Cambridge University Press.

Macrae, C. N., Bodenhausen, G. V., & Milne, A. B. (1998). Saying no to unwanted thoughts: Self-focus and the regulation of mental life. *Journal of Personality and Social Psychology, 74,* 578–589.

Macrae, C. N., Bodenhausen, G. V., Milne, A. B., & Jetten, J. (1994). Out of mind but back in sight: Stereotypes on the rebound. *Journal of Personality and Social Psychology, 67,* 808–817.

Macrae, C. N., Bodenhausen, G. V., Milne, A. B., & Wheeler, V. (1996). On resisting the temptation for simplification: Counterintentional effects of stereotype suppression on social memory. *Social Cognition, 14,* 1–20.

Maddux, W. W., Barden, J., Brewer, M. B., & Petty, R. E. (2005). Saying no to negativity: The effects of context and motivation to control prejudice on automatic evaluative responses. *Journal of Experimental Social Psychology, 41,* 19–35.

Martin, L. L., Seta, J. J., & Crelia, R. A. (1990). Assimilation and contrast as a function of people's willingness and ability to expend effort in forming an impression. *Journal of Personality and Social Psychology, 59,* 27–37.

Martin, L., Tesser, A., & McIntosh, W. (1993). Wanting but not having: The effects of unattained goals on thoughts and feelings. In D. M. Wegner & J. W. Pennebaker (Eds.), *The handbook of mental control* (pp. 552–572). New York, NY: Prentice Hall.

McCaslin, M. J., Petty, R. E., & Wegener, D. T. (2010). Self-enhancement and theory based correction processes. *Journal of Experimental Social Psychology, 6,* 830–835.

Monteith, M. J., Sherman, J. W., & Devine, P. G. (1998). Suppression as a stereotype control strategy. *Personality and Social Psychology Review, 2,* 63–82.

Monteith, M. J., Spicer, C., & Tooman, G. (1998). Consequences of stereotype suppression: Stereotypes on AND not on the rebound. *Journal of Experimental Social Psychology, 34,* 355–377.

Mussweiler, T., & Damisch, L. (2008). Going back to Donald: How comparisons shape judgmental priming effects. *Journal of Personality and Social Psychology, 95,* 1295–1315.

Newman, L., Duff, K., Hedberg, D., & Blistein, J. (1996). Rebound effects in impression formation: Assimilation and contrast effects following thought suppression. *Journal of Experimental Social Psychology, 32,* 460–483.

Nisbett, R. E., & Wilson, T. D. (1977). Telling more than we can know: Verbal reports on mental processes. *Psychological Review, 84,* 231–259.

Ostrom, T. M., & Upshaw, H. S. (1968). Psychological perspective and attitude change. In A. G. Greenwald, T. C. Brock, & T. M. Ostrom (Eds.), *Psychological foundations of attitudes* (pp. 217–242). New York, NY: Academic Press.

Ottati, V. C., & Isbell, L. M. (1996). Effects of mood during exposure to target information on subsequently reported judgments: An online model of misattribution and correction. *Journal of Personality and Social Psychology, 71,* 39–53.

Petty, R. E. (1994). Two routes to persuasion: State of the art. In G. d'Ydewalle, P. Eelen, & P. Bertelson (Eds.) *International perspectives on psychological science* (Vol. 2, pp. 229–247). Hillsdale, NJ: Lawrence Erlbaum Associates.

Petty, R. E., Briñol, P., & Tormala, Z. L. (2002). Thought confidence as a determinance of persuasion: The self-validation hypothesis. *Journal of Personality and Social Psychology, 82*, 722–741.

Petty, R. E., Briñol, P., Tormala, Z. L., & Wegener, D. T. (2007). The role of meta-cognition in social judgment. In E. T. Higgins & A. W. Kruglanski (Eds.), *Social psychology: Handbook of basic principles* (2nd ed., pp. 254–284). New York, NY: Guilford Press.

Petty, R. E., & Cacioppo, J. T. (1984). The effects of involvement on response to argument quantity and quality: Central and peripheral routes to persuasion. *Journal of Personality and Social Psychology, 46*, 69–81.

Petty, R. E., & Cacioppo, J. T. (1986). *Communication and persuasion: Central and peripheral routes to persuasion.* New York, NY: Springer-Verlag.

Petty, R. E., DeMarree, K. G., Briñol, P., Horcajo, J., & Strathman, A. J. (2008). Need for cognition can magnify or attenuate priming effects in social judgment. *Personality and Social Psychology Bulletin, 34*, 900–912.

Petty, R. E., & Wegener, D. T. (1993). Flexible correction processes in social judgment: Correcting for context-induced contrast. *Journal of Experimental Social Psychology, 29*, 137–165.

Petty, R. E., Wegener, D. T., & White, P. (1998). Flexible correction processes in social judgment: Implications for persuasion. *Social Cognition, 16*, 93–113.

Petty, R. E., Wheeler, S, C., & Bizer, G. Y. (1999). Is there one persuasion process or more? Lumping versus splitting in attitude change theories. *Psychological Inquiry, 10*, 156–163.

Plant, E. A., & Devine, P. G. (1998). Internal and external motivation to respond without prejudice. *Journal of Personality and Social Psychology, 75*, 811–832.

Priester, J. R., Wegener, D. T., Petty, R. E., & Fabrigar, L. R. (1999). Examining the psychological processes underlying the sleeper effect: The elaboration likelihood model explanation. *Media Psychology, 1*, 27–48.

Pryor, J. B., Reeder, G. D., Yeadon, C., & Hesson-McInnis, M. (2004). A dual process model of reactions to perceived stigma. *Journal of Personality and Social Psychology, 87*, 436–452.

Schul, Y., & Burnstein, E. (1985). When discounting fails: Conditions under which individuals use discredited information in making a judgment. *Journal of Personality and Social Psychology, 49*, 894–903.

Schwarz, N., & Bless, H. (1992). Constructing reality and its alternatives: An inclusion/exclusion model of assimilation and contrast effects in social judgment. In L. L. Martin & A. Tesser (Eds.), *The construction of social judgments* (pp. 217–245). Hillsdale, NJ: Lawrence Erlbaum Associates.

Schwarz, N., & Clore, G. (1983). Mood, misattribution, and judgments of well-being: Informative and directive functions of affective states. *Journal of Personality and Social Psychology, 45*, 513–523.

Schwarz, N., Strack, F., & Mai, H. P. (1991). Assimilation and contrast effects in part–whole question sequences: A conversational logic analysis. *Public Opinion Quarterly, 55*, 3–23.

Sczesny, S., & Kühnen, U. (2004). Meta-cognition about biological sex and gender-stereotypic physical appearance: Consequences for the assessment of leadership competence. *Personality and Social Psychology Bulletin, 30*, 13–21.

Sherif, M., & Hovland, C. I. (1961). *Social judgment: Assimilation and contrast effects in communication and attitude change.* New Haven, CT: Yale University Press.

Silva, P., Garcia-Marques, T., & Wegener, D. T. (2010). *Ironic consequences of attempts to regulate source attractiveness effects on persuasion.* Unpublished manuscript. Lisbon, Portugal.

Stanovich, K. E. (1999). *Who is rational? Studies of individual differences in reasoning.* Mahwah, NJ: Lawrence Erlbaum Associates.

Stapel, D. A., & Koomen, W. (2001). The impact of interpretation versus comparison mindsets on knowledge accessibility effects. *Journal of Experimental Social Psychology, 37,* 134–149.

Stapel, D. A., Martin, L. L., & Schwarz, N. (1998). The smell of bias: What instigates correction processes in social judgments? *Personality and Social Psychology Bulletin, 24,* 797–806.

Strack, F. (1992). The different routes to social judgments: Experiential versus informational based strategies. In L.L. Martin & A. Tesser (Eds.), *The construction of social judgments* (pp. 249–275). Hillsdale, NJ: Lawrence Erlbaum Associates.

Strack, F., & Deutsch, R. (2004). Reflective and impulsive determinants of social behavior. *Personality and Social Psychology Review, 8* (3), 220–247.

Strack, F., & Mussweiler, T. (2001). Resisting influence: Judgmental correction and its goals. In J. Forgas & K. Williams (Eds.), *Social influence processes: Direct and indirect influences* (pp. 199–212). New York, NY: Psychology Press.

Strack, F., Schwarz, N., Bless, H., Kübler, A., & Wänke, M. (1993). Awareness of the influence as a determinant of assimilation versus contrast. *European Journal of Social Psychology, 23,* 53–62.

Thompson, W. C., Fong, G. T., & Rosenhan, D. L. (1981). Inadmissible evidence and juror verdicts. *Journal of Personality and Social Psychology, 40,* 453–463.

Wan, E., Rucker, D. D., Tormala, Z. L., & Clarkson, J. (2010). The effect of regulatory depletion on attitude certainty. *Journal of Marketing Research, 47,* 531–541.

Wegener, D. T., & Carlston, D. E. (2005). Cognitive processes in attitude formation and change. In D. Albarracin, B. Johnson, & M. Zanna (Eds.), *The handbook of attitudes* (pp. 493–542). Mahwah, NJ: Lawrence Erlbaum Associates.

Wegener, D. T., Clark, J. K., & Petty, R. E. (2006). Not all stereotyping is created equal: Differential consequences of thoughtful versus nonthoughtful stereotyping. *Journal of Personality and Social Psychology, 90,* 42–59.

Wegener, D. T., & Claypool, H. M. (1999). The elaboration continuum by any other name does not smell as sweet. *Psychological Inquiry, 10,* 176–181.

Wegener, D. T., Dunn, M., & Tokusato, D. (2001). The flexible correction model: Phenomenology and the use of naive theories in avoiding or removing bias. In G. B. Moskowitz (Ed.), *Cognitive social psychology: The Princeton symposium on the legacy and future of social cognition* (pp. 277–290). Mahwah, NJ: Lawrence Erlbaum Associates.

Wegener, D. T., & Petty, R. E. (1995). Flexible correction processes in social judgment: The role of naive theories in corrections for perceived bias. *Journal of Personality and Social Psychology, 68,* 36–51.

Wegener, D. T., & Petty, R. E. (1997). The flexible correction model: The role of naive theories of bias in bias correction. In M. P. Zanna (Ed.), *Advances in experimental social psychology* (Vol. 29, pp. 141–208). Mahwah, NJ: Lawrence Erlbaum Associates.

Wegener, D. T., & Petty, R. E. (2001). Understanding effects of mood through the elaboration likelihood and flexible correction models. In L. L. Martin & G. L. Clore (Eds.) *Theories of mood and cognition: A user's guidebook* (pp. 177–210). Mahwah, NJ: Lawrence Erlbaum Associates.

Wegener, D. T., Petty, R. E., & Dunn, M. (1998). The metacognition of bias correction: Naive theories of bias and the flexible correction model. In V. Yzerbyt, G. Lories, & B. Dardenne (Eds.), *Metacognition: Cognitive and social dimensions* (pp. 202–227). London, England: Sage.

Wegner, D. M., & Wenzlaff, R. (1996). Mental control. In E. T. Higgins & A. W. Kruglanski (Eds.), *Social psychology: Handbook of basic principles* (pp. 466–492). New York, NY: Guilford Press.

Wegner, D. M. (1994). Ironic processes of mental control. *Psychological Review, 101,* 34–52.

Wegner, D. M., & Erber, R. (1992). The hyperaccessibility of suppressed thoughts. *Journal of Personality and Social Psychology, 63,* 903–912.

Wegner, D. M., Schneider, D. J., Carter, S., III, & White, L. (1987). Paradoxical effects of thought suppression. *Journal of Personality and Social Psychology, 53,* 409–418.

Wenzlaff, R., & Wegner, D. M. (2000). Thought suppression. *Annual Review of Psychology, 51,* 59–91.

Wilson, T. D., & Brekke, N. (1994). Mental contamination and mental correction: Unwanted influences on judgments and evaluations. *Psychological Bulletin, 116,* 117–142.

Wyer, N. A. (2007). Motivational influences on compliance with and consequences of instructions to suppress stereotypes. *Journal of Experimental Social Psychology, 43,* 417–424.

Wyer, N. A., Sherman, J. W., & Stroessner, S. J. (2000). The roles of motivation and ability in controlling the consequences of stereotype suppression. *Personality and Social Psychology Bulletin, 26,* 13–25.

Wyer, R. S., & Budesheim, T. L. (1987). Person memory and judgments: The impact of information that one is told to disregard. *Journal of Personality and Social Psychology, 53,* 14–29.

Yzerbyt, V. Y., Corneille, O., Dumont, M., & Hahn, K. (2001). The dispositional inference strikes back: Situational focus and dispositional suppression in causal attribution. *Journal of Personality and Social Psychology, 81,* 365–376.

Section II

Self and Identity

6

What Do I Think About Who I Am?
Metacognition and the Self-Concept

KENNETH G. DEMARREE and
KIMBERLY RIOS MORRISON

INTRODUCTION

*T*he self-concept plays an important role in how people think about and act
in their social worlds (Baumeister, 1998). A person's self-concept is a representation of his or her own characteristics, including traits, identities, relationships, and goals (DeMarree, Petty, & Briñol, 2007a; Swann & Bosson, 2010),
and is inextricably tied to his or her other mental representations (Greenwald &
Pratkanis, 1984). Because of the importance that self-views are thought to play in
human cognition, it is crucial for psychologists to understand the nature, origins,
and consequences of these self-views.

In this chapter, we focus on the role of metacognitive processes in advancing
psychologists' understanding of the self. In so doing, we address some of the most
important questions relating to the self. Do a person's self-views matter and, if so,
when, why, and how? Where do self-views come from? Is the self the same across
cultures? How are self-views maintained? Metacognitive factors offer novel insight
into these questions and others.

Metacognition refers to people's thoughts about their thoughts or thought processes (Dunlosky & Metcalfe, 2009; Petty, Briñol, Tormala, & Wegener, 2007; see
also Briñol & DeMarree, Chapter 1, this volume). The first-order thoughts (primary thoughts) that are the focus of the current chapter are related to a person's
self-concept or self-evaluation (e.g., I am shy; I am a good person), whereas the
second-order thoughts (secondary thoughts) are reflections upon these primary
thoughts (e.g., "I'm not really sure how shy or how good a person I am."). In this
chapter, we discuss how secondary cognitions can influence the strength of a person's self-conceptions, the very nature of the self-concept, and how the nature and

operation of these secondary cognitions can vary across cultures, as well as meta-cognitive processes related to defending self-views.

SELF-STRENGTH

People's beliefs about themselves vary in a number of important ways: Some self-beliefs are very consequential (e.g., they predict people's behavior and thought patterns), whereas others are not. Some self-beliefs are long-lasting and resistant to change, whereas others are unstable and easily shifted. These characteristics represent the strength of a person's self-views. Strong self-views, like strong attitudes (Petty & Krosnick, 1995; Visser & Holbrook, Chapter 2, this volume), are resistant to change, stable over time, and predictive of behavior and thoughts (DeMarree, Petty, & Briñol, 2007b; Krosnick & Petty, 1995). A number of properties of self-views predict their strength, including several metacognitive variables.

Although much of the research on self-strength has used concepts also studied in the attitudes literature, such as certainty and importance (for reviews, see Petty & Krosnick, 1995; Visser, Bizer, & Krosnick, 2006), some unique strength variables (e.g., self-concept clarity) have been examined primarily by self researchers. In this section, we briefly introduce several metacognitive self-strength variables and discuss the consequences of each. Before proceeding, we should note that the term "strength" does not necessarily connote a positive quality (DeMarree et al., 2007b). For example, someone with "strong" low self-esteem is likely to see the world in a much more pessimistic way than someone with "weak" low self-esteem, potentially opening that person up to depression and other negative outcomes. In other words, strength refers to the durability and impact of the primary cognition (i.e., self-view), which can itself be adaptive or maladaptive to the individual.

Certainty

Metacognitive certainty refers to the extent to which a person is convinced of a belief and views the belief as valid (DeMarree et al., 2007a; Gross, Holtz, & Miller, 1995; Petty et al., 2007). Applied to the self, two people might each believe that they are outgoing (primary thought). However, one of these people might be convinced that this belief is correct, whereas the other person might hold some reservations about the validity of this belief (both secondary thoughts).

When a person holds a self-view with high rather than low certainty, the self-view tends to be more predictive of behavior (e.g., Swann & Ely, 1984) and information processing (e.g., Pelham & Swann, 1989), more stable over time (e.g., Pelham, 1991), and more resistant to change (e.g., Swann & Ely, 1984; for a review, see DeMarree et al., 2007a). For example, Swann and Ely (1984) found that participants who were certain (relative to uncertain) of their level of extraversion behaved more consistently with these self-beliefs during an interaction. Furthermore, when participants interacted with someone whose expectations about their level of extraversion countered their self-beliefs, those low (but not high) in certainty changed their behavior to align with their partner's expectations.

In addition to affecting specific self-views (e.g., beliefs about one's intelligence or attractiveness), certainty has also been found to influence the strength of the thoughts on which these self-views might be based. For example, Briñol and Petty (2003, Study 4) had participants list either three strengths or three weaknesses about themselves using either their dominant or their nondominant hand. Briñol and Petty argued that thoughts written with a person's nondominant hand are more difficult to express and appear shaky and unclear, both of which lower participants' confidence in the thoughts listed, even though the thoughts themselves should be similar (both of these predictions were confirmed by manipulation checks). People who wrote with their dominant hands ultimately evinced self-perceptions congruent with the valence of the thoughts listed (e.g., lower self-esteem if they wrote about their weaknesses), whereas those who wrote with their nondominant hands did not (Briñol & Petty, 2003; see also Briñol, Petty, & Wagner, 2009). Thus, metacognitive confidence in self-relevant thoughts appears to affect the strength of these *thoughts* in much the same way that confidence affects the strength of self-views and attitudes.

Importance

Importance refers to the psychological significance that a person attaches to a given self-view or attitude (e.g., Boninger, Krosnick, Berent, & Fabrigar, 1995; DeMarree et al., 2007b). That is, it is the metacognitive assessment that a self-view (e.g., I am a talented jet-skier) is psychologically meaningful (e.g., it is important to me to be a talented jet-skier). Like certainty, importance has been studied extensively in both the self and the attitudes literatures.

As the importance of self-views increases, their strength also increases. Importantly held self-views, relative to self-views held with low importance, are more stable over time (Pelham, 1991) and more resistant to change (Eisenstadt & Leippe, 1994). They are also more predictive of a person's thoughts and judgments than self-views held with low importance (Pelham & Swann, 1989). For example, in the consumer domain, Aaker (1999) has found that people prefer brands with "personalities" that match their own (e.g., exciting, sophisticated) over brands that do not match—especially when the specific personality dimension is important to their self-concept (for further discussion of metacognition in the consumer domain, see Rucker & Tormala, Chapter 16, this volume).

Self-Concept Clarity

The self-concept clarity (SCC) scale (Campbell et al., 1996) measures the confidence, consistency, and stability of the self-concept and self-evaluation (e.g., "In general, I have a clear sense of who I am and what I am" or "My beliefs about myself often conflict with one another" [reversed]). In a sense, all of a person's self-knowledge represents the primary cognition in this case, whereas clarity is the secondary cognition. The SCC scale was developed to explain differences in the self-conceptions of individuals high and low in self-esteem; the rationale is that the self-conceptions of individuals with high self-esteem are clearer than those of individuals with low self-esteem (Campbell, 1990; Campbell et al., 1996). Because of this initial focus, most of the research on SCC has examined its relationships to mental health and adjustment (e.g., Bigler, Neimeyer, & Brown, 2001; Vartanian, 2009).

However, some research has also examined strength consequences of self-concept clarity. For example, the SCC scale predicts the stability of self-descriptions over a 4-month period (Campbell et al., 1996) as well as greater day-to-day stability of self-esteem (Kernis, Paradise, Whitaker, Wheatman, & Goldman, 2000). Furthermore, when people encounter negative life events, higher SCC is associated with decreased fluctuations of self-esteem assessed with an implicit measure (DeHart & Pelham, 2007). In addition, because unclear self-views are not useful in guiding judgment and behavior, people with low SCC are more prone to seek out potentially self-informative social comparisons (Butzer & Kuiper, 2006).

Although research on SCC has generated considerable interest in the strength of individuals' self-views, some caution should be exercised when considering clarity findings. First, is clarity truly associated with self-esteem, or are these relationships an artifact of the overly high self-esteem scores found in study samples? Because the self-esteem distribution in college student samples typically lies well above the midpoint of self-esteem scales, self-esteem level becomes confounded with self-esteem extremity. It is possible that people with very low self-esteem (who are underrepresented in these samples) are just as high in self-concept clarity as their counterparts with very high self-esteem. This is important because research on attitudes indicates that extremity itself is associated with strength consequences (Fazio & Zanna, 1978).

Another concern is whether the SCC scale is tapping a new construct or several existing constructs. Inspection of the items reveals some conceptual overlap with the attitude strength construct of subjective (felt) ambivalence, as well as certainty (see Visser & Holbrook, Chapter 2, this volume). Specifically, items such as "My beliefs about myself often conflict with one another" seem to represent the conflict and confusion typically captured by measures of subjective ambivalence (see Priester & Petty, 1996), whereas items such as "In general, I have a clear sense of who I am and what I am" seem more consistent with measures of certainty (see Petrocelli, Tormala, & Rucker, 2007). Finally, SCC is a general assessment of the perceived strength of the self, but might be less useful in predicting the strength of a specific self-view (e.g., it might not predict the stability of one's self-perceived attractiveness).

In sum, clear self-concepts tend to be more stable than unclear self-concepts. Similarly to confidence and importance, SCC predicts stability over time and resistance to change. Although some precautions should be noted when this scale is used, it provides a useful tool for examining the global strength of the self.

Other Variables Associated With Strength

As described previously, metacognitive variables such as certainty, importance, and clarity are associated with strength consequences. However, some nonmetacognitive variables are also associated with strength. For example, the accessibility (DeMarree, Petty, & Strunk, 2010) and objective ambivalence (DeMarree,

Morrison, Wheeler, & Petty, 2011; Riketta & Ziegler, 2007) of self-views have been found to predict strength outcomes (e.g., resistance to change) over and above metacognitive strength variables. Research on attitudes suggests that the many variables associated with strength might be distinct constructs (Krosnick & Petty, 1995) and that they might exert their influence via different psychological processes (Visser et al., 2006) or produce different outcomes (Visser, Krosnick, & Simmons, 2003). For example, accessibility and certainty might both increase the likelihood that a self-view will predict behavior, generally speaking.

However, they might do so in different situations (e.g., moderating the effects of attitudes in spontaneous versus deliberative situations, respectively; Fazio & Towles-Schwen, 1999; Petty et al., 2007 or via different psychological mechanisms (e.g., by affecting hypothesis generation versus validation, respectively; see Kruglanski, 1990). For example, a person whose high self-esteem is accessible might be more likely than someone whose high self-esteem is inaccessible to generate automatically and then test the hypothesis that ambiguous self-information is positive. However, if he or she is being thoughtful, this person might further consider whether his or her initial inclination (that this self-information was positive) is valid or not—something that might be affected by certainty in self-esteem, rather than accessibility. Because of the complexity of potential strength effects in both the attitudes and self domains (DeMarree et al., 2007b), we recommend measuring multiple indicators of strength to lend insight into why and under what conditions specific strength variables will produce specific consequences.

IMPLICIT THEORIES AND THE SELF

The discussion of self-strength focused on metacognitive judgments about the content of specific self-views (e.g., certainty in one's level of extraversion, importance of being intelligent); however, another important type of metacognition involves implicit theories about how the self operates in general. Implicit theories can refer to many different constructs, including our beliefs about how much we have changed (see Schryer & Ross, Chapter 8, this volume) or how we will react to future events (Wilson & Gilbert, 2005). One heavily researched area on implicit theories is Dweck and colleagues' work on self-theories (e.g., Dweck, Chiu, & Hong, 1995).

Self-Theories

Dweck describes two distinct types of self-theories. Entity theorists believe that people's self-attributes are fixed and stable, whereas incremental theorists believe that people's self-attributes are malleable and can be changed through experience and effort. These differences in beliefs have a wide range of implications for self-relevant processes. For example, people with incremental (versus entity) theories of intelligence tend to blame failure on their lack of effort (versus ability), seek out tasks that allow them to improve (versus demonstrate) their abilities, and exert additional effort following failure (Dweck et al., 1995). As a result of these differences in how entity and incremental theorists approach ability-relevant tasks, differences in the trajectory of scholastic performance have been documented, with incremental theorists demonstrating a positive (improving) trajectory and entity theorists demonstrating a negative (declining) trajectory over time (Blackwell, Trzesniewski, & Dweck, 2007).

Other implicit theories that can be applied to the self-concept include cultural beliefs about the inevitability of memory loss in old age (Levy & Langer, 1994), stereotypes about gender differences in mathematical ability (e.g., Steele & Ambady, 2006), and self-efficacy, or one's confidence in his or her ability to accomplish particular tasks (Bandura, 1982). Thus, people's metacognitive beliefs about how the self operates can have important consequences for performance and motivation.

Perceived Origin of Self-Related Thoughts

Although we have focused our discussion on one type of implicit self-relevant theory, it is worth noting that metacognitive theories can apply to the self in many different ways. For example, they can refer to the origin of self-knowledge and abilities, such as whether a person knows that his or her liking of a restaurant comes from his or her own personal experience or through secondhand information (e.g., a friend's recommendation). They can also refer to whether or not a particular thought is attributed to the self, such as when information active in memory does not have a clear origin (e.g., because it is subliminally primed; see Wheeler & DeMarree, 2009).

When a concept is active in memory and a person does not know why, he or she might try to explain where this thought came from and, in so doing, might mistakenly (or correctly) attribute the thought to the self. In the case of priming, when the prime-activated content is attributed to the self, it can impact self-evaluations and corresponding behavior (Wheeler & DeMarree, 2009). Factors that increase the likelihood that mental contents of ambiguous origin will be perceived as stemming from the self include self-ambiguity (DeMarree et al., 2011; Morrison, DeMarree, Wheeler, & Petty, 2010), self-focused attention (DeMarree & Loersch, 2009), or a combination of these factors (Wheeler, Morrison, DeMarree, & Petty, 2008). For example, people who have ambivalent self-conceptions (e.g., people who view themselves as both aggressive and peaceful) are more likely to change in response to a relevant prime (e.g., African American stereotype) because the self-concept is less clear and people mistakenly attribute the activated mental contents as stemming from the self. In this case, the primary cognition is the one activated by the prime and the secondary cognition is the explanation of its origin.

Of course, if other targets are available, applicable, ambiguous, and salient, the activated mental contents could appear to stem from these other targets (see, for example, Smeesters, Wheeler, & Kay, 2010). This, in turn, can have implications for the self (e.g., "If I am primed with an extremely intelligent person such as Einstein, any activated intelligence will be attributed to that person, so I might view myself as less intelligent by comparison"; see Dijksterhuis et al., 1998; Wheeler & DeMarree, 2009; Wheeler, DeMarree, & Petty, 2007).

CULTURE AND SELF-RELATED METACOGNITION

People's cultural environments have profound influence over the ways that they think about themselves (e.g., Markus & Kitayama, 1991; Spencer-Rodgers & Peng, 2005). For example, people from societies that construe the self in an interdependent fashion (e.g., East Asia) see themselves as inherently interconnected to others, whereas people from societies that construe the self in an independent manner (e.g., North America) see themselves as distinct from others (Markus & Kitayama, 1991). Cultural differences in how the self is defined and in how the self operates in relation to the social environment have a number of implications for self-relevant metacognitive processes. We highlight several of these implications next.

Changes in Primary Cognition of Interest

In many cultures—particularly Western cultures that see the self as an independent entity—global individual differences often provide a meaningful level of analysis to study a person's behavior. For example, a person might be extraverted across a wide range of social settings. However, in many non-Western cultures, a person's traits might instead be constrained to more specific role relationships. This means that a person might be extraverted when with Fred, but introverted when with Diane. Indeed, research has shown that East Asians tend to describe themselves more in terms of their social roles and identities than do North Americans, whereas North Americans tend to describe themselves more in terms of abstract traits (e.g., intelligent, kind) than do their East Asian counterparts (Bond & Cheung, 1983; Rhee, Uleman, Lee, & Roman, 1995).

These cultural differences in how people define themselves might determine what the most relevant primary cognitions are when considering metacognitive processes, such as those that produce strength. For someone whose global self-beliefs are most relevant (e.g., "I am an extravert."), the certainty or importance of this belief might moderate the extent to which this belief predicts future behavior, such as resistance to change (Swann & Ely, 1984). However, for people who define themselves by their social roles and identities, the strength of global self-beliefs (e.g., "I am certain that I am an extravert.") might not help to predict behavior. Instead, the certainty or importance of the more specific, contextually dependent self-beliefs (e.g., "I am certain that I am an extravert when I am with Fred"; see DeMarree et al., 2007a, for further discussion) or the strength of beliefs about one's social relationships rather than individual characteristics (e.g., "I am certain that I fit in with my peer group"; Morrison, Johnson, & Wheeler, in press) might be most relevant.

Changes in Implicit Theories

Entity and Incremental Theories   The greater cross-situational consistency of North Americans' self-descriptions relative to those of East Asians can have implications for implicit theories of the self. Given that North Americans tend to describe themselves in terms of general traits and characteristics regardless of context, they should be more likely than East Asians to believe that the overall self-concept is fixed and stable. By contrast, because East Asians' self-descriptions tend to change according to specific roles and situations, they should be more likely than North Americans to believe that the overall self-concept is malleable.

Supporting this idea, research has shown that North Americans (compared to East Asians) more strongly endorse entity theories of various self-attributes, whereas East Asians (compared to North Americans) more strongly endorse incremental theories of these attributes (Heine et al., 2001). However, East Asians, to a greater extent than North Americans, believe that their social roles are immutable and that they must change themselves to adapt to these roles (Su et al., 1999). Thus, the direction and magnitude of cultural differences in implicit self-theories, much like spontaneous self-descriptions, may depend on how the "self" is defined (i.e., in terms of abstract traits versus social relationships).

Dialectical Thinking

Another culture-relevant construct that involves implicit theories is dialectical thinking (Nisbett, Peng, Choi, & Norenzayan, 2001; Spencer-Rodgers & Peng, 2005). Dialectical thinking is a style of thought common in East Asian countries that is derived from the region's philosophical and religious history. Dialectical thinking includes several implicit theories about the nature of the world, including the self. Among these are the principle of contradiction, which holds that two opposing sides (e.g., good and evil) are inherently interconnected; the principle of change, which holds that the concepts used to define any object are likely to change over time; and the principle of holism, which holds that nothing can be understood independently of its context (Nisbett et al., 2001; Spencer-Rodgers & Peng, 2005).

Implicit theories that stem from dialectical thinking styles have a number of implications for the self. For example, people high in dialecticism are more likely to be comfortable with holding contradictory self-beliefs (e.g., believing that they are both introverted and extraverted) and to accept these self-beliefs as part of who they are. By contrast, upon recognizing inconsistencies such as these, people low in dialecticism might make attempts to change their self-beliefs to be more consistent with one another. This leads people high (versus low) in dialecticism to view the self as containing both positive and negative attributes (Spencer-Rodgers, Peng, Wang, & Hou, 2004) or as possessing inconsistent traits (Spencer-Rodgers, Boucher, Mori, Wang, & Peng, 2009).

In addition, as dialecticism increases, so too does variability in participants' spontaneous self-descriptions (e.g., "I am practical" may be juxtaposed with "I am a dreamer"; Spencer-Rodgers et al., 2009). That is, metacognitive beliefs about the nature of the self can vary across cultures and hence can affect the content of people's primary self-beliefs differentially. Another way to frame dialectical thinking is that, as dialectical thinking styles change, people's naïve theories about whether ambivalence is good or bad shift (cf. Briñol, Petty, & Tormala, 2006), with dialectical thinkers being more positive (or at least less negative) about ambivalence and, as such, more likely to rely on and less likely to change ambivalently held self-views. Thus, metacognitive processes have implications for understanding *both* the content and operation of self-knowledge.

METACOGNITION AND SELF-DEFENSE

One theme that pervades the literature on the self is that self-enhancement and self-protection can be powerful motives that guide a person's thought and behavior (Alicke & Sedikides, 2009; Sedikides, 1993; Sedikides & Gregg, 2008). People often seek to boost or restore self-views when their views are threatened. As with the research described before, metacognitive constructs are important to understanding how an individual responds to potential self-related threats, as well as how a person attempts to restore threatened self-views. Next, we discuss some examples of how metacognitive constructs are related to each of these processes.

Contingencies of Worth

One area of research examines the idea that one's self-esteem is often contingent on situational factors. Such contingencies involve the perception (the secondary cognition) that a person's self-esteem (the primary cognition) depends on a specific event, outcome, or perception (e.g., academic performance, social acceptance). Contingencies have been studied in several forms, including contingencies in global self-evaluation (e.g., Kernis, 2003; Kernis & Goldman, 2006; Leary & Baumeister, 2000) as well as in specific domains (e.g., athleticism, intelligence; Crocker, Karpinski, Quinn, & Chase, 2003; Crocker & Wolfe, 2001). Individuals who are contingent in a given domain view attaining success in that domain as critical to their global self-worth (Crocker & Wolfe, 2001). That is, they have metacognitive knowledge about how success or failure in a domain will impact their self-evaluation. This knowledge is assessed using self-report items such as "My self-esteem is influenced by my academic performance" (academic competence contingency) or "My self-esteem would suffer if I did something unethical" (virtue contingency) (Crocker, Luhtanen, Cooper, & Bouvrette, 2003).

Such contingencies lead people to approach and engage in activities that are likely to offer success while they avoid those that will produce failure (Crocker & Knight, 2005; Crocker & Park, 2004; Crocker & Wolfe, 2001). In addition, when faced with success or failure, contingent individuals experience increases or decreases in their state self-evaluation and will often engage in defensive processes to restore feelings of worth (Crocker & Knight, 2005; Crocker & Wolfe, 2001). For example, when interviewed about negative life events (e.g., instances in which they had engaged in self-destructive behaviors), contingent individuals were more verbally defensive during the interview than were noncontingent individuals (Kernis, Lakey, & Heppner, 2008).

In many respects, contingencies of self-worth are similar to the concept of importance discussed before. Recall that importance can refer to the centrality of a specific self-view or attitude to one's overall self-concept. In the case of academic contingencies, for example, individuals might feel that it is important for them to have an extremely high level of intelligence. Thus, their perceived level of intelligence would function as a primary cognition, whereas the importance (contingency) they place on their intelligence would function as a secondary cognition. Research on attitudes has shown that as attitude importance increases, so too do selective exposure and processing of information relevant to the attitude (e.g., Holbrook, Berent, Krosnick, Visser, & Boninger, 2005; Visser et al., 2003). That is, people with highly important attitudes seek and think more about information that is consistent rather than inconsistent with their attitudes (Holbrook et al., 2005). In research on the self, this might be analogous to contingent individuals approaching and engaging more in activities that are likely to offer success relative to failure (see Crocker & Knight, 2005; Crocker & Wolfe, 2001).

In addition, when attacked, important attitudes produce more defensive thoughts (e.g., counterarguing the attacking message), negative affective reactions, and feelings of irritation than do unimportant attitudes, thus leading to increased resistance to change (Zuwerink & Devine, 1996). Similarly, when inconsistent information in a contingent domain is unavoidable (e.g., a person experiences failure), contingent individuals often experience negative affective states (e.g., Crocker, Sommers, & Luhtanen, 2002) and respond in a defensive manner (Kernis et al., 2008). Thus, much as negative affect can motivate people to reduce inconsistency between their thoughts, feelings, or behaviors (Festinger, 1957; Higgins, 1987, 1997), the negative affect created by a threat to an important attitude or a contingent self-view can initiate similar processes. Because these negative affective reactions appear to motivate self-defense, such reactions could ultimately lead contingent individuals to be more resistant than noncontingent individuals to self-change at the trait level—an idea that has yet to be tested.

By combining perspectives on contingencies of worth and attitude importance, we may be able to gain insight into the mechanisms by which we maintain our evaluations. At the very least, research in these domains shows how a metacognitive judgment about a self-view ("My self-esteem is contingent on my ability in this domain.") or attitude ("This attitude is important to who I am.") can have important consequences for a person's day-to-day life.

Compensatory Confidence

The preceding discussion of contingencies of worth centered on people's reactions to success or failure in contingent domains and on the ways in which people may seek to restore or maintain their self-evaluations (e.g., when their self-esteem level is threatened by failure). However, people may also experience and react against threats to their self-certainty (for a review of self-related certainty and doubt, see Arkin, Oleson, & Carroll, 2010). Just as individuals, at least in Western cultures, are motivated to have high self-esteem, so too are they motivated to maintain a consistent, coherent, and confident self-concept (Aronson, 1969; Swann, Rentfrow, & Guinn, 2003). As such, when people are induced to feel uncertain about the self, they often compensate by claiming certainty in other areas of their lives—in other words, by claiming the level of certainty that they wish to attain.

Self-uncertainty can be manipulated in many ways, including having participants reflect upon a personal dilemma (McGregor, Zanna, Holmes, & Spencer, 2001), having participants write about the aspects of their lives that make them uncertain (Hogg, Sherman, Dieselhuis, Maitner, & Moffitt, 2007), or giving participants bogus feedback that their personality traits are inconsistent (Stapel &

Tesser, 2001). These inductions of doubt ironically lead people to report greater conviction in their political attitudes (McGregor et al., 2001), identify more strongly with important social groups (e.g., nationality, political party; Hogg et al., 2007), express opinions that they consider to be self-defining (i.e, minority opinions, Morrison & Wheeler, 2010; Morrison, Wheeler, & Miller, 2011), and claim that their material possessions reflect "who they are" (Morrison & Johnson, 2011). These defensive responses to self-uncertainty emerge independently of any differences in mood or state self-esteem triggered by the uncertainty manipulation (McGregor et al., 2001).

People can also be made to feel uncertain about their specific self-attributes, in addition to their overall self-concept. The consequences of these two types of self-uncertainty largely parallel one another. Specifically, both types of uncertainty lead people to exhibit defensive cognitions and behaviors, in an attempt to appear as certain as they would like to be. For example, in a recent set of experiments (Gao, Wheeler, & Shiv, 2009), participants used either their dominant or nondominant hands to write about three instances in which they had demonstrated a particular trait (e.g., intelligence). Participants in the nondominant (relative to dominant) hand condition reported less confidence that they possessed that trait, similarly to participants in the Briñol and Petty (2003) study described earlier. However, participants who had been induced to doubt a specific self-view (versus control participants) were also more likely to select a product that symbolized this self-view (e.g., a palm pilot in the case of intelligence). Ironically, then, participants were most likely to exhibit behavior consistent with their "shaken" self-views. Such behavior (i.e., the product choices) produced subsequent increases in confidence in the self-view; participants who were not given the opportunity to select these products did not exhibit increases in confidence (for a related discussion, see DeMarree et al., 2007a).

Thus, although uncertainty about the self—in general or in relation to specific traits—can produce temporary drops in confidence, it may ultimately trigger a greater (perhaps inauthentic) sense of conviction, so long as people are provided with a means of restoring their confidence in their threatened self-concept. Future research should investigate additional conditions under which uncertainty manipulations produce feelings of doubt versus defensive confidence. For example, it may be that self-uncertainty leads people to report greater conviction only after some time has elapsed (see McGregor & Marigold, 2003; McGregor et al., 2001), similarly to the delayed effects of other types of threat (e.g., mortality salience; Pyszczynski, Greenberg, & Solomon, 1999).

In addition, it is possible that some variables (e.g., social consensus information, repeated experience) are especially likely to produce genuine confidence, whereas other sources (e.g., one's desire to be confident or appear confident to others) are especially likely to produce compensatory or defensive confidence (see DeMarree et al., 2007a). This raises further questions about whether "genuine" and "compensatory" confidence have similar effects on thoughts and behaviors and whether people are aware of the authenticity of their confidence (which is a metacognition about confidence itself). To date, no research has examined these questions.

One important aspect of the research reviewed in this section is that a person's metacognitions are subject to some of the same basic principles that their primary cognitions are. That is, much like a person might have a desired level of self-esteem, so too might they have a desired level of certainty in that self-esteem (or any other judgment; e.g., Chaiken, Liberman, & Eagly, 1989). As such, people can engage in the regulation of self-related certainty or other metacognitions, and this certainty regulation can in turn affect the operation of a primary cognition.

CONCLUSION

In this chapter, we have reviewed some of the ways that metacognition and metacognitive processes have produced novel insight into the content and operation of the self. We have discussed how metacognitive variables and processes can help determine which self-views predict behavior and thought and are stable over time (i.e., are strong), explain differences in people's beliefs about how the self operates, vary across cultures, and predict and result from self-defensive processes. In each of these cases, it is important to consider not only people's self-characteristics per se, which might predict their judgments and behaviors, but also what they think about these characteristics and the very nature of their self-concepts.

REFERENCES

Aaker, J. L. (1999). The malleable self: The role of self-expression in persuasion. *Journal of Marketing Research, 36,* 45–57.

Alicke, M. D., & Sedikides, C. (2009). Self-enhancement and self-protection: What they are and what they do. *European Review of Social Psychology, 20,* 1–48.

Arkin, R. M., Oleson, K. C., & Carroll, P. J. (Eds.). 2010. *The uncertain self: A handbook of perspectives from social and personality psychology.* New York, NY: Psychology Press.

Aronson, E. (1969). The theory of cognitive dissonance: A current perspective. In L. Berkowitz (Ed.), *Advances in experimental social psychology* (Vol. 4, pp. 1–34). New York, NY: Academic Press.

Bandura, A. (1982). Self-efficacy mechanism in human agency. *American Psychologist, 37,* 122–147.

Baumeister, R. F. (1998). The self. In D. T. Gilbert, S. T. Fiske, & G. Lindzey (Eds.), *The handbook of social psychology* (4th ed., Vol. 1, pp. 680–740). New York, NY: Oxford University Press.

Bigler, M., Neimeyer, G. J., & Brown, E. (2001). The divided self revisited: Effects of self-concept clarity and self-concept differentiation on psychological adjustment. *Journal of Social and Clinical Psychology, 20,* 396–415.

Blackwell, L. S., Trzesniewski, K. H., & Dweck, C. S. (2007). Implicit theories of intelligence predict achievement across an adolescent transition: A longitudinal study and an intervention. *Child Development, 78,* 246–263.

Bond, M. H., & Cheung, T.-S. (1983). College students' spontaneous self-concept: The effect of culture among respondents in Hong Kong, Japan, and the United States. *Journal of Cross-Cultural Psychology, 14,* 153–171.

Boninger, D. S., Krosnick, J. A., Berent, M. K., & Fabrigar, L. R. (1995). The causes and consequences of attitude importance. In R. E. Petty & J. A. Krosnick (Eds.), *Attitude strength: Antecedents and consequences* (pp. 159–189). Hillsdale, NJ: Lawrence Erlbaum Associates.

Briñol, P., & Petty, R. E. (2003). Overt head movements and persuasion: A self-validation analysis. *Journal of Personality and Social Psychology, 84,* 1123–1139.

Briñol, P., Petty, R. E., & Tormala, Z. L. (2006). The meaning of subjective ease and its malleability. *Psychological Science, 17,* 200–206.

Briñol, P., Petty, R. E., & Wagner, B. (2009). Body posture effects on self-evaluation: A self-validation approach. *European Journal of Social Psychology, 39,* 1053–1064.

Butzer, B., & Kuiper, N. A. (2006). Relationships between the frequency of social comparisons and self-concept clarity, intolerance of uncertainty, anxiety, and depression. *Personality and Individual Differences, 41,* 167–176.

Campbell, J. D. (1990). Self-esteem and clarity of the self-concept. *Journal of Personality and Social Psychology, 59,* 538–549.

Campbell, J. D., Trapnell, P. D., Heine, S. J., Katz, I. M., Lavallee, L. F., & Lehman, D. R. (1996). Self-concept clarity: Measurement, personality correlates, and cultural boundaries. *Journal of Personality and Social Psychology, 70,* 141–156.

Chaiken, S., Liberman, A., & Eagly, A. H. (1989). Heuristic and systematic information processing within and beyond the persuasion context. In J. S. Uleman & J. A. Bargh (Eds.), *Unintended thought* (pp. 212–252). New York, NY: Guilford Press.

Crocker, J., Karpinski, A., Quinn, D. M., & Chase, S. K. (2003). When grades determine self-worth: Consequences of contingent self-worth for male and female engineering and psychology majors. *Journal of Personality and Social Psychology, 85,* 507–516.

Crocker, J., & Knight, K. M. (2005). Contingencies of self-worth. *Current Directions in Psychological Science, 14,* 200–203.

Crocker, J., Luhtanen, R. K., Cooper, M. L., & Bouvrette, A. (2003). Contingencies of self-worth in college students: Theory and measurement. *Journal of Personality and Social Psychology, 85,* 894–908.

Crocker, J., & Park, L. E. (2004). The costly pursuit of self-esteem. *Psychological Bulletin, 130,* 392–414.

Crocker, J., Sommers, S. R., & Luhtanen, R. K. (2002). Hopes dashed and dreams fulfilled: Contingencies of self-worth and graduate school admissions. *Personality and Social Psychology Bulletin, 28,* 1275–1286.

Crocker, J., & Wolfe, C. T. (2001). Contingencies of self-worth. *Psychological Review, 108,* 593–623.

DeHart, T., & Pelham, B. W. (2007). Fluctuations in state implicit self-esteem in response to daily negative events. *Journal of Experimental Social Psychology, 43,* 157–165.

DeMarree, K. G., & Loersch, C. (2009). Who am I and who are you? Priming and the influence of self versus other focused attention. *Journal of Experimental Social Psychology, 45,* 440–443.

DeMarree, K. G., Morrison, K. R., Wheeler, S. C., & Petty, R. E. (2011). Self-ambivalence and resistance to subtle self-change attempts. *Personality and Social Psychology Bulletin, 37,* 674–686.

DeMarree, K. G., Petty, R. E., & Briñol, P. (2007a). Self-certainty: Parallels to attitude certainty. *International Journal of Psychology and Psychological Therapy, 7,* 159–188.

DeMarree, K. G., Petty, R. E., & Briñol, P. (2007b). Self and attitude strength parallels: Focus on accessibility. *Social and Personality Psychology Compass, 1,* 441–468.

DeMarree, K. G., Petty, R. E., & Strunk, D. R. (2010). Self-esteem accessibility as attitude strength: On the durability and impactfulness of accessible self-views. *Personality and Social Psychology Bulletin, 36,* 628–641.

Dijksterhuis, A., Spears, R., Postmes, T., Stapel, D., Koomen, W., van Knippenberg, A., & Scheepers, D. (1998). Seeing one thing and doing another: Contrast effects in automatic behavior. *Journal of Personality and Social Psychology, 75,* 862–871.

Dunlosky, J., & Metcalfe, J. (2009). *Metacognition.* Thousand Oaks, CA: Sage.

Dweck, C. S., Chiu, C.-Y., & Hong, Y.-Y. (1995). Implicit theories and their role in judgments and reactions: A world from two perspectives. *Psychological Inquiry, 6,* 267–285.

Eisenstadt, D., & Leippe, M. R. (1994). The self-comparison process and self-discrepant feedback: Consequences of learning you are what you thought you were not. *Journal of Personality and Social Psychology, 67,* 611–626.

Fazio, R. H., & Towles-Schwen, T. (1999). The MODE model of attitude–behavior processes. In S. Chaiken & Y. Trope (Eds.), *Dual process theories in social psychology* (pp. 97–116). New York, NY: Guilford Press.

Fazio, R. H., & Zanna, M. P. (1978). Attitudinal qualities relating to the strength of the attitude–behavior relationship. *Journal of Experimental Social Psychology, 14,* 398–408.

Festinger, L. (1957). *A theory of cognitive dissonance.* Palo Alto, CA: Stanford University Press.

Gao, L., Wheeler, S. C., & Shiv, B. (2009). The "shaken self": Product choices as a means of restoring self-view confidence. *Journal of Consumer Research, 36,* 29–38.

Greenwald, A. G., & Pratkanis, A. R. (1984). The self. In R. S. Wyer, Jr. & T. K. Srull (Eds.), *Handbook of social cognition* (Vol. 3, pp. 129–178). Hillsdale, NJ: Lawrence Erlbaum Associates.

Gross, S. R., Holtz, R., & Miller, N. (1995). Attitude certainty. In R. E. Petty & J. A. Krosnick (Eds.), *Attitude strength: Antecedents and consequences* (pp. 215–245). Hillsdale, NJ: Lawrence Erlbaum Associates.

Heine, S. J., Kitayama, S., Lehman, D. R., Takata, T., Ide, E., Leung, C., et al. (2001). Divergent consequences of success and failure in Japan and North America: An investigation of self-improving motivations and malleable selves. *Journal of Personality and Social Psychology, 81,* 599–615.

Higgins, E. T. (1987). Self-discrepancy: A theory relating self and affect. *Psychological Review, 94,* 319–340.

Higgins, E. T. (1997). Beyond pleasure and pain. *American Psychologist, 52,* 1280–1300.

Hogg, M. A., Sherman, D. K., Dierselhuis, J., Maitner, A. T., & Moffitt, G. (2007). Uncertainty, entitativity, and group identification. *Journal of Experimental Social Psychology, 43,* 135–142.

Holbrook, A. L., Berent, M. K., Krosnick, J. A., Visser, P. S., & Boninger, D. S. (2005). Attitude importance and the accumulation of attitude-relevant knowledge in memory. *Journal of Personality and Social Psychology, 88,* 749–769.

Kernis, M. H. (2003). Toward a conceptualization of optimal self-esteem. *Psychological Inquiry, 14,* 1–26.

Kernis, M. H., & Goldman, B. M. (2006). A multicomponent conceptualization of authenticity: Research and theory. In M. P. Zanna (Ed.), *Advances in experimental social psychology* (Vol. 38). San Diego, CA: Academic Press.

Kernis, M. H., Lakey, C. E., & Heppner, W. L. (2008). Secure versus fragile high self-esteem as a predictor of verbal defensiveness: Converging findings across three different markers. *Journal of Personality, 76,* 477–512.

Kernis, M. H., Paradise, A. W., Whitaker, D. J., Wheatman, S. R., & Goldman, B. N. (2000). Master of one's psychological domain? Not likely if one's self-esteem is unstable. *Personality and Social Psychology Bulletin, 26,* 1297–1305.

Krosnick, J. A., & Petty, R. E. (1995). Attitude strength: An overview. In R. E. Petty & J. A. Krosnick (Eds.), *Attitude strength: Antecedents and consequences* (pp. 1–24). Mahwah, NJ: Lawrence Erlbaum Associates.

Kruglanski, A. W. (1990). Lay epistemic theory in social-cognitive psychology. *Psychological Inquiry, 1,* 181–197.

Leary, M. R., & Baumeister, R. F. (2000). The nature and function of self-esteem: Sociometer theory. In M. P. Zanna (Ed.), *Advances in experimental social psychology* (Vol. 32, pp. 1–62). San Diego, CA: Academic Press.

Levy, B., & Langer, E. (1994). Aging free from negative stereotypes: Successful memory in China and among the American deaf. *Journal of Personality and Social Psychology, 66,* 989–997.

Markus, H. R., & Kitayama, S. (1991). Culture and the self: Implications for cognition, emotion, and motivation. *Psychological Review, 98,* 224–253.

McGregor, I., & Marigold, D. C. (2003). Defensive zeal and the uncertain self: What makes you so sure? *Journal of Personality and Social Psychology, 85,* 838–852.

McGregor, I., Zanna, M. P., Holmes, J. G., & Spencer, S. J. (2001). Compensatory conviction in the face of personal uncertainty: Going to extremes and being oneself. *Journal of Personality and Social Psychology, 80,* 472–488.

Morrison, K. R., DeMarree, K. G., Wheeler, S. C., & Petty, R. E. (2010). *Actual-desired self-discrepancies and resistance to subtle self-change attempts.* Unpublished manuscript, University of Chicago, Chicago, IL.

Morrison, K. R., & Johnson, C. S. (2011). When what you have is who you are: Self-uncertainty leads to seeing values in possessions. *Personality and Social Psychology Bulletin, 37,* 639–651.

Morrison, K. R., Johnson, C. S., & Wheeler, S. C. (in press). Not all selves feel the same uncertainty: Assimilation to primes among individualists and collectivists. *Social Psychological and Personality Science.*

Morrison, K. R., & Wheeler, S. C. (2010). Nonconformity defines the self: The role of minority opinion status in self-concept clarity. *Personality and Social Psychology Bulletin, 36,* 297–308.

Morrison, K. R., Wheeler, S. C., & Miller, D. T. (2011). Compensatory opinion expression: Self-uncertainty reduces conformity to the majority. Unpublished manuscript, University of Chicago, Chicago, IL.

Nisbett, R. E., Peng, K., Choi, I., & Norenzayan, A. (2001). Culture and systems of thought: Holistic versus analytic cognition. *Psychological Review, 108,* 291–310.

Pelham, B. W. (1991). On confidence and consequence: The certainty and importance of self-knowledge. *Journal of Personality and Social Psychology, 60,* 518–530.

Pelham, B. W., & Swann, W. B. (1989). From self-conceptions to self-worth: On the sources and structure of global self-esteem. *Journal of Personality and Social Psychology, 57,* 672–680.

Petrocelli, J. V., Tormala, Z. L., & Rucker, D. D. (2007). Unpacking attitude certainty: Attitude clarity and attitude correctness. *Journal of Personality and Social Psychology, 92,* 30–41.

Petty, R. E., Briñol, P., Tormala, Z. L., & Wegener, D. T. (2007). The role of meta-cognition in social judgment. In E. T. Higgins & A. W. Kruglanski (Eds.), *Social psychology: Handbook of basic principles* (2nd ed., pp. 254–284). New York, NY: Guilford Press.

Petty, R. E., & Krosnick, J. A. (1995). *Attitude strength: Antecedents and consequences.* Mahwah, NJ: Lawrence Erlbaum Associates.

Priester, J. R., & Petty, R. E. (1996). The gradual threshold model of ambivalence: Relating the positive and negative bases of attitudes to subjective ambivalence. *Journal of Personality and Social Psychology, 71,* 431–449.

Pyszczynski, T., Greenberg, J., & Solomon, S. (1999). A dual-process model of defense against conscious and unconscious death-related thoughts. *Psychological Review, 106,* 835–845.

Rhee, E., Uleman, J. S., Lee, H. K., & Roman, R. J. (1995). Spontaneous self-descriptions and ethnic identities in individualistic and collectivistic cultures. *Journal of Personality and Social Psychology, 69,* 142–152.

Riketta, M., & Ziegler, R. (2007). Self-ambivalence and reactions to success versus failure. *European Journal of Social Psychology, 37,* 547–560.

Sedikides, C. (1993). Assessment, enhancement, and verification determinants of the self-evaluation process. *Journal of Personality and Social Psychology, 65,* 317–338.

Sedikides, C., & Gregg, A. P. (2008). Self-enhancement: Food for thought. *Perspectives on Psychological Science, 3,* 102–116.

Smeesters, D., Wheeler, S. C., & Kay, A. C. (2010). Indirect prime-to-behavior effects: The role of perceptions of the self, others, and situations in connecting primed constructs to social behavior. In M. P. Zanna (Ed.), *Advances in experimental social psychology* (Vol. 42, pp. 259–317). New York, NY: Elsevier.

Spencer-Rodgers, J., Boucher, H. C., Mori, S. C., Wang, L., & Peng, K. (2009). The dialectical self-concept: Contradiction, change, and holism in East Asian cultures. *Personality and Social Psychology Bulletin, 35,* 29–44.

Spencer-Rodgers, J., & Peng, K. (2005). The dialectical self: Contradiction, change, and holism in the East Asian self-concept. In R. M. Sorrentino, D. Cohen, J. M. Olson, & M. P. Zanna (Eds.), *Culture and social behavior: The Ontario symposium* (pp. 224–249). Mahwah, NJ: Lawrence Erlbaum Associates.

Spencer-Rodgers, J., Peng, K., Wang, L., & Hou, Y. (2004). Dialectical self-esteem and East–West differences in psychological well-being. *Personality and Social Psychology Bulletin, 30,* 1416–1432.

Stapel, D. A., & Tesser, A. (2001). Self-activation increases social comparison. *Journal of Personality and Social Psychology, 81,* 742–750.

Steele, J. R., & Ambady, N. (2006). "Math is hard!" The effect of gender priming on women's attitudes. *Journal of Experimental Social Psychology, 42,* 426–436.

Su, S. K., Chiu, C.-Y., Hong, Y.-Y., Leung, K., Peng, K., & Morris, M. W. (1999). Self-organization and social organization: American and Chinese constructions. In T. R. Tyler, R. M. Kramer, & O. P. John (Eds.), *The psychology of the social self* (pp. 193–222). Mahwah, NJ: Lawrence Erlbaum Associates.

Swann, W. B., & Bosson, J. K. (2010). Self and Identity. In S. T. Fiske, D. Gilbert, & G. Lindzey (Eds.), *Handbook of social psychology* (5th ed., Vol. 1, pp. 589–628). Hoboken, NJ: John Wiley & Sons.

Swann, W. B., & Ely, R. J. (1984). A battle of wills: Self-verification versus behavioral confirmation. *Journal of Personality and Social Psychology, 46,* 1287–1302.

Swann, W. B., Rentfrow, P. J., & Guinn, J. S. (2003). Self-verification: The search for coherence. In M. R. Leary & J. P. Tangney (Eds.), *Handbook of self and identity* (pp. 367–383). New York, NY: Guilford Press.

Vartanian, L. R. (2009). When the body defines the self: Self-concept clarity, internalization, and body image. *Journal of Social and Clinical Psychology, 28,* 94–126.

Visser, P. S., Bizer, G. Y., & Krosnick, J. A. (2006). Exploring the latent structure of strength related attitude attributes. In M. P. Zanna (Ed.), *Advances in experimental social psychology* (Vol. 38, pp. 1–67). New York, NY: Academic Press.

Visser, P. S., Krosnick, J. A., & Simmons, J. P. (2003). Distinguishing the cognitive and behavioral consequences of attitude importance and certainty: A new approach to testing the common-factor hypothesis. *Journal of Experimental Social Psychology, 39,* 118–141.

Wheeler, S. C., & DeMarree, K. G. (2009). Multiple mechanisms of prime-to-behavior effects. *Social and Personality Psychology Compass, 3,* 566–581.

Wheeler, S. C., DeMarree, K. G., & Petty, R. E. (2007). Understanding the role of the self in prime to behavior effects: The active-self account. *Personality and Social Psychology Review, 11,* 234–261.

Wheeler, S. C., Morrison, K. R., DeMarree, K. G., & Petty, R. E. (2008). Does self-consciousness increase or decrease priming effects? It depends. *Journal of Experimental Social Psychology, 44,* 882–889.

Wilson, T. D., & Gilbert, D. T. (2005). Affective forecasting: Knowing what to want. *Current Directions in Psychological Science, 14*, 131–134.

Zuwerink, J. R., & Devine, P. G. (1996). Attitude importance and resistance to persuasion: It's not just the thought that counts. *Journal of Personality and Social Psychology, 70*, 931–944.

7

Metacognitive Processes in the Self-Regulation of Goal Pursuit

ANJA ACHTZIGER, SARAH E. MARTINY,
GABRIELE OETTINGEN, and PETER M. GOLLWITZER

INTRODUCTION

*I*t is Thursday morning; you are a professional soccer player whose team lost the semifinal of the World Cup last night. You are frustrated and depressed because of the poor performance of your team. However, in a few days you and your team will compete for third place and your team has set itself the goal to succeed in this final match. How will you manage to commit strongly to the goal to perform well in this last match? How will you get yourself to train intensively, focused on the upcoming challenge, rather than to avoid the soccer field, ruminating about your recent loss?

To reach goals, we often need to override or alter dominant response tendencies that are deemed inappropriate. This process of altering dominant response tendencies into goal-directed behavior is coined *self-regulation* (e.g., Bandura, 1989; Carver & Scheier, 1981; Metcalfe & Mischel, 1999; Vohs & Baumeister, 2004). Self-regulation comprises monitoring, controlling, and changing our thoughts, emotions, impulses, and performance (Baumeister, Heatherton, & Tice, 1994). In order to break bad habits and to resist temptation, self-regulation orchestrates cognitive, metacognitive, affective, and volitional processes that reflect the self's ability to regulate itself.

Research has shown that people differ in their self-regulatory abilities and that high self-control is positively associated with desirable outcomes in a broad variety of domains (e.g., success in school and work and mental health), whereas low self-control is associated with less desired outcomes (Baumeister et al., 1994; Duckworth & Seligman, 2005; Friese & Hofmann, 2009; Hofmann, Friese, & Strack, 2009; Mischel, Shoda, & Peake, 1988; Shoda, Mischel, & Peake, 1990;

Tangney, Baumeister, & Boone, 2004; Wolfe & Johnson, 1995). Thus, skilful self-regulation is a crucial ability for effective human functioning.

In the present chapter, we will first discuss the important role of metacognitive processes in the self-regulation of goal pursuit. We will present and extend Nelson's model of metacognition (1996) by discussing the role of three metacognitive strategies: planning, monitoring, and controlling. Then, these three strategies and their role in goal setting and goal striving will be discussed within the theoretical framework of the mind-set theory of action phases (Gollwitzer, 1990; Heckhausen & Gollwitzer, 1987). Afterward, the fantasy realization theory (Oettingen, 1999; Oettingen, Pak, & Schnetter, 2001), the theory of intentional action control (Gollwitzer, 1993, 1999), and a recent intervention technique to promote self-regulation of goal attaining and goal striving (mental contrasting with implementation intentions: MCII; Oettingen & Gollwitzer, 2010) will be introduced. Finally, we will address the issues of consciousness versus nonconsciousness in self-regulation, and we end by pointing to the role of positive thinking and counterfactual thinking in modern self-regulation approaches.

METACOGNITION IN SELF-REGULATION

The importance of metacognition in the self-regulation of goal pursuit has been highlighted by several researchers (e.g., Gollwitzer & Schaal, 1998; Nelson, 1996). Nelson (1996) argued that we need to distinguish between the object-level and the meta-level. The object-level is defined as the current state (i.e., reality), whereas the meta-level contains a desired end state including one's goals and ideas about how the object-level can be used to obtain the goals—that is, one's strategies to reach the goals. At the object-level there are only cognitions concerning external objects (e.g., "The contest for third place will be a difficult match"), whereas at the meta-level there are cognitions concerning cognitions of external objects (e.g., "Why am I thinking that this is going to be a difficult match?").

In line with recent theoretical work on metacognition (e.g., Petty, Briñol, Tormala, & Wegener, 2007), the first category of thoughts can be labeled *primary cognition* and the second category as *secondary cognition*. Two processes connect the meta-level with the object-level: *monitoring*, which refers to information flowing from the object-level to the meta-level, and *control*, which describes information flowing from the meta-level to the object-level. Through monitoring, the meta-level is informed about the state of the object-level; through control, the object-level is informed by the meta-level about what actions to take to reach the set goal represented in the meta-level. Thus, planning, monitoring, and controlling refer to secondary cognition.

In recent models of metacognition in different domains, such as metacognitive processes in emotional intelligence (e.g., Briñol, Petty, & Rucker, 2006) or metacognition in self-regulated learning (e.g., Boekaerts, 1996), three, rather than two, metacognitive strategies are proposed to enable goal pursuit: *planning, monitoring,* and *controlling*. All three strategies comprise secondary cognition because they do not focus on external objects, but rather refer to cognitions of cognitions. In line with Nelson's assumptions, monitoring implies a higher level cognitive activity that examines the process of reaching a goal. Whenever the result of the monitoring process indicates that the realized action does not lead to the established goal, control processes are engaged to change the individual's behavior and thoughts so that the set goal is attained.

However, in recent models, planning goal pursuit is seen as a separate metacognitive strategy in which one cognitively designs actions to be accomplished to attain the desired goal (e.g., by planning future control processes). In Nelson's model, planning is one component of control because his examples of control processes include the selection of strategies and the allocation of time to a certain task. Thus, we consider planning to be one component of the control aspect— although a most important one. All three of these metacognitive strategies play a central role in the overarching theoretical framework of the following chapter— namely, the mind-set theory of action phases (Gollwitzer, 1990, 2011; Heckhausen & Gollwitzer, 1987).

SELF-REGULATION IN GOAL SETTING AND GOAL STRIVING

In social psychological research, the processes of deciding which goal to pursue and how to pursue it are subsumed by the term "motivation." Both early and more recent theories of motivation (e.g., Ajzen, 1991; Atkinson, 1957; Bandura, 1997; Carver & Scheier, 1998; Gollwitzer, 1990) suggest that people prefer to choose goals that are desirable and feasible. This means that when they *set a goal*, people weigh the incentive value of reaching different goals with the expectancy of actually reaching these goals. Then, they choose the alternative with the best combined outcome (e.g., Atkinson, 1957). Even though setting the right goal is an important step in the direction of effective human functioning, it is only the first step. Whether the desired goal is indeed attained depends on how well the process of *goal striving* is executed. Whereas early research on motivation mainly focused on factors influencing goal setting, more recently the attention of researchers has shifted to factors influencing the success of goal striving (for an overview see Bargh, Gollwitzer, & Oettingen, 2010). An important theory combining both aspects of motivation is the *mind-set theory of action phases* (Gollwitzer, 1990, 2011). This theory will be outlined in the following section.

The Mind-Set Theory of Action Phases

This theory describes the sequential process of goal setting, goal striving (i.e., planning and acting), and the reflection on and evaluation of both processes. It postulates that these elements are characteristic of different phases, distinguishing four separate stages in goal pursuit. The first phase, the so-called *predecisional phase*, is characterized by goal setting. Here, as postulated by earlier theories of motivation (e.g., Atkinson, 1957), people consider the desirability and feasibility of each alternative wish before turning one of these wishes into a binding goal. In terms of Nelson's model of metacognition (1996), reflecting on the desirability and feasibility of one's wishes is a component of the metacognitive strategy of *monitoring* because it requires a flow of information from the object-level to the meta-level (for a similar argument, see Gollwitzer & Schaal, 1998). Commitment to goal attainment is high when goals are attractive (i.e., when the expected outcomes are evaluated positively) and feasible (i.e., when one's ability to implement the required goal-directed behaviors is assessed positively).

When a goal is set, the predecisional phase ends and the first of two volitional phases begins: the *preactional* phase. The focus of the preactional phase is to plan how to pursue one's goal, including the when and where of action to reach the goal. Thus, in this phase the focus is clearly laid on the process of planning how to implement the goal. In Nelson's model, this is part of the control component (i.e., secondary cognition) that ensures the flow of information from the meta-level to the object-level. In a third stage, the *actional* phase, the plans made must be realized in the form of action. In the actional phase, *monitoring* and *control* as secondary cognition may or may not take place, depending on specific aspects of the person (e.g., working memory capacity), the situation (e.g., time), and the goal (e.g., the specificity of the goal). However, in the last phase, the *postactional* phase, people concentrate fully on evaluating their goal pursuit. The postactional phase addresses two main questions: First, did I achieve the goal I intended to achieve? Second, does the actual value of the achieved goal meet the expected value? The results of these evaluation processes influence future goal setting and goal striving, thereby influencing primary cognition (i.e., the object-level) through secondary cognition (i.e., the meta-level), as in the control component of Nelson's model of metacognition.

The mind-set theory of action phases further states that the decision to strive for a certain goal is a psychologically significant event, leading to a certain mindset that affects cognition and behavior (e.g., Gollwitzer, 1990, 2011; Gollwitzer & Bayer, 1999; Taylor & Gollwitzer, 1995; for a review, see Achtziger & Gollwitzer, 2010). More precisely, the predecisional phase is characterized by a *deliberative mind-set*. This mind-set is defined by an openness to all relevant information with the goal of maximizing the likelihood of reaching an objective judgment concerning the desirability and feasibility of the different goal alternatives. In contrast, the *implemental mind-set* occurs in the postdecisional and preactional phase and is characterized by increased processing of information concerning the planning of goal striving that is the when, where, and how of realizing the goal.

Numerous studies have supported the main assumptions of the mindset theory of action phases (e.g., Gollwitzer, Heckhausen, & Ratajczak, 1990; Gollwitzer & Kinney, 1989), but two crucial questions have been left unanswered: (1) Do strategies exist that enhance people's goal commitment and goal striving for feasible goals? (2) How can people make sure to reach the goals they have set themselves? More precisely, how do people master the problems inherent in goal striving, such as seizing opportunities to act, warding off distractions, and compensating for failures? Empirical evidence suggests that there are self-regulatory strategies that can improve goal commitment as well as goal striving. In the following, two strategies will be discussed: mental contrasting as a strategy to increase goal commitment and implementation intentions as a strategy to improve goal striving.

The Fantasy Realization Theory

Mental contrasting, as described in fantasy realization theory (Oettingen et al., 2001), is a self-regulatory strategy that can be used in the predecisional phase to improve goal setting by increasing goal commitment to feasible goals (e.g., Oettingen, Mayer, Stephens, & Brinkmann, 2010). Mental contrasting (Oettingen, 1999) refers to the following process: People first imagine a desired future and attaining it (e.g., winning an important soccer match) and then reflect on the present reality that may impede realizing the desired future (e.g., having little time for preparation). The conjoint elaboration of the positive future and the negative reality makes both future and reality simultaneously accessible and thereby highlights obstacles standing in the way of attaining the desired future. Research suggests that mental contrasting helps people to make up their mind about whether to commit to a goal by scrutinizing the feasibility of achieving it. When perceived feasibility is high, people strongly commit to attaining the goal; when perceived feasibility is low, they form either a weak goal commitment or none at all.

Instead of mental contrasting, people may only *indulge* in a positive future or only *dwell* on the negative reality. When this occurs, people fail to recognize that they need to act on the status quo in order to arrive at the desired future. As a consequence, expectations are not consulted and goal commitments stemming solely from focusing on either a positive future or a negative reality will fail to be expectancy dependent. The level of goal commitment is then determined by the *a priori commitment* that the person holds with respect to attaining the desired future, rather than the feasibility of achieving it. Thus, only mental contrasting succeeds in raising commitment when expectations of success are high and in lowering commitment when expectations of success are low.

Empirical Evidence for the Fantasy Realization Theory   So far, a large number of studies have tested the effects of mental contrasting, indulging (focusing on positive future outcomes only), and dwelling (focusing on the negative reality only) on goal commitment and goal striving (Oettingen, 2000; Oettingen, Hönig, & Gollwitzer, 2000; Oettingen, Mayer, Thorpe, Janetzke, & Lorenz, 2005; Oettingen et al., 2001). All of these studies found empirical support for the effectiveness of mental contrasting. For instance, in one experiment, adolescent students had to mentally contrast the positive future of excelling in mathematics (participants imagined feelings of pride, increasing their job prospects, etc.) with the negative reality (participants reflected on being distracted by peers, feeling lazy, etc.). Two weeks after the experiment, students in the mental contrasting condition who initially had high expectations that they could achieve the desired goal (i.e., excel in math) received better course grades and teachers rated them as exerting more effort compared to students in the indulging and dwelling conditions (Oettingen et al., 2001, Study 4). The same pattern of results emerged in schoolchildren starting to learn a foreign language (Oettingen et al., 2000, Study 1), in students wishing to solve an interpersonal problem (Oettingen et al., 2001, Studies 1 and 3), and in students being offered the opportunity to get to know an attractive stranger (Oettingen, 2000, Study 1).

Recently, Oettingen and colleagues have turned to analyzing the processes underlying the creation of strong goal commitments by mental contrasting (e.g., energization; Oettingen et al., 2009) and to answering the question of how people can be taught to mentally contrast their desires and concerns as a metacognitive strategy. This research focuses on teaching individuals the cognitive procedure of mental contrasting in a way so that it will be used not only for a specific concern, but also for everyday desires and concerns in general. For instance, Oettingen, Mayer, and Brinkmann (2010) taught German personnel managers how to perform mental contrasting by working through a specific work-related problem (e.g., giving constructive feedback to their coworkers). After 2 weeks, it was observed that managers who then completed a mental contrasting exercise reported better time management, more ease of decision making, and more effective project completion in general, compared to those who performed a control exercise (i.e., thinking about the same issues but not contrasting desired future outcomes with reality).

The Role of Metacognition in the Fantasy Realization Theory   How does mental contrasting fit into recent metacognitive frameworks? Thinking of mental contrasting from a metacognitive perspective, it becomes clear that people who mentally contrast their concerns and desires do compare the current state (on the object-level; primary cognition) with positive outcomes of a to-be-attained future state (represented on the meta-level as secondary cognition). Thus, they inform the meta-level about obstacles on the object-level (i.e., in present reality) and their model or mental representation of their concerns and desires becomes updated. Moreover, mental contrasting should influence willingness to plan (i.e., control) because it increases commitment to feasible goals. Finally, it should enable people to realize what the main obstacles to goal pursuit are so that they are in a position to plan specifically how to deal with these obstacles as soon as they occur (for a detailed discussion of this point, see "Mental Contrasting With Implementation Intentions" later in this chapter).

The Theory of Intentional Action Control

Whereas the fantasy realization theory focuses on increasing goal commitment in the predecisional phase (i.e., the improvement of goal setting), the theory of intentional action control deals with the problem of how set goals can be reached (i.e., the improvement of goal striving). Based on the mind-set theory of action phases, the theory of intentional action control (Gollwitzer, 1993, 1999) argues that one of the reasons for the intention–behavior gap, or why people do so poorly in transforming their intentions into action, lies in the failure to spell out *how* they want to realize their goals. It is suggested that most people lack the metacognitive knowledge of how to form action plans in order to support their goal striving. Not thinking carefully about relevant opportunities, hindrances, and instrumental goal-directed behavior results in failing to initiate goal-directed behavior (e.g., Brandstaetter, Lengfelder, & Gollwitzer, 2001) and failing to shield one's goals from external distractions (e.g., Gollwitzer & Schaal, 1998) and negative inner states (e.g., anxiety and nervousness: Achtziger, Gollwitzer, & Sheeran, 2008; ego-depletion and feelings of incompleteness: Bayer, Gollwitzer, & Achtziger, 2010).

In order to elucidate the intention–behavior gap, Gollwitzer (1993, 1999) differentiates between two kinds of intentions: goal intentions and implementation intentions. Goal intentions are goals in the common sense and are defined as desired end states that a person wants to attain. They have the format of "I intend to do X" (e.g., "I want to win the upcoming soccer match."). Implementation intentions are if–then plans defining when, where, and how a person wants to act to reach his or her desired goal. Action plans in the form of implementation intentions have the format of "if situation Y arises, then I will perform behavior Z" (e.g., "If player X calls on me to pass the ball, then I will carefully pass the ball.").

Empirical Evidence for the Theory of Intentional Action Control

These action plans operate in the service of goals, and in numerous studies they have been found to support strongly goal attainment in a broad variety of domains. For instance, Orbell, Hodgkins, and Sheeran (1997) found that women who had been given the goal of performing regular breast self-examinations greatly benefited from forming implementation intentions. Similar patterns of results have emerged for participating in voluntary cancer screening (Sheeran & Orbell, 2000), resuming functional activity after hip replacement surgery (Orbell & Sheeran, 2000), reducing consultations for emergency contraception and pregnancy testing among teenage girls (Martin, Sheeran, Slade, Wright, & Dibble, 2009), and increasing attendance for psychotherapy (Sheeran, Aubrey, & Kellett, 2007; for a review, see Achtziger & Gollwitzer, 2010; Gollwitzer & Sheeran, 2006).

In most studies examining the effects of implementation intentions, goal intentions and if–then plans were assigned to participants by the experimenters and worded so that they could easily be employed as they were highly appropriate to the predetermined critical situations. In everyday life, people are confronted with all kinds of expected and unexpected situations with which they must deal effectively to reach their goals. It therefore seems crucial to teach people to form their own if–then plans as new situations emerge as a useful metacognitive strategy for supporting their goal striving. In one early study (Murgraff, White, & Phillips, 1996), participants were instructed to form their own individual if–then plans by explaining the advantage of linking a specified viable opportunity for action initiation to a goal-directed behavior. By forming their own individual implementation intentions, participants who suffered from alcohol problems learned to control their excessive drinking behavior.

Recently, Achtziger and colleagues (2008, Study 2) taught people how to form implementation intentions that could control disruptive inner states (e.g., nervousness, anxiety). Participants were tennis players and, in this study, they found it easy to follow the if–then planning instructions. Most importantly, they performed better in the subsequent tennis match compared to earlier matches and compared to participants who learned only to form goal intentions. These findings suggest that teaching people how to form implementation intentions as a metacognitive strategy of the self-regulation of goal striving is possible and effective.

The question arises whether there is a meaningful metacognition-related distinction between various forms of implementation intentions. One might wonder whether we can only speak about metacognitive implementation intentions if both parts of these plans (the "if" and the "then") are related to thoughts. Numerous studies have shown that quite different forms of implementation intentions are effective. There are examples of if–then plans in which only the "if" part or only the "then" part is related to thoughts; nevertheless, these plans are effective. Implementation intentions can hence be metacognitive (if both parts define thoughts), partly metacognitive (if only one of the two parts defines a thought), or not metacognitive at all (if neither of the two parts defines thoughts).

Recently, Gollwitzer, Wieber, Myers, and McCrea (2010) have argued that "if" parts that specify thoughts are more integrative and therefore might imply more critical situations than the mere specification of certain external situations themselves. Moreover, Adriaanse, de Ridder, and de Wit (2009, Study 1) have shown that motivational cues (specified as thoughts in the "if" parts of implementation intentions) can help to enhance healthy food consumption. Implementation intentions in this study were partly metacognitive because only the "if" part (but not the "then" part) of the plan was related to thoughts. Achtziger et al. (2008) have shown that implementation intentions that are metacognitive in the sense that both of their parts define thoughts are also quite effective (e.g., "If I feel self-abandoned, then I will tell myself, 'I can win this match.'").

The Role of Metacognitions in the Theory of Intentional Action Control   Interestingly, implementation intentions can be seen as both a monitoring process and a control process. The *formation* of implementation intentions reflects a *monitoring* process, in the terms of Nelson's metacognition model (1996), because this act of will uses specific cues at the object-level (i.e., the when, where, and how of goal-directed behaviors; primary cognition) in order to support goal striving and goal attainment. When people form implementation intentions on their own, they first carefully think about situational cues in order to decide in which situation it would be best to implement their goal-directed behaviors. Moreover, these goal-directed behaviors are subjected to a reality check in order to determine their instrumentality for goal attainment. Thus, these cues at the object-level (or primary cognition) inform the formation of the plan at the meta-level (i.e., secondary cognition).

After forming the implementation intention, a mental representation (or model) of this action plan is established on the meta-level as a secondary cognition. This representation is in a state of heightened activation, leading to a heightened cognitive accessibility of the if–then plan (Achtziger, Bayer, & Gollwitzer, 2010; Gollwitzer, 1999). From the moment this representation is stored on the meta-level, it guides goal striving by *controlling* behavior (i.e., by facilitating the implementation of the goal-directed behavior specified in the "then" component of the implementation intention). This action control process in turn affects the object-level (i.e., the current state of the world in the sense of primary cognition) for the purpose of goal attainment. However, after an implementation intention has been realized, it can be assumed that people check whether the respective superordinate goal has been met. Accordingly, a new process of *monitoring* in the sense of secondary cognition is initiated that compares the current state (i.e., the object-level) with the desired end state (represented on the meta-level).

Mental Contrasting With Implementation Intentions

Recently, Oettingen and Gollwitzer (2010) explored whether it is possible to construct an intervention that teaches people to use an integrated combination of the two self-regulation strategies of mental contrasting and implementation intentions so that people can become effective self-regulators of their goal setting and goal striving in everyday life. This intervention that combines mental contrasting (MC) with implementation intentions (II) is called MCII. The procedure was expected to be especially effective because in order to maximize their beneficial effects, implementation intentions require that strong goal commitments be in place (Achtziger et al., 2010, Study 2; Sheeran, Webb, & Gollwitzer, 2005, Study 1).

Mental contrasting creates such strong commitments. Additionally, mental contrasting supports the identification of obstacles that hinder goal striving. These same obstacles can then be addressed by if–then plans by specifying these critical situations in the "if" component of an implementation intention and then linking these obstacles to goal-directed responses in the "then" component. Moreover, mental contrasting is known to increase the readiness to form if–then plans (Oettingen et al., 2001, Study 3; Oettingen & Kappes, 2009); accordingly, an intervention such as MCII that explicitly suggests forming implementation intentions after mental contrasting is likely to show even stronger effects than the deployment of just one of the two strategies.

Empirical Evidence for MCII   The impact of the MCII intervention on behavior change was tested in various studies targeting different types of problem behaviors. For instance, the impact of MCII on improving mobility in a sample of chronic back pain patients was examined by Christiansen, Oettingen, Dahme, and Klinger (2010). Participants were randomly assigned to either a control group (i.e., standard outpatient back pain program) or an intervention group (i.e., this program plus the MCII intervention). The experimental condition involved (in addition to the standard back pain program) two one-half hour sessions. In the first session, participants engaged in mental contrasting about realizing fantasies related to improved mobility, and during the second session, participants identified behaviors in response to the obstacles generated in the first session to serve as the focus of an implementation intention (e.g., "If I am afraid of causing damage to myself, then I will remember that movement is good against pain."). The dependent variables for this study were physical strength, appropriate lifting behavior, and pain severity, after 10 days and after 3 months, in comparison to respective pre-intervention baseline measures.

The findings indicate that MCII, in conjunction with the standard treatment, improved physical mobility (strength and lifting) in chronic back pain patients beyond the standard treatment. This was true for subjective and objective measures of physical mobility. These effects were independent of participants' experienced pain, which did not significantly differ between conditions during and after treatment. In further intervention studies using MCII to target health behavior, the combination of mental contrasting with implementation intentions was shown to be effective in inducing stable behavior change with respect to exercising (over 4 months; Stadler, Oettingen, & Gollwitzer, 2009) and healthy eating (over 2 years; Stadler, Oettingen, & Gollwitzer, 2010).

Given that MCII as a metacognitive strategy is expected to improve self-regulation in general, the impact of MCII trainings has also been examined on broader variables such as self-discipline in everyday life. In line with the conceptualization of self-discipline suggested by Tangney et al. (2004), the following key components of self-regulation were examined in one study (Oettingen, Barry, Guttenberg, & Gollwitzer, 2011, Study 2): time management, project completion, and the feeling of being on top of things. Undergraduate participants were assigned to an MCII intervention group or to a control group. As dependent measures, participants rated self-discipline at two time points: immediately following the intervention and once again 1 week after the intervention. The results showed that the MCII intervention enhanced participants' reports of self-discipline in terms of time management, project completion, and feeling on top of things over the time period of 1 week, and in comparison to control group participants (who either addressed the same type of thought content, reflecting on it in a different way, or used the MCII way of reflection on different thought content). Apparently, the MCII intervention empowered individuals with self-regulatory skills, first by helping them to commit to feasible rather than unfeasible goals and then by helping them to achieve the goals effectively.

In sum, this powerful yet simple combination of mental contrasting with implementation intentions seems to help people to meet their goals or, when taught as a metacognitive strategy, to improve the self-regulation of goal setting and goal implementation in general.

CONSCIOUSNESS AND NONCONSCIOUSNESS IN GOAL PURSUIT

Traditional models of motivation are based on an agentic, conscious self that deliberately sets goals (e.g., Atkinson, 1957; Gollwitzer, 1990). However, within the last two decades researchers have argued that there is an alternative route to goal attainment: the nonconscious mode of goal striving (see Bargh et al., 2010). Social cognition research has shown that the activation of a goal can also be achieved outside awareness. This can, for example, be accomplished by subliminally presented goal-relevant cues. Although not consciously perceived, subliminally presented cues have repeatedly been shown to initiate goal striving successfully (e.g., Bargh, 1989, 2006).

Similarities Between Conscious and Nonconscious Goal Pursuit

Early research on nonconscious goal striving focused on its similarities to conscious goal striving, demonstrating that nonconscious and conscious goal striving have similar outcomes (Bargh, Gollwitzer, Chai, Barndollar, & Troetschel, 2001). For example, researchers showed that nonconscious and conscious goal striving have the same affective and motivational consequences. Chartrand and Bargh (2002) gave participants an anagram task that was either easy or impossible to solve. By indicating that it was merely a filler task, the experimenter downplayed the importance of the task to the participants. For those participants who were previously primed with achievement, but not the control group, working on the easy anagrams resulted in improved mood and increased motivation, whereas working on difficult anagrams resulted in depressed mood and lower motivation to perform a subsequent task. Thus, even when participants were not aware of the primed goal, the activation of an achievement goal influenced their affective and motivational reaction to their performance, as has been shown when people consciously strive for goals.

Differences Between Conscious and Nonconscious Goal Pursuit

Recently, research has started to elucidate the differences between conscious and nonconscious goal striving. For instance, Oettingen, Grant, Smith, Skinner, and Gollwitzer (2006) argued that people who strive for nonconscious goals are acting in an explanatory vacuum; that is, they do not know why they are doing what they are doing. As a consequence, when explanations of one's actions are demanded (e.g., because one acts against an established norm), nonconscious goal strivers have a disadvantage because they cannot access the nonconscious goal that is driving their behavior. Nonconscious goal strivers therefore try to fill this explanatory vacuum by coming up with potential goals that might have caused their behavior. They are thus found to accept readily any suggestions for such goals as provided by their situational surroundings (Parks-Stamm, Oettingen, & Gollwitzer, 2010). From the perspective of Nelson's metacognition model (1996), acting in an explanatory vacuum reflects a disconnection between the meta-level and the object-level and thus between primary and secondary cognition. It appears that information does not flow freely between the two levels, or at least it does not occur on a conscious level.

Implementation Intentions as a Tool for Automatic Goal Striving

As a control metacognitive strategy, implementation intentions appear to automate the control of primary cognition by secondary cognition, thereby automating some of the metacognitive tasks necessary for self-regulation. For example, Stewart and Payne (2008) demonstrated that implementation intentions can control automatic aspects of cognition. Thus, action control by forming implementation intentions can be understood as a conscious attempt to turn conscious goal striving into automatic goal striving. This type of automaticity is in the service of the superordinate goal and it can thus be understood as strategic automaticity (Gollwitzer & Schaal, 1998).

THE ROLE OF THINKING POSITIVELY ABOUT THE FUTURE IN THE SELF-REGULATION OF GOAL PURSUIT

Until now we have discussed how our representations of goals influence our behavior, what strategies can be used to ensure that we choose and commit to the right goals, and how we can handle problems arising in the process of goal striving. The following section will focus on a different aspect of metacognition in goal pursuit by asking how thinking about possible futures (i.e., desired end states) impacts goal pursuit.

On the one hand, research has shown that optimistic thinking about the future can foster motivation and performance, whereas pessimistic thinking seems to dampen it (e.g., Bandura, 1997; Taylor & Brown, 1988). Accordingly, optimistic thinking is associated with successful cognitive and self-regulatory problem solving and with setting high standards and aspirations. Such beliefs about the future, or expectancy judgments, pertain to self-efficacy expectations (i.e., whether one can perform a certain behavior; Bandura, 1997) and outcome expectations (i.e., whether performing a certain behavior will lead to the desired outcome; Bandura, 1997) as general expectations (i.e., whether a certain event will occur; e.g., Oettingen & Wadden, 1991) or as generalized expectations (i.e., whether the future in general will be positive or negative; Scheier & Carver, 1992).

On the other hand, some forms of thinking positively about the future, such as those based less on past experiences and thus less influenced by performance history, seem not always to be beneficial for effortful action, performance, and well-being. For example, wishful thinking that is mainly unrelated to concrete past experiences is linked to lower performance and well-being compared to planning future behavior and confrontational coping styles (e.g., Lengua & Sandler, 1996; Reid, Dubow, & Carey, 1995). Experimental research on how self-regulatory thoughts affect task completion also showed that positive thoughts are not always beneficial for effort and performance. For example, Goodhart (1986) reported unfavorable effects of positive task-related thoughts or images on success in solving anagrams.

These studies are in line with the Oettingen and Mayer (2002) proposition that there are actually two distinguishable types of thinking about the future with differential effects on motivation and performance. *Beliefs about the future* (expectations about feasibility) should be differentiated from mere *positive images* (fantasies) depicting future events. Beliefs are expectancy judgments that assess the probability of occurrence of certain events (i.e., feasibility), whereas images are solely fantasies that contain future events, neglecting information about the feasibility of the event. Positive expectancy judgments, then, are beliefs that a desired event is likely to occur; positive fantasies about the future, in contrast, are positively experienced images of future desired events that emerge in one's stream of thought.

Oettingen and Mayer (2002) found that the experienced positivity of fantasies predicted low effort and low success over various periods of time (from 2 weeks to 2 years). This correlation held true for different life domains (professional, interpersonal, academic, and health) and for people of different ages (young adults, the elderly). In all of these studies, high expectations of success were associated with the positivity of experienced fantasies. When expectations were controlled for, the authors found that the detrimental effects of positively fantasizing about the future were even stronger. This strongly suggests that positive fantasies about future events can have negative effects on both effort and success.

But even optimistic beliefs can hamper goal striving when they lead to adopting an avoidant coping style linked to low effort, performance, and well-being (e.g., Lengua & Sandler, 1996; Reid et al., 1995). For example, avoiding information about upcoming medical procedures in order to remain optimistic and to control one's negative feelings prior to medical procedures has been shown to be less beneficial than mentally facing the painful future events, for both children and adults (Peterson, Oliver, & Saldana, 1997; Taylor & Clark, 1986). Avoidant coping with future stressors is linked to neuroticism (Bolger, 1990), sadness, and anger (Spirito, Stark, & Tyc, 1994). Further, avoidant coping seems to impede achieving mastery of the problem at hand, especially when mastery cannot be achieved with ignorance, but rather demands vigilance and effortful action (Carver, Scheier, & Weintraub, 1989; Lazarus, 1983). In line with this work, empirical evidence shows that students reporting habitually denying stressful events in order to cope with them felt more threatened by an upcoming exam than students who used less denial (Carver & Scheier, 1994).

In sum, thinking positively about the future is not always beneficial. Most interestingly, if it simply implies fantasizing about desired end states, including neither *monitoring*—that is, comparing the desired end state (as a secondary cognition) with the actual reality (i.e., primary cognition)—nor *planning*, then it will hinder goal attainment.

THE ROLE OF COUNTERFACTUAL THINKING ON THE SELF-REGULATION OF GOAL PURSUIT

Counterfactual thinking is defined as thinking about how a past event could have been better or worse, and thus it can be understood as the reflection of "what might have been" (Galinsky, Liljenquist, Kray, & Roese, 2005; Kray et al., 2010). The literature distinguishes two kinds of counterfactuals: upward counterfactuals and downward counterfactuals. Upward counterfactuals are defined as if–then statements indicating how a previous outcome could have been better. For example, the professional soccer player might think after losing the semifinal, "If only I had practiced my passes harder, then I would not have failed in the match." Downward counterfactuals refer to thoughts about how an outcome could have been worse. For example, the soccer player might think, "At least I completed several good passes in the game; I could have done worse."

A large body of literature has documented the consequences of these thoughts for subsequent behavior and affect (for reviews, see Epstude & Roese, 2008; Markman & McMullen, 2003; Sanna, Carter, & Small, 2006). Overall, empirical evidence has shown that counterfactual thoughts are positively related to preparation, task effort, and performance. Upward counterfactuals are particularly beneficial for subsequent performance (Markman, McMullen, & Elizaga, 2008; Roese, 1994).

Several explanations for this effect have been postulated. For instance, Roese and colleagues (Epstude & Roese, 2008; Roese, 1994; Smallman & Roese, 2009) have suggested that counterfactual thoughts affect performance by identifying useful strategies and thus support the formation of plans as metacognitive strategies. For example, one could easily convert the counterfactual "If only I had practiced my passes harder, then I would not have failed in the match" into the implementation intention of "Whenever I am called for a training session to prepare for an upcoming match, then I will practice passing very seriously."

In addition, counterfactual thoughts might improve performance by mobilizing effort (Epstude & Roese, 2008; Markman & McMullen, 2003). Upward counterfactual thinking involves evaluating the outcome relative to a higher standard, likely producing disappointment with one's actual goal progress. Theories of effort mobilization (e.g., Brehm & Self, 1989) and discrepancy reduction (Carver & Scheier, 1999) both suggest that such disappointment increases effort and persistence. Consistent with this account, the performance benefits of upward counterfactual thinking appear to be limited to situations in which the individual is dissatisfied with the outcome (Markman et al., 2008). However, upward counterfactual thoughts can also have negative effects on motivation when people have the desire to excuse poor performances and protect self-esteem (McCrea, 2008).

To summarize, counterfactual thinking can have positive effects on motivation and performance because, among other benefits, it facilitates the forming of implementation intentions. Thinking about why one failed and how one could have succeeded already implies the deployment of metacognitive strategies. When one asks oneself why one failed, this can be understood as a type of retrospective monitoring, comparing the past reality (primary cognition) to the desired end state (secondary cognition). Identifying how one could have succeeded is likely to influence one's planning in the future whenever a similar goal is formed.

CONCLUSION

The goal of this chapter was to outline the importance of metacognition in the self-regulation of goal pursuit. To summarize, metacognition as already described in Nelson's model (1996) plays an important role in the self-regulation of goal pursuit because it helps us to understand the way in which important and effective self-regulatory strategies that enhance goal commitment (mental contrasting) and goal striving (implementation intentions) work. Whereas goal striving can be conscious as well as nonconscious, forming implementation intentions is a tool that transforms conscious goal striving into automatic goal striving.

On the one hand, we reviewed research suggesting that optimistic thinking that leads to avoidant coping styles or positive fantasies that are independent of past behavior and do not take the feasibility of the desired future into account will not have positive effects on goal attainment. Upward counterfactuals ("what might have been"), on the other hand, can have positive effects on motivation and performance.

Turning back to our example at the beginning of the chapter: What should the professional soccer player do after the failure of his team in the semifinal to ensure his commitment and motivation for the next match? In our opinion, he should mentally contrast the desired future of winning the third-place prize to the present reality in order to increase his goal commitment to train for the next match. He should do counterfactual thinking about the lost match ("If only I had passed to the best players, then I would not have failed in the match.") and form respective implementation intentions ("If I get the ball, then I will carefully pass it to Schweinsteiger."). And what should he avoid doing? He should not adhere to optimistic beliefs ("We will win anyway.") or indulge in positive fantasies ("We will celebrate the victory extensively.").

REFERENCES

Achtziger, A., Bayer, U. C., & Gollwitzer, P. M. (2010). *Committing oneself to implementation intentions: Attention and memory effects for selected situational cues.* Manuscript submitted for publication.

Achtziger, A., & Gollwitzer, P. M. (2010). Motivation and volition during the course of action. In J. Heckhausen & H. Heckhausen (Eds.), *Motivation and action.* London, England: Cambridge University Press.

Achtziger, A., Gollwitzer, P. M., & Sheeran, P. (2008). Implementation intentions and shielding goal striving from unwanted thoughts and feelings. *Personality and Social Psychology Bulletin, 34,* 381–393.

Adriaanse, M., de Ridder, D., & de Wit, J. (2009). Finding the critical cue: Implementation intentions to change one's diet work best when tailored to personally relevant reasons for unhealthy eating. *Personality and Social Psychology Bulletin, 35,* 60–71.

Ajzen, I. (1991). The theory of planned behavior. *Organizational Behavior and Human Decision Processes, 50,* 179–211.

Atkinson, J. W. (1957). Motivational determinants of risk-taking behavior. *Psychological Review, 64,* 359–372.

Bandura, A. (1989). Human agency in social cognitive theory. *American Psychologist, 44,* 1175–1184.

Bandura, A. (1997). *Self-efficacy: The exercise of control.* New York, NY: Freeman.

Bargh, J. A. (1989). Conditional automaticity: Varieties of automatic influence on social perception and cognition. In J. Uleman & J. A. Bargh (Eds.), *Unintended thought.* New York, NY: Guilford.

Bargh, J. A. (2006). What have we been priming all these years? On the development, mechanisms, and ecology of unconscious social behavior. *European Journal of Social Psychology, 36,* 147–168.

Bargh, J. A., Gollwitzer, P. M., Chai, A. L., Barndollar, K., & Troetschel, R. (2001). Automated will: Nonconscious activation and pursuit of behavioral goals. *Journal of Personality and Social Psychology, 81,* 1014–1027.

Bargh, J. A., Gollwitzer, P. M., & Oettingen, G. (2010). Motivation. In S. Fiske, D. Gilbert, & G. Lindzey (Eds.), *Handbook of social psychology* (5th ed., pp. 268–316). New York, NY: John Wiley & Sons.

Baumeister, R. F., Heatherton, T. F., & Tice, D. M. (1994). *Losing control: How and why people fail at self-regulation.* San Diego, CA: Academic Press.

Bayer, U. C., Gollwitzer, P. M., & Achtziger, A. (2010). Staying on track: Planned goal striving is protected from disruptive internal states. *Journal of Experimental Social Psychology, 46,* 505–514.

Boekaerts, M. (1996). Self-regulated learning at the junction of cognition and motivation. *European Psychologist, 1,* 100–112.

Bolger, N. (1990). Coping as a personality process: A prospective study. *Journal of Personality and Social Psychology, 59,* 525–537.

Brandstaetter, V., Lengfelder, A., & Gollwitzer, P. M. (2001). Implementation intentions and efficient action initiation. *Journal of Personality and Social Psychology, 81,* 946–960.

Brehm, J. W., & Self, E. (1989). The intensity of motivation. *Annual Review of Psychology, 40,* 109–131.

Briñol, P., Petty, R. E., & Rucker, D. D. (2006). The role of meta-cognitive processes in emotional intelligence. *Psicothema, 18,* 26–33.

Carver, C. S., & Scheier, M. F. (1981). *Attention and self-regulation: A control-theory approach to human behavior.* New York, NY: Springer.

Carver, C. S., & Scheier, M. F. (1994). Situational coping and coping dispositions in a stressful transaction. *Journal of Personality and Social Psychology, 66,* 184–195.

Carver, C. S., & Scheier, M. F. (1998). *On the self-regulation of behavior.* Cambridge, England: Cambridge University Press.

Carver, C. S., & Scheier, M. F. (1999). Themes and issues in the self-regulation of behavior. In R. S. Wyer, Jr. (Ed.), *Perspectives on behavioral self-regulation: Advances in social cognition* (Vol. XII, pp. 1–105). Mahwah, NJ: Lawrence Erlbaum Associates.

Carver, C. S., Scheier, M. F., & Weintraub, J. K. (1989). Assessing coping strategies: A theoretically based approach. *Journal of Personality and Social Psychology, 56,* 267–283.

Chartrand, T., & Bargh, J. (2002). Nonconscious motivations: Their activation, operation, and consequences. *Self and motivation: Emerging psychological perspectives* (pp. 13–41). Washington, DC: American Psychological Association.

Christiansen, S., Oettingen, G., Dahme, B., & Klinger, R. (2010). A short goal-pursuit intervention to improve physical capacity: A randomized clinical trial in chronic back pain patients. *Pain, 149,* 444–452.

Duckworth, A. L., & Seligman, M. E. P. (2005). Self-discipline outdoes IQ in predicting academic performance of adolescents. *Psychological Science, 16,* 939–944.

Epstude, K., & Roese, N. J. (2008). The functional theory of counterfactual thinking. *Personality and Social Psychology Review, 12,* 168–192.

Friese, M., & Hofmann, W. (2009). Control me or I will control you: Impulses, trait self-control, and the guidance of behavior. *Journal of Research in Personality, 43,* 795–805.

Galinsky, A. D., Liljenquist, K. A., Kray, L. J., & Roese, N. J. (2005). Finding meaning from mutability: Making sense and deriving significance through counterfactual thinking. In D. R. Mandel, D. J. Hilton, & P. Catellani (Eds.), *The psychology of counterfactual thinking* (pp. 110–125). New York, NY: Routledge.

Gollwitzer, P., Wieber, F., Myers, A., & McCrea, S. (2010). How to maximize implementation intention effects. In C. R. Agnew, D. E. Carlston, W. G. Graziano, & J. R. Kelly (Eds.), *Then a miracle occurs: Focusing on behavior in social psychological theory and research* (pp. 137–161). New York, NY: Oxford University Press.

Gollwitzer, P. M. (1990). Action phases and mind-sets. In E. T. Higgins & R. M. Sorrentino (Eds.), *The handbook of motivation and cognition: Foundations of social behavior* (Vol. 2, pp. 53–92). New York, NY: Guilford Press.

Gollwitzer, P. M. (1993). Goal achievement: The role of intentions. *European Review of Social Psychology, 4,* 141–185.

Gollwitzer, P. M. (1999). Implementation intentions: Strong effects of simple plans. *American Psychologist, 54,* 493–503.

Gollwitzer, P. M. (2011). Mindset theory of action phases. In P. Van Lange, A. W. Kruglanski, & E. T. Higgins (Eds.), *Handbook of theories of social psychology* (pp. 526–545). London, England: Sage Publications.

Gollwitzer, P. M., & Bayer, U. (1999). Deliberative versus implemental mindsets in the control of action. In S. Chaiken & Y. Trope (Eds.), *Dual-process theories in social psychology* (pp. 403–422). New York: Guilford Press.

Gollwitzer, P. M., Heckhausen, H., & Ratajczak, H. (1990). From weighing to willing: Approaching a change decision through pre- or postdecisional mentation. *Organizational Behavior and Human Decision Processes, 45*, 41–65.

Gollwitzer, P. M., & Kinney, R. F. (1989). Effects of deliberative and implemental mind-sets on the illusion of control. *Journal of Personality and Social Psychology, 56*, 531–542.

Gollwitzer, P. M., & Schaal, B. (1998). Metacognition in action: The importance of implementation intentions. *Personality and Social Psychology Review, 2*, 124–136.

Gollwitzer, P. M., & Sheeran, P. (2006). Implementation intentions and goal achievement: A meta-analysis of effects and processes. *Advances in Experimental Social Psychology, 38*, 69–119.

Goodhart, D. E. (1986). The effects of positive and negative thinking on performance in an achievement situation. *Journal of Personality and Social Psychology, 51*, 117–124.

Heckhausen, H., & Gollwitzer, P. (1987). Thought contents and cognitive functioning in motivational versus volitional states of mind. *Motivation and Emotion, 11*, 101–120.

Hofmann, W., Friese, M., & Strack, F. (2009). Impulse and self-control from a dual-systems perspective. *Perspectives on Psychological Science, 4*, 162–176.

Kray, L. J., George, L. G., Liljenquist, K. A., Galinsky, A. D., Tetlock, P. E., & Roese, N. J. (2010). From what might have been to what must have been: Counterfactual thinking creates meaning. *Journal of Personality and Social Psychology, 98*, 106–118.

Lazarus, A. A. (1983). From achievement to enjoyment. *Psychotherapy in Private Practice, 1*, 39–42.

Lengua, L. J., & Sandler, I. N. (1996). Self-regulation as a moderator of the relation between coping and symptomatology in children of divorce. *Journal of Abnormal Child Psychology, 24*, 681–701.

Markman, K. D., & McMullen, M. N. (2003). A reflection and evaluation model of comparative thinking. *Personality and Social Psychology Review, 7*, 244–267.

Markman, K. D., McMullen, M. N., & Elizaga, R. A. (2008). Counterfactual thinking, persistence, and performance: A test of the reflection and evaluation model. *Journal of Experimental Social Psychology, 44*, 421–428.

Martin, J., Sheeran, P., Slade, P., Wright, A., & Dibble, T. (2009). Implementation intention formation reduces consultations for emergency contraception and pregnancy testing among teenage women. *Health Psychology, 28*, 762–769.

McCrea, S. M. (2008). Self-handicapping, excuse making, and counterfactual thinking: Consequences for self-esteem and future motivation. *Journal of Personality and Social Psychology, 95*, 274–292.

Metcalfe, J., & Mischel, W. (1999). A hot-/cool-system analysis of delay of gratification: Dynamics of willpower. *Psychological Review, 106*, 3–19.

Mischel, W., Shoda, Y., & Peake, P. K. (1988). The nature of adolescent competencies predicted by preschool delay of gratification. *Journal of Personality and Social Psychology, 54*, 687–696.

Murgraff, V., White, D., & Phillips, K. (1996). Moderating binge drinking: It is possible to change behavior if you plan it in advance. *Alcohol and Alcoholism, 31*, 577–582.

Nelson, T. O. (1996). Consciousness and metacognition. *American Psychologist, 51*, 102–116.

Oettingen, G. (1999). Free fantasies about the future and the emergence of developmental goals. In J. Brandtstädter & R. M. Lerner (Eds.), *Action & self-development: Theory and research through the life span* (pp. 315–342). Thousand Oaks, CA: Sage.

Oettingen, G. (2000). Expectancy effects on behavior depend on self-regulatory thought. *Social Cognition, 18*, 101–129.

Oettingen, G., Barry, H., Guttenberg. K. B., & Gollwitzer, P. M. (2011). *Self-regulation of time management: Mental contrasting with implementation intentions*. Manuscript submitted for publication.

Oettingen, G., & Gollwitzer, P. M. (2010). Strategies of setting and implementing goals: Mental contrasting and implementation intentions. In J. E. Maddux & J. P. Tangney (Eds.), *Social psychological foundations of clinical psychology* (pp. 114–135). New York: Guilford Press.

Oettingen, G., Grant, H., Smith, P. K., Skinner, M., & Gollwitzer, P. M. (2006). Nonconscious goal pursuit: Acting in an explanatory vacuum. *Journal of Experimental Social Psychology, 42*, 668–675.

Oettingen, G., Hönig, G, & Gollwitzer, P. M. (2000). Effective self-regulation of goal attainment. *International Journal of Educational Research, 33*, 705–732.

Oettingen, G., & Kappes, A. (2009). Mental contrasting of the future and reality to master negative feedback. In K. D. Markman, W. M. P. Klein, & J. A. Suhr (Eds.), *Handbook of imagination and mental simulation* (pp. 395–412). New York, NY: Psychology Press.

Oettingen, G., & Mayer, D. (2002). The motivating function of thinking about the future: Expectations versus fantasies. *Journal of Personality and Social Psychology, 83*, 1198–1212.

Oettingen, G., Mayer, D., & Brinkmann, B. (2010). Mental contrasting of future and reality: Managing the demands of everyday life in health care professionals. *Journal of Personnel Psychology, 9*, 138–144.

Oettingen, G., Mayer, D., Sevincer, A. T., Stephens, E. J., Pak, H., & Hagenah, M. (2009). Mental contrasting and goal commitment: The mediating role of energization. *Personality and Social Psychology Bulletin, 35*, 608–622.

Oettingen, G., Mayer, D., Stephens, E. J., & Brinkmann, B. (2010). Mental contrasting and the self-regulation of helping relations. *Social Cognition, 28*, 490–508.

Oettingen, G., Mayer, D., Thorpe, J. S., Janetzke, H., & Lorenz, S. (2005). Turning fantasies about positive and negative futures into self-improvement goals. *Motivation and Emotion, 29*, 237–267.

Oettingen, G., Pak, H., & Schnetter, K. (2001). Self-regulation of goal setting: Turning free fantasies about the future into binding goals. *Journal of Personality and Social Psychology, 80*, 736–753.

Oettingen, G., & Wadden, T. A. (1991). Expectation, fantasy, and weight loss: Is the impact of positive thinking always positive? *Cognitive Therapy and Research, 15*, 167–175.

Orbell, S., Hodgkins, S., & Sheeran, P. (1997). Implementation intentions and the theory of planned behavior. *Personality and Social Psychology Bulletin, 23*, 953–962.

Orbell, S., & Sheeran, P. (2000). Motivational and volitional processes in action initiation: A field study of implementation intentions. *Journal of Applied Social Psychology, 30*, 780–797.

Parks-Stamm, E. J., Oettingen, G., & Gollwitzer, P. M., (2010). Making sense of one's actions in an explanatory vacuum: The interpretation of nonconscious goal striving. *Journal of Experimental Social Psychology, 46*, 531–542.

Peterson, L., Oliver, K. K., & Saldana, L. (1997). Children's coping with stressful medical procedures. In S. A. Wolchik & I. N. Sandler (Eds.), *Handbook of children's coping: Linking theory and intervention* (pp. 333–360). New York, NY: Plenum Press.

Petty, R., Briñol, P., Tormala, Z., & Wegener, D. (2007). The role of metacognition in social judgment. *Social psychology: Handbook of basic principles* (2nd ed., pp. 254–284). New York, NY: Guilford Press.

Reid, G. J., Dubow, E. F., & Carey, T. C. (1995). Developmental and situational differences in coping among children and adolescents with diabetes. *Journal of Applied Developmental Psychology, 16*, 529–554.

Roese, N. (1994). The functional basis of counterfactual thinking. *Journal of Personality and Social Psychology, 66,* 805–818.

Sanna, L., Carter, S., & Small, E. (2006). The road not taken: Counterfactual thinking over time. In L. J. Sanna & E. C. Chang (Eds.), *Judgments over time: The interplay of thoughts, feelings, and behaviors* (pp. 163–181). New York, NY: Oxford University Press.

Scheier, M. F., & Carver, C. S. (1992). Effects of optimism on psychological and physical well-being: Theoretical overview and empirical update. *Cognitive Therapy and Research, 16,* 201–228.

Sheeran, P., Aubrey, R., & Kellett, S. (2007). Increasing attendance for psychotherapy: Implementation intentions and the self-regulation of attendance-related negative affect. *Journal of Consulting and Clinical Psychology, 75,* 853–863.

Sheeran, P., & Orbell, S. (2000). Using implementation intentions to increase attendance for cervical cancer screening. *Health Psychology, 19,* 283–289.

Sheeran, P., Webb, T. L., & Gollwitzer, P. M. (2005). The interplay between goal intentions and implementation intentions. *Personality and Social Psychology Bulletin, 31,* 87–98.

Shoda, Y., Mischel, W., & Peake, P. K. (1990). Predicting adolescent cognitive and self-regulatory competencies from preschool delay of gratification: Identifying diagnostic conditions. *Developmental Psychology, 26,* 978–986.

Smallman, R., & Roese, N. (2009). Counterfactual thinking facilitates behavioral intentions. *Journal of Experimental Social Psychology, 45,* 845–852.

Spirito, A., Stark, L. J., & Tyc, V. L. (1994). Stressors and coping strategies described during hospitalization by chronically ill children. *Journal of Clinical Child Psychology, 23,* 314–322.

Stadler, G., Oettingen, G., & Gollwitzer, P. M. (2009). Physical activity in women: Effects of a self-regulation intervention. *American Journal of Preventive Medicine, 36,* 29–34.

Stadler, G., Oettingen, G., & Gollwitzer, P. M. (2010). Intervention effects of information and self-regulation on eating fruits and vegetables over two years. *Health Psychology, 29,* 274–283.

Stewart, B., & Payne, B. (2008). Bringing automatic stereotyping under control: Implementation intentions as efficient means of thought control. *Personality and Social Psychology Bulletin, 34,* 1332–1345.

Tangney, J., Baumeister, R., & Boone, A. (2004). High self-control predicts good adjustment, less pathology, better grades, and interpersonal success. *Journal of Personality, 72,* 271–322.

Taylor, S. E., & Brown, J. (1988). Illusion and well-being: A social psychological perspective on mental health. *Psychological Bulletin, 103,* 193–210.

Taylor, S. E., & Clark, L. F. (1986). Does information improve adjustment to noxious medical procedures? In M. Sake & R. F. Kidd (Eds.), *Advances in applied social psychology* (Vol. 4, pp. 1–28). Hillsdale, NJ: Lawrence Erlbaum Associates.

Taylor, S. E., & Gollwitzer, P. M. (1995). Effects of mindset on positive illusions. *Journal of Personality and Social Psychology, 69,* 213–226.

Vohs, K., & Baumeister, R. (2004). Ego depletion, self-control, and choice. *Handbook of experimental existential psychology* (pp. 398–410). New York, NY: Guilford Press.

Wolfe, R., & Johnson, S. (1995). Personality as a predictor of college performance. *Educational and Psychological Measurement, 55,* 177–185.

8

People's Thoughts About Their Personal Pasts and Futures

EMILY SCHRYER and MICHAEL ROSS

INTRODUCTION

*M*ost people spend a lot of time thinking about themselves. They consider their beliefs and why they think the way they do; they ponder their pasts and probable futures. Psychologists label the process of thinking about thoughts "metacognition"[1] (Dunlosky & Metcalfe, 2009; Petty, Briñol, Tormala, & Wegener, 2007). Metacognition is a dynamic process. In the process of thinking about their beliefs, people alter the form and content of their beliefs (Jost, Kruglanski, & Nelson, 1998). As people explore their pasts and futures, they construct their own realities and identities: who they were, who they are, and who they want to be.

In the present chapter, we discuss how people think about their personal pasts and futures. Recall and forecasts depend importantly on each other. Although the temporal orientation differs, recall and forecasting have much in common. Both are constructive processes that occur in the present. Both memories and predictions reflect and contribute to people's current self-conceptions. Both are influenced by preferences, goals, and metacognitive processes such as theories, norms, and feelings of accessibility. In the current chapter, we analyze how motivational and metacognitive processes shape people's conceptions of their pasts and futures.

Some authors distinguish between "constructions" and "reconstructions" when discussing recollections and forecasts. For example, Johnson and Sherman (1990) reserved the term "reconstruction" for revisions of initial constructions of the past or future. It is often difficult, however, for researchers to discriminate initial constructions from reconstructions, especially after the fact. In the current chapter, we use the term construction to describe all recollections and forecasts. In adopting this label, we do not intend to imply anything about their accuracy.

RECALLING PERSONAL PASTS

Look back on time with kindly eyes,
He doubtless did his best;
How softly sinks his trembling sun
In human nature's west!

Emily Dickinson, *Collected Poems*, p. 185

Effects of Current Beliefs

Social psychologists have demonstrated the effects of current beliefs on memory by altering people's beliefs and then assessing their recall of earlier attitudes and behaviors pertinent to their new beliefs (e.g., Goethals & Reckman, 1973; Murray & Holmes, 1993; Ross, 1989; Ross, McFarland, Conway, & Zanna, 1983; Ross, McFarland, & Fletcher, 1981; Sanitioso, Kunda, & Fong, 1990). People tend to recall thinking and acting in ways that are consistent with their new preferences. In a classic study, Goethals and Reckman (1973) changed students' attitudes toward busing to promote school integration in the United States. In an initial session, the researchers assessed students' attitudes toward a variety of topics including busing to achieve racial integration. In a second seemingly unrelated session, a student confederate armed with persuasive arguments convinced students who were initially pro- or antibusing to change their attitudes. Students later remembered their initial beliefs about busing as being more consistent with their current changed attitude than they actually were.

How do experimental manipulations of preferences exert their influence on personal recall? One answer is that when people remember past mental states, their recall is guided by metacognitive theories. Ross (1989) noted that people often use theories of stability to infer their earlier characteristics, judgments, and behaviors. To see how this might work, let us suppose that a man is trying to remember how he felt about a politician 5 years ago. Such memories are often difficult to retrieve because people do not typically maintain a mental catalogue of their past attitudes or judgments arranged chronologically. Rather than simply admit ignorance, however, people often use the information available to construct their earlier assessments. According to Ross (1989), two sources of information are generally available to people: their current standing (e.g., how they feel about the politician right now) and their theories about the stability of different attributes over time. People often presume that attitudes, judgments, and actions are fairly stable over time. As a consequence, people tend to infer that their past attitudes were very similar to their current opinions. Using a theory of stability to reconstruct past attitudes can lead people astray if they have changed their beliefs in the interim.

It is possible to argue that participants in social psychology experiments are relatively oblivious to their attitude change because of the design of the studies. Social psychological researchers typically use subtle manipulations to alter people's attitudes. Researchers also tend to mislead participants about the true purposes of the research, which allegedly have nothing to do with attitude change. Under such circumstances, individuals may apply a theory of stability because they have been duped into thinking that their attitudes are unchanged. Perhaps people are more aware of belief change in their everyday lives and less likely to infer stability.

There are many examples, however, of people's tendency to overestimate the stability of their beliefs in naturalistic settings (Ross, 1989) in which attitudes may change slowly and almost imperceptibly. For example, McFarland and Ross (1987) asked members of dating couples to evaluate their partners and their relationships at two sessions months apart. At the second session, participants were asked to recall their earlier evaluations. Participants whose attitudes became more favorable over time recalled more positive evaluations than they had provided earlier. Those whose attitudes became less favorable recalled more negative evaluations than they had reported earlier. Even in the absence of nefarious experimenters, then, people tend to exaggerate the consistency between their past and current beliefs.

We suggest that people use metacognitive theories to construct aspects of the past that they cannot readily retrieve from memory. However, people may exaggerate their stability even when they could potentially retrieve information that is either consistent or inconsistent with their current beliefs. People's current beliefs may prime the subset of memories that is consistent with their beliefs so that belief-consistent memories are more accessible. For example, Sanitioso and colleagues (1990) persuaded participants that either extraversion or introversion was important to academic success. In a seemingly unrelated task, participants were asked to produce autobiographical memories of times when they were shy or outgoing. Those participants who believed that extraversion was preferable more readily recalled more autobiographical memories of times when they were outgoing than times when they were shy. The opposite was true when participants were told that introversion was preferable.

This research on the effects of theories on recall makes it seem that people can readily construct pasts that satisfy their wishes. However, there are limits to the effect of current theories and preferences on recall, as clearly demonstrated in a study conducted by Kunda and Fong (1990). These researchers induced participants to believe that extroversion is psychologically superior to introversion, or the reverse. Participants who believed that extroversion was superior more readily recalled engaging in extroverted behaviors than did those who now supposed that introversion was superior. In addition to reflecting their current preferences, however, participants' recall also depended on their chronic self-knowledge. Participants who had previously indicated that they were introverts more readily recalled introverted behaviors than did self-proclaimed extroverts, regardless of their experimentally assigned preferences. People's current beliefs did not completely eliminate the effects of their prior self-knowledge.

If people recall information that is both consistent and inconsistent with their current attitudes or preferences, do they assign equal weighting to the two types of information when inferring their prior beliefs? Perhaps not. People may tend to perceive personal consistency even in the face of variable recollections. Research on metacognition suggests that people will regard previous information that is consistent with their current attitudes as more valid (Tormala, Briñol, & Petty, 2006; Tormala, Petty, & Briñol, 2002). Therefore, people may tend to judge past attitudes or behaviors that are inconsistent with their current preferences as erroneous or atypical and thus not representative of either their prior or current beliefs.

Finally, note that the relationship between current beliefs and recall is reciprocal. Current beliefs influence recall and recall, in turn, affects current beliefs. For example, people's commitment to new beliefs is increased when they recall behaving in line with those beliefs in the past (Lydon, Zanna, & Ross, 1988). The selective recall of information that is consistent with beliefs helps to establish the validity of the newly formed attitudes.

Perceiving Improvement

In looking backward, people do not always perceive consistency. Sometimes they infer that they must have changed. A theory of change can be evoked by an event or intervention that people believe ought to affect them. For example, Conway and Ross (1984) asked students in a study skills course to evaluate their progress following completion of the course. As is the case with many self-improvement programs, the study skills course was ineffective. With its emphasis on strategies and skills, however, the course seemed useful and participants assumed that it was. Participants could potentially derive support for their illusory theory of improvement by exaggerating their current study skills, demeaning their prior study skills, or both. Conway and Ross suspected that reality constraints would prevent people from exaggerating their current skills to any great degree. The students knew that they were not working incredibly hard or effectively right then. Consequently, they might be more inclined to find evidence for improvement in the past. As predicted, participants in the study skills course manufactured illusory improvement by exaggerating how awful their study skills were before they took the course. Conway and Ross suggested that this type of memory bias can help explain why people often seem to overstate the benefits of other types of ineffective self-improvement programs.

People typically choose to engage in study-skills programs because they expect benefits. In contrast, few people choose to experience traumatic life events. Despite the manifold differences between completing a self-improvement program and encountering trauma, the two experiences do share a common element: In both cases, individuals often presume that they have experienced personal growth. Following a traumatic life event, individuals tend to suppose that they are better people than they used to be (McFarland & Alvaro, 2000). McFarland and Alvaro observed that people's belief in personal growth following trauma is, at least in part, illusory. People's theory of improvement is supported not so much by postevent growth, but rather by their tendency to derogate their pre-event attributes. Thus, the improvement that people associate with both self-improvement programs and traumatic life events reflects people's tendencies to revise their personal histories.

Even in the absence of interventions or trauma, people may theorize that they have improved over time. In particular, people seem to possess a theory of development that implies growth on many characteristics as they progress from adolescence to middle age (Ross & Wilson, 2003). Studying various groups of people including Canadian and Japanese university students, middle-aged

Canadians, and celebrities, Wilson and Ross (2000, 2001, 2003) reported that people regarded themselves as getting better over time on most favorable attributes (e.g., self-confidence). Consistent with cultural norms, Japanese students were less enthusiastic about themselves than were their Canadian counterparts, but both groups evaluated their current self more favorably than they did earlier selves (Ross, Heine, Wilson, & Sugimori, 2005). Similarly, middle-aged participants' ratings of their social skills, common sense, and self-confidence indicated that they viewed themselves as improving steadily with age (Wilson & Ross, 2001). Although they perceived others as improving as well, they regarded their own improvement as much more substantial.

What is the basis of theories of personal improvement? One obvious possibility is that people do improve with age and experience. Wilson and Ross did not reject the prospect of actual improvement, but they argued that individuals seem to exaggerate their personal progress (e.g., as compared to others). Wilson and Ross (2001) studied a group of participants over time and found that participants perceived personal improvement where little or none had occurred, according to contemporaneous evaluations. Moreover, as in the study skills and trauma experiments, participants seemed to manufacture illusory improvement by demeaning their earlier selves (Wilson & Ross, 2001, 2003). Wilson and Ross suggested that this criticism of earlier selves helps people to think well of their current selves—that they are much better now than they used to be, particularly on dimensions that they care about.

Not surprisingly, people's perception of improvement over time varies according to the traits in question. People are particularly motivated to perceive personal improvement on attributes that are important to them (Wilson & Ross, 2001). The ironic implication of their desire for improvement on important attributes is that people are more critical of past selves on dimensions that matter to them (Wilson & Ross, 2001, Study 6). By being hypercritical of past but not present selves, people can exaggerate their progress in critical domains.

We have assumed that people feel better by contrasting their present selves to inferior past selves, but this is not always the case. An unfavorable evaluation of a past self can sometimes negatively impact the present self. It is fairly safe to criticize past selves that feel sufficiently distant that their successes and faults do not reflect directly on the current self (that was the old me). To criticize a past that feels subjectively close is more problematic: The criticism may then apply almost as well to the current self. Wilson and Ross (2001) demonstrated the importance of subjective temporal distance by depicting the same point in time (the beginning of the academic term) as either recent or fairly distant. Participants evaluated their earlier, beginning-of-the-term self more harshly when the start of term was presented as farther away in time. When the start of the term was presented as recent, participants rated their beginning-of-the-term self just as favorably as they rated their current self.

In related research, Wilson and Ross showed that recollections of the same past experiences have different effects on current evaluations, depending on whether people remember the episodes as subjectively near or far away in time. Wilson and Ross (2003) used experimental manipulations to lead participants to feel temporally close or far away from negative or positive past experiences. In one study, university students were asked to think back to their high school experiences. To alter perceptions of distance, Wilson and Ross asked participants to place their senior year of high school on a time line. Participants were assigned a time line spanning either a long period (birth to present day) or a relatively brief period (high school to present day). They placed their senior year closer to the present day on the time line spanning a long period and reported feeling temporally closer to that year. Participants' current self-evaluations constituted the primary dependent variable. Participants' evaluations of their current selves were directly affected by experiences that they experienced as more recent. For instance, participants who had reported being popular in high school (in a questionnaire completed weeks before the study) felt more socially successful today when they were in the experimental condition that led them to feel close to, rather than distant from, high school. Those who had reported being unpopular in high school perceived themselves to be less socially successful today when they were induced to feel close to, rather than distant from, high school.

Subjective Experiences of Time

In the research we described by Wilson and Ross, the experience of subjective time was an independent variable: experimentally induced variations in feelings' subjective distance affected people's evaluations of a past self. Dating back at least to William James, psychologists have also examined the subjective experience of time as a dependent variable. Most of this research examines factors that affect people's perceptions of the length of short intervals, usually minutes or hours (Block, 1989). The factors studied are typically aspects of the situation, such as whether participants are occupied with tasks or idle during the target interval (e.g., Block, 1989).

In recent years, social psychologists have studied the subjective perception of much longer time intervals and variables more relevant to self-evaluations, such as the valence of the remembered episodes. For example, Ross and Wilson (2002) controlled for actual time and examined feelings of subjective distance from past episodes that potentially have negative or positive implications for the current self. In their theory of temporal self-appraisal, Ross and Wilson hypothesized that people would distance past episodes that potentially had negative implications for evaluations of current selves (e.g., failures). By temporally distancing a negative episode, people can render it less relevant to their current self. Although regarding a negative episode as distant is not the same as forgetting it, the psychological consequences may be comparable. Distancing helps individuals to put their undesirable behavior and outcomes behind them. The episode belongs to an "old me," not the current self. Temporal self-appraisal theory also hypothesizes that people should feel relatively close to a past episode that has favorable implications for the current self (e.g., successes). By keeping such episodes temporally close, people can continue to take credit for them.

In one study testing the theory, Ross & Wilson (2002) randomly assigned participants to remember the course in the previous semester in which they received either their best or worst grade. After reporting their grade, participants indicated how temporally distant they felt from the target course on a scale with end points labeled "feels like yesterday" and "feels far away." Participants felt more temporally distant from the course in which they obtained a relatively low grade, even though the actual passage of time was identical in the two conditions. In subsequent research, Ross and Wilson found that this asymmetry in temporal distance reflects a tendency both to pull favorable outcomes forward in subjective time and push unflattering outcomes backward, though the latter effect may be somewhat stronger. They also found that the asymmetry was obtained for personal outcomes, but not for the outcomes of acquaintances. This self–other discrepancy points to the functional significance of feelings of subjective distance. The asymmetry reflects a motivation to protect one's own self-regard rather than a general tendency to perceive unflattering events as farther away than flattering events.

SELF-PREDICTIONS

> But Mousie, thou are no thy-lane,
> In proving foresight may be vain:
> The best laid schemes o' Mice an' Men,
> Gang aft agley,
> An' lea'e us nought but grief an' pain,
> For promis'd joy!

Robert Burns, "To a Mouse"

Self-predicting involves thinking about events, experiences, and mental states that have not yet occurred. Anyone can predict, but doing so with accuracy is another matter entirely. In every area of human knowledge, well-trained experts commonly offer inaccurate forecasts (Sarewitz & Pielke, 2000). Weather forecasters are the only experts with a strong record of success. However, weather forecasters have the advantage of being able to alter their predictions as the target date approaches—an opportunity that is not available to all forecasters.

Intuitively, it seems reasonable to expect that people would be accurate self-predictors because they possess self-expertise and, unlike meteorologists, they can influence future outcomes. Yet psychological research casts doubt on people's forecasting abilities. We begin our analysis of future thinking by examining some of the preferences and theories that guide people's self-predictions. We then discuss prediction accuracy and the factors that influence people's forecasts.

Optimism About the Future: Theories of Change and Improvement

Thinking about the future is a process of construction with constraints. Memories of the past are constrained by what actually happened. Thoughts about the future are constrained by what could probably happen. Unconstrained imaginings about the future are usually dubbed fantasies. Most adults and children are capable of distinguishing fantasies from more realistic forecasts. A 40-year-old couch potato who fantasizes playing in the NFL knows that his likelihood of doing so is about zero.

Even people's supposedly realistic forecasts often seem rather optimistic, however. People's theories of improvement extend to the future. They are aware that bad things have happened to them in the past and could happen in the future, but they generally predict that they will experience fewer negative life events in the future. Newby-Clark and Ross (2003) compared university students' views of their pasts and futures by asking them to recall and anticipate personally significant episodes. Participants spontaneously recalled affectively mixed pasts that contained both "highs" and "lows," but they anticipated consistently positive futures.

People also expect to experience fewer unpleasant events than their peers (Hoorens, Smits, & Shepperd, 2008). For example, people predict that their own chances of developing serious illnesses or experiencing serious accidents are much lower than their peers' (Weinstein, 1980). This illusion of future invulnerability generalizes to close others. People view friends or family members as being equally invulnerable to negative events (Perloff & Fetzer, 1986).

When thinking about the future, people often focus on their goals (Karniol & Ross, 1996). They create scenarios that detail how they will obtain their preferred outcomes and devote relatively little thought to the possibility that bad things will happen to them (Buehler, Griffin, & Ross, 1994; Kahneman & Tversky, 1979; Newby-Clark & Ross, 2003). For example, in considering possible negative life events such as divorce, physical ailments, and traffic accidents, people suppose that they and close others will take actions that promote their well-being and safety, but that others will not undertake similar evasive behaviors (Perloff & Fetzer, 1986). They thus create scenarios that justify their beliefs that they and their loved ones are uniquely invulnerable.

A striking demonstration of optimism concerns people's predictions about their own memory. People consistently underestimate the extent to which they will forget information (Kornell & Bjork, 2009). When it comes to their own memory, people tend to adopt a theory of stability. Individuals regard their memory and knowledge as enduring and discount forgetting (Kornell & Bjork, 2009). For example, Koriat, Bjork, Sheffer, and Bar (2004) assigned word pairs to participants and asked them how likely they would be to remember the word pairs at varying intervals (10 minutes, a day, and a week later). Participants were relatively insensitive to the fact that they would forget more word pairs over time. The rate at which they actually forgot the words was much steeper than they predicted. In everyday life, people who exaggerate their memory prowess may fail to record such information as birthdays, appointments, the names of their new neighbors, or telephone messages, with embarrassing consequences.

Self-Predictions Can Be Accurate

In many studies, people's predictions can be informative even in the presence of an optimistic prediction bias. In Buehler and his associates' (1994) studies of the planning fallacy, people underestimated, often considerably, how long they would take to complete various projects. Nonetheless, their predictions were often strongly related to their actual completion times (with correlations sometimes exceeding $r = .7$). Compared to others in the sample, people who predicted that they would finish their projects in a shorter time actually took less time. MacDonald and Ross (1999) found that romantic partners were too optimistic about how long their relationships would last. However, the relationships of participants who predicted a shorter time ended sooner than the relationships of those who predicted a longer time. Koehler and Poon (2006) reported that participants were much too optimistic about their likelihood of donating blood. Nonetheless, those who predicted that their probability of donation was high were more likely to donate 1–3 weeks later than those who predicted that their probability of donation was lower.

That predictions are at least somewhat accurate should not be surprising, given the findings from a set of studies on the effects of prediction on behaviors. Sherman (1980) established the paradigm for these studies by studying people's predictions for whether they would be willing to engage in socially desirable (e.g., collect money for the Cancer Society) or undesirable (e.g., write an essay contrary to their beliefs) behaviors if asked in the future. Comparing forecasts from participants who were asked to predict their responses to responses of participants who were actually presented with the requests, Sherman found that predictors overestimated the likelihood of engaging in socially desirable behaviors and underestimated the probability of engaging in socially undesirable behaviors.

Sherman also included a condition in which he asked participants to predict what they would do and then assessed what they actually did. Although prediction and requests were separated by days or weeks and allegedly associated with different organizations, participants in this condition brought their behavior in line with their predictions. Compared to participants in the request-only conditions, participants in predict-followed-by-request conditions exhibited greater resistance to socially undesirable requests and more compliance with socially desirable requests. Sherman suggested that participants were motivated to behave consistently with their predictions—their predictions helped them determine what they ought to do. As a consequence, errors in prediction were self-erasing. It is also probably important to the self-prophecy effect that participants in these studies are predicting fairly straightforward behaviors; for the most part, participants can control whether or not the target behaviors occur (Gregory, Cialdini, & Carpenter, 1982; Levav & Fitzsimons, 2006).

Often dubbed the "self-prophecy effect," the self-erasing effects of errors in prediction have been demonstrated in a variety of contexts. For example, participants who are first asked for a prediction are more likely to vote (Greenwald, Carnot, Beach, & Young, 1987), more likely to recycle (Sprott, Spangenberg, & Perkins, 1999), and less likely to cheat in the classroom (Spangenberg & Obermiller, 1997). The self-prophecy effect is strongest when, in the absence of a prior prediction, people possess firm beliefs about the appropriateness of certain behaviors (e.g., recycling, exercise) but often fail to engage in these actions (perhaps because of the effort or time required) (Sprott, Spangenberg, & Fisher, 2003).

Self-Predictions Can Be Inaccurate

Research demonstrating inaccuracy and bias in forecasts is strikingly similar in form to research on the self-prophecy effect, with its emphasis on accuracy in prediction.

Researchers first assess people's plans, intentions, or expectations for their personal futures and subsequently determine what they actually do. Participants tend to be much too confident in quite inaccurate predictions. For example, Vallone, Griffin, Lin, and Ross (1990) asked Stanford students to predict a variety of behaviors in the coming academic year (e.g., whether or not they would visit San Francisco). In these and many other studies (e.g., Chapin, 2001; Kahneman & Snell, 1992; Koriat et al., 2004), people's predictions were not nearly as correct as they expected them to be. One reason that these studies show little or no self-prophecy effect is that forecasts are not limited to contexts in which people possess firm beliefs about the appropriateness or importance of certain behaviors.[2]

Researchers have offered a number of explanations for people's overconfidence in the accuracy of their predictions. Individuals tend to base their predictions on scenarios in which they imagine that the future will unfold in line with their current plans and intentions (Kahneman & Tversky, 1979). They often fail or even refuse to entertain the possibility of plausible alternative scenarios in which their plans or intentions would be stymied (Buehler et al., 1994; Kahneman & Tversky, 1979; Newby-Clark, Ross, Buehler, Koehler, & Griffin, 2000). People also attribute too much behavioral control to themselves, underestimating the effects of chance factors, situational influences, or other people on their behavior and outcomes. For example, in the Vallone et al. (1990) study, participants' ability to visit San Francisco would likely depend on factors that may be somewhat out of their control, such as the availability of time, funds, transportation, and company. They thereby underestimated the difficulty they sometimes confronted in translating their intentions into behavior (Griffin, Dunning, & Ross, 1990; Koehler & Poon, 2006; Koehler, White, & John, 2011; Vallone et al., 1990). Finally, people's intentions and preferences are not as stable as they imagine.

Individuals tend to underestimate the likelihood of changing their intentions and preferences over time as they encounter new experiences or alterations in physical states (e.g., hunger or fatigue) (Dunning, Griffin, Milojkovic, & Ross, 1990; Koehler & Poon, 2006; Loewenstein, 1996). This tendency to overemphasize stability should be familiar to the reader: We have already noted how people often exaggerate the stability of their beliefs and other attributes.

One of the intriguing findings in this literature is that people often possess (or could seek) information at the time of their forecasts that would yield more accurate predictions. Kahneman and Tversky (1979) argued that individuals should examine base rates to increase the accuracy of their forecasts rather than rely on speculative scenarios. Many researchers have confirmed the effectiveness of using base rates in the service of self-predictions (Dunning & Story, 1991; Osberg & Shrauger, 1986; Shrauger, Mariano, & Walter, 1998; Vallone et al., 1990).

Despite their potential usefulness, people do not spontaneously pay much heed to base rates when generating self-predictions. Even when people are familiar with personal or other people's base rates, they typically regard the information as irrelevant to their predictions (Buehler et al., 1994; Dunning et al. 1990). For example, Buehler, Griffin, and Ross (1994, 2002) studied the planning fallacy: people's pervasive tendency to underestimate how long it will take them to complete various tasks. They found that, although people were often aware that they had underestimated completion times in the past, they did not alter their predictions—even when reminded of their prior prediction errors. Instead, they attributed their past failures to complete tasks on time to idiosyncratic circumstances that were unlikely to repeat (e.g., computer problems or illness). People may often be correct in predicting that a particular circumstance will not recur. They fail to appreciate, however, that the likelihood that *something* will happen to impede their progress is quite high.

Are there any circumstances in which people do make spontaneous use of base rates? Yes—when predicting the futures of other people, rather than of themselves. MacDonald and Ross (1999) asked the college roommates of romantic partners to predict how long the relationships would last. Roommates seemed to base their predictions for other people's relationships at least in part on base rates, and their predictions were more accurate and less optimistic than those offered by the romantic partners themselves. Epley and Dunning (2000) found that participants overestimated their likelihood of engaging in various generous or selfless actions (e.g., donating to charity). They were more accurate in their predictions for other people, in part because they considered base rates when forecasting the actions of others; however, they ignored base rates when predicting their own behavior. When predicting their own behaviors, participants indicated that they would be wonderfully generous, apparently focusing more on how they believed they should act rather than how they had acted in the past.

When offering self-predictions, people also seem to ignore the potential importance of situational factors on their behavior, even when the information is available when they tender their predictions. Buehler et al. (1994) found that people dramatically underestimated the effects of deadlines on the completion times. Although people optimistically predicted that they would finish tasks well in advance of deadlines, they tended to finish at or near the deadline.

A more recent study again reveals that foreseeable situational factors have a much greater impact on behavior than on predictions. Koehler and Poon (2006) asked university students to estimate their probability of participating in a Web study several weeks in the future. Some of the students were informed that their participation was very important to the graduate student conducting the study. Others were told that their participation was helpful, but not crucial. In addition, some students were told that they would receive an e-mail reminding them of the study at the appropriate time (which they did receive). The remaining students were neither promised nor sent the e-mail.

The importance manipulation, which varied the social desirability of volunteering, affected predictions. Relative to those in the low-importance condition, students in the high-importance condition predicted that they would be more likely to volunteer. In contrast, the anticipated presence or absence of reminders had no significant effect on predictions. Students predicted that they would behave in line with their intentions, whether or not they would receive reminders. The reminder manipulation probably had no effect on predictions, in part because students in the no reminder condition overestimated their memory prowess.

Interestingly, the effects of the two experimental manipulations on actual volunteering were the precise opposite of their effects on predictions. The importance manipulation did not affect volunteering. In contrast, the situational factor—the presence or absence of reminders—significantly affected participation. Participants were more likely to volunteer if they received reminders.

Even when the accuracy of predictions is important to the self, people still ignore situational factors more than they ought to. Koehler and colleagues (2011) asked co-op students (university students who alternate study and work semesters) how much money they intended to save during their work term. Half of the students were told that they would be e-mailed a biweekly link to a website where they could report their savings progress. Students' initial predictions of how much they would save were not affected by whether or not they would be regularly reminded of their savings goals. Biweekly reporting, however, had a significant effect on saving. Participants who provided regular reports of their savings came much closer to their savings goals than those who did not.

Perhaps people simply lack correct intuitions about the impact of social desirability and situational factors such as reminders on behavior. This does not seem to be the case, however. They are aware, at least when it comes to predicting the behavior of other people. Koehler and Poon (2006) asked another group of participants to estimate the probability that the original participants had taken part in the Web study. Each of these observer participants was yoked to one of the original participants and provided with the importance and reminder information offered to that participant. Observers were less optimistic than the actors themselves, although still far too optimistic. More important, observers intuited the impact of the manipulations. They correctly inferred that the importance manipulation would have no impact and that reminders would enhance participation in the Web study. In a follow-up study, students predicted that other students who had the opportunity to use a savings monitoring software package would save more money, but that such a program would have no effect on their own behavior (Koehler et al., 2011).

The finding that outsiders offer more accurate predictions has been obtained in other studies as well (e.g., Buehler et al., 1994). Lacking information about their target's intentions or optimistic scenarios for the future, observers use information with greater predictive validity, such as base rates or contextual information (such as reminders). In contrast, when making self-predictions, people seem to rely heavily on their intentions and associated scenarios of the future that show how they will convert their intentions into action.

Intentions often reflect people's perceptions of the desirability of actions—what they ought to do rather than what might be more feasible. According to Trope and Liberman's theory of temporal construal (2003) and related research (e.g., Liberman & Trope, 1998), people typically predict that they will act in normatively appropriate ways when forecasting their more distant future behaviors. Conversely, people are more influenced by practical concerns, such as the amount of effort required, when predicting their more immediate behaviors. Consistent with Trope and Liberman's (2003) theory, participants in the prediction studies conducted by Koehler and others appear to focus on the desirability rather than the feasibility of their future actions when the actions are weeks away (as is often the case in these studies). In contrast, people's actual behaviors (and likely their more immediate predictions) are more influenced by factors related to feasibility, such as the presence or absence of reminders.

Trope and Liberman (2003) examined how people's predictions vary depending on the actual proximity of events. The subjective experience of time is also psychologically important. Some future events feel more imminent than other events that will occur at about the same time. For example, just as people feel subjectively closer to past successes than failures (Ross & Wilson, 2002), people feel subjectively closer in time to predicted successes than predicted failures (Peetz, Wilson, & Strahan, 2009). Peetz et al. found that this difference in subjective experience had implications for behavior. Participants who felt subjectively closer to an aptitude test prepared more for the test and performed better than those who felt farther away.

CONCLUDING COMMENTS: WHY ARE PEOPLE SO CONFIDENT OF THEIR ABILITY TO REMEMBER AND PREDICT?

In many psychology experiments, participants are far too confident about the accuracy of both their memories and their predictions. How do they maintain this confidence in the face of everyday experiences that could demonstrate their inadequacies in both domains? One answer is that their everyday experiences in both domains probably support their confidence in their abilities rather than emphasize their inadequacies. They may forget some events, such as the occasional birthday, but the routine of daily life helps them to get through their days without too many memory errors. People's memory and knowledge structures are less stable than they imagine, but the routine of everyday life provides a different form of stability. Most days, people are where they are supposed be, doing what they are supposed to do, and interacting with the same people whose names they know well. Forgetting is likely not a dominant aspect of most people's everyday experiences. Finally, even when people do make errors in personal memory, they may be unaware of their mistakes.

As for predictions, they too are likely confirmed on a daily basis. The structure and routine of people's everyday lives ensure that they will not encounter many surprises. The days unfold pretty much as people expect them to happen. Also, and perhaps more importantly, people are not typically wedded to a single prediction in everyday life, as they are in most psychology experiments. Although there is little research on the topic, it seems likely that, similarly to meteorologists, people alter their predictions over time to reflect changing realities, including shifts in situations, preferences, and intentions. However, people are not just too confident in their original predictions; they are also too optimistic. In this sense, people resemble meteorologists who initially predict sunshine when the evidence points to rain, but shift to predicting rain as the storm looms.

Suppose that people do change their predictions over time. Are they more likely to recall their accurate or inaccurate predictions after the target event has occurred? We propose that people more readily recall accurate forecasts, a proposal that is consistent with research on the hindsight bias (Fischhoff & Beyth, 1975). People's accurate predictions should be more accessible for a variety of reasons, including recency (more accurate forecasts will typically be more recent), outcomes (e.g., rain), and prime consonant predictions (predictions of rain), and people recall their successes more readily rather than their failures (Mischel, Ebbesen, & Zeiss, 1976). Thus, everyday errors in prediction are likely self-erasing in a different sense than Sherman (1980) intended. Errors in prediction are self-erasing in that correct predictions replace false ones and false predictions subsequently become relatively inaccessible to recall.

A combination of factors may provide individuals with the compelling meta-cognitive illusion that they are superior rememberers and forecasters—an illusion that is evident in the overconfidence they demonstrate in psychological experiments. One implication of this metacognitive illusion is that people should feel little need to test the accuracy of their recollections or alter the process by which they make predictions (e.g., by incorporating information such as base rates or situational factors). Why trifle with success? Our somewhat pessimistic conclusion, then, is that people will tend to persist in generating less optimal recollections and predictions than they could, given the information available to them.

NOTES

1. For the purposes of the current chapter, we define metacognition as the process of thinking about one's own thoughts and not thinking about the thoughts of other individuals.
2. Some of the studies that show overconfidence, however, are remarkably similar to studies that show self-prophecy effects (e.g., Koehler & Poon, 2006). As far as we know, no one has offered a compelling explanation of the differing findings.

REFERENCES

Block, R. A. (1989). A contextualistic view of time and mind. In J. T. Fraser (Ed.), *Time and mind: Interdisciplinary issues: The study of time* (pp. 61–79). Madison, CT: International Universities Press Inc.

Buehler, R., Griffin, D., & Ross, M. (1994). Exploring the "planning fallacy": Why people underestimate their task completion times. *Journal of Personality and Social Psychology, 67*, 366–381.

Buehler, R., Griffin, D., & Ross, M. (2002). Inside the planning fallacy: The causes and consequences of optimistic time predictions. In T. Gilovich, D. Griffin, & D. Kahneman (Eds.), *Heuristics and biases: The psychology of intuitive judgment* (pp. 250–270). New York, NY: Cambridge University Press.

Chapin, J. (2001). It won't happen to me: The role of optimistic bias in African American teens' risky sexual practices. *Howard Journal of Communications, 12*, 49–59.

Conway, M., & Ross, M. (1984). Getting what you want by revising what you had. *Journal of Personality and Social Psychology, 47*, 738–748.

Dickinson, E. (1993). *Emily Dickinson: Collected poems.* New York, NY: Barnes & Noble.

Dunlosky, J., & Metcalfe, J. (2009). *Metacognition.* Thousand Oaks, CA: Sage Publications Inc.

Dunning, D., Griffin, D. W., Milojkovic, J. D., & Ross, L. (1990). The overconfidence effect in social prediction. *Journal of Personality and Social Psychology, 58*, 568–581.

Dunning, D., & Story, A. L. (1991). Depression, realism, and the overconfidence effect: Are the sadder wiser when predicting future actions and events? *Journal of Personality and Social Psychology, 61*, 521–532.

Epley, N., & Dunning, D. (2000). Feeling "holier than thou": Are self-serving assessments produced by errors in self or social prediction? *Journal of Personality and Social Psychology, 79*, 861–875.

Fischhoff, B., & Beyth, R. (1975). "I knew it would happen": Remembered probabilities of once-future things. *Organizational Behavior and Human Performance, 13*, 1–16.

Goethals, G. R., & Reckman, R. F. (1973). The perception of consistency in attitudes. *Journal of Experimental Social Psychology, 9*, 491–501.

Greenwald, A. G., Carnot, C. G., Beach, R., & Young, B. (1987). Increasing voting behavior by asking people if they expect to vote. *Journal of Applied Psychology, 72*, 315–318.

Gregory, W. L., Cialdini, R. B., & Carpenter, K. M. (1982). Self-relevant scenarios as mediators of likelihood estimates and compliance: Does imagining make it so? *Journal of Personality and Social Psychology, 43*, 89–99.

Griffin, D. W., Dunning, D., & Ross, L. (1990). The role of construal processes in over-confident predictions about the self and others. *Journal of Personality and Social Psychology, 59*, 1128–1139.

Hoorens, V., Smits, T., & Shepperd, J. A. (2008). Comparative optimism in the spontaneous generation of future life-events. *British Journal of Social Psychology, 47*, 441–451.

Johnson, M. K., & Sherman, S. J. (1990). Constructing and reconstructing the past and the future in the present. In E. T. Higgins & R. M. Sorrentino (Eds.), *Handbook of motivation and cognition: Foundations of social behavior* (Vol. 2, pp. 482–526). New York, NY: Guilford Press.

Jost, J. T., Kruglanski, A. W., & Nelson, T. O. (1998). Social metacognition: An expansionist review. *Personality and Social Psychology Review, 2*, 137–154.

Kahneman, D., & Snell, J. (1992). Predicting a changing taste: Do people know what they will like? *Journal of Behavioral Decision Making, 5*, 187–200.

Kahneman, D., & Tversky, A. (1979). Prospect theory: An analysis of decision under risk. *Econometrica, 47*, 263–291.

Karniol, R., & Ross, M. (1996). The motivational impact of temporal focus: Thinking about the future and the past. *Annual Review of Psychology, 47*, 593–620.

Koehler, D. J., & Poon, C. S. K. (2006). Self-predictions overweight strength of current intentions. *Journal of Experimental and Social Psychology, 42*, 517–524.

Koehler, D. J., White, R. J., & John L. K. (2011). Good intentions, optimistic self-predictions, and missed opportunities. *Social Psychological and Personality Science, 2*, 90–96.

Koriat, A., Bjork, R. A., Sheffer, L., & Bar, S. K. (2004). Predicting one's own forgetting: The role of experience-based and theory-based processes. *Journal of Experimental Psychology: General, 133*, 643–656.

Kornell, N., & Bjork, R. A. (2009). A stability bias in human memory: Overestimating remembering and underestimating learning. *Journal of Experimental Psychology: General, 138*, 449–468.

Kunda, Z., & Fong, G. T. (1990). Motivated recruitment of autobiographical memories. *Journal of Personality and Social Psychology, 59*, 229–241.

Levav, J., & Fitzsimons, G. J. (2006). When questions change behavior. *Psychological Science, 17*, 207–213.

Liberman, N., & Trope, Y. (1998). The role of feasibility and desirability considerations in near and future decisions: A test of temporal construal theory. *Journal of Personality and Social Psychology, 75*, 5–18.

Loewenstein, G. (1996). Out of control: Visceral influences on behavior. *Organizational Behavior and Human Decision Processes, 65,* 272–292.

Lydon, J., Zanna, M. P., & Ross, M. (1988). Bolstering attitudes by autobiographical recall: Attitude persistence and selective memory. *Personality and Social Psychology Bulletin, 14,* 78–86.

MacDonald, T. K., & Ross, M. (1999). Assessing the accuracy of predictions about dating relationships: How and why do lovers' predictions differ from those made by observers? *Personality and Social Psychology Bulletin, 25,* 1417–1429.

McFarland, C., & Alvaro, C. (2000). The impact of motivation on temporal comparisons: Coping with traumatic events by perceiving personal growth. *Journal of Personality and Social Psychology, 79,* 327–343.

McFarland, C., & Ross, M. (1987). The relation between current impressions and memories of self and dating partners. *Personality and Social Psychology Bulletin, 13,* 228–238.

Mischel, W., Ebbesen, E. B., & Zeiss, A. M. (1976). Determinants of selective memory about the self. *Journal of Consulting and Clinical Psychology, 44,* 92–103.

Murray, S. L., & Holmes, J. G. (1993). Seeing virtues in faults: Negativity and the transformation of interpersonal narratives in close relationships. *Journal of Personality and Social Psychology, 65,* 707–722.

Newby-Clark, I. R., & Ross, M. (2003). Conceiving the past and future. *Personality and Social Psychology Bulletin, 29,* 807–818.

Newby-Clark, I. R., Ross, M., Buehler, R., Koehler, D., & Griffin, D. (2000). People focus on optimistic scenarios and disregard pessimistic scenarios while predicting task completion times. *Journal of Experimental Psychology: Applied, 6,* 171–182.

Osberg, T. M., & Shrauger, J. S. (1986). Self-prediction: Exploring the parameters of accuracy. *Journal of Personality and Social Psychology, 51,* 1044–1057.

Peetz, J., Wilson, A. E., & Strahan, E. J. (2009). So far away: The role of subjective temporal distance to future goals in motivation and behavior. *Social Cognition, 27,* 475–495.

Perloff, L. S., & Fetzer, B. K. (1986). Self-other judgments and perceived vulnerability to victimization. *Journal of Personality and Social Psychology, 50,* 502–510.

Petty, R. E., Briñol, P., Tormala, Z. L., & Wegener, D. T. (2007). The role of metacognition in social judgment. In A. W. Kruglanski & E. T. Higgins (Eds.), *Social psychology: Handbook of basic principles* (pp. 254–284). New York, NY: Cambridge University Press.

Ross, M. (1989). Relation of implicit theories to the construction of personal histories. *Psychological Review, 96,* 341–357.

Ross, M., Heine, S. J., Wilson, A. E., & Sugimori, S. (2005). Cross-cultural discrepancies in self-appraisals. *Personality and Social Psychology Bulletin, 31,* 1175–1188.

Ross, M., McFarland, C., Conway, M., & Zanna, M. P. (1983). Reciprocal relation between attitudes and behavior recall: Committing people to newly formed attitudes. *Journal of Personality and Social Psychology, 45,* 257–267.

Ross, M., McFarland, C., & Fletcher, G. J. (1981). The effect of attitude on the recall of personal histories. *Journal of Personality and Social Psychology, 40,* 627–634.

Ross, M., & Wilson, A. E. (2002). It feels like yesterday: Self-esteem, valence of personal past experiences, and judgments of subjective distance. *Journal of Personality and Social Psychology, 82,* 792–803.

Ross, M., & Wilson, A. E. (2003). Autobiographical memory and conceptions of self: Getting better all the time. *Current Directions in Psychological Science, 12,* 66–69.

Sanitioso, R., Kunda, Z., & Fong, G. T. (1990). Motivated recruitment of autobiographical memories. *Journal of Personality and Social Psychology, 59,* 229–241.

Sarewitz, D., & Pielke Jr., R. A. (2000). Prediction in science and policy. In D. Sarewitz, R. A. Pielke, & F. Byerly, Jr. (Eds.), *Prediction, science, decision making and the future of nature* (pp. 11–22). Washington, DC: Island Press.

Sherman, S. J. (1980). On the self-erasing nature of errors of prediction. *Journal of Personality and Social Psychology, 39,* 211–221.

Shrauger, J. S., Mariano, E., & Walker, T. J. (1998). Depressive symptoms and accuracy in the prediction of future events. *Personality and Social Psychology Bulletin, 24,* 880–892.

Spangenberg, E. R., & Obermiller, C. (1997). To cheat or not to cheat? Reducing cheating by requesting self-prophecy. *Marketing Education Review, 6,* 95–103.

Sprott, D. E., Spangenberg, E. R., & Fisher, R. (2003). The importance of normative beliefs to the self-prophecy effect. *Journal of Applied Psychology, 88,* 423–431.

Sprott, D. E., Spangenberg, E. R., & Perkins, A. (1999). Two more self-prophecy experiments. In L. Scott & E. J. Arnould (Eds.), *Advances in consumer research* (Vol. 26, pp. 621–626). Provo, UT: Association for Consumer Research.

Tormala, Z. L., Briñol, P., & Petty, R. E. (2006). When credibility attacks: The reverse impact of source credibility on persuasion. *Journal of Experimental Social Psychology, 42,* 684–691.

Tormala, Z. L., Petty, R. E., & Briñol, P. (2002). Ease of retrieval effects in persuasion: A self-validation analysis. *Personality and Social Psychology Bulletin, 28,* 1700–1712.

Trope, Y., & Liberman, N. (2003). Temporal construal. *Psychological Review, 110,* 403–421.

Vallone, R. P., Griffin, D. W., Lin, S., & Ross, L. (1990). Overconfident prediction of future actions by self and others. *Journal of Personality and Social Psychology, 58,* 582–592.

Weinstein, N. D. (1980). Unrealistic optimism about future life events. *Journal of Personality and Social Psychology, 39,* 806–820.

Wilson, A. E., & Ross, M. (2000). The frequency of temporal-self and social comparisons in people's personal appraisals. *Journal of Personality and Social Psychology, 78,* 928–942.

Wilson, A. E., & Ross, M. (2001). From chump to champ: People's appraisals of their earlier and present selves. *Journal of Personality and Social Psychology, 80,* 572–584.

Wilson, A. E., & Ross, M. (2003). The identity function of autobiographical memory: Time is on our side. *Memory, 11,* 137–149.

9

Metacognition and the Social Animal

LISA K. SON, NATE KORNELL, BRIDGID FINN,
and JESSICA F. CANTLON

INTRODUCTION

*M*etacognition, at its most basic level, is cognition about cognition. For instance, *metamemory* involves judgments and beliefs about memory (Dunlosky & Metcalfe, 2009). In an ideal world, metacognitive processes would provide a perfect reflection of the mind's contents, the way a mirror does. But research has shown repeatedly that metacognition is, at best, a distorted mirror: Predictions of future knowledge and judgments of current knowledge are subject to bias and are frequently inaccurate. The current chapter seeks to answer why, with all of its inaccuracies, metamemory survives as one of the most critical mental processes for any individual in a social world.

Here we consider the link between self-knowledge and knowledge of others and distinguish between three types of metacognition: metamemory, self-awareness, and other-awareness. Using data from a range of populations, including nonhuman animals, adult humans, children, and individuals with autism, we present evidence for a distinction between fast, heuristic-based metacognition and slower, more deliberate metacognition. We claim that without fast, heuristic metamemory processes, which do not necessarily depend on language or self-awareness, our memory systems would be of little value. Moreover, we postulate that metamemory is a key step in allowing individuals to develop into social beings. Taken together, the findings suggest that metacognition is crucial for an understanding of our own uncertainties, as well as the knowledge and intentions of others.

THE ROLE OF METAMEMORY

Over the past century, memory science has focused on how experiences are inscribed in memory, how these traces of the memories are stored in the mind, and how knowledge that has been committed to memory can be recalled at a later time. Over the past few decades, metamemory research has emerged as a new psychological subfield. And while the features of metamemory are linked to those of memory, the two faculties have been thought to be distinct. Consider the following illustration of the difference. Imagine that you learn that Emily Brontë wrote *Jane Eyre* and judge that you are confident that you will always remember this. Your metamemory may be absolutely accurate; that is, you thought you would remember the author and, when asked later, you do. Unfortunately (for you), Charlotte Brontë, not Emily, wrote *Jane Eyre*. Thus, your metamemory can be accurate when your memory is inaccurate. The reverse can also be true: You might know that Charlotte was the author of *Jane Eyre,* but be mistaken, at the metamemory level, in thinking that you will be able to remember that information later.

The use of metamemory is ubiquitous in everyday communication. For example, in response to a question about how well one did on a test, the answer, "I got a perfect score," is very different from "I'm not certain, but I may have gotten a perfect score" because "I'm not certain" and "may" signal uncertainty. They are, in other words, indicators of one's confidence, or lack thereof, in one's knowledge. We constantly produce such signals without much thought, and we understand them just as automatically. The simple act of saying, "I don't know," which many preschool children can do fluently and accurately, signals that people can report a lack of memory confidence from an early age. (Note, however, that the ability to say "I don't know" accurately depends on the child's age and the question the child is asked; for example, children sometimes say they can name an object, or know what it is, even when they do not; see Marazita & Merriman, 2004.)

In line with the preceding examples, empirical research on metamemory has relied on introspection and verbal self-reports. In a typical metamemory experiment, participants study information and give numerical ratings of how sure they are to remember that information later. It is well known, of course, that self-report data can be inaccurate, unreliable, and difficult to interpret (e.g., Nisbett & Wilson, 1977). However, this inaccuracy may be the essence of metamemory. That is, metamemory *is* what people believe about their own memories, whether it is accurate or not.

What is the role of metamemory? A memory is essentially a belief. Metamemory is one's strength or conviction in that belief. Retrieving a memory that is divorced from a feeling of confidence is like receiving a message from an unreliable source. A memory system that endorsed everything with equal confidence would be of little value unless it was free of gaps and errors. Metamemory allows us to recognize—and express—the gaps and errors in our memories. As a result, metamemory can be a check, or restraint, on memory. We learn not to trust our memories when we are not sure that they are accurate (for example, if someone looks only sort of familiar, we restrain ourselves from running toward them and giving them a big hug). In addition, we do not communicate false information to others (or, at least, we qualify the information by saying "I think" or "maybe"). And while metamemory is not perfect either, it serves the vital function of monitoring situations in which memory is not perfect so that the contents of the memory may be interpreted and conveyed to others appropriately.

Metamemory requires knowledge about our own knowledge. The ability to understand our own internal states may serve as a stepping stone to a variety of other higher level cognitive functions. Consider *theory of mind*, which refers to an awareness of our own mental states as well as an understanding that others have similar mental states. It is thought that theory of mind allows us to make inferences about the minds and behaviors of others. The major difference between metamemory and theory of mind is that the former refers to knowledge about the self, while the latter refers to knowledge about another. The two types of metacognition seem to be intimately related. For example, feelings of uncertainty may allow us to recognize that others can have similar feelings of doubt. Perhaps the universal ability to assess one's own uncertainty is a precursor for the complexities of human society, where individuals make room for debate, persuasion, sarcasm, humor, and even deception.

In the remainder of the chapter, we review some of the research on knowledge about the self, knowledge about others, and the link between the two. We begin with a discussion of the basic metamemory abilities that humans share with nonhuman animals.

METAMEMORY WITHOUT LANGUAGE

Within the science of metamemory, participants have typically reported their metamemory judgments verbally. But is language necessary for metamemory? And how did metamemory evolve? Did it coevolve with language, or is the ability linked to other prelinguistic cognitive abilities? These questions have led some to explore metamemory abilities in nonhuman animals. For the remainder of this chapter, we shall use the term "animals" to refer to nonhuman animals.

Understanding metacognition in the animal mind is of theoretical interest for a number of reasons. First, if an animal can make metamemory judgments, we can conclude that metamemory does not require language. Second, examining a nonverbal species allows for a relatively pure assay of metamemory mechanisms, without concurrent contamination by an interior monologue (at least the type of monologue that can exist in humans). Finally, discovering the mental capacities in animals can help unravel the development of human behaviors and abilities.

The most fundamental method of exerting control over one's internal representations is to decide which representations to acknowledge and which to ignore. One example of this kind of cognitive control is *directed forgetting*, in which an individual selectively chooses *not* to remember something. There is good evidence that animals engage in directed forgetting in order to reallocate memory to more important information. Roper, Kaiser, and Zentall (1995) presented pigeons with a delayed match-to-sample task in which a sample stimulus was presented, followed by a cue that indicated whether or not they would be tested on the sample color. If a "remember" cue was presented, after a delay the animal was shown the sample stimulus and a distractor stimulus. Correct responses produced a reward. If a "forget" cue was presented, the animal was not tested on the sample; instead, there was an unrelated discrimination task after the delay.

Occasionally, however, there was a "pop quiz," which tested the pigeons' memories for the "to-have-been-forgotten" sample. On these pop quiz trials, the pigeons' memories for the sample were much worse than on the standard "remember" trials, indicating that they had abandoned the memory when they were presented with the "forget" cue but not after the "remember" cue. Similar evidence of directed forgetting in animals has been reported in studies that used a variety of other task manipulations (e.g., Roper, Chaponis, & Blaisdell, 2005; Zentall, Roper, & Sherburne, 1995). These data illustrate that even animals can actively control their memory processes. More generally, these animals appear to possess an ability to manipulate their own mental states. The question then becomes: Do the animals know it?

How might one test metamemory in a nonverbal species? One approach has been to ask animals to perform a task in which they choose between two stimuli (such as a square densely populated with dots compared to a sparsely populated square) and are given a third option: to skip or "escape" the trial and move on to another trial. These tasks have shown that Rhesus macaque monkeys and other animals tend to escape on particularly difficult trials (see Smith & Washburn, 2005), such as when the target stimuli are not easily distinguishable due to having similar dot densities. This suggests that animals might know that they "do not know."

A task that involves making judgments about stimuli that are currently being presented may qualify as metacognition, but it does not involve making a judgment about one's internal memory state. Hampton's (2001) prospective task directly investigated metamemory. Monkeys were shown sample pictures; after a delay, they saw the sample picture again, along with distractor pictures. The subjects' task was to select the sample. However, after seeing the sample and prior to receiving the test, the monkeys could sometimes opt out of taking the test. On mandatory trials, they had to take the test. The monkeys were more accurate on self-selected test trials than on mandatory trials, suggesting that the monkeys opted out when they knew they did not know the answer. Crucially, they did so when no external stimuli were available as cues at the time of their decision (see also Smith & Washburn, 2005, for metamemory performance using the escape procedure).

Another approach has been to ask animals to make retrospective judgments after they take a memory test. In one such task, monkeys performed a memory task and were then asked to "bet" on the accuracy of their memories (Kornell, Son, & Terrace, 2007). They first studied six images that were presented sequentially on a touch-sensitive computer screen. After viewing these images, one of the six images was presented along with eight distractors and the task was to touch the picture that had already been seen in the initial exposure sequence. Once a monkey had touched his choice, he placed a bet. Betting high risk meant that he would earn three tokens if his recognition response had been right, but lose three tokens if it had been wrong. Betting low risk meant that he would earn one token, regardless of accuracy. Tokens were accumulated at the bottom of the screen and could be exchanged for food pellets when a criterion was reached.

The monkeys in this task acted metacognitively; that is, they tended to choose high risk after correct responses and low risk after incorrect responses. Moreover, they did so within the first few trials of transferring to this task. (The monkeys had previously been trained to respond metacognitively in other, perceptual, tasks; see Son & Kornell, 2005.) It seems, then, that they had learned a broad metacognitive skill that could generalize to new circumstances. They appear to have represented two internal responses: a recognition response and a confidence judgment. These data do not necessarily imply that the monkeys had conscious awareness of their confidence in their memories. But they do imply that the animals could monitor their confidence in their own memories (for recent reviews of animal metacognition research, see Kornell, 2009; Smith, 2009; Terrace & Son, 2009).

CONSCIOUSNESS AND METACOGNITION

Does metacognition—and metamemory in particular—require consciousness and/or self-awareness? Historically, metacognition has often been interpreted as a conscious introspection into the mind linked to language and to self-reflection. As Aristotle said, "Remembering, as we have conceived it, essentially implies consciousness of itself" (350 B.C.). Clearly, some metamemory judgments are conscious—for example, one can be irritatingly aware of feeling that a lost answer is "on the tip of my tongue"—but do all metamemory states require consciousness? If so, the fact that nonverbal animals exhibit accurate metamemory has important implications.

The simple answer appears to be no. Even humans are not always conscious of their metacognitive judgments. In one study, participants were presented with questions and were asked to judge as quickly as possible whether they knew the answer. In another condition, participants had to retrieve the answer. The data demonstrated that people were able to make the judgments—which were accurate—*prior to* having retrieved the answer and thus too quickly to have made a conscious assessment of its accuracy (Reder & Schunn, 1996). We have argued that these findings, in addition to the monkey data, suggest that some metacognitive processes do not require consciousness (e.g., Son & Kornell, 2005).

Remember, however, that Kornell and colleagues' (2007) metamemory task required monkeys to bet on their responses. Recently, Persaud, McLeod, and Cowey (2007) have argued that the ability to make appropriate wagers after completing a task is an objective measure of conscious awareness. They used three tasks that generally do not involve conscious awareness: blindsight, artificial grammar learning, and the Iowa gambling task. Their participants performed the tasks well, but they could not make appropriate post-task wagers; that is, they rarely bet more after correct responses than they did after errors. Once the conditions were changed to elicit conscious decision making, participants made appropriate wagers. The authors conclude: "This double dissociation suggests that placing a wager is a special sort of decision, one that is closely related to being aware" (p. 260).

As described previously, Kornell et al. (2007) found evidence that monkeys could make accurate wagers about their memories. Does that mean that monkeys have conscious awareness? A monkey's experience is clearly very different from a human's, in part because it is not linguistic. Consciousness is a kind of continuum: Humans have extremely flexible, creative conscious experiences, including the ability to reexperience past events and imagine future events. However, monkeys, though they may be aware of their surroundings and the recent past, seem to be stuck in the moment.

Proving anything about another being's experience—even another human—is not possible. In the absence of proof, what is needed is converging evidence of awareness in animals. For example, a hemianopic monkey (i.e., a monkey with blindsight) that can discriminate between stimuli presented in an area of its visual field will, nonetheless, fail to report seeing a stimulus presented in that area in a signal detection task, as though it lacks awareness of what it sees in that area (Cowey & Stoerig, 1995). At this stage, it seems clear that monkeys have metacognitive abilities. Evidence is accumulating that monkeys have their own sort of awareness; it is not a sure thing, but it may be worth a wager.

HEURISTICS VERSUS ANALYTICAL PROCESSES

All metamemory is not created equal (Kornell, 2009). For instance, a "tip of the tongue" experience is clearly conscious. The ability to decline to answer a question because of a lack of confidence, though, does not appear to require self-awareness. Moreover, the mechanisms underlying various metamemory processes may differ. Some judgments may be based on a very fast assessment of how familiar one is with the cue or question (Metcalfe, Schwartz, & Joaquim, 1993). Other judgments may be based on a slower, but more direct, retrieval of the target from memory (Koriat & Levy-Sadot, 2001). Imagine, for instance, that you had practiced the problem 27 + 41 repeatedly. If you are then presented with the problem 27 × 41, you may judge (too quickly) that you know the answer and, as a result, choose not to calculate but rather to retrieve the answer from memory. Unfortunately, having based your judgment on only the rapid familiarity of the numbers and not the operation and having limited your time, the likelihood of solving the problem accurately is close to nil (Reder & Ritter, 1992).

It appears that some metacognitive processes require effort. Others are based on heuristic processes (e.g., based on familiarity), and these processes allow humans and other animals to make metacognitive judgments (such as "I know" or "I don't know") quickly and automatically. One negative result of this could be that experts, in situations within their own area of expertise, display a larger degree of overconfidence (or the belief that they know more than they actually do) than do novices. After all, experts are bound to be more familiar with the context (e.g. Oskamp, 1965; Son & Kornell, 2010).

In humans, at least, there are effortful metacognitive processes that are slower, perhaps more likely to involve language, and more likely to become conscious. That is, humans have the luxury of mulling over thoughts and judgments, even after having made numerous quick (and maybe less than accurate) judgments. Furthermore, how much humans mull over their own thoughts can vary from very little interpretation to extensive interpretation (see Petty & Briñol, 2009). And it is this deeper type of metacognition that may give rise to an understanding of the self and of others.

SELF-AWARENESS AND OTHER-AWARENESS

Like many other primates, humans are an intensely social species. We spend much of our time, effort, and resources on fostering and manipulating social relationships with kin and others. Successfully creating alliances is crucial for our well-being and survival. Theory of mind, or an awareness of another's mind, is a key ability because it allows us to predict what others will do, how they will react to what we do, and how we can manipulate them.

Psychologists have long debated whether self-awareness or other-awareness comes first. In his comprehensive review, Carruthers (2008) summarizes four different possibilities for the emergence of self- and other-awareness. As a first possibility, he proposes that the two skills—dubbed *metacognition* and *mind reading*—are independent. In the second, he proposes that they come from the same fundamental faculty. In the third, he provides evidence for self-awareness being a necessity for other-awareness, and in the fourth model, vice versa. While there are mixed conclusions, we examine a fundamental question raised by Carruthers's review: Could metacognition have evolved to allow for an awareness of others?

One way to approach this question is to examine the relationship between self-awareness and other-awareness in animals. In 1970, Gallup challenged the notion that animals lacked self-awareness by publishing his classic studies on mirror self-recognition. In the study, when preadolescent chimpanzees encountered a mirror for the first time, they made social gestures to the image they saw. After a few days of experience with the mirror, however, such other-directed responses began to wane. At the same time, self-directed responses began to increase. After being marked with a red, odorless dye while unconscious, the chimpanzees touched the marked area on their own bodies (rather than on the mirror) a significant number of times, suggesting that they understood the reflection to be themselves. Remarkably, when Gallup followed up on his original study using chimpanzees raised in isolation, none showed signs of mirror self-recognition (Gallup, McClure, Hill, & Bundy, 1971). One interpretation is that because chimpanzees have had experience with others, they were able to view themselves as another might view them.

The view that other-awareness comes before self-awareness is not a recent one. In 1912, Cooley wrote that the concept of the self was dependent on social interaction. Mead (1934) also proposed that a self-concept is formed as one experiences how others view oneself.

Not all social animals have been able to pass the mirror self-recognition test. While great apes (Gallup, 1970), elephants (Plotnik, de Waal, & Reiss, 2006), dolphins (Reiss & Marino, 2001), and pigs (Broom, Sena, & Moynihan, 2009) have passed, monkeys (who were able to express metamemory) have failed (see Roma et al., 2007). This supports the theory that metamemory—at least the kind that monkeys possess—does not depend on being self-aware. Rather, the ability to express certainty and uncertainty allows monkeys to be cautious and perceptive in an uncertain world. In other words, monkeys may not be self-aware, but they may still have metamemory abilities.

ULTIMATE METACOGNITION: KNOWLEDGE OF OTHERS

Even animals that are not considered to be self-aware can be spectacularly good at responding to the behaviors of others. The ability to know the contents of another's mind may be *the* most sophisticated level of metacognitive skill—and also among the most useful for a social animal. Take, for instance, the complex acts of deception, cheating, and stealing. Researchers have suggested that these malicious behaviors were the evolutionary catalyst for metacognitive processes, especially within the social domain (Cosmides & Tooby, 1994). The data from social reasoning studies of nonhuman primates seem to support this view.

A study by Hare, Call, Agnetta, and Tomasello (2000) showed that subordinate chimpanzees follow the gaze of dominant chimpanzees in order to decide whether or not to raid a food cache that is equidistant between them. In the study, animals were held in enclosures on opposite sides of a large room. Caches of fruit were placed in the middle of the room either in plain view of both animals or in view of only one of the animals (due to the clever placement of a visual barrier). The important finding was that subordinate chimpanzees would not approach the food cache when the dominant chimp had seen it. But, when the dominant chimpanzee had not seen the food cache, subordinate animals readily approached the cache.

A related study by Flombaum and Santos (2005) further supported these findings by showing that rhesus monkeys selectively steal food from humans who cannot see them stealing. Thus, although monkeys and apes are notoriously bad at inferring mental states from eye gaze during traditional theory-of-mind tasks (cf. Povinelli & Eddy, 1996), they succeed at using eye gaze to predict another animal's behavior in a competitive task. In short, deception, cheating, and stealing are three competitive behaviors that seem to play a privileged role in metacognitive reasoning within the social domain.

Though less frequently observed than competitive behaviors in animals, the three altruistic behaviors of helping, informing, and sharing have recently been studied in chimpanzees and in human children (Warneken & Tomasello, 2009). These studies have revealed important similarities in the cooperative acts of these groups. For example, when children and chimpanzees observe a human companion drop a pen or a sponge, they will rush to retrieve it for the companion, even in the absence of any reinforcement or feedback (Warneken & Tomasello, 2006). Thus, both children and chimpanzees understand the immediate intention of their human companion to maintain possession of an object, and both groups are motivated to participate in that goal.

But there are important differences in the altruistic behaviors of children and chimpanzees. Sharing and informing are two behaviors in which human children engage much more frequently than other primates. From 12 months of age, when they know the location of an object lost by an adult, children will actively lead the adult to that object (Liszkowski, Carpenter, Striano, Tomasello, 2006). Brownell, Svetlova, and Nichols (2009) showed that 25-month-olds who are given a choice between delivering food only to themselves or to themselves and a companion will choose to share. In contrast, chimpanzees tested in a comparable paradigm do not exhibit the same sharing instinct and instead choose randomly between the selfish and sharing options (which give them the same payoff). These findings indicate that chimpanzees have a deep lack of familiarity with or faith in a system of cooperation. In fact, some have argued that even the cooperative and altruistic behaviors in which chimpanzees do engage, such as proximal helping, have selfish origins (see Warneken & Tomasello, 2009).

Studies that permit chimpanzees to behave cooperatively or altruistically toward kin or other conspecifics have yielded slightly more evidence for altruism in chimpanzees (see de Waal, 2008, for a review). These studies suggest that the natural behaviors of chimpanzees might include more unselfish acts and emotions, such as empathy, than can be observed in artificial experiments with human agents. However, regardless of the testing modality, the extent to which apes engage in spontaneous altruistic and cooperative acts differs from that observed in human behavior. And, importantly, nonhuman primates interact competitively more than they interact cooperatively (Muller & Mitani, 2005). However, some of the differences between humans and nonhuman primates might be linked to the uniquely human ability to communicate large amounts of information efficiently (Warnecken & Tomasello, 2009).

The explanation of why nonhuman primates do not engage in a level of cooperative and altruistic behavior that is comparable to their competitive abilities is an open pursuit. Different social interactions could rely on qualitatively different metacognitive mechanisms (Warneken & Tomasello, 2009). Alternatively, quantitative differences in the amount or kind of information that serves as the input to metacognitive reasoning could be a crucial factor. Informing, for example, requires the representation of the goal states of others, whereas stealing only requires that another's gaze be tracked. Thus, there may be broad differences in "difficulty" between the metacognitive inferences required by competitive and cooperative acts. Such differences could contribute to asymmetries in the forms of nonhuman primate metacognition.

One possibility is that metacognition emerged earliest within the competitive social domain because the information within that domain had more "meaningful" content and better organization (and was more easily afforded metacognitive assessments). Social relations, kin relations, mating, and dominance are considered the central focus of a primate's existence. Overall, many more competitive exchanges have been reported in observations of ape and monkey social interactions than cooperative exchanges. Thus, based on sheer frequency, nonhuman primates would be expected to have more detailed (and therefore more "meaningful") representations of competition than of altruism or cooperation.

Whether competitive social behaviors were *the* catalyst for the evolution of metacognition is a matter of speculation because it is impossible to reconstruct our evolutionary history. Social information may have played a role in the emergence of metacognition because it emerged earliest as a sufficiently rich knowledge system, or metacognitive processes might have emerged independently within social and nonsocial domains (rather than emerging from a single core process). In that regard, evidence from studies of the development of social and nonsocial forms of metacognition in human children might better reveal the relations among varieties of metacognitive reasoning.

SELF-AWARENESS AND OTHER-AWARENESS IN CHILDREN

What can we learn from the development of a self-awareness and theory of mind in young children? An early and ongoing line of inquiry has been directed toward the development of children's metamemory abilities, or the understanding of one's own memory processes and its contents (e.g., Brown, 1987; Finn & Metcalfe, 2011; Metcalfe & Kornell, 2003). Data have shown that, compared to adults, children make relatively poor use of their judgments (e.g., Bisanz, Vesonder, & Voss, 1978), particularly because young children often have an unrealistic self-concept about the capacity of their memories. For example, a study by Kreutzer, Leonard, and Flavell (1975) found that kindergarteners were convinced that they always remembered well, with 30% of the children convinced that they never forgot anything. (In normal conversation, however, many children in kindergarten or younger can accurately report that they forgot something.) Much research has shown that children are overconfident in their memories (e.g., Flavell, Friedrichs, & Hoyt, 1970) and remain overly optimistic even after experience and feedback on a similar task (Finn & Metcalfe, 2011).

In parallel, research on metacognition has focused on how and when children begin to understand the mental world. This area of research dates back to the work of Piaget and Vygotsky and targets the development of theory of mind. Children's understanding of mental concepts, like thinking, understanding, and belief, has been a focus of theory-of-mind research (Wellman & Estes, 1986). By around 2.5–3 years of age, children begin to use the words "think" and "remember" (Limber, 1973; Shatz, Wellman, & Silber, 1983), suggesting a nascent awareness of their mental world. However, theory of mind continues to coalesce throughout childhood. For example, Wellman and Johnson (1979) showed that 3-year-olds were not able to distinguish between remembering and forgetting, but that children were usually able to make this distinction by the age of 4.

Beyond age 4, children do seem to have a better grasp of the distinction between mental verbs (e.g., remembering versus forgetting; Johnson & Wellman, 1980; Kreutzer et al., 1975; Wellman, 1985), but research suggests that they are still developing a clear understanding of their mental worlds. For example, Flavell, Green, and Flavell (2000) tested 5-year-olds, 8-year-olds, and adults on tasks designed to investigate their ability to introspect. The 5-year-old children showed some ability to report their introspections, but in comparison to the older children and the adults, their reports reflected that they were less aware of their thoughts. Indeed, the 5-year-olds often denied having had thoughts at all.

It would be hard to overstate the importance of understanding one's own mental states. But the ability to understand and respond to the mental states of others is equally important (Jost, Kruglanski, & Nelson, 1998). It is crucial in allowing people to create the rich social and interpersonal relationships that help to define the *Homo sapiens,* or *Homo psychologicus* as characterized by Humphrey (1984). Some have postulated that how we think about thinking itself should also be considered within the context of our assessments about the mental states of others (Nelson, Kruglanski, & Jost, 1998; Perner, 1991). Thus, as noted in the context of animal research, self-awareness and other-awareness seem to be strongly connected.

The relationship between self-awareness and other-awareness is complicated by a rapid development in language and complex behaviors in children between the ages of 3 and 5. Some behaviors, while seemingly correlated with theory of mind, may simply be conditioned responses. Thus, it is important to distinguish between theory of mind and "theory of behavior." If I am able to predict that you will give me a candy bar if I give you a dollar, does that imply theory of mind? Or does it just mean that I've learned from experience that my behavior leads to yours? Clearly, if you are a vending machine, I do not need (nor should I use) theory of mind to predict your behavior. Yet it can be difficult to distinguish between theory of mind and theory of behavior in another actor. This difficulty has led many researchers to employ false-belief tasks in which a theory of behavior would lead to one prediction, but a theory of mind would lead to the opposite.

False-belief tasks assess a person's understanding that others can have beliefs that are different from one's own or distinct from reality. In one of the classic tasks testing false belief—often called the *Sally–Anne task* (Wimmer & Perner, 1983)—a child is shown a doll named Sally and a doll named Anne. Sally puts her marble in a basket and then leaves the room. After Sally leaves, Anne moves the marble from Sally's basket into her own box. Then Sally returns to the room. The children are asked where they think Sally will look for her marble. The question can only be answered correctly if the children understand that Sally believes something different from what the child knows to be true. The literature on false-belief tasks suggests that children younger than 3.5 years are not able to represent others' beliefs appropriately (Wellman, Cross, & Watson, 2001). The ability to make the correct assessment about what the other person will believe is thought to be in place around 4 years of age (Wellman et al., 2001). In a sense, such tasks put self-awareness and other-awareness in conflict with each other.

By adulthood, most people interpret others' behavior in mentalistic terms effortlessly (Baron-Cohen, 1995). Indeed, our inclination to think in terms of others' minds is so strong that we attribute beliefs and intentions to inanimate objects (Adolphs, 1999; Heider & Simmel, 1944). Our ability to "read minds" helps us make predictions about others' behaviors and helps us to understand why they do what they do. It also helps us to avoid being deceived and to deceive others (Byrne & Whiten, 1988). In essence, theory of mind allows us to be more certain about our unfolding social world.

What if an adult did not have the ability to read other mental states? This is the case for the subset of individuals with autism, who are not able to ascribe minds to others in a usual manner. Researchers like Gopnik (1993) discussed how frightening they imagine such "mindblindness" to be. Gopnik writes:

> This is what it's like to sit round the dinner table....Around me bags of skin are draped over chairs, and stuffed into pieces of cloth, they shift and protrude in unexpected ways...Imagine that the noisy skin bags suddenly moved toward you and their noises grew loud and you had no idea why, no way of explaining them or predicting what they would do next. (quoted in Baron-Cohen, 1995, p. 5)

Children with autism are much less likely to pass false-belief tasks than typically developing children or even children with Down syndrome (e.g., Baron-Cohen, Leslie, & Frith, 1985; Leslie & Frith, 1988). They are also less likely to engage in spontaneous pretend play (Lewis & Boucher, 1988) and to predict what kinds of emotions someone might have given their beliefs (Baron-Cohen, 1995). Thus, lacking an awareness of others can often reduce an individual's ability to participate in society.

There are two main competing theories regarding the development of theory of mind. The modular class of theories proposes that there is a special, innate structure implicated in theory of mind (see, for example, Baron-Cohen, 1995; Leslie, 1991, 1994). Developmental differences in theory-of-mind tasks arise because the brain structures involved in theory-of-mind judgments are still maturing. The second class of theory proposes a general mechanism that supports, but is not specifically designed for, theory of mind. Perner and colleagues (e.g., Perner & Lang, 1999) have argued that theory-of-mind abilities are tied to the development of executive control, including the inhibition of irrelevant thoughts. Research in support of this theory has shown that there is a positive correlation between executive control—which is implicated in much metacognitive function—and performance on a theory-of-mind task (for a review, see Moses, Carlson, & Sabbagh, 2005). Underlying both theories is a deep connection between self-awareness and other-awareness.

THE ROLE OF LANGUAGE AND SOCIETY

Metamemory is often inaccurate (Dunlosky & Bjork, 2008). Overconfidence, or not knowing that you do not know, is among the most common human biases (Son & Kornell, 2010). We began the chapter by likening metacognition to a distorted mirror that provides a somewhat distorted picture of one's mind. One way to support metacognition is to improve how accurately it reflects actual memory. Do language abilities support metacognition? Studies have shown that when people are trained to use verbalization strategies (e.g., Beurhing & Kee, 1987) or to be more aware of their own thinking (Moreno & Saldana, 2005), overall metamemory accuracy and performance improve. Thus, perhaps human metamemory is more sophisticated when it is entwined with language and self-awareness.

We have suggested that no single mechanism underlies all types of metamemory. For humans, the metamemory process is often entwined with language. Animal metamemory clearly develops independently of language. It is important to keep in mind that, at the end of the day, decision making is the reason metacognition is important. Animals, as well as humans, make decisions all the time, and most decisions are made without language. While humans can take advantage of the benefits that language offers, we should not diminish the need for a fundamental metamemory ability to assess what we do and do not know. Indeed, data have shown that monkeys, like humans, are more likely to seek information particularly when they lack information (Kornell et al., 2007). Thus, even the most primitive type of metamemory plays a role in affecting subsequent decisions.

CONCLUSION

Human metacognition develops gradually. The data, ranging from nonhuman animals to children to individuals with autism, have shown that an awareness of our own thoughts can stem from the awareness of others in the world and their actions. Similarly, by knowing what we know and what we do not know, we can learn to understand the uncertainties of others.

Animals appear to make decisions based on a rudimentary type of metamemory. Humans seem to share this level of metamemory, but human metacognition has evolved beyond the simple metamemory abilities of animals. On the whole, humans seem to possess at least three levels of metacognition: automatic metamemory, self-awareness, and other-awareness. Each of these levels may have different, if overlapping, underlying mechanisms. And perhaps timing could be used as a proxy for various levels: A fast/familiar response could indicate an automatic metacognition that does not require conscious thought; a slower and deliberate response would indicate that consciousness—either of oneself or another—was present. While the levels may differ mechanistically, they are equal in importance for the individual.

To thrive in an intensely social world requires humans (and perhaps other animals) to know themselves and to find ways to know the secret thoughts of others. Metamemory, in the form of certainty monitoring, helps us to distinguish accurate memories from false ones, which allows us to be truthful. Theory of mind helps us to deceive, cheat, and manipulate, as well as to communicate, cooperate, share, and empathize.

REFERENCES

Adolphs, R. (1999). Social cognition and the human brain. *Trends in Cognitive Sciences, 3,* 469–479.

Aristotle. (350 B.C.). *On memory and reminiscence.* Translation by J. I. Beare.

Baron-Cohen, S. (1995). *Mindblindness: An essay on autism and theory of mind.* Boston, MA: MIT Press/Bradford Books.

Baron-Cohen, S., Leslie, A. M., & Frith, U. (1985). Does the autistic child have a "theory of mind"? *Cognition, 21,* 37–46.

Beurhing T., & Kee, D. W. (1987). Developmental relationships among metamemory, elaborative strategy use and associative memory. *Journal of Experimental Child Psychology, 44,* 377–400.

Bisanz, G. L., Vesonder, G. T., & Voss, J. F. (1978). Knowledge of one's own responding and the relation of such knowledge to learning. *Journal of Experimental Child Psychology, 25,* 116–128.

Broom, D. M., Sena, H., & Moynihan, K. L. (2009). Pigs learn what a mirror image represents and use it to obtain information. *Animal Behavior, 78,* 1037–1041.

Brown, A. L. (1987). Metacognition, executive control, self-regulation, and other more mysterious mechanisms. In F. E. Weinert & R. H. Kluwe (Eds.), *Metacognition, motivation and understanding.* Mahwah, NJ: Lawrence Erlbaum Associates.

Brownell, C. A., Svetlova, M., & Nichols, S. (2009). To share or not to share: When do toddlers respond to another's needs? *Infancy, 14,* 117–130.

Byrne, R. W., and Whiten, A. (Eds.). (1988). *Machiavellian intelligence: Social expertise and the evolution of intellect in monkeys, apes, and humans.* New York, NY: Oxford University Press.

Carruthers, P. (2008). Metacognition in animals: A skeptical look. *Mind & Language, 23,* 58–89.

Cooley, C. H. (1912). Valuation as a social process. *Psychological Bulletin, 9,* 441–450.

Cosmides, L., & Tooby, J. (1994). Beyond intuition and instinct blindness—Toward an evolutionarily rigorous cognitive science. *Cognition, 50,* 41–77.

Cowey, A., & Stoerig, P. (1995). Blindsight in monkeys. *Nature, 373,* 247–249.

de Waal, F. B. M. (2008). Putting the altruism back into altruism: The evolution of empathy. *Annual Review of Psychology, 59,* 279–300.

Dunlosky, J., & Bjork, R. A. (Eds.). (2008). *A handbook of metamemory and memory.* Hillsdale, NJ: Psychology Press.

Dunlosky, J., & Metcalfe, J. (2009). *Metacognition.* Beverly Hills, CA: Sage.

Finn, B., & Metcalfe, J. (2011). *Incurable optimism: Children's multi-trial judgments of learning.* Manuscript in preparation.

Flavell, J. H., Friedrichs, A. G., & Hoyt, J. D. (1970). Developmental changes in memorization processes. *Cognitive Psychology, 1,* 324–340.

Flavell, J. H., Green, F. L., & Flavell, E. R. (2000). Development of children's awareness of their own thoughts. *Journal of Cognition and Development 1,* 97–112.

Flombaum, J. I., & Santos, L. R. (2005). Rhesus monkeys attribute perceptions to others. *Current Biology, 15,* 447–452.

Gallup, G. G. (1970). Chimpanzees: Self-recognition. *Science, 167*(3914), 86–87.

Gallup, G. G., McClure, M. K., Hill, S. D., & Bundy, R. A. (1971). Capacity for self-recognition in differentially reared chimpanzees. *Psychological Record, 21,* 69–74.

Gopnik, A. (1993). How we know our minds: The illusion of first-person knowledge of intentionality. *Behavioral and Brain Sciences, 16,* 1–15, 90–101.

Hampton, R. R. (2001). Rhesus monkeys know when they remember. *Proceedings of the National Academy of Sciences of the United States of America, 98,* 5359–5362.

Hare, B., Call, J., Agnetta, B., & Tomasello, M. (2000). Chimpanzees know what conspecifics do and do not see. *Animal Behavior, 59,* 771–785.

Heider, F., & Simmel, M. (1944). An experimental study of apparent behavior. *American Journal of Psychology, 57,* 243–259.

Humphrey, N. (1984). *Consciousness regained. 12. The color currency of nature* (pp. 146–152). Oxford, England: Oxford University Press.

Johnson, C. N., & Wellman, H. (1980). Children's developing understanding of mental verbs: Remember, know, and guess. *Child Development, 51,* 1095–1102.

Jost, J. T., Kruglanski, A. W., & Nelson, T. O. (1998). Social metacognition: An expansionist review. *Personality and Social Psychology Review, 2,* 137–154.

Koriat, A., & Levy-Sadot, R. (2001). The combined contributions of the cue-familiarity and accessibility heuristics to feelings of knowing. *Journal of Experimental Psychology: Learning, Memory, & Cognition, 27,* 34–53.

Kornell, N. (2009). Metacognition in humans and animals. *Current Directions in Psychological Science, 18,* 11–15.

Kornell, N., Son, L. K., & Terrace, H. S. (2007). Transfer of metacognitive skills and hint seeking in monkeys. *Psychological Science, 18,* 64–71.

Kreutzer, M. A., Leonard, C., & Flavell, J. H. (1975). An interview study of children's knowledge about memory. *Monographs of the Society for Research in Child Development, 40*(1, serial no. 159).

Kuhn, D. (1999). A developmental model of critical thinking. *Educational Researcher, 28,* 16–25.

Leslie, A. M. (1991). Theory of mind impairment in autism. In A. Whiten (Ed.), *Natural theories of mind: Evolution, development and simulation of everyday mind reading* (pp. 63–77). Oxford, England: Basil Blackwell.

Leslie, A. M. (1994). Pretending and believing: Issues in the theory of mind ToM. *Cognition, 50,* 211–238.

Leslie, A. M., & Frith, U. (1988). Autistic children's understanding of seeing, knowing and believing. *British Journal of Developmental Psychology, 6,* 315–324.

Lewis, V., & Boucher, J. (1988). Spontaneous, instructed and elicited play in relatively able autistic children. *British Journal of Developmental Psychology, 6,* 325–339.

Limber, J. (1973). The genesis of complex sentences. In T. Moore (Ed.), *Cognitive development and the acquisition of language.* New York, NY: Academic Press.

Liszkowski, U., Carpenter, M., Striano, T., & Tomasello, M. (2006). Twelve- and 18-month-olds point to provide information for others. *Journal of Cognition and Development, 7,* 173–187.

Marazita, J. M., & Merriman, W. E. (2004). Young children's judgment of whether they know names for objects: The metalinguistic ability it reflects and the processes it involves. *Journal of Memory and Language, 51,* 458–472.

Mead, G. (1934). *Mind, self, and society from the standpoint of a social behaviorist.* Chicago, IL: University of Chicago Press.

Metcalfe, J., & Kornell, N. (2003). The dynamics of learning and allocation of study time to a region of proximal learning. *Journal of Experimental Psychology: General, 132,* 530–542.

Metcalfe, J., Schwartz, B. L., & Joaquim, S. G. (1993). The cue familiarity heuristic in metacognition. *Journal of Experimental Psychology: Learning, Memory, and Cognition, 19,* 851–861.

Moreno, F. J., & Saldana, D. (2005). Use of a computer-assisted program to improve metacognition in persons with severe intellectual disabilities. *Research in Developmental Disabilities, 26,* 341–357.

Moses, L. J., Carlson, S. M., & Sabbagh, M. A. (2005). On the specificity of the relation between executive function and children's theories of mind. In W. Schneider, R. Schumann-Hengsteler, & B. Sodian (Eds.), *Young children's cognitive development: Interrelationships among executive functioning, working memory, verbal ability, and theory of mind* (pp. 131–145). Mahwah, NJ: Lawrence Erlbaum Associates.

Muller, M., & Mitani, J. C. (2005). Conflict and cooperation in wild chimpanzees. In P. J. B. Slater, J. Rosenblatt, C. Snowdon, T. Roper, & M. Naguib (Eds.), *Advances in the study of behavior* (pp. 275–331). New York, NY: Elsevier.

Nelson, T. O., Kruglanski, A. W., & Jost, J. T. (1998). Knowing thyself and others: Progress in metacognitive social psychology. In V. Y. Yzerbyt, G. Lories, & B. Dardenne (Eds.), *Metacognition: Cognitive and social dimensions* (pp. 69–89). Thousand Oaks, CA: Sage.

Nisbett, R. E., & Wilson, T. D. (1977). Telling more than we can know: Verbal reports on mental processes. *Psychological Review, 84,* 231–259.

Oskamp, S. (1965). Overconfidence in case-study judgments. *Journal of Consulting Psychology, 29,* 261–265.

Perner, J. (1991). *Understanding the representational mind.* Cambridge, MA: MIT Press.

Perner, J., & Lang, B. (1999). Theory of mind and executive function: Is there a developmental relationship? In S. Baron-Cohen, H. Tager-Flusberg, & D. Cohen (Eds.), *Understanding other minds: Perspectives from autism and developmental cognitive neuroscience* (2nd ed., pp. 150–181). Oxford, England: Oxford University Press.

Persaud, N., McLeod, P., & Cowey, A. (2007). Post-decision wagering objectively measures awareness. *Nature Neuroscience, 10,* 257–261.

Petty, R. E., & Briñol, P. (2009). Implicit ambivalence: A meta-cognitive approach. In R. E. Petty, R. H. Fazio, & P. Briñol (Eds.), *Attitudes: Insights from the new implicit measures* (pp. 119–161). New York, NY: Psychology Press.

Plotnik, J. M., de Waal, F. B. M., & Reiss, D. (2006). Self-recognition in an Asian elephant. *Proceedings of the National Academy of Sciences of the United States of America, 103*(45), 17053–17057.

Povinelli, D. J., & Eddy, T. J. (1996). Factors influencing young chimpanzees' (*Pan troglodytes*) recognition of attention. *Journal of Comparative Psychology, 110,* 336–345.

Reder, L., & Schunn, C. (1996). Metacognition does not imply awareness: Strategy choice is governed by implicit learning and memory. In L. Reder (Ed.), *Implicit memory and metacognition.* Mahwah, NJ: Lawrence Erlbaum Associates.

Reder, L. M., & Ritter, F. E. (1992). What determines initial feeling of knowing? Familiarity with question terms, not with the answer. *Journal of Experimental Psychology: Learning, Memory, and Cognition, 18,* 435–451.

Reiss, D., & Marino, L. (2001). Mirror self-recognition in the bottlenose dolphin: A case of cognitive convergence. *Proceedings of the National Academy of Sciences of the United States of America, 98,* 5937–5942.

Roma, P. G., Silberberg, A., Huntsberry, M. E., Christensen, C. J., Ruggiero, A. M., & Suomi, S. J. (2007). Mark tests for mirror self-recognition in Capuchin monkeys (*Cebus apella*) trained to touch marks. *American Journal of Primatology, 69,* 989–1000.

Roper, K. L., Chaponis, D. M., & Blaisdell, A. R. (2005). Transfer of directed-forgetting cues across discrimination tasks with pigeons. *Psychonomic Bulletin & Review, 12,* 1005–1010.

Roper, K. L., Kaiser, D. H., & Zentall, T. R. (1995). True directed forgetting in pigeons may occur only when alternative working-memory is required on forget–cue trials. *Animal Learning & Behavior, 23,* 280–285.

Shatz, M., Wellman, H. M., & Silber, S. (1983). The acquisition of mental verbs: A systematic investigation of the first reference to mental state. *Cognition, 14,* 301–321.

Smith, J. D. (2009). The study of animal metacognition. *Trends in Cognitive Sciences, 13,* 389–396.

Smith, J. D., & Washburn, D. A. (2005). Uncertainty monitoring and metacognition by animals. *Current Directions in Psychological Science, 14,* 19–24.

Son, L. K., & Kornell, N. (2005). Metaconfidence judgments in rhesus macaques: Explicit versus implicit mechanisms. In H. S. Terrace & J. Metcalfe (Eds.), *The missing link in cognition: Origins of self-knowing consciousness.* Oxford, England: Oxford University Press.

Son, L. K., & Kornell, N. (2010). The virtues of ignorance. *Behavioral Processes, 83,* 207–212.

Terrace, H. S., & Son, L. K. (2009). Comparative metacognition. *Current Opinion in Neurobiology, 19,* 67–74.

Warneken, F., & Tomasello, M. (2006). Altruistic helping in human infants and young chimpanzees. *Science, 311,* 1301–1303.

Warneken, F., & Tomasello, M. (2009). Varieties of altruism in children and chimpanzees. *Trends in Cognitive Science, 13,* 397–402.

Wellman, H. M. (1985). The child's theory of mind: The development of conceptions of cognition. In S. Yussen (Ed.), *The growth of reflection in children.* San Diego, CA: Academic Press.

Wellman, H. M., Cross, D., & Watson, J. (2001). Meta-analysis of theory-of-mind development: The truth about false belief. *Child Development, 62,* 655–684.

Wellman, H. M., & Estes, D. (1986). Early understanding of mental entities: A reexamination of childhood realism. *Child Development, 57,* 910–923.

Wellman, H. M., & Johnson, C. N. (1979). Understanding of mental processes: A developmental study of remember and forget. *Child Development, 50,* 79–88.

Wimmer, H., & Perner, J. (1983). Beliefs about beliefs: Representation and constraining function of wrong beliefs in young children's understanding of deception. *Cognition, 13*, 41–68.

Zentall, T. R., Roper, K. L., & Sherburne, L. M. (1995). Most directed forgetting in pigeons can be attributed to the absence of reinforcement on forget trials during training or to other procedural artifacts. *Journal of the Experimental Analysis of Behavior, 63*, 127–137.

Section *III*

Experiential Metacognition

10

The Experience of Thinking
Metacognitive Ease, Fluency, and Context

LAWRENCE J. SANNA and KRISTJEN B. LUNDBERG

Only so much do I know, as I have lived.

Ralph Waldo Emerson, "The American Scholar" (1837)

INTRODUCTION

People's thoughts are accompanied by a variety of metacognitive experiences—subjective experiences of thinking or thinking processes—which influence the conclusions that are drawn from what they are thinking about. As when watching a sunrise in the physical world we not only notice the heightening trajectory but also experience the sun's beauty, warmth, and light, so too in the psychological world do we not only consider the content of our thoughts but also experience whether our thinking is easy, fluent, and associated with emotions or bodily sensations. There are many perspectives that describe how people form judgments on the basis of declarative information, such as the content of thoughts that come to mind and are applied at the time of judgment (for reviews, see Förster & Liberman, 2007; Higgins, 1996; Wyer & Srull, 1989). However, there is more to thinking than just *what* comes to mind—such as experiential information like metacognitive experiences that also affect judgments (for reviews, see Alter & Oppenheimer, 2009; Jost, Kruglanski, & Nelson, 1998; Koriat, 1993; Petty, Briñol, Tormala, & Wegener, 2007; Schwarz, Sanna, Skurnik, & Yoon, 2007). As in the Emerson quote opening this chapter, knowing is imparted through experiencing.

We focus our chapter on people's metacognitive experiences of "ease"—namely, the ease or difficulty of thought generation and retrieval, the fluency of processing information, and the contextual theories that people hold about the self and/or external world that are used to interpret these experiences. Generating thoughts, retrieving examples, and processing new information can be experienced subjectively on a continuum from easy to difficult. It is critical to understand metacognitive experiences because they often produce surprising, counterintuitive effects by qualifying—even reversing—consequences predicted on the basis of thought content alone.

Viewed in this way, one approach to characterizing metacognition that is in line with the theme of this book is that there is a first level of primary cognition, including declarative information such as thought content, and a second level of metacognitive experiences that reflect on the first level, including experiential feelings of ease, fluency, emotions, and bodily sensations. Metacognitive experiences, along with their interpretation in particular contexts, influence the conclusions that people draw from what they are thinking about beyond thought content. Human judgment thus cannot be fully understood without accounting for metacognitive experiences.

The first section of our chapter addresses ease of thought generation and retrieval, and the second section addresses fluency of processing information. Both sections highlight how numerous variables, ranging from the nature of the task at hand to a person's bodily sensations, potentially affect subjective ease or difficulty. The third section addresses some of the varied contexts that further influence people's interpretations of ease experiences. Throughout, we inform our discussions with reference to a general model of human judgment and metacognitive experiences (Figure 10.1; see also Sanna & Schwarz, 2006, 2007; Schwarz et al., 2007). This model suggests that experiences of ease and fluency can be more fully understood within the framework of (a) declarative information such as accessible thought content, (b) experiential information such as the metacognitive experiences, (c) perceived informational value of experiences, and (d) naïve theories used to interpret experiences. The chapter concludes by noting relations between metacognitive ease and other phenomena.

METACOGNITIVE MODEL OF JUDGMENT

We suggest that judgments are a joint function of thought content (accessible declarative information), and accompanying metacognitive experiences (associated experiential information; the top oval in Figure 10.1). As a default, people consider metacognitive experiences relevant to what they are thinking about; otherwise, why would they be having these particular experiences right now while thinking about this issue? Hence, people will draw on their metacognitive experiences as a source of information that qualifies the implications of accessible thought content (lower left-hand box, following the solid lines).[1]

Exactly what people conclude from their metacognitive experiences depends on the nature of the experience (e.g., ease of thought generation or retrieval, processing fluency, emotions, bodily sensations) and on the particular naïve theory of the self and/or external world that is applied (the context represented by the perimeter box). However, if the informational value of the metacognitive experience to the judgment at hand is discredited or discounted (e.g., Sanna & Schwarz,

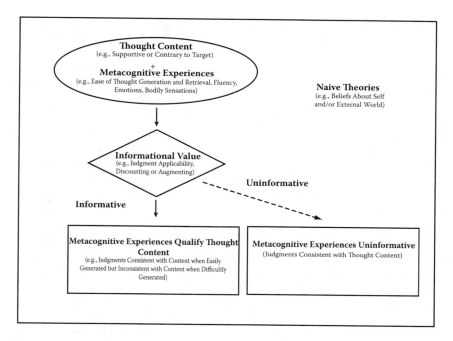

Figure 10.1 Model of human judgment and metacognitive experiences. Solid arrows indicate the default path (i.e., metacognitive experiences are informative and qualify judgments); dashed arrow indicates the path where metacognitive experiences are rendered uninformative to the judgment at hand. (Adapted from Sanna, L. J., & Schwarz, N. 2006. *Current Directions in Psychological Science, 15,* 172–176; Sanna, L. J., & Schwarz, N. 2007. *Social Cognition, 25,* 185–202; and Schwarz, N. et al. 2007. *Advances in Experimental Social Psychology, 39,* 127–161.)

2003), judgments will be based solely on accessible declarative information, such as thought content alone (lower right-hand box, following the dashed arrow). Each of these components and its operation are described in more detail within the following sections.

EASE OF THOUGHT GENERATION AND RETRIEVAL

Metacognitive experiences pertaining to ease of thought generation and retrieval influence a wide range of judgments, following the seminal research pitting accessible thought content against accessibility experiences by Schwarz et al. (1991; for a review, see Schwarz, 1998). If only thought content mattered, people's judgments should be consistent with what comes to mind to the extent that more thoughts are generated or examples are retrieved. However, empirically, exactly the opposite happens. For example, people infer that they are less assertive after recalling many rather than few examples of assertiveness (Schwarz et al., 1991), conclude that they are in less close relationships when listing many rather than few instances of closeness (Broemer, 2001), hold attitudes less confidently when listing many rather than few supportive arguments (Haddock, Rothman, Reber, & Schwarz, 1999), and like products less when more positive attributes are brought to mind (Wänke, Bohner, & Jurowitsch, 1997). These findings are opposite to that which would be predicted on the basis of thought content alone, but are readily predicted by accounting for metacognitive experiences of ease.

The importance of metacognitive experiences can be exemplified by research on the emergence and attenuation of bias, such as hindsight bias. Hindsight bias (Fischhoff, 1975) refers to people's belief that they "knew it all along" after outcomes are known in contrast to when outcomes are unknown, such as when making foresight predictions. Although there are many reasons for the bias, most theories share the presumption that hindsight bias will be greater when many rather than few reasons for the known outcome come to mind (for reviews, see Christensen-Szalanski & Willham, 1991; Guilbault, Bryant, Posavac, & Brockway, 2004; Hawkins & Hastie, 1990). Conversely, thinking about alternative outcomes in an attempt "to convince oneself that it might have turned out otherwise" (Fischhoff, 1982, p. 343) is the most frequently recommended debiasing strategy for eliminating hindsight bias. However, an exclusive focus on thought content misses the important role of metacognitive experiences in judgment and ignores the fact that this debiasing strategy could profoundly backfire.

Such an effect was demonstrated by Sanna, Schwarz, and Small (2002; see also Sanna, Schwarz, & Stocker, 2002). For example, Sanna, Schwarz, and Small (2002, Exp. 1) asked participants to read a story of a battle in the British–Gurkha war (Fischhoff, 1975) and were told that the British won. Some participants listed either two or 10 thoughts supporting this outcome (British winning), whereas other participants listed either two or 10 thoughts supporting the alternative outcome (Gurkha winning). Following the previously discussed logic, if only thought content mattered, hindsight bias should be greater when listing 10 rather than two thoughts supporting a British victory (known outcome); conversely, hindsight bias should be lesser when listing 10 rather than two thoughts supporting a Gurkha victory (alternative outcome).

However, exactly the opposite happened (see Figure 10.2): Listing more thoughts favoring the known outcome, experienced as difficult, *decreased* hindsight bias; listing more thoughts favoring alternative outcomes, likewise experienced as difficult, *increased* hindsight bias (for reviews, see Sanna, 2007; Sanna & Schwarz, 2006). These findings were replicated for other well-known biases, such as planning fallacy, affective forecasting impact bias, and confidence changes over time (Sanna & Schwarz, 2004).

Several lines of research indicate that these findings are due to metacognitive experiences and not, for example, to differences in the quality of thoughts listed:

- In related research, external raters find no quality differences between the first and last two examples listed (Schwarz et al., 1991).
- Yoked participants who merely read thoughts generated by others—who are deprived of the generation experience—are more influenced by thought numbers, in contrast to those who list them (Wänke, Bless, & Biller, 1996).

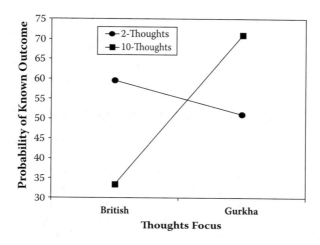

Figure 10.2   Mean probability of known outcome in percentages (0%–100% scale). All participants were told that the British won. British focus thus represents the known outcome, whereas Gurkha focus represents the alternative outcome. (Adapted from Sanna, L. J. et al. 2002, Exp. 1. *Memory & Cognition, 30*, 1288–1296.)

• Conceptually identical effects are obtained when holding constant thought numbers and manipulating feelings of difficulty via bodily sensations (Sanna, Schwarz, & Small, 2002, Exp. 2), facial feedback from contracting the corrugator muscle resulting in a furrowed brow, conveying a sense of mental effort paralleling difficult thought listing (e.g., Strack & Neumann, 2000).

Replicating the prior hindsight bias pattern, participants listing five thoughts favoring a British victory (known outcome) considered a British victory less likely when furrowing their brows than when they did not; participants listing five thoughts favoring a Gurkha victory (alternative outcome) considered a British victory more likely when furrowing their brows than when they did not (Sanna, Schwarz, & Small, 2002, Exp. 2).

Summary

Metacognitive experiences relating to ease or difficulty of thought generation and retrieval influence judgments across a wide variety of domains. These experiences are important to consider because they provide information in their own right and qualify—even reverse—the conclusions that people draw from thought content. As the hindsight bias examples illustrate, thinking about an issue only results in bias when supportive reasons come to mind easily; conversely, thinking about alternatives only attenuates bias when contrary reasons come to mind easily.

In contrast, when thought generation or retrieval is difficult, people's conclusions are opposite to the implications of accessible thought content, even to the extent of producing a backfiring of a frequently recommended debiasing strategy.

Metacognitive experiences of ease or difficulty may be produced not only by the thought generation task itself or by manipulating bodily sensations like facial feedback, but also by a host of other variables (for a review, see Schwarz, 2004). In short, judgments resulting from thought generation and retrieval cannot be fully understood without accompanying metacognitive ease experiences.

FLUENCY OF PROCESSING INFORMATION

Numerous variables can also influence the metacognitive experiences people have when processing new information, known as *processing fluency* (for reviews, see Jacoby, Kelley, & Dywan, 1989; Oppenheimer, 2008; Schwarz, 2004). These variables include perceptual, linguistic, conceptual, or embodied cognitive factors, among others; in fact, viewed broadly, thought generation and retrieval ease may be classified as types of fluency (for a review, see Alter & Oppenheimer, 2009). Processing fluency affects a wide range of judgments. For example, when processing is fluent versus disfluent, people judge statements as truer (McGlone & Tofighbakhsh, 2000), infer that names are more famous (Jacoby, Kelley, Brown, & Jasechko, 1989), conclude that examples are better category members (Whittlesea & Leboe, 2000), and assume more social consensus (Weaver, Garcia, Schwarz, & Miller, 2007). Importantly, people may draw such conclusions even when processing fluency is due solely to factors unrelated to the actual judgments at hand, like high figure–ground contrast, easy-to-read print font, rhyming presentation format, or preceding semantic primes (Schwarz et al., 2007). Metacognitive experiences of fluency are generated by so many cognitive operations that they could potentially influence judgments in almost any situation (Alter & Oppenheimer, 2009).

The importance of fluency experiences can be exemplified by research on feelings of familiarity in various judgment domains. Familiar information is easier to process than novel information. Presumably informed by this correct observation, people also draw the reverse inference and conclude from ease of processing that information must be familiar. Thus, any number of variables that affect processing fluency may influence the subjective sense of familiarity (for a review, see Schwarz et al., 2007). For example, the illusion of truth effect finds that statements are viewed as truer simply because they are repeated often (Begg, Anas, & Farinacci, 1992). Skurnik, Yoon, Park, and Schwarz (2005) presented younger and older adults with health-related statements (e.g., "aspirin destroys tooth enamel") labeled true or false one, two, or three times. (All statements were, in fact, true.)

Both groups correctly recognized statements as labeled true or false immediately after presentation. However, after a 3-day delay, warnings backfired and became recommendations for older adults: That is, they were more likely to infer a statement was true the more times it was presented, whether or not it was originally labeled true or false. Older adults, who show a decreasing ability to remember context, could not recall whether the statement was originally marked true or false, but they still experienced the more frequently presented statements as highly familiar, leading them to accept them as true.

Exploring processing fluency in hindsight bias, Werth and Strack (2003) exposed participants to general knowledge questions and answers (e.g., "How high is the Eiffel Tower?"—"300 m") and asked them to report what they would have answered had they not been given the solutions. Questions and answers were presented in colors that were either easy or difficult to read against a background. Participants believed more strongly that they "knew" the correct answer all along when the material was easy rather than difficult to read—after all, the answer would not feel "familiar" had they not known it earlier.

Harley, Carlsen, and Loftus (2004) identified a visual hindsight bias that is similarly driven by processing fluency. Participants were asked to identify degraded photos of celebrity faces as they were resolved to full clarity, and then they predicted how others would perform at this task. Having just seen the faces, participants mistook their own processing fluency to mean that naïve observers would identify the faces earlier or that others "saw the faces all along." As with thought generation and retrieval ease, fluent processing of outcomes increased hindsight bias, whereas disfluent processing of outcomes decreased hindsight bias—and even small changes in variables like readability of the print or visual clarity affected people's judgments.

Fluency-based impressions of familiarity can also impact risk judgments. It stands to reason that if something is familiar and elicits no negative memories, then it has not hurt us in the past. For example, Song and Schwarz (2009) presented to participants a series of 12-letter words identified as food additives and asked them to rate how hazardous or harmful the substance was. Easy-to-pronounce names (e.g., magnalroxate) were rated as less harmful than difficult-to-pronounce names (e.g., hnegripitrom). Additionally, this effect was mediated by the perceived novelty of the names.

Alter and Oppenheimer (2006) similarly found that, in the absence of other diagnostic information, people will use the fluency of a stock's name and ticker symbol to infer risk and predict future performance. For real-life initial public offerings of companies listed on the New York Stock Exchange and American Stock Exchange, those with easy-to-pronounce ticker symbols (e.g., KAR) outperformed those with difficult-to-pronounce ticker symbols (e.g., RDO). Although this difference was largest on the first day of trading ($85.35 favoring fluent stocks per $1,000 investment), the fluent stocks still outperformed the disfluent stocks by a margin of $20.25 a year later. Thus, fluency of pronunciation, a variable that is seemingly irrelevant to the actual judgment task at hand (e.g., choosing among stock investment options), affected people's perceptions of risk.

Summary

People's judgments are influenced by whether information is easy or difficult to process in ways that are not predicted by knowing only declarative information. As our examples illustrate, people infer that statements are more truthful simply because they have been presented more often, that they or others knew outcomes all along simply because they are easy to read or clearly visible, and that assumed risk is less simply because food additives or stock-ticker names are easy to pronounce. Metacognitive experiences of fluency or disfluency may be influenced not only by the manipulations illustrated in our examples but also by a whole host of other variables (for a review, see Alter & Oppenheimer, 2009).

As with thought generation and retrieval ease, people's metacognitive experiences of fluency are critical in determining judgments. When the object of judgment can be fluently processed, people's conclusions are consistent with the content of their thoughts; when the object of judgment is disfluent to process, conclusions are opposite to the content of their thoughts. This is true even when processing fluency is due solely to factors unrelated to the actual judgment tasks at hand. Because metacognitive experiences of fluency are ubiquitous across so many cognitive operations, they may be generated by nearly any form of thinking (Oppenheimer, 2008).

INTERPRETING METACOGNITIVE EXPERIENCES IN CONTEXT

As noted earlier, people draw on both declarative and experiential information by default, resulting in the interaction of thought content and metacognitive experiences illustrated in Figure 10.1. However, the meaning of metacognitive experiences is malleable and must be interpreted within context. On a general level, this can be seen by the diverse judgments that are influenced by metacognitive ease experiences. For example, in addition to those already described, wide-ranging inferences about bicycle usage (Aarts & Dijksterhuis, 1999), liking for politicians (Haddock, 2002), heart disease vulnerability (Rothman & Schwarz, 1998), attributions of intelligence (Oppenheimer, 2006), and temporal event distance (Sanna, Chang, & Carter, 2004), among many others, are influenced by metacognitive experiences of ease or difficulty. In short, the judgmental target focuses people on the most meaningful interpretations of their metacognitive experiences; for example, when people are thinking about bicycle usage, metacognitive experiences will correspondingly be interpreted as pertaining to bicycle usage unless there is reason to question this inference. Hence, on a specific level, the impact of metacognitive experiences is also a function of its perceived informational value.

Perceived Informational Value

Beginning with Schwarz et al. (1991), numerous studies have shown that once people attribute metacognitive experiences of ease or difficulty to a source that is irrelevant to the judgment task at hand, metacognitive experiences no longer influence judgments (dashed arrow from diamond in Figure 10.1). This logic is in line with broader proposals that people will generally use any subjective experiences, like moods, emotions, bodily sensations, and so on, as a cue to judgment by default unless they become aware that the subjective experience is due to a source that is irrelevant to the judgment task at hand (for a review, see Schwarz & Clore, 2007). For example, Schwarz et al. (1991) found that participants used experienced thought generation ease to guide their judgments of self-assertiveness, unless the experimenter drew their attention to distracting background music. Under these conditions, participants attributed the difficulty of retrieving many examples of assertiveness to the music playing rather than to their own lack of assertiveness. That is, judgments were no longer influenced by metacognitive experiences. Participants instead relied on the numbers of assertiveness examples they retrieved, or thought content. Many other contextual variables can analogously influence people's disuse of metacognitive experiences (for reviews, see Schwarz, 1998, 2004).

Like attributions made to external sources, attributions made to internal sources, such as one's own lack of knowledge, can render metacognitive experiences uninformative for judgments unrelated to one's knowledge (see Schwarz, 1998). Sanna and Schwarz (2003) provided direct evidence for this in a study of hindsight bias during the 2000 U.S. presidential election. Participants were asked to predict the outcome of the popular vote 1 day prior to the November 7 election. Following an extended court battle over disputed election outcomes in Florida, the Democratic candidate, Gore, conceded the election to the Republican candidate, Bush, on December 13, 2000. On December 14, participants were asked to recall their preelection predictions, made on November 6. The actual election result was that the Gore–Lieberman ticket led the Bush–Cheney ticket by a small popular vote difference of 0.32%. Prior to the election, participants had predicted a clear victory for Gore–Lieberman, with a lead of 4.71%. After the election, participants who were asked merely to recall their preelection prediction recalled that they did predict a Gore–Lieberman win, but at a much smaller margin of 0.58%. This result replicates hindsight bias.

Further, participants who listed 12 ways that Gore–Lieberman could have won the election before recalling their predictions concluded that they had never expected them to win by a large margin (0.61%)—even though they had predicted a large margin of victory for Gore–Lieberman over Bush–Cheney prior to the election (5.26%). In other words, participants who found it difficult to generate thoughts supporting a Gore–Lieberman win now concluded that it was less likely in comparison with their initial predictions. However, more importantly here, when other participants were first asked how much they knew about politics before making judgments, they attributed their difficulty of generating 12 thoughts to their own lack of political expertise, rendering metacognitive experiences uninformative with regard to Gore–Lieberman's preelection likelihood of winning. In this case, participants drew on the content of their thoughts despite their difficulty and concluded that Gore–Lieberman could have won instead—even *overestimating* the margin of victory that they predicted for Gore–Lieberman prior to the election (7.52%). A parallel study, using the outcome of a college football game, produced comparable results (see Sanna & Schwarz, 2003).

People do not require explicit encouragement to discount their metacognitive experiences, as in the preceding examples. Instead, they sometimes spontaneously discount the informativeness of metacognitive experiences when they recognize on their own that it emanates from an irrelevant source. For example, Oppenheimer (2004) found that people underestimated the prevalence of surnames like Bush and Clinton (U.S. presidents) relative to equally common but not famous names like Stevenson and Woodall. People discounted the role of name availability when there was an obvious reason for the names being mentally available, leading to an overcorrection for fame on commonality judgments. Thus, discounting can be quite nuanced and context specific.

However, despite diverse instantiations and whether encouraged or spontaneous, informativeness has strikingly uniform effects on judgments. When people attribute their metacognitive experiences to an irrelevant source, they discount it as useful information regardless of how the inference is generated. Further, although most research has focused on discounting metacognitive experiences, the use of such experiences presumably can be augmented under certain conditions. For example, people may discount low ease or disfluency when it is attributed to an inhibiting cause (e.g., noise next door), but they may augment high ease or fluency as particularly informative under these conditions (for reviews of relevant findings in diverse domains, see Kelley & Rhodes, 2002; Schwarz, 2004).

Naïve Theories of Self and/or World

Just as context helps determine the perceived informational value of metacognitive experiences, so too does context help to determine the meaning of experiences that are viewed as relevant. A growing body of research indicates that the inferences people draw from given metacognitive experiences depend on the naïve theories of self and/or external world that are brought to bear on the task. These naïve theories can also be quite malleable (for reviews, see Alter & Oppenheimer, 2009; Petty et al., 2007; Schwarz, 2004; Schwarz et al., 2007; represented by the perimeter box in Figure 10.1).

For example, Winkielman and Schwarz (2001) asked participants to recall either four or 12 childhood events that were happy or sad. Some participants were told that unpleasant events are poorly represented in memory, whereas others were told that pleasant events are poorly represented. Participants recalling 12 events (a difficult task) inferred their childhood was less happy when the suggested naïve theory implied that unpleasant events were harder to remember than when told that pleasant events were harder to remember. Briñol, Petty, and Tormala (2006) similarly demonstrated that subjective interpretations of metacognitive ease experiences could be varied depending upon whether the naïve theory that was suggested to participants implied that it was either a positive or negative cue for attitude change.

Because influences of naïve theories are often subtle, context specific, and malleable, they are sometimes difficult to specify. However, within the same domain, people often share common naïve theories that lead them to the same conclusions, irrespective of how the metacognitive experience is instantiated. For example, much of the previously described research can be interpreted as compatible with a common naïve theory at the heart of Tversky and Kahneman's (1973) availability heuristic: When there are many (few) examples or reasons, it is easy (difficult) to bring some to mind. Applying this particular naïve theory, people infer from the experienced ease or difficulty that there are many or few reasons of the sought after type, giving rise to the effects reviewed previously. Hence, the metacognitive experience of ease or difficulty of thought generation or retrieval and the fluency or disfluency of processing new information leads to judgments consistent with the implications of thought content when the experience is easy and to judgments that are opposite to the implications of thought content when the experience is difficult. Thought generation ease may also increase confidence in thought content, and thought generation difficulty may decrease confidence in thought content (Tormala, Petty, & Briñol, 2002).

People may hold a variety of other naïve theories. For example, one naïve theory holds that recent events are easier to recall than distant events, making ease of recall a cue for temporal distance (Sanna et al., 2004; Sanna, Chang, Carter, & Small, 2006; see also Ross & Wilson, 2002). Other naïve theories hold that important events are easier to recall than unimportant ones and that thought generation is easier when one has high rather than low expertise, making ease a cue for importance and expertise (e.g., Schwarz, Cho, & Xu, 2005). Drawing on these naïve theories, people may consider ease of thought generation or fluency more informative and difficulty or disfluency less informative when the event is distant rather than recent and unimportant rather than important and when they lack rather than have domain expertise or confidence. In short, different naïve theories suggest that people's metacognitive experiences can have very different implications depending on the context. Given that the meanings of metacognitive experiences appear to be highly malleable, it would seem that critically important questions for future research are to further understand the determinants of their application and use.

Summary

The reviewed research indicates that the meaning of metacognitive experiences is malleable and must be interpreted within context. This can be seen by the diverse judgments influenced by metacognitive experiences. The judgmental target normally focuses people on the most meaningful interpretation of metacognitive experiences, unless there is reason to question its relevance. Thus, the impact of metacognitive experiences is a function of perceived informational value. Once people attribute metacognitive experiences of ease or difficulty to a source irrelevant to the judgment task at hand, they no longer influence judgments; this is in line with general proposals about subjective experiences (see Schwarz & Clore, 2007).

Naïve theories of the self and/or external world also influence how people interpret metacognitive experiences that are viewed as relevant to the judgment task. This malleability of meaning sometimes makes accounting for naïve theories difficult. However, within context, people often share common naïve theories. For example, much of the research in this chapter is compatible with a naïve theory at the heart of the availability heuristic. This can imply frequency, probability, recency, and so on, depending upon the context. In short, naïve theories influence the specific meaning that people derive from metacognitive ease experiences.

FURTHER CONJECTURES AND CONCLUSIONS

In this final section, we offer some further conjectures relating metacognitive experiences to other phenomena and suggest some future research. Our proposed model can account for previous content-focused theories, as well as make novel and unique predictions. It converges with content-based models by predicting thought-content congruent judgments when metacognitive experiences imply ease or fluency or when the relevance of the metacognitive experience to the judgment at hand is discredited. It differs from content-based models by predicting that metacognitive experiences implying ease or fluency are more influential when they are considered informative than when they are not. And, most importantly, it makes predictions that are opposite to thought-content based models when metacognitive experiences imply difficulty or disfluency.

While cognition and metacognition are used to refer to primary and secondary cognition, thinking does not happen in a vacuum. Metacognitive experiences will naturally accompany nearly all forms of thinking (Oppenheimer, 2008; Schwarz, 2004). That is, the experience of thinking includes metacognitive experiences, just as jumping into a swimming pool full of water includes the experiences of wetness, buoyancy, and temperature. Metacognitive experience *is* part and parcel of the thinking process.

Metacognition Over Time

To date, little is known about metacognitive experiences over time. This may be an especially promising avenue for future research because most real-life decisions transpire over time. In contrast, research has thus far mainly considered metacognitive influences at only one point: when making judgments immediately after generating thoughts (for a review, see Schwarz et al., 2007). Practically, investigating metacognitive experiences over time is important because people often come back to earlier generated reasons, either by formally reading previously generated lists or by simply reconsidering thoughts (for a review, see Plous, 1993). Theoretically, this is important because, as suggested by Robinson and Clore (2002), subjective experiences are not well represented in memory and quickly fade over time.

Consistent with this idea, Sanna, Kennedy, Chang, and Miceli (2009, Exp. 1) found that, after a University of North Carolina men's basketball win over rival Duke University, students viewed the game outcome as less inevitable when generating 12 versus 3 thoughts supporting a Carolina win a day after (see Figure 10.3). Hence, judgments were influenced by metacognitive experiences, consistent with results described previously. However, when participants merely read earlier generated reasons a week afterward, judgments were consistent with the numbers of thoughts listed, or thought content. Thus, metacognitive experiences apparently faded over time, and students came to completely different conclusions depending upon when judgments were made (see Sanna et al., 2009). There also might be instances when metacognitive experiences are relatively stable over time, such as if thoughts accompanied by feelings of ease are better integrated in memory (Petty, Briñol, & DeMarree, 2007). Future research could explore these possibilities.

Changes in other metacognitive experiences, such as moods or emotions (Schwarz & Clore, 2007), may also occur over time and influence conclusions that people draw from thinking. For example, suppose initial exposure to an outcome elicits feelings of high surprise and curtails hindsight bias (e.g., Ofir & Mazursky, 1997). But surprising events also may elicit more explanatory activity than unsurprising events as people attempt to make sense of what happened (for reviews, see Pezzo & Pezzo, 2007; Wilson & Gilbert, 2008). When plausible explanations for outcomes later come to mind easily (or if someone else provides explanations), hindsight bias may creep in: "I was surprised but I should have expected this."

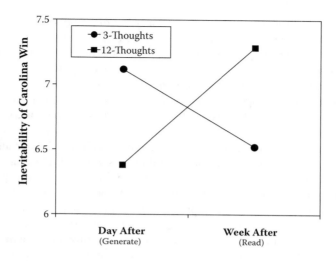

Figure 10.3   Mean rated inevitability of a University of North Carolina at Chapel Hill men's basketball win (0- to 10-point scale). Participants generated thoughts supporting a Carolina win over Duke. Participants in the 3- and 12-thoughts conditions generated thoughts 1 day after the game and read previously generated thoughts 1 week afterward, respectively. (Adapted from Sanna, L. J. et al. 2009, Exp. 1. *Journal of Experimental Social Psychology, 45*, 940–946.)

This may be particularly likely when outcomes are especially important, striking, or impactful. At first, the initial shock of the outcome elicits strong surprise, and the conclusion is that events were very unpredictable. However, as people make sense of what happened, potential causes become highly accessible, which may result in the conclusion that the event could have been foreseen and, in fact, might or even should have been prevented. Public discourse following the 9/11 terror attacks in the United States is consistent with this conjecture (for a review, see Wirtz, 2006). Media coverage may further change the metacognitive experiences of ease associated with representing event outcomes and their causes through frequent repetition.

Mere Exposure and Affective Responses

The experience of ease or fluency may be experienced as pleasant, eliciting positive affect that can even be measured physiologically (Winkielman & Cacioppo, 2001). Positive affect derived from fluency may relate to other classic phenomena, such as the mere exposure effect (Zajonc, 1968; for a review, see Bornstein, 1989), whereby repeated exposure to an initially neutral stimulus leads to gradually increased liking and positive evaluations.[2] In fact, several researchers have suggested that mere exposure effects are due to increased processing fluency and/or feelings of familiarity that result from repeated exposure (Bornstein & D'Agostino, 1994; Jacoby, Kelley, & Dywan, 1989), although these have not always been labeled as metacognitive experiences per se (see Alter & Oppenheimer, 2009).

For example, the perceptual fluency/attribution model of Bornstein and D'Agostino (1994) may explain why mere exposure effects are stronger when people are unaware that they have been exposed to the stimuli. People prefer stimuli more under brief (e.g., 5 ms) versus longer (e.g., 500 ms) exposure times. The interpretation is that once people attribute fluency to prior exposure (e.g., recognizing more exposure under longer presentation times), using ease as a cue to liking is discounted (Bornstein & D'Agostino, 1994)—an idea that also appears compatible with our present model.

Following this reasoning, future research may examine whether any variable that increases metacognitive experiences influences affect and evaluations. There is accumulating evidence for this, even under conditions of single exposure. For example, Reber, Winkielman, and Schwarz (1998) presented to participants pictures of everyday objects and manipulated processing fluency via visual priming. Depending on condition, pictures of target objects were preceded by subliminally presented highly degraded contours of either the target picture or a different picture. The target pictures that were preceded by matched contours were recognized faster, suggesting high fluency, and were liked more than pictures preceded by mismatched contours. Moreover, the effects of processing fluency were eliminated when participants attributed their positive affect to music playing in the background (for a review of implications for broader aesthetic judgments, see Reber, Schwarz, & Winkielman, 2004).

Also interesting is that speedy thinking can similarly produce positive affect (for a review, see Pronin & Jacobs, 2008). Thus, fluent processing elicits positive affect and fast thinking elicits positive affect. Although thought speed may be influenced by variables apart from fluency, exploring further relationships between these two perspectives could prove interesting, as is whether fluency (and perhaps fast thinking) may sometimes also lead to negative affect (see Note 2).

Metacognition and Processing Strategies

Finally, future research should explore the possible implications of metacognitive experiences for processing strategies. On a general level, people can process information in a heuristic, automatic, and effortless way (System 1) or in a systematic, controlled, and effortful way (System 2; for a review, see Kahneman, 2003). To date, not much is known about how metacognitive experiences influence the choice of specific processing strategies. However, given strong parallels with other sources of experiential information (e.g., moods, emotions, bodily sensations; Schwarz & Clore, 2007), it is intriguing to speculate that metacognitive experiences would likewise exert influences on strategy choice.

Generally, information suggesting to people that the situation is benign induces more heuristic, automatic, and effortless processing, whereas information suggesting to people that the situation is problematic induces more systematic, controlled, and effortful processing (see Schwarz, 2004). This may be because benign situations do not necessitate our immediate attention and effort while problematic situations do. Difficulty in processing new information may analogously be taken to mean that something is wrong and that greater effort is required to resolve the problem, with processing disfluency resulting in more detail-oriented, effortful, and analytic strategies.

Song and Schwarz (2008) provided support for this idea using the Moses illusion (see Erickson & Mattson, 1981). That is, when people are asked, "How many animals of each kind did Moses take on the ark?" most answer "two," even though the biblical protagonist is Noah. However, when participants read the Moses question in difficult-to-read print font, as opposed to easy-to-read font, they more likely take an analytic approach and report that the question cannot be answered as asked because Moses did not build an ark. Similarly, Alter, Oppenheimer, Epley, and Eyre (2007) found that manipulations that increased processing disfluency improved participants' performances on reasoning tasks that benefited from analytic processing.

Other evidence is consistent with the idea that low motivation, manipulated through low personal relevance or happy moods (Rothman & Schwarz, 1998; Ruder & Bless, 2003), fosters greater reliance on using metacognitive experiences of ease or fluency. But still other evidence suggests that high motivation fosters greater reliance on using ease or fluency in judgments (Tormala et al., 2002; Wänke & Bless, 2000). It is possible that feelings of ease may affect judgments via multiple processes.

For example, when motivation and ability to think are low, ease may operate as a simple cue (e.g., availability), but when motivation and ability to think are high, ease may operate by affecting thought-confidence (Petty & Briñol, 2008). Likewise, in the few thoughts versus many thoughts paradigm, ease of retrieval may affect the proportion of requested versus unrequested cognitions (Tormala, Falces, Briñol, & Petty, 2007), although this may have difficulty with findings that do not vary thought numbers (e.g., varying facial expressions [Sanna, Schwarz, & Small, 2002] or print font [Alter et al., 2007]). Clearly, the degree to which metacognitive experiences influence processing strategies and to which motivations influence the use of metacognitive experiences is ripe for more integrative research.

CODA

Several perspectives have identified the importance of accessible declarative information, such as thought content, in influencing people's judgments (for reviews, see Förster & Liberman, 2007; Higgins, 1996; Wyer & Srull, 1989). However, research has increasingly identified the equally important influence of experiential information, like people's metacognitive experiences, in judgments (for reviews, see Alter & Oppenheimer, 2009; Jost et al., 1998; Koriat, 1993; Petty, Briñol, Tormala, et al., 2007; Schwarz et al., 2007).

Our main objective in this chapter was to review some of the accumulating evidence on metacognitive experiences of "ease"—namely, the ease or difficulty of thought generation and retrieval and fluency of processing information. People's naïve theories about the self and/or world further influence whether these metacognitive experiences are viewed as informative and how metacognitive experiences are interpreted. We used a general model of human judgment and metacognitive experiences as an organizing framework (see also Sanna & Schwarz, 2006, 2007; Schwarz et al., 2007), but we recognize that there can be other ways to characterize this growing literature. Nonetheless, our primary point remains: There is more to thinking than just what comes to mind. As in the Emerson quote opening this chapter, when it comes to thinking, it is also the *experience* that matters.

ACKNOWLEDGMENT

We thank the Better Decision Making (betterdecisionmaking.org) Laboratory members at the University of North Carolina at Chapel Hill and the editors of this book for their helpful comments on this chapter.

NOTES

1. Several other lines of research similarly demonstrate that the default process is that people presume that any thoughts that come to mind or feelings they are having while thinking about X are in fact "about" X; otherwise, why would they be having these thoughts or feelings at this point in time? Hence, people are likely to find their metacognitive experiences informative by default *unless* their attention is drawn to influences that call the informational value of those metacognitive experiences into question for the judgment at hand (for reviews, see Clore et al., 2001; Higgins, 1998; Schwarz & Clore, 2007).
2. This applies to initially neutral stimuli. For example, repeated exposure to initially negative stimuli can make those stimuli even more negative (Cacioppo & Petty, 1989; Grush, 1976). One possibility is that repeated exposure may increase the perceived validity of people's assessments, whether positive or negative (Kruglanski, Freund, & Bar-Tal, 1996).

REFERENCES

Aarts, H., & Dijksterhuis, A. (1999). How often did I do it? Experienced ease of retrieval and frequency estimates of past behavior. *Acta Psychologica, 103*, 77–89.

Alter, A. L., & Oppenheimer, D. M. (2006). Predicting short-term stock fluctuations by using processing fluency. *Proceedings of the National Academy of Sciences USA, 103*, 9369–9372.

Alter, A. L., & Oppenheimer, D. M. (2009). Uniting the tribes of fluency to form a metacognitive nation. *Personality and Social Psychology Review, 13*, 219–235.

Alter, A. L., Oppenheimer, D. M., Epley, N., & Eyre, R. N. (2007). Overcoming intuition: Metacognitive difficulty activates analytic reasoning. *Journal of Experimental Psychology: General, 136*, 569–576.

Begg, J. M., Anas, A., & Farinacci, S. (1992). Dissociation of processes in belief: Source recollection, statement familiarity, and the illusion of truth. *Journal of Experimental Psychology: General, 121*, 446–458.

Bornstein, R. F. (1989). Exposure and affect: Overview and meta-analysis of research 1968–1987. *Psychological Bulletin, 106*, 265–289.

Bornstein, R. F., & D'Agostino, P. R. (1994). The attribution and discounting of perceptual fluency: Preliminary tests of a perceptual fluency/attributional model of the mere exposure effect. *Social Cognition, 12*, 103–128.

Briñol, P., Petty, R. E., & Tormala, Z. (2006). The malleable meaning of subjective ease. *Psychological Science, 17*, 200–206.

Broemer, P. (2001). Ease of recall moderates the impact of relationship-related goals on judgments of interpersonal closeness. *Journal of Experimental Social Psychology, 37,* 261–266.

Cacioppo, J. T., & Petty, R. E. (1989). Effects of message repetition on argument processing, recall, and persuasion. *Basic and Applied Social Psychology, 10,* 3–12.

Christensen-Szalanski, J. J. J., & Willham, C. F. (1991). The hindsight bias: A meta-analysis. *Organizational Behavior and Human Decision Processes, 48,* 147–168.

Clore, G. L., Wyer, R. S., Dienes, B., Gasper, K., Gohm, C. L., & Isbell, L. (2001). Affective feelings as feedback: Some cognitive consequences. In L. L. Martin & G. L. Clore (Eds.), *Theories of mood and cognition: A user's handbook* (pp. 27–62). Mahwah, NJ: Lawrence Erlbaum Associates.

Emerson, R. W. (1837). The American scholar. Retrieved March 7, 2010, from http://www.emersoncentral.com/amscholar.htm

Erickson, T. A., & Mattson, M. F. (1981). From words to meaning: A semantic illusion. *Journal of Verbal Learning and Verbal Behavior, 20,* 540–552.

Fischhoff, B. (1975). Hindsight ≠ foresight: The effect of outcome knowledge on judgments under uncertainty. *Journal of Experimental Psychology: Human Perception and Performance, 1,* 288–299.

Fischhoff, B. (1982). Debiasing. In D. Kahneman, P. Slovic, & A. Tversky (Eds.), *Judgment under uncertainty: Heuristics and biases* (pp. 422–444). New York, NY: Cambridge University Press.

Förster, J., & Liberman, N. (2007). Knowledge activation. In A. Kruglanski & E. T. Higgins (Eds.), *Social psychology: Handbook of basic principles* (2nd ed., pp. 201–231). New York, NY: Guilford Press.

Guilbault, R. L., Bryant, F. B., Posavac, E. J., & Brockway, J. H. (2004). A meta-analysis of research on hindsight bias. *Basic and Applied Social Psychology, 26,* 103–117.

Grush, J. E. (1976). Attitude formation and mere exposure phenomena: A nonartifactual explanation of empirical findings. *Journal of Personality and Social Psychology, 33,* 281–290.

Haddock, G. (2002). It's easy to like or dislike Tony Blair: Accessibility experiences and the favorability of attitude judgments. *British Journal of Social Psychology, 93,* 257–267.

Haddock, G., Rothman, A. J., Reber, R., & Schwarz, N. (1999). Forming judgments of attitude certainty, intensity, and importance: The role of subjective experiences. *Personality and Social Psychology Bulletin, 25,* 771–782.

Harley, E. M., Carlsen, K. A., & Loftus, G. R. (2004). The "saw-it-all-along" effect: Demonstrations of visual hindsight bias. *Journal of Experimental Psychology: Learning, Memory, and Cognition, 30,* 960–968.

Hawkins, S. A., & Hastie, R. (1990). Hindsight: Biased judgments of past events after the outcomes are known. *Psychological Bulletin, 107,* 311–327.

Higgins, E. T. (1996). Knowledge activation: Accessibility, applicability, and salience. In E. T. Higgins & A. Kruglanski (Eds.), *Social psychology: Handbook of basic principles* (pp. 133–168). New York, NY: Guilford Press.

Higgins, E. T. (1998). The aboutness principle: A pervasive influence on human inference. *Social Cognition, 16,* 173–198.

Huntsinger, J. R. (in press). Mood and trust in intuition interactively orchestrate correspondence between implicit and explicit attitudes. *Personality and Social Psychology Bulletin.*

Jacoby, L. L., Kelley, C. M., Brown, J., & Jasechko, J. (1989). Becoming famous overnight: Limits on the ability to avoid unconscious influences of the past. *Journal of Personality and Social Psychology, 56,* 326–338.

Jacoby, L. L., Kelley, C. M., & Dywan, J. (1989). Memory attributions. In H. L. Roediger & F. I. M. Craik (Eds.), *Varieties of memory and consciousness: Essays in honor of Endel Tulving* (pp. 391–422). Hillsdale, NJ: Lawrence Erlbaum Associates.

Jost, J. T., Kruglanski, A. W., & Nelson, T. O. (1998). Social metacognition: An expansionist review. *Personality and Social Psychology Review, 2,* 137–154.

Kahneman, D. (2003). A perspective on judgment and choice: Mapping bounded rationality. *American Psychologist, 58,* 697–720.

Kelley, C. M., & Rhodes, M. G. (2002). Making sense and nonsense of experience: Attributions in memory and judgment. *The Psychology of Learning and Motivation, 41,* 293–320.

Koriat, A. (1993). How do we know what we know? The accessibility model of the feeling of knowing. *Psychological Review, 100,* 609–639.

Kruglanski, A. W., Freund, T., & Bar Tal, D. (1996). Motivational effects in the mere exposure paradigm. *European Journal of Social Psychology, 26,* 479–499.

McGlone, M. S., & Tofighbakhsh, J. (2000). Birds of a feather flock conjointly (?): Rhyme as reason in aphorisms. *Psychological Science, 11,* 424–428.

Ofir, C., & Mazursky, D. (1997). Does a surprising outcome reinforce or reverse the hindsight bias? *Organizational Behavior and Human Decision Processes, 69,* 51–57.

Oppenheimer, D. M. (2004). Spontaneous discounting of availability in fluency judgment tasks. *Psychological Science, 15,* 100–105.

Oppenheimer, D. M. (2006). Consequences of erudite vernacular utilized irrespective of necessity: Problems with using long words needlessly. *Applied Cognitive Psychology, 20,* 139–156.

Oppenheimer, D. M. (2008). The secret life of fluency. *Trends in Cognitive Sciences, 12,* 237–241.

Petty, R. E., & Briñol, P. (2008). Persuasion: From single to multiple to meta-cognitive processes. *Perspectives on Psychological Science, 3,* 137–147.

Petty, R. E., Briñol, P., & DeMarree, K. G. (2007). The meta-cognitive model (MCM) of attitudes: Implications for attitude measurement, change, and strength. *Social Cognition, 25,* 657–686.

Petty, R. E., Briñol, P., Tormala, Z. L., & Wegener, D. T. (2007). The role of metacognition in social judgment. In A. W. Kruglanski & E. T. Higgins (Eds.), *Social psychology: Handbook of basic principles* (2nd ed., pp. 254–284). New York, NY: Guilford Press.

Pezzo, M. V., & Pezzo, S. P. (2007). Making sense after failure: A motivated model of hindsight bias. *Social Cognition, 25,* 147–164.

Plous, S. (1993). *The psychology of judgment and decision making.* New York, NY: McGraw-Hill.

Pronin, E., & Jacobs, E. (2008). Thought speed, mood, and the experience of mental motion. *Perspectives on Psychological Science, 3,* 461–485.

Reber, R., Schwarz, N., & Winkielman, P. (2004). Processing fluency as aesthetic pleasure: Is beauty in the perceiver's processing experience? *Personality and Social Psychology Review, 8,* 364–382.

Reber, R., Winkielman, P., & Schwarz, N. (1998). Effects of perceptual fluency on affective judgments. *Psychological Science, 9,* 45–48.

Robinson, M. D., & Clore, G. L. (2002). Belief and feeling: Evidence for an accessibility model of emotion self-report. *Psychological Bulletin, 128,* 934–960.

Ross, M., & Wilson, A. E. (2002). It feels like yesterday: Self-esteem, valence of personal past experiences, and judgments of subjective distance. *Journal of Personality and Social Psychology, 82,* 792–803.

Rothman, A. J., & Schwarz, N. (1998). Constructing preferences of vulnerability: Personal relevance and the use of experiential information in health judgments. *Personality and Social Psychology Bulletin, 24,* 1053–1064.

Ruder, M., & Bless, H. (2003). Mood and the reliance on the ease of retrieval heuristic. *Journal of Personality and Social Psychology, 85,* 20–32.

Sanna, L. J. (2007). When imagination is difficult: Metacognitive experiences at the fault lines of reality. *Behavioral and Brain Sciences, 30,* 464–465.

Sanna, L. J., Chang, E. C., & Carter, S. E. (2004). All our troubles seem so far away: Temporal pattern to accessible alternatives and retrospective team appraisals. *Personality and Social Psychology Bulletin, 30,* 1359–1371.

Sanna, L. J., Chang, E. C., Carter, S. E., & Small, E. M. (2006). The future is now: Prospective temporal self-appraisals among defensive pessimists and optimists. *Personality and Social Psychology Bulletin, 32,* 727–739.

Sanna, L. J., Kennedy, L. A., Chang, E. C., & Miceli, P. M. (2009). When thoughts don't feel like they used to: Changing feelings of subjective ease in judgments of the past. *Journal of Experimental Social Psychology, 45,* 940–946.

Sanna, L. J., & Schwarz, N. (2003). Debiasing the hindsight bias: The role of accessibility experiences and (mis)attributions. *Journal of Experimental Social Psychology, 39,* 287–295.

Sanna, L. J., & Schwarz, N. (2004). Integrating temporal biases: The interplay of focal thoughts and accessibility experiences. *Psychological Science, 15,* 474–481.

Sanna, L. J., & Schwarz, N. (2006). Metacognitive experiences and human judgment: The case of hindsight bias and its debiasing. *Current Directions in Psychological Science, 15,* 172–176.

Sanna, L. J., & Schwarz, N. (2007). Metacognitive experiences and hindsight bias: It's not just the thought (content) that counts! *Social Cognition, 25,* 185–202.

Sanna, L. J., Schwarz, N., & Small, E. M. (2002). Accessibility experiences and the hindsight bias: I knew it all along versus it could never have happened. *Memory & Cognition, 30,* 1288–1296.

Sanna, L. J., Schwarz, N., & Stocker, S. L. (2002). When debiasing backfires: Accessible content and accessibility experiences in debiasing hindsight. *Journal of Experimental Psychology: Learning, Memory, and Cognition, 28,* 497–502.

Schwarz, N. (1998). Accessible content and accessibility experiences: The interplay of declarative and experiential information in judgment. *Personality and Social Psychology Review, 2,* 87–99.

Schwarz, N. (2004). Metacognitive experiences in consumer judgment and decision making. *Journal of Consumer Psychology, 14,* 332–348.

Schwarz, N., Bless, H., Strack, F., Klumpp, G., Rittenauer-Schatka, H., & Simons, A. (1991). Ease of retrieval as information: Another look at the availability heuristic. *Journal of Personality and Social Psychology, 61,* 195–202.

Schwarz, N., Cho, H., & Xu, J. (2005, July). *Diverging inferences from identical inputs: The role of naive theories.* Paper presented at the European Association of Experimental Social Psychology, Würzburg, Germany.

Schwarz, N., & Clore, G. L. (2007). Feelings and phenomenal experiences. In A. W. Kruglanski & E. T. Higgins (Eds.), *Social psychology: Handbook of basic principles* (2nd ed., pp. 385–407). New York, NY: Guilford Press.

Schwarz, N., Sanna, L. J., Skurnik, I., & Yoon, C. (2007). Metacognitive experiences and the intricacies of setting people straight: Implications for debiasing and public information campaigns. *Advances in Experimental Social Psychology, 39,* 127–161.

Skurnik, I., Yoon, C., Park, D. C., & Schwarz, N. (2005). How warnings about false claims become recommendations. *Journal of Consumer Research, 31,* 713–724.

Song, H., & Schwarz, N. (2008). Fluency and the detection of distortions: Low processing fluency attenuates the Moses illusion. *Social Cognition, 26,* 791–799.

Song, H., & Schwarz, N. (2009). If it's difficult to pronounce, it must be risky: Fluency, familiarity, and risk perception. *Psychological Science, 20,* 135–138.

Strack, F., & Neumann, R. (2000). Furrowing the brow may undermine perceived fame: The role of facial feedback in judgments of celebrity. *Personality and Social Psychology Bulletin, 26,* 762–768.

Tormala, Z. L., Falces, C., Briñol, P., & Petty, R. E. (2007). Ease of retrieval effects in social judgment: The role of unrequested cognitions. *Journal of Personality and Social Psychology, 93,* 143–157.

Tormala, Z. L., Petty, R. E., & Briñol, P. (2002). Ease of retrieval effects in persuasion: The roles of elaboration and thought confidence. *Personality and Social Psychology Bulletin, 28,* 1700–1712.

Tversky, A., & Kahneman, D. (1973). Availability: A heuristic for judging frequency and probability. *Cognitive Psychology, 5,* 207–232.

Wänke, M., & Bless, H. (2000). The effects of subjective ease of retrieval on attitudinal judgments: The moderating role of processing motivation. In H. Bless & J. P. Forgas (Eds.), *The message within: The role of subjective experience in social cognition and behavior* (pp. 143–161). Philadelphia, PA: Psychology Press.

Wänke, M., Bless, H., & Biller, B. (1996). Subjective experiences versus content of information in the construction of attitude judgments. *Personality and Social Psychology Bulletin, 22,* 1105–1113.

Wänke, M., Bohner, G., & Jurowitsch, A. (1997). There are many reasons to drive a BMW: Does imagined ease of argument generation influence attitudes? *Journal of Consumer Research, 24,* 170–177.

Weaver, K., Garcia, S. M., Schwarz, N., & Miller, D. T. (2007). Inferring the popularity of an opinion from its familiarity: A repetitive voice can sound like a chorus. *Journal of Personality and Social Psychology, 92,* 821–833.

Werth, L., & Strack, F. (2003). An inferential approach to the knew-it-all-along phenomenon. *Memory, 11,* 411–419.

Whittlesea, B. W. A., & Leboe, J. P. (2000). The heuristic basis of remembering ad classification: Fluency, generation, and resemblance. *Journal of Experimental Psychology: General, 129,* 84–106.

Wilson, T. D., & Gilbert, D. T. (2008). Explaining away: A model of affective adaptation. *Perspectives on Psychological Science, 3,* 370–386.

Winkielman, P., & Cacioppo, J. T. (2001). Mind at ease puts a smile on the face: Psychophysiological evidence that processing facilitation leads to positive affect. *Journal of Personality and Social Psychology, 81,* 989–1000.

Winkielman, P., & Schwarz, N. (2001). How pleasant was your childhood? Beliefs about memory shape inferences from experienced difficulty of recall. *Psychological Science, 12,* 176–179.

Wirtz, J. J. (2006). Responding to surprise. *Annual Review of Political Science, 9,* 45–65.

Wyer, R. S., & Srull, T. K. (1989). *Memory and cognition in its social context.* Hillsdale, NJ: Lawrence Erlbaum Associates.

Zajonc, R. B. (1968). Attitudinal effects of mere exposure. *Journal of Personality and Social Psychology, 9,* 1–27.

11

Emotion and Social Metacognition

JEFFREY R. HUNTSINGER and GERALD L. CLORE

Emotion is the atmosphere in which thought is steeped, that which lends to thought its tone or temperature, that to which thought is often indebted for half its power.

Hugh Reginald Haweis, "Schubert and Chopin" (1866, p. 92)

INTRODUCTION

Cognition concerns knowledge about the world, including how it is acquired, organized, and used (Neisser, 1976). It involves knowing that particular objects have particular attributes (e.g., that cats have sharp claws) and whether particular propositions are true or false (e.g., that tigers hate cinnamon). By contrast, metacognition concerns knowledge not about the world, but rather about one's own cognitive processes (Flavell, 1976, 1979; Koriat & Levy-Saldot, 1999). When a person notices that she is finding something difficult to learn, she is engaging in metacognition. This kind of metacognitive feedback is crucial for regulating one's thought processes. Noticing that one is finding something difficult to learn, for example, may lead one to take a different approach to the task.

In this chapter, we are concerned with the metacognitive functions of affect. The realization that one is making poor progress on a cognitive task is likely to elicit not only metacognitive thoughts but also affective feelings, and it is presumably those feelings that would actually motivate a change in tactics. Metacognitive thoughts can lead one to shift mental gears, but the beauty of affective feedback about cognition is that the mental gear shifting is then automated.

Although affect and cognition have been traditionally assumed to be independent or even conflicting forces within the mind, more recent research suggests that they are intimately intertwined and that affect plays important and functional roles in cognitive processing. Indeed, when affective input is silenced or otherwise disrupted, the ability to make even the most mundane decisions is severely impaired (Damasio, 1994). Thus, whereas we usually think of cognition as having the often thankless task of controlling emotion, in this chapter, we focus on the other side of the relationship. We describe the critical role of affect as a guide to cognition—a metacognitive guide. In taking this perspective, we therefore concur with the Reverend Haweis, author of the quotation at the beginning of this chapter, when he asserts that, without affective input, cognition loses much of its power.

How does affect guide cognition? There are several aspects to its influence. Affective reactions regulate attention, memory, and cognitive processing more generally. The arousal dimension specifically conveys information about the urgency or importance of objects and events, which in turn guides attention and memory (Storbeck & Clore, 2008). One attends to current sources of arousal (Zillman, 1978), and one tends to remember material that is followed by states of arousal (e.g., Cahill & Alkire, 2003). The valence dimension of affect, on the other hand, involves embodied information about value. Information about the goodness or badness of objects, including of one's own thoughts, is conveyed in the goodness or badness of affective feelings. Such self-referential evaluation turns out to be a powerful force in shaping our mental lives.

Although much of our research has focused on this ability of affective valence to regulate cognitive processing (e.g., Clore & Huntsinger, 2009), we assume that experiences other than affective valence can have similar influences on thought. A person might feel confident in his thoughts as a result of emotions that implicate certainty, such as anger (Tiedens & Linton, 2001). Arousal, too, is likely to energize people to act on accessible thoughts and inclinations (Corson & Verrier, 2007). And feelings of power (Smith & Trope, 2006) might also promote the use of accessible information. But whether valence, certainty, arousal, or power is the active element in a given situation, the same informational principles apply, so affective influences depend on people's implicit attributions (Schwarz & Clore, 1983) and hence on the particular objects to which the experiences seem to apply (Clore & Huntsinger, 2009).

Research on the affective regulation of thinking styles often employs procedures for inducing emotional moods. Assigning participants randomly to mood conditions and observing performance effects on cognitive tasks allows investigators to map the cognitive consequences of affective states. There now exists an extensive literature on the role of affect in regulating cognitive processing. In general, positive affect tends to lead to top-down processing, including the use of primed cognitions, stereotypes, and expectations, whereas negative affect tends to inhibit their use.

These kinds of cognitive consequences of positive and negative affect have been repeatedly documented, and a variety of explanations have been offered to account for them. Among them is the hypothesis that positive affect elicits heuristic processing (Schwarz & Clore, 2007), a global focus (Gasper & Clore, 2002), relational processing (Storbeck & Clore, 2005), widened attention (Derryberry & Tucker, 1994), substantive processing (Forgas, 2001), or a Piagetian process of assimilation (Fiedler, 2001).

Despite the variety of explanations that have been offered, all have one thing in common. All assume that positive affect elicits a distinctive cognitive style and that negative affect elicits a different cognitive style. Another possibility, however, is that the task-relevant information from affect serves a more general metacognitive function of validating or invalidating whatever processing inclination is accessible at the time.

In this chapter, we review research that leads us to believe that the influence of affect on cognition is like that of reward in that it is not dedicated to any one cognitive outcome. We argue that positive and negative affective states, such as moods, simply signal the value or validity of whatever thoughts and responses happen to be in mind at the moment. Positive affect serves as a "go signal" that encourages the use of mental content and negative affect serves as a "stop signal" that discourages use of such content. Thus, rather than assuming a direct or dedicated connection between affect and styles of cognitive processing, this view implies that the impact of affect on cognition should be quite malleable and depend on what thoughts and responses happen to be in mind at the time (see Clore & Huntsinger, 2009, for a review).

This influence of affect on cognition may usefully be conceived of as metacognitive. Metacognition involves our thoughts about our own thoughts and thought processes (Petty, Briñol, Tormala, & Wegener, 2007). We may, for example, feel confident in our belief that iguanas make fantastic pets, that the Clash is a great band, or that focusing on the details of the situation is appropriate. Such higher order thoughts then guide whether or not accessible mental content and thought processes inform judgments and guide responses.

At first glance it might seem peculiar that we should need information about our own cognitive processes because they are processes that we ourselves have generated. But much of our mental activity occurs beyond the reach of introspection (Wilson, 2002), and an important function of affective experience, then, is to provide conscious feedback or information about the ongoing workings of the cognitive system (Simon, 1967). Because positive affect is pleasant and negative affect is unpleasant, the feedback about the value of current thoughts and thought processes is also motivating. As such, affect acts as a stage manager of cognitive activity, including metacognitive activity, as it unfolds.

This chapter is organized as follows. In the first part, we review research consistent with the idea that affect moves cognition by providing metacognitive information about the value of accessible mental content and thought processes. This research shows that the link between affect and cognition is flexibly responsive to what thoughts and response tendencies happen to be in mind at the moment. The second part focuses on what is termed affective coherence versus affective incoherence. Affective beliefs are hypotheses about the evaluative state of the world or the self that can be either validated or invalidated by other coactivated affective cues like those from feelings or bodily states. Affective coherence occurs when affective and bodily cues validate affective concepts, and affective incoherence occurs when such cues invalidate affective concepts. The picture that emerges from this research is that whether or not embodied affect agrees with activated concepts about affect plays an important metacognitive role in ongoing cognitive activity.

AFFECT AS METACOGNITIVE INFORMATION

We argue that affect regulates cognition by providing a ready source of information that people draw on when making metacognitive inferences about their own thoughts and thought processes. The information provided by affect is about the value of whatever thoughts and response tendencies happen to be in mind at the moment, which then guides the extent to which people draw on or use such thoughts and responses (Clore & Huntsinger, 2007, 2009). Positive affect signals that accessible thoughts and responses are valuable and encourages their use, whereas negative affect signals that they are not valuable and discourages their use.

From this viewpoint, rather than being dedicated to one or another kind of cognitive process, as is often assumed, the influence of affect on cognition should depend on its object or what it is about. In other words, affective influences on cognition should be flexibly responsive to changing goals, thoughts, and response inclinations. Whether positive or negative affect leads people to focus on the forest or the trees, for example, should depend on which perceptual focus happens to be dominant at the moment. Similarly, whether positive affect or negative affect leads to greater or lesser stereotyping should depend on whether stereotypical thoughts or counterstereotypical thoughts are most accessible in any particular cognitive moment.

Depending on the particular metacognitive question posed, the information about value conferred by affect on accessible thoughts and responses may be experienced in different ways. The positive value conferred on accessible thoughts by positive affect may make them seem particularly valid or it may lead people to have great confidence in them. In terms of accessible responses or styles of cognitive processing, positive affect may lead people to view them as particularly useful or appropriate ways of dealing with incoming information, navigating interactions with other people, or more generally acting in the world. Negative affect should have just the opposite effect. Though the information conveyed by affect about accessible thoughts and responses may be experienced in different ways, in each case it should regulate whether or not people rely on such thoughts and responses.

In what follows, we review research spanning a variety of domains and outcomes that illustrates this metacognitive influence of affect on cognition. Along the way, we pay particular attention to studies that document the flexible impact of affect on cognition, and point out when results of this research are more consistent with a metacognitive influence of affect than with the idea that positive and negative affect promote different cognitive styles.

Thoughts: Signaling the Value of Accessible Attitudes

The idea that affect regulates the use of accessible thoughts by signaling their value is illustrated in recent research examining the influence of mood on the implicit association task (Huntsinger, Sinclair, & Clore, 2009). After listening to music to induce happy or sad moods, participants completed several implicit measures of attitudes. These included racial attitudes assessed in the implicit association test (IAT) by comparing reaction times to endorse positive and negative associations to typical African American names (e.g., Rashan, Yolanda) in comparison to European American names (e.g., John, Heidi). As in other unselected, largely non-Black samples, mildly negative associations with African American names tend to be the dominant, most accessible responses. An additional experiment also varied mood, but used the IAT to measure gender-relevant attitudes toward English versus math.

Compared to men, the most accessible response for women tended to be negative to math relative to English. Happy moods were found to empower and sad moods to block the use of accessible attitudes toward African Americans and toward academic subjects. Specifically, compared to those in sad moods, participants in happy moods displayed the negative attitudes toward African Americans usually seen on such measures, and female participants in happy moods also displayed a stereotypical pattern of academic attitudes (i.e., favoring English over math).

Follow-up analyses on these data using a process-dissociation procedure (Payne, 2001) revealed that, consistent with the current metacognitive view, these mood effects were in fact due to differences in the use of accessible attitudes, rather than to mood-related differences in style or depth of cognitive processing, as is often assumed (e.g., Schwarz & Clore, 2007).

Goals: Signaling the Value of Goals Versus Goal Progress

When determining whether to pursue a goal, people often reflect on its feasibility or desirability. Such metacognitive judgments about goal feasibility and desirability then shape goal adoption (Gollwitzer & Schaal, 1998). People often draw on their affective reactions to different goals when making judgments about whether or not to pursue them (Schwarz & Bohner, 1996). In such instances, positive affect signals that accessible goals are feasible or desirable, whereas negative affect signals just the opposite. In research consistent with this idea, Fishbach and Labroo (2007) found that happy people worked harder on a task than sad people when a self-improvement goal was accessible, but less hard when a mood-maintenance goal was accessible.

A similar pattern was recently found for adoption or rejection of interpersonal goals—in this case, the goals to affiliate with or gain social distance from others. When people have the goal to affiliate with others, they allow their attitudes, self-beliefs, and affective states to adjust toward those of an interaction partner, a process called "social tuning." As with other goals, this research found that positive moods facilitated the adoption of activated interpersonal goals. When the goal to affiliate with a partner was in mind, positive mood led to the alignment of both implicit and explicit racial attitudes of partners, whereas negative moods did not lead to such alignment (Huntsinger & Sinclair, 2010).

People may also reflect on their progress during goal pursuit or whether goal pursuit is going well or poorly. Judgments about goal progress can then influence whether people redouble or reduce their efforts to accomplish the goal, depending on the implied information about goal progress. Thus, when positive affect implies better progress than necessary, it leads to reduced effort, and when negative affect implies inadequate progress, it leads to increased effort (Martin, Ward, Achee, & Wyer, 1993).

People can also ask themselves whether their goal pursuit is enjoyable. When positive affect provides a "yes" answer, people continue the goal pursuit. When negative affect provides a "no" answer, this leads people to stop goal pursuit (Martin et al., 1993).

Implicit–Explicit Attitude Relations: Signaling the Value of Implicit Attitudes for Explicit Attitude Reports

Affect also regulates correspondence between implicit attitudes and explicit attitudes by conferring value on accessible implicit attitudes, which then regulate whether they inform explicit attitude reports (Huntsinger & Smith, 2009). Implicit attitudes reflect automatic tendencies to respond in a positive or negative fashion toward an attitude object; explicit attitudes reflect more controlled evaluative tendencies (Gawronski & Bodenhausen, 2006). But people typically base their explicit attitude reports on their automatic or implicit attitudes (Gawronski & Bodenhausen, 2006). Whether this occurs or not depends on the validation or invalidation of the implicit attitude by other accessible thoughts. In addition to such cognitive validation of implicit attitudes, however, factors such as mood may provide affective validation (Huntsinger & Smith, 2009). In multiple studies and in different attitude domains, positive moods have been found to promote congruence between implicit–explicit attitudes, whereas negative moods lead to a dissociation between implicit and explicit attitudes.

In addition, changing the object of affect can reverse the impact of mood on implicit–explicit attitude correspondence. In the research discussed earlier, affect informed people about the value of accessible implicit attitudes, whereas in other research (Huntsinger, in press), affect informed people about the value of momentarily accessible inclinations to trust or distrust intuition. Whether out of habit or only temporarily, people who trust their intuitions, as compared to those who distrust their intuitions, allow their implicit attitudes to inform their explicit attitude reports (Jordan, Whitfield, & Zeigler-Hill, 2007).

Thus, in that research (e.g., Huntsinger, in press) priming trust in intuition led people in positive but not negative moods to incorporate their implicit attitudes into their explicit attitude reports. By contrast, priming distrust in intuition resulted in the opposite pattern, so people in positive moods were then less likely than those in negative moods to incorporate their implicit attitudes into their explicit attitude reports. It should be noted that, in this research, both the measurement of participants' implicit attitudes and the priming task occurred before the mood induction, which precludes the possibility that mood influenced either the expression of implicit attitudes or the effectiveness of the priming task.

Persuasion: Signaling the Value of Processing Styles Versus Message-Relevant Thoughts

Some of the research we are discussing concerns metacognitive influences of affect on *how* people think (e.g., processing studies), whereas others concern such influences on *what* people think (e.g., judgment studies). Studies of affect and persuasion involve both. In terms of our current metacognitive analysis, the influence of affect on persuasion should depend on whether affect is experienced as feedback about accessible styles of thought or about specific thoughts while reading a persuasive appeal.

Influences on processing can be seen in many past studies in which moods are induced before receipt of the persuasive appeals (e.g., Bless, Bohner, Schwarz, & Strack, 1990; Mackie & Worth, 1989). In such cases, affect may shape the processing of persuasive messages by conferring value on accessible styles of information processing. If participants are motivated to conserve cognitive effort, as is sometimes assumed, they should process incoming information in a superficial or heuristic fashion. Positive affect would then validate this accessible style of processing, leading to equal persuasion by weak and strong arguments. Negative affect, on the other hand, should invalidate that accessible processing style, leading to more careful attention to the messages and greater persuasion by strong rather than weak arguments (Schwarz, Bless, & Bohner, 1991).

The second kind of influence can be seen in more recent studies in which, rather than moods being induced before receipt of persuasive appeals, they are induced afterward. Under these conditions, affect is experienced not as validation or invalidation of a heuristic or systematic mode of thought, but rather as validation or invalidation of the specific thoughts that came to mind while reading the persuasive messages (Briñol, Petty, & Barden, 2007).

In research by Briñol et al. (2007), for example, participants first were exposed to persuasive appeals consisting of either strong arguments or weak arguments and then wrote down their thoughts, which tended to be positive for strong arguments and negative for weak arguments. Positive or negative moods were then induced and participants rated their agreement with the persuasive appeal. Positive mood validated thoughts about the messages so that participants were persuaded more by strong than by weak arguments. In contrast, negative mood invalidated such thoughts, reversing these effects.

Stereotyping: Signaling the Value of Stereotypes Versus Counterstereotypes

Stereotypes represent knowledge about social groups and they frequently come to mind whenever people encounter or merely consider members of stereotyped groups (Fiske, 1998). As with any other thoughts, when stereotypes are in mind, positive affect confers positive value on them, promoting their use, and negative affect confers negative value on them, blocking their use. Thus, in a jury decision-making task, people in happy moods are more likely than those in sad moods to impose a harsher sentence on a defendant if that person is a member of a social group associated with criminality or violence (Bodenhausen, Kramer, & Susser, 1994). When people form impressions of others, stereotypes are more likely to creep into the impressions of people in happy moods than into those of people in sad moods (Lambert, Khan, Lickel, & Fricke, 1997).

But this research examined only downstream judgments, leaving open the question of whether affect shapes the activation or application of stereotypes. That is, does affect regulate whether stereotypes come to mind or does it mainly control stereotype use once the stereotype is already activated? Recent research favors the former view, in which the impact of affect occurs at the stereotype activation stage (Huntsinger et al., 2009; Experiment 1). The outcome of interest was performance on Payne's (2001) weapon-identification task, in which participants are briefly exposed to either a Black or a White face and then indicate as quickly as possible whether a briefly presented image is of a weapon or a tool. Typically, errors that occur after exposure to a Black face involve seeing tools as weapons, whereas errors after exposure to a White face involve seeing weapons as tools (Payne, 2001). We found that positive moods led to more of these stereotypical errors than negative moods.

We then applied process-dissociation analyses (Payne, 2001) to decompose that performance into estimates of automatic and controlled processing. They revealed that mood influenced the automatic activation of race-related stereotypes, rather than the controlled application of already activated stereotypes. Our interpretation of this finding is that, in situations likely to elicit a stereotype automatically, negative affect hampers the automatic use and hence the activation of the stereotype, rather than that positive and negative affect are linked to distinctly different styles of processing.

A similar influence of affect on the use of stereotypical knowledge can be seen in recent research on affective regulation of social category priming. When primed with the category "elderly," for example, people walk more slowly down a hallway and express more conservative social attitudes (Dijksterhuis, Chartrand, & Aarts, 2007). If affect confers value on accessible thoughts, including primed social categories, then people in positive moods should be more likely than those in negative moods to display such effects. Several studies support this reasoning (Ashton-James, Huntsinger, Clore, & Chartrand, 2009). Participants in this research experienced a happy or sad mood induction and then completed a task that primed the social category "elderly" or "young." The outcome of interest here was participants' walking speeds and social attitudes. As predicted, happy moods led to slower walking speed and more conservative attitudes after the category "elderly" was primed compared to the category "young." Conversely, sad moods did not lead participants to display the attitudes and behavior stereotypically associated with the primed social category.

The consistent capacity of positive affect to increase reliance on stereotypes compared to negative affect appears to suggest some dedicated or express connection between affect and stereotyping. But another way of understanding this link is that stereotypes often spring to mind whenever people encounter or merely entertain thoughts about members of stereotyped groups (Bargh, 1997); therefore, positive affect simply confers value on this highly accessible response. If this is the case, then the link between affect and stereotyping should vary according to the accessibility of stereotype-relevant thoughts and responses. When, for example, thoughts and responses that undermine or counter stereotyping are most accessible, positive affect should lead to less stereotyping than negative affect. When such thoughts and responses are not present in the mind, positive affect should lead to more stereotyping than negative affect.

Such flexibility in the link between affect and stereotyping was demonstrated in recent research (e.g., Huntsinger, Sinclair, Dunn, & Clore, 2010). In this research, happy moods reduced stereotyping compared to negative moods among individuals for whom the goal to be egalitarian was chronically or temporarily accessible. In the absence of egalitarian goals, happy moods increased stereotyping compared to negative moods. Similarly, among individuals for whom counterstereotypic thoughts were made accessible from exposure to strong female leaders or through formation of counterstereotypic implementation intentions (e.g., think safe in the presence of African Americans), happy moods reduced stereotyping compared to sad moods. The opposite influence of happy and sad moods was found among individuals for whom such thoughts were not accessible. It should be noted that, in several of these studies, the manipulation of counterstereotypic thoughts occurred prior to the mood manipulation, thereby excluding the possibility that the observed differences in stereotyping occurred because mood influenced the efficacy of the thought manipulation.

The results of this research are difficult to reconcile with perspectives that assume a direct, exclusive connection between affect and the use of stereotypes— whether because positive affect instigates heuristic processing, use of preexisting general knowledge structures, or a global focus. If there were such a connection, then people in positive moods should display greater stereotyping than those in negative moods, regardless of the presence or absence of egalitarian response tendencies or exposure to counterstereotypic exemplars. In contrast, our results suggest that affect is not inextricably connected to the use of stereotypes and that previously observed relationships between affect and stereotyping are reversed when counterstereotypic responses are more accessible.

Global–Local Focus: Signaling the Value of Perceptual Styles

When peering out at the world, people in positive moods tend to focus on the "forest," whereas those in negative moods focus on the "trees." This tendency has been found for a variety of outcomes. When judging the similarity between a series of geometric figures, people in positive moods tend to base their similarity judgments on the global features of the stimuli more than do people in negative moods (Gasper & Clore, 2002). Similarly, when forming impressions of others, people in happy moods are more likely to rely on global information, such as stereotypes, whereas those in negative moods are more likely to rely on local information, such as specific behaviors (Isbell, 2004). A similar pattern emerges in studies of autobiographical recall. People in positive moods describe events from the past using more global, abstract representations; those in negative moods use more local, concrete representations (Beukeboom & Semin, 2005, 2006).

As with stereotypes, the apparent consistency of the link between positive and negative affect and a global versus local focus, respectively, led many to propose that affect regulates people's focus of attention (see Schwarz & Clore, 2007, for a review). Although people certainly possess the capacity to shift between a global and local focus, in most circumstances a global focus dominates (Navon, 1977), and most experimental contexts only reinforce this tendency. Therefore, rather than instigating a global focus, positive affect may merely be conferring value on this already accessible way of viewing the world. If this is the case, then making a local focus most accessible should reverse the link between affect and a global versus local perceptual focus.

This idea was recently examined in the context of perceptual judgments (Huntsinger, Clore, & Bar-Anan, 2010). Across two different measures of perceptual focus, when a global focus was most accessible, people in happy moods displayed a tendency to focus on the forest, whereas those in sad moods focused on the trees. However, when a local focus was made most accessible, this pattern reversed. Then, people in happy moods focused on the trees, whereas those in sad moods focused on the forest. Importantly, in both studies there was not a hint of a direct effect of mood on perceptual style, and the manipulation of perceptual focus in one experiment occurred prior to the manipulation of mood, thereby ruling out the prospect that the success of the perceptual focus manipulation varied as a consequence of participants' moods.

Creativity: Signaling the Value of Thoughts and Focus

Other than a global versus local focus, perhaps the most commonly assumed direct connection between affect and cognitive processing concerns creativity. Across a variety of different tasks, including Dunker's candle task and the remote associates test, people in positive moods typically display greater creativity and flexibility in their thinking than do those in negative moods (Baas, De Dreu, & Nijstad, 2008; Isen, 1987). Does positive affect directly instigate greater cognitive flexibility and a divergent thinking style? Certainly that is one possibility, but, as with a global–local focus, the affect experienced during creativity tasks may simply be conferring positive or negative value on accessible thoughts and response tendencies.

When contemplating unusual uses for a brick, for example, mood may signal the value of thoughts that come to mind (e.g., "a brick would make for a clever hood ornament"), which then influence whether they are reported during the task. Because they view accessible thoughts as valid and valuable, people in positive moods should be more likely to report those thoughts than people in negative moods. This may then contribute to mood-related differences in divergent and creative thinking. Just such a pattern was found in recent research. While completing a creativity task, people in negative moods were less likely than those in positive moods to report thoughts that came to mind (Gasper, 2004). However, this difference in reporting thoughts, and hence in apparent creativity, disappeared when participants were encouraged to write down whatever thoughts came to mind while completing the task. Thus, what appears to be an affective influence on what types of thoughts come to mind during a creativity task (e.g., Isen, 1987) may sometimes be an influence on whether or not people rely on whatever thoughts come to mind.

But, presumably, mood can also influence creative generation as well as creative responding on occasion. One alternative approach to understanding mood effects on creative thought generation is to assume that many creativity tasks are probably among the more enjoyable tasks that participants in psychology experiments encounter. If so, participants may spontaneously adopt an enjoyment focus when completing creativity tasks in laboratory experiments, which may underlie many of the mood-related differences in creativity found in past research (see Wyer, Clore, & Isbell, 1999). If this is the case, then manipulating the framing of a creativity task should break the link between affect and creativity. Consistent with this idea, when a task is framed in a way that stresses enjoyment, people in positive moods, compared to those in negative moods, devote more time to the task and thus come up with more creative responses (Martin et al., 1993). But when performance rather than enjoyment is stressed, people in positive moods devote less time to the task and thus come up with less creative responses than those in negative moods.

Additional evidence for malleability in the affect–creativity link comes from studies that vary whether participants are instructed to focus on similarities or differences. In one study of this sort (Murray, Sujan, Hirt, & Sujan, 1990), participants were induced into a happy or sad mood prior to completing a measure of categorization breadth in which they grouped TV shows into meaningful categories. During this task, some participants were instructed to focus on the differences between the TV shows and others were instructed to focus on their similarities. When a focus on differences was accessible, people in positive moods displayed a greater breadth of categorization than those in negative moods—the standard link between affect and creativity. When a focus on similarities was accessible, by contrast, people in positive moods displayed a lesser breadth of categorization than those in negative moods.

Summary

In this section we reviewed evidence showing that the influence of affect on cognition is metacognitive in that affect provides a source of embodied information that people draw on when making inferences about currently accessible thoughts and styles of thinking. Positive affect confers positive value and negative affect confers negative value on accessible thoughts and mental styles, which regulates how people process information and whether they rely on particular thoughts.

As this research shows, and in contrast to the idea that positive and negative affect are tied to particular cognitive outcomes, the impact of affect on cognition is quite variable. Positive affect can encourage one to focus on the forest or the trees, depending on which perceptual focus is most dominant at the moment. Similarly, positive affect does not invariably lead to greater stereotyping and creativity than negative affect; again, this connection depends on what thoughts and responses happen to be accessible at the moment. It should be noted, however, that as research by Petty (Wegener & Petty, 2001) has shown, affect can have multiple effects on cognition even in the same experiment. Our position is therefore that one way in which affect influences cognition is by validating accessible thoughts, inclinations, and styles of thinking. The flexibility of this process can be seen in the research reviewed in the next section.

AFFECTIVE (IN)COHERENCE: COGNITIVE CONSEQUENCES

This section concerns the cognitive consequences of what is called *affective coherence* and *incoherence*. One way to view evaluative beliefs is as hypotheses about the value of objects in the world, including the self. Principal sources of data for such hypotheses are one's own affective feelings and bodily cues. We speak of affective coherence when such subjective experiences are consistent with evaluative beliefs and of affective incoherence when they are inconsistent with evaluative beliefs.

Epistemic Consequences of Affective Coherence

When subjective experience fails to validate evaluative beliefs about the self, a person is confronted with an epistemic problem. When this happens during cognitive tasks, it may interfere with ongoing cognitive activity, leading to a decrease in performance. This idea was examined in recent research in which momentary affective feelings were made to be either consistent or inconsistent with people's theories about whether they were generally happy or unhappy individuals (Tamir, Robinson, & Clore, 2002). A measure of extraversion–introversion was used as the measure of general beliefs about the self because extraverts reliably report believing themselves to be happier individuals than do introverts. Consistent with hypotheses about the effects of affective incoherence, when induced moods produced feelings that were incompatible with participants' beliefs about themselves as more or as less happy individuals, their performance on a reaction-time task suffered. Thus, happy extraverts who found themselves in a sad mood and unhappy introverts who felt momentarily happy were both relatively slow in making simple choices in comparison to those with feelings and beliefs that were in harmony.

Similar kinds of performance effects have been found in research employing several different forms of affective coherence and incoherence (Centerbar, Schnall, Clore, & Garvin, 2008). In four experiments, happy or sad concepts were primed—in some cases using the sentence unscrambling technique (Srull & Wyer, 1979) and in some cases using subliminal exposure to the same happy or sad words. Of interest was the degree to which various affective experiences would serve as a kind of "evidence" for the validity of happy or sad concepts that had been activated through subtle or unconscious priming.

In one experiment, the experiential "evidence" came from happy or sad feelings due to a musical mood induction. In another, the experiential evidence came from muscular feedback relevant from having participants flex either their obicularis (smile) or corrugator (frown) muscles. In two other experiments, the evidence came from having participants engage in arm muscle flexion (approach) or extension (avoidance) by pressing up or down on the top or bottom of a desktop.

In each of these experiments, participants were asked at the end to recall as much as they could of a story that they had read earlier in the study. Analyses of their free recall showed the same pattern in each case. When affective feelings and bodily cues were inconsistent with affective ideas that had been primed, participants were able to recall significantly less of the story than those whose activated cognitions were validated by the affective feedback from feelings, expressions, and actions.

Affective Coherence Influences the Value of Accessible Mental Content

As discussed by Centerbar et al. (2008), one way to understand the influence of affective coherence and incoherence is that they elicit feelings of fluency and disfluency, respectively. Evidence consistent with this idea comes from the finding that, as in the case of fluency experiences, experiences of affective coherence are associated with increased feelings of positive affect.

Research on fluency has generally explored its effects on judgment, finding that fluency experiences lead to more positive judgments than disfluency experiences (Oppenheimer, 2008; Reber, Schwarz, & Winkielman, 2004). However, recent research suggests that fluency and disfluency may also serve as cues to the value or validity of accessible mental content, with fluency validating and disfluency invalidating accessible thoughts and responses. Evidence of fluency and disfluency directly changing the judged value or validity of accessible thoughts comes from research examining ease of retrieval effects on persuasion and judgment (Tormala, Falces, Briñol, & Petty, 2007; Tormala, Petty, & Briñol, 2002). In this research, fluency was shown to enhance and disfluency to reduce confidence in accessible thoughts, which then was shown to play a pivotal role in whether such thoughts impacted judgments. This influence of fluency on the subjective value of available mental content has also been shown for primed concepts in impression formation tasks, such as the now classic Donald paradigm (Häfner & Stapel, 2010).

The possibility of a link between affective coherence and incoherence and the use of accessible mental content was recently explored in a series of studies (Huntsinger, 2009; Huntsinger & Graupner, 2010). The idea was that if affective coherence produces feelings of fluency, then it should enhance the subjective value or validity of accessible thoughts. If affective incoherence produces feelings of disfluency, then it should have just the opposite effect on the use of accessible thoughts. Affective coherence and incoherence were again manipulated in different ways in these experiments, including by inducing matches or mismatches in state and trait affect in several studies and by creating matches or mismatches in affective feelings and primed affective concepts in others.

The role of affective coherence in validating accessible thoughts and responses is further shown in research examining its impact on persuasion (Huntsinger & Graupner, 2010). In two studies, affective coherence (vs. incoherence) was induced prior to participants reading persuasive messages advocating implementation of comprehensive exams for graduating seniors. In addition to the manipulation of affective coherence, these studies also manipulated the strength of the arguments in the persuasive messages (Study 1) and expertise of the source advocating such exams (Study 2). In these studies, affective coherence and incoherence should have been experienced as validation or invalidation, respectively, of available styles of thought and led to differences in how participants processed the messages.

Given people's general inclination to conserve cognitive resources, affective coherence should have validated this tendency and led to superficial or heuristic processing. Affective incoherence, on the other hand, should have invalidated this inclination and led to more careful or systematic processing. Consistent with this idea, affective coherence led participants to be equally persuaded by weak versus strong messages (Study 1) and to be more persuaded by an expert than an inexpert source. Affective incoherence, by contrast, led participants to be persuaded more by strong than weak appeals and to be equally persuaded by expert and nonexpert sources.

In a third study, affective coherence was induced after participants read persuasive appeals containing either strong or weak arguments, but before they reported their attitudes toward comprehensive exams. Thus, similarly to the research by Briñol et al. (2007), rather than validating accessible styles of processing, in this situation affective coherence should have validated or invalidated the specific thoughts that came to mind while reading the persuasive messages. Consistent with this idea, affective coherence led participants to be more persuaded by strong versus weak persuasive appeals, whereas affective incoherence led to the opposite pattern of persuasion. Participants were also asked about their confidence in the thoughts that came to mind reading the persuasive messages. As expected, affective coherence led to greater confidence in such thoughts than did affective incoherence. Mediation analyses revealed that this difference in thought confidence mediated the relation between affective coherence and persuasion discussed before. Accordingly, this research provides direct evidence for the role of affective coherence (vs. incoherence) in shaping the subjective value of accessible mental content, which in turn shapes whether people rely on this content.

Also consistent with the idea that affective coherence influences the perceived value of accessible thoughts, in other studies White participants experiencing affective coherence were more likely than those experiencing incoherence to display stereotypical attitudes toward African Americans and also to show a general preference for arts over math, which is commonly found on the IAT (Huntsinger, 2009, Studies 1 and 2). A similar pattern was found for performance on Payne's weapon-identification task, where affective coherence led to more stereotypical mistakes on this task than affective incoherence (Study 3). In each study, process-dissociation analyses indicated that variation in the expression of implicit attitudes and stereotypes was driven by changes in the automatic use of accessible thoughts, rather than changes in the amount or style of cognitive processing. Affective coherence and affective incoherence were also found to affect the extent to which primed social categories influenced behavior (Study 4) and chronically accessible perceptual styles dominated visual processing (Study 5).

CODA

In this chapter, we took the perspective that affect acts as a guide to cognition—a metacognitive guide, to be precise. We reviewed evidence showing that the influence of affect on cognition is metacognitive in that affect provides a source of embodied information that people draw on when making inferences about currently accessible thoughts and styles of thinking. Positive affect confers positive value and negative affect confers negative value on accessible thoughts and cognitive styles; this regulates how people process information and whether they rely on particular thoughts. As this research shows, and in contrast to the idea that positive and negative affect are tied to particular cognitive outcomes, the impact of affect on cognition is quite variable and depends on the thoughts and responses that happen to be in mind at any given cognitive moment.

The second half of this chapter concerned the cognitive consequences of affective coherence and incoherence. Affective beliefs are hypotheses about the evaluative state of the world or the self that can be validated or invalidated by other coactivated affective cues like those from feelings or bodily states. Affective coherence occurs when affective and bodily cues validate affective concepts, and affective incoherence occurs when such cues invalidate affective concepts.

As our research shows, affect regulates thought by serving as information about the suitability of one's current thoughts or cognitive orientation in a specific task situation. The success of affective reactions in promoting this alignment, however, might be moderated by emotional intelligence or other factors affecting the individual's ability to read his or her own affective reactions accurately, which might in turn be moderated by the intensity of such reactions (for a longer list, see Gohm & Clore,[*] 2000).

In addition, to the extent that such processes involve metacognitive activity, one might expect it to be moderated by variation in motivation and attentional resources. However, that expectation assumes that metacognitive activity necessarily involves controlled rather than automatic processes. But some of the cognitions and inclinations that affective reactions appear to validate are unconscious. Hence, their validation may not involve controlled processing and might not therefore require cognitive resources. For example, some metacognitive validations might be rather nonspecific. Rather than validating one's particular thought, as in a persuasion experiment, affect and fluency experiences might validate one's general cognitive orientation to a task. Feeling positive, fluent, or in the groove, or having an experience of flow might promote a current line of thought more or less automatically.

To be effective, the process would presumably involve a tacit interpretive frame in which feelings of positivity and fluency signify the appropriateness of one's current thoughts, ideas, and cognitive approach. Such metacognitive messages might not then be moderated by factors such as one's need for cognition or the availability of attentional resources. Our reasoning here is simply that because cognitions are not subject to the limitations of conscious, controlled processing,

[*] Gerald L. Clore acknowledges the support of NIMH Grant # MH50074.

cognitions about cognitions, or metacognitions, might not be subject to such limitations either.

REFERENCES

Ashton-James, C., Huntsinger, J. R., Clore, G. L., & Chartrand, T. L. (2009). *Affective regulation of social category priming.* Unpublished manuscript.

Baas, M., De Dreu, C. K. W., & Nijstad, B. A. (2008). A meta-analysis of 25 years of research on mood and creativity: Hedonic tone, activation, or regulatory focus? *Psychological Bulletin, 134,* 779–806.

Bargh, J. A. (1997). The automaticity of everyday life. In R. S. Wyer, Jr. (Ed.), *The automaticity of everyday life: Advances in social cognition* (Vol. 10, pp. 1–61). Mahwah, NJ: Lawrence Erlbaum Associates.

Beukeboom, C. J., & Semin, G. R. (2005). Mood and representations of behavior: The how and why. *Cognition and Emotion, 19,* 1242–1251.

Beukeboom, C. J., & Semin, G. R. (2006). How mood turns on language. *Journal of Experimental Social Psychology, 42,* 553–566.

Bless, H., Bohner, G., Schwarz, N., & Strack, F. (1990). Mood and persuasion: A cognitive response analysis. *Personality and Social Psychology Bulletin, 16,* 331–345.

Bodenhausen, G. V., Kramer, G., & Susser, K. (1994). Happiness and stereotypic thinking in social judgment. *Journal of Personality and Social Psychology, 66,* 621–632.

Briñol, P., Petty, R. E., & Barden, J. (2007). Happiness versus sadness as a determinant of thought confidence in persuasion: A self-validation analysis. *Journal of Personality and Social Psychology, 93,* 711–727.

Cahill, L., & Alkire, M. T. (2003). Epinephrine enhancement of human memory consolidation: Interaction with arousal at encoding. *Neurobiology of Learning and Memory, 79,* 194–198.

Centerbar, D. B., Schnall, S., Clore, G. L., & Garvin, E. (2008). Affective incoherence: When affective concepts and embodied reactions clash. *Journal of Personality and Social Psychology, 94,* 560–578.

Clore, G. L., & Huntsinger, J. R. (2007). How emotions inform judgment and regulate thought. *Trends in Cognitive Sciences, 9,* 393–399.

Clore, G. L., & Huntsinger, J. R. (2009). How the object of affect guides its impact. *Emotion Review, 1,* 39–54.

Corson, Y., & Verrier, N. (2007). Emotions and false memories: Valence or arousal? *Psychological Science, 18,* 208–211.

Damasio, A. (1994). *Descartes' error: Emotions, reason, and the human brain.* New York, NY: Avon Books.

Derryberry, D., & Tucker, D. M. (1994). Motivating the focus of attention. In P. Niedenthal & S. Kitayama (Eds.), *The heart's eye: Emotional influences in perception and attention.* New York, NY: Academic Press.

Dijksterhuis, A., Chartrand, T. L., & Aarts, H. (2007). Automatic behavior. In J. A. Bargh (Ed.), *Social psychology and the unconscious.* Philadelphia, PA: Psychology Press.

Fiedler, K. (2001). Affective states trigger processes of assimilation and accomodation. In L. L. Martin & G. L. Clore (Eds.), *Theories of mood and cognition: A user's handbook* (pp. 85–98). Mahwah, NJ: Lawrence Erlbaum Associates.

Fishbach, A., & Labroo, A. A. (2007). Be better or be merry: How mood affects self-control. *Journal of Personality and Social Psychology, 93,* 158–173.

Fiske, S. T. (1998). Stereotyping, prejudice, and discrimination. In D. T. Gilbert, S. T. Fiske, & G. Lindzey (Eds.), *Handbook of social psychology* (4th ed., Vol. 2, pp. 357–411). New York, NY: McGraw–Hill.

Flavell, J. H. (1976). Metacognitive aspects of problem solving. In L. B. Resnick (Ed.), *The nature of intelligence* (pp. 231–236). Hillsdale, NJ: Lawrence Erlbaum Associates.

Flavell, J. H. (1979). Metacognition and cognitive monitoring: A new area of cognitive-developmental inquiry. *American Psychologist, 34,* 906–911.

Forgas, J. P. (2001). The affect infusion model (AIM): An integrative theory of mood effects on cognition and judgments. In L. L. Martin & G. L. Clore (Eds.), *Theories of mood and cognition* (pp. 99–134). Mahwah, NJ: Lawrence Erlbaum Associates.

Gasper, K. (2004). Permission to seek freely? The effect of happy and sad moods on generating old and new ideas. *Creativity Research Journal, 16,* 215–229.

Gasper, K., & Clore, G. L. (2002). Attending to the big picture: Mood and global vs. local processing of visual information. *Psychological Science, 13,* 34–40.

Gawronski, B., & Bodenhausen, G. V. (2006). Associative and propositional processes in evaluation: An integrative review of implicit and explicit attitude change. *Psychological Bulletin, 132,* 692–731.

Gohm, C. L., & Clore, G. L. (2003). Affect as information: An individual differences approach. In L. Feldman Barrett & P. Salovey (Eds.) *The wisdom of feelings: Processes underlying emotional intelligence* (pp. 89–113). New York, NY: Guilford Press.

Gollwitzer, P. M., & Schaal, B. (1998). Metacognition in action: The importance of implementation intentions. *Personality and Social Psychology Review, 2,* 124–136.

Häfner, M., & Stapel, D. A. (2010). Information to go: Fluency enhances the usability of primed information. *Journal of Experimental Social Psychology, 46,* 73–84.

Haweis, H. R. (1866). Schubert and Chopin. *Contemporary Review, 2,* 80–102.

Huntsinger, J. R. (2009). *Affective (in)coherence regulates subjective value of accessible mental content: Implicit attitudes, social categories, and perceptual styles.* Unpublished manuscript.

Huntsinger, J. R. (in press). Mood and trust in intuition interactively orchestrate correspondence between implicit and explicit attitudes. *Personality and Social Psychology Bulletin.*

Huntsinger, J. R., Clore, G., & Bar-Anan, Y. (2010). Mood and global–local focus: Priming a local focus reverses the link between mood and global–local processing. *Emotion, 10*(5), 722–726.

Huntsinger, J. R., & Graupner, J. (2010). *Affective (in)coherence and persuasion.* Unpublished manuscript.

Huntsinger, J. R., & Sinclair, S. (2010). If it feels right, go with it: Affective regulation of affiliative social tuning. *Social Cognition, 28,* 290–305.

Huntsinger, J. R., Sinclair, S., & Clore, G. L. (2009). Affective regulation of implicitly measured attitudes and stereotypes: Automatic and controlled processes. *Journal of Experimental Social Psychology, 45,* 560–566.

Huntsinger, J. R., Sinclair, S., Dunn, E., & Clore, G. (2010). Affective regulation of automatic stereotype activation: It's the (accessible) thought that counts. *Personality and Social Psychology Bulletin, 36,* 564–577.

Huntsinger, J. R., & Smith, C. T. (2009). First thought, best thought: Positive mood maintains and negative mood disrupts implicit-explicit attitude correspondence. *Personality and Social Psychology Bulletin, 35,* 187–197.

Isbell, L. (2004). Not all happy people are lazy or stupid: Evidence of systematic processing in happy moods. *Journal of Experimental Social Psychology, 40,* 341–349.

Isen, A. (1987). Positive affect, cognitive processes, and social behavior. *Advances in Experimental Social Psychology, 20,* 203–253.

Jordan, C. H., Whitfield, M., & Zeigler-Hill, V. (2007). Intuition and the correspondence between implicit and explicit self-esteem. *Journal of Personality and Social Psychology, 93,* 1067–1079.

Koriat, A., & Levy-Sadot, R. (1999). Processes underlying metacognitive judgments: Information-based and experience-based monitoring of one's own knowledge. In S. Chaiken & Y. Trope (Eds.), *Dual process theories in social psychology* (pp. 483–502). New York, NY: Guilford Press.

Lambert, A. J., Khan, S. R., Lickel, B. A., & Fricke, K. (1997). Mood and the correction of positive versus negative stereotypes. *Journal of Personality and Social Psychology, 72,* 1002–1016.

Mackie, D. M., & Worth, L. T. (1989). Cognitive deficits and the mediation of positive affect in persuasion. *Journal of Personality and Social Psychology, 57,* 27–40.

Martin, L. L., Ward, D. W., Achee, J. W., & Wyer, R. S. (1993). Mood as input: People have to interpret the motivational implication of their moods. *Journal of Personality and Social Psychology, 64,* 317–326.

Murray, N., Sujan, H., Hirt, E. R., & Sujan M. (1990). The influence of mood on categorization: A cognitive flexibility interpretation. *Journal of Personality and Social Psychology, 59,* 411–425.

Navon, D. (1977). Forest before trees: The precedence of global features in visual perception. *Cognitive Psychology, 9,* 353–383.

Neisser, U. (1976). *Cognition and reality: Principles and implications of cognitive psychology.* Gordonsville, VA: W. H. Freeman.

Oppenheimer, D. M. (2008). The secret life of fluency. *Trends in Cognitive Science, 12,* 237–241.

Payne, B. K. (2001). Prejudice and perception: The role of automatic and controlled processes in misperceiving a weapon. *Journal of Personality and Social Psychology, 81,* 181–192.

Petty, R. E., Briñol, P., Tormala, Z. L., & Wegener, D. T. (2007). The role of metacognition in social judgment. In A. W. Kruglanski & E. T. Higgins (Eds.), *Social psychology: Handbook of basic principles* (2nd ed., pp. 254–284). New York, NY: Guilford Press.

Reber, R., Schwarz, N., & Winkielman, P. (2004). Processing fluency and aesthetic pleasure: Is beauty in the perceiver's processing experience? *Personality and Social Psychology Review, 8,* 364–382.

Schwarz, N., Bless, H., & Bohner, G. (1991). Mood and persuasion: Affective states influence the processing of persuasive communications. *Advances in Experimental Social Psychology, 23,* 161–197.

Schwarz, N., & Bohner, G. (1996). Feelings and their motivational implications: Moods and the action sequence. In P. M. Gollwitzer & J. A. Bargh (Eds.), *The psychology of action: Linking cognition and motivation to behavior* (pp. 119–145). New York, NY: Guilford Press.

Schwarz, N., & Clore, G. L. (1983). Mood, misattribution, and judgments of well-being: Informative and directive functions of affective states. *Journal of Personality and Social Psychology, 45,* 513–523.

Schwarz, N., & Clore, G. L. (2007). Feelings and phenomenal experiences. In E. T. Higgins & A. Kruglanski (Eds.), *Social psychology: A handbook of basic principles* (Vol. 2). New York, NY: Guilford Press.

Simon, H. (1967). Motivational and emotional controls of cognition. *Psychological Review, 74,* 29–39.

Smith, P. K., & Trope, Y. (2006). You focus on the forest when you're in charge of the trees: Power priming and abstract information processing. *Journal of Personality and Social Psychology, 90,* 578–596.

Srull, T. K., & Wyer, R. S. (1979). The role of category accessibility in the interpretation of information about persons: Some determinants and implications. *Journal of Personality and Social Psychology, 37,* 1660–1672.

Storbeck, J., & Clore, G. L. (2005). With sadness comes accuracy, with happiness, false memory: Mood and the false memory effect. *Psychological Science, 16,* 785–791.

Storbeck, J., & Clore, G. L. (2008). Affective arousal as information: How affective arousal influences judgments, learning, and memory. *Social and Personality Psychology Compass, 2,* 1824–1843.

Tamir, M., Robinson, M. D., & Clore, G. L. (2002). The epistemic benefits of trait-consistent mood states: An analysis of extraversion and mood. *Journal of Personality and Social Psychology, 83,* 663–677.

Tiedens, L. Z., & Linton, S. (2001). Judgment under emotional certainty and uncertainty: The effects of specific emotions and their associated certainty appraisals on cognitive processing. *Journal of Personality and Social Psychology, 81,* 973–988.

Tormala, Z. L., Falces, C., Briñol, P., & Petty, R. E. (2007). Ease of retrieval effects in social judgment: The role of unrequested cognitions. *Journal of Personality and Social Psychology, 93,* 143–157.

Tormala, Z. L., Petty, R. E., & Briñol, P. (2002). Ease of retrieval effects in persuasion: A self-validation analysis. *Personality and Social Psychology Bulletin, 28,* 1700–1712.

Wegener, D. T., & Petty, R. E. (2001). Understanding effects of mood through the elaboration likelihood and flexible correction models. In L. L. Martin & G. L. Clore (Eds.), *Theories of mood and cognition: A user's guidebook* (pp. 177–210). Mahwah, NJ: Lawrence Erlbaum Associates.

Wilson, T. W. (2002). *Strangers to ourselves: Discovering the adaptive unconscious.* Cambridge, MA: Harvard University Press.

Wyer, R. S., Clore, G. L., & Isbell, L. (1999). Affect and information processing. *Advances in Experimental Social Psychology, 31,* 3–78.

Zillman, D. (1978). Attribution and misattribution of excitatory reactions. In J. H. Harvey & W. J. Ickes (Eds.), *New directions in attribution research* (Vol. 2). Hillsdale, NJ: Lawrence Erlbaum Associates.

12

Embodied Validation
Our Bodies Can Change and Also Validate Our Thoughts

PABLO BRIÑOL, RICHARD E. PETTY,
and BENJAMIN C. WAGNER

INTRODUCTION

E *mbodied persuasion* refers to the idea that people's own behaviors can impact their attitudes (i.e., their likes and dislikes). As one example, when we smile, we tend to see everything in a more positive light than when we frown. Also, when we nod our heads, we tend to like things better than when we shake our heads. In one early embodiment study, individuals who were induced to nod their heads (i.e., agreement behavior) while listening to a persuasive message over headphones were more favorable to the proposal than people who were induced to shake their heads (i.e., disagreement behavior) while listening to the same message (Wells & Petty, 1980). Other research has found that information presented while performing an approach behavior (e.g., using one's hands to pull up from underneath a table) is evaluated more positively than information presented during an avoidance behavior (e.g., pushing down on a table top surface; Cacioppo, Priester, & Bernston, 1993). Similar findings have been found for a large number of behaviors, postures, and bodily movements (for a recent review on embodied persuasion, see Briñol & Petty, 2008).

Although the ability of bodily movements to influence attitudes seems to be a well-established phenomenon, most research on this topic has not focused on the psychological mechanisms by which the body affects attitudes. Understanding these processes is essential in order to predict *whether, when, and how* attitudes will change, as well as to predict whether, when, and how attitudes will result in further behavioral changes. That is, although we might often like something more when we smile (vs. frown) or when we nod (vs. shake) our heads, it is important to understand the processes responsible for these changes in evaluation so that we can appreciate the consequences of these embodied attitudes.

Consistent with the elaboration likelihood model (ELM) of persuasion (Petty & Cacioppo, 1986), we argue that the psychological processes relevant to embodied attitude change can be organized into a finite set that operates at different points along an elaboration continuum. Under low-thinking conditions, bodily responses, like other variables, can influence attitudes via a variety of low-effort processes. When the likelihood of thinking is relatively high, these same bodily responses can impact persuasion by affecting the direction of the thoughts that come to mind or by serving as a piece of evidence (argument). Furthermore, body postures and actions can influence attitudes by influencing the amount of thinking when elaboration is not constrained to be very low or high.

We begin the present chapter by reviewing how our body can influence these psychological processes, focusing on primary or first-order cognition. Primary thoughts are those that occur at a direct level of cognition and involve our initial associations of some object with some attribute. Following a primary thought, people can also generate other thoughts, which occur at a second level and involve reflections on the first-level thoughts. *Metacognition* refers to these second-order thoughts, or thoughts about other thoughts or thought processes (Petty, Briñol, Tormala, & Wegener, 2007).

In the second part of the chapter, we focus on this secondary form of cognition, describing recent work on embodiment that reveals that our body can influence attitudes by affecting confidence in our thoughts—a metacognitive process called self-validation. According to the *self-validation* perspective (Petty, Briñol, & Tormala, 2002), although our body can serve as a cue for or influence the amount and direction of thoughts, it can also affect what we think about our thoughts, especially the extent to which we are certain in the validity of these thoughts. We refer to this idea as *embodied validation*. In line with this metacognitive process, in the second part of the chapter, we describe different lines of research revealing that the confidence (or doubt) that emerges from bodily responses can magnify (or attenuate) the effect of anything that is currently available in people's minds. The research described in that section is organized around the content of the primary thoughts that are validated (or invalidated) by the body, ranging from thoughts in response to persuasion to emotional thoughts and other primed psychological constructs.

Third, we distinguish among the processes by which bodily responses operate and specify the conditions under which metacognitive processes such as self-validation are particularly likely to occur. A final section compares self-validation with other metacognitive perspectives, highlighting the unique features of our framework. In closing this chapter, we outline some general conclusions and highlight a number of current and future issues relevant to the research on embodied change and validation.

BODILY RESPONSES AFFECT PRIMARY COGNITION

The ELM has described four ways in which our body, like any other variable present in the persuasion setting, can affect attitudes: (1) serving as a simple cue, (2) affecting the extent of information processing by influencing motivation or ability to think, (3) affecting the direction of processing (i.e., introducing a bias to the ongoing thinking), and (4) serving as a piece of substantive evidence (i.e., an argument). In this section we briefly describe how our bodily responses can influence attitudes by affecting each of these primary cognition processes at different points along the elaboration continuum (see also Briñol & Petty, 2008).

Bodily Responses Serve as Simple Cues to Persuasion

Our body posture, our facial expressions, and the way we move can all influence our opinions in very subtle ways. In fact, because bodily responses belong to our physical nature, researchers have tended to think that they have to operate in our minds through very simple, automatic mechanisms. Indeed, our actions can influence our opinions on a topic even when we do not think about the information we receive (Cacioppo, Marshall-Goodell, Tassinary, & Petty, 1992) showed that neutral Chinese ideographs (i.e., irrelevant stimuli for the sample of participants) presented during arm flexion were subsequently evaluated more favorably than ideographs presented during arm extension (for another classic example using facial expressions, see Stepper & Strack, 1993; Strack, Martin, & Stepper, 1988).

Aside from using mere associations such as with arm flexion, smiling, or head nodding, people can also rely on simple heuristics when forming or changing attitudes. For instance, people can draw direct inferences about their attitudes based on their body states (e.g., if my heart is beating fast, I must like this object; Bem, 1972; Valins, 1966). Thus, the body can serve as a simple cue to persuasion when motivation and ability to think are low.

Bodily Responses Influence the Amount of Thinking

Our bodies can also make us think about things to a greater or lesser degree. Our postures, facial expressions, and movements sometimes distract us from what is going on, but at other times those same actions can help us to think about things. That is, bodily responses can affect the amount of thinking a person does. Because people tend to think less when they are happy, secure, and confident rather than sad or doubtful (e.g., Briñol, Petty, & Barden, 2007; Tiedens & Linton, 2001), people might think less when smiling than when frowning, or when nodding the head than when shaking it.

In an early demonstration that body posture can affect susceptibility to a persuasive communication by affecting the extent of thinking, Petty, Wells, Heesacker, Brock, and Cacioppo (1983) asked undergraduate students to try new headphones to rate the headphones' qualities. Some participants were then told to stand while testing the headphones, whereas others were told to lie down while testing them.

Importantly, a persuasive message was played for participants as they "tested" the headphones. The message consisted of either strong or weak arguments favoring a tuition increase at their university. Consistent with the idea that posture can affect thinking, this study showed that although reclining participants were differentially persuaded by the strong and weak arguments (i.e., suggesting that they paid careful attention to the message), standing participants were not. Importantly, the body affects the amount of thinking, particularly when the person has not decided whether to think carefully about the topic or issue.

Recent research has demonstrated that not only body postures but also other embodied variables can influence attitude change by affecting how much people think about persuasive proposals. For example, Jostmann, Lakens, and Schubert (2009) found that participants holding a heavy (vs. light) clipboard were more persuaded by strong rather than weak arguments, suggesting that they engaged in more processing of the proposal. This finding may suggest that just as weight makes people invest more physical effort in dealing with material objects, it also makes people invest more cognitive effort in dealing with ideas.

Important practical implications flow from the possibility that embodied manipulations can induce persuasion by affecting the amount of thinking in which the individual engages. For example, the practice of brainwashing often involves a massive assault on the body in which the victim is frequently starved, drugged, tortured, and emotionally agitated. In other domains, attempts at persuasion may involve the direct control of a person's behavior, including alteration in appearance (e.g., clothing, posture, hairstyle), public behaviors (e.g., self-criticism), and escalation of commitment, in which a recruit is asked, over time, to engage in increasingly costly behaviors that are hard to undo (e.g., donating his or her personal possessions to the group, recruiting new members). The combination of physical deprivation and behavior modification has been argued to reduce a person's motivation and ability to think, thus rendering that person more susceptible to what would ordinarily have been weak arguments (e.g., faulty logic, incomplete verification, erroneous and stereotypical information; for a review, see Baron, 2000). These simplistic, weak messages could presumably be easily counterargued if people were not so physically depleted (e.g., Wheeler, Briñol, & Hermann, 2007).

Bodily Responses Influence the Direction of Thinking

Our bodies can influence persuasion not only by affecting the amount of thinking but also by affecting the direction of that thinking. Obviously, for the body to influence thoughts, people need to be thinking. One extensively explored idea is that bodily responses can shape attitudes by affecting the valence (i.e., positivity or negativity) of the thoughts that come to mind when thinking about an attitude object. For example, in the original research on head movements and persuasion, Wells and Petty (1980) speculated that participants' past experiences had made nodding compatible with "approval" and favorable thinking, whereas head shaking was more compatible with "disapproval" and unfavorable thinking. In line with the Wells and Petty proposal about behavior biasing thinking, Neumann, Förster, and Strack (2003) argued that overt behaviors can directly trigger compatible thoughts that facilitate encoding and processing of evaluatively congruent information (Förster & Strack, 1996).

Bodily Responses Serving as Arguments

When the amount of thinking is high, people assess the relevance of *all* of the information in the context that comes to mind in order to determine the merits of the attitude object under consideration. That is, people can examine their own bodily responses as possible arguments or reasons for favoring or disfavoring the attitude object. For example, when thinking carefully, people can be influenced by their own bodily information, such as smiling when rating how good they look that day.

In sum, it might be helpful for some people to know that their actions can influence their likes and dislikes. In fact, our bodies can provide us with valuable information in many cases (e.g., elevated heart rate and stomach butterflies when encountering a person inform us that we like that person). However, if people who believe that their judgments are somehow biased or influenced by their bodily actions do not want this to occur, they may adjust their judgments in a direction opposite to the expected bias (*correction processes;* Wegener & Petty, 1997; see Chapter 5, this volume).

BODILY RESPONSES AFFECT SECONDARY COGNITION

In the first section, we have seen how the body can influence attitudes by serving as a simple cue and by affecting either the amount or direction of thinking. Recently, we have proposed that behavior not only can influence what people think about attitude objects, but also can impact what people think about their own thoughts (i.e., metacognition). This idea is referred to as the *self-validation hypothesis* (Petty et al., 2002). The key notion is that generating thoughts is not sufficient for these thoughts to have an impact on judgments. Rather, one must also have confidence in one's thoughts.

The main idea behind the concept of *embodied validation* is that people's own behaviors can impact their judgments by affecting thought confidence. In other words, the confidence that emerges from one's body and its position or movements can magnify the effect of anything that is currently available in people's minds, including not only thoughts about a persuasive message, but also other cognitions, emotions, goals, and so forth. That is, confidence applies to whatever mental contents are salient and available at the time (see Briñol & Petty, 2009a, for a review). In this section, we describe research on self-validation organized around the content of the primary cognitions that are validated by the confidence that emerges from the body.

Bodily Responses Validate Thoughts in Response to a Persuasive Message

Consider the research on head nodding described earlier, which had assumed that moving one's head in a vertical (versus horizontal) manner produced more positive attitudes either because vertical head nodding biased thinking in a favorable direction or because head nodding served as a relatively simple affective cue (Wells & Petty, 1980). The self-validation hypothesis suggests another possibility. Specifically, this hypothesis suggests that just as vertical head movements from others give us confidence in what we are saying, our own vertical head movements can give us confidence in what we are thinking.

In the first series of studies on embodied validation, Briñol and Petty (2003) found that head movements affected the confidence people had in their thoughts and thereby had an impact on attitudes. Thus, when people listened through headphones to strong arguments advocating that students be required to carry personal identification cards on campus, vertical head movements led to more favorable attitudes than horizontal movements, as would be expected if vertical movements increased confidence in one's favorable thoughts. However, when people listened to weak arguments in favor of the identification cards, vertical movements led to less favorable attitudes than horizontal movements, as would be expected if vertical movements increased confidence in one's negative thoughts.

This was the first study on the effects of head movements through self-validation processes, and it was conducted in a traditional persuasion setting in which attitudes changed with respect to a particular proposal. Having demonstrated that body movements can determine the extent of influence by affecting thought confidence, we have started to examine whether our bodies can validate other kinds of thoughts and thus whether other social psychological phenomena can similarly benefit from a consideration of self-validation processes. We next describe how our bodily responses not only can validate thoughts in response to a persuasive proposal, but also can validate other kinds of cognitions, such as self-related thoughts, emotional thoughts, and primed thoughts.

Bodily Responses Validate Self-Relevant Thoughts

The confidence that our body makes us feel applies to whatever the salient or available mental contents are at the time. Thus, the self-validation framework can be applied to attitude domains other than traditional persuasive messages about external issues. Consider recent work on attitudes about oneself (i.e., self-esteem). In one example of research applying self-validation to self-evaluation (Briñol & Petty, 2003, Experiment 4), participants were asked, as part of a presumed graphology study, to think about and write down their best or worst qualities (i.e., thought-direction manipulation) using their dominant or nondominant hands (i.e., overt behavior manipulation). Then, participants rated the confidence in the thoughts they listed and reported their self-esteem. Writing with the nondominant hand happens infrequently and is very difficult, so whatever is written with the nondominant may appear "shaky"; thus, we expected and found that using the nondominant hand decreased the confidence with which people held the thoughts they had listed. As a consequence, the effect of the direction of thoughts (i.e., positive vs. negative) on state self-esteem was significantly greater when participants wrote their thoughts with their dominant hand than when they wrote their thoughts with their nondominant hand.

That is, writing positive thoughts about oneself with the dominant hand increased self-esteem relative to writing positive thoughts with the nondominant hand, but writing negative thoughts with the dominant hand resulted in the reverse pattern. When writing about the things we do not like about ourselves, we feel better if we use the nondominant (vs. dominant) hand. This pattern of findings is interesting because it reveals that people do not feel too badly about themselves even after listing negative self-relevant thoughts in objectively unattractive handwriting. This is a unique implication of the self-validation logic.

In another more recent illustration, Briñol, Petty, and Wagner (2009) asked participants to think about and write down their best or worst qualities while sitting with their backs erect, pushing their chests out (i.e., confident posture), or while sitting slouched forward with their backs curved (i.e., doubtful posture). Then, participants completed a number of measures, including self-esteem. In line with the self-validation hypothesis, it was predicted and found that the thoughts generated about the self only affected self-attitudes in the confident posture. Conceptually similar to the previous study, the effect of the direction of thoughts on self-esteem was greater when participants wrote their thoughts in the confident rather than the doubtful body posture. Thus, this research demonstrated that relatively static body responses, such as postures, are able to influence individuals' reliance on their own thoughts; previous research had shown that reliance on one's thoughts could be influenced by more dynamic behaviors such as head movements.

These two studies demonstrated that inducing doubts about possessing positive qualities tended to undermine self-esteem, whereas inducing doubts about possessing negative qualities tended to enhance self-esteem. Importantly, both studies showed that these changes in self-evaluation were mediated by changes in certainty about the self-beliefs that were listed; these changes in certainty were, in turn, provoked by different bodily responses. Subsequent research has replicated these effects on self-thoughts using other validating variables (for a review, see Briñol, DeMarree, & Petty, 2010).

Other Bodily Responses (Facial Expressions) Validate Self-Relevant Thoughts

The experiments described before reveal that bodily responses such as head movements and handwriting can influence self-evaluation by affecting the confidence with which people hold their self-related thoughts. In this section, we describe three lines of research in which other bodily responses (i.e., facial expressions) affected self-attitudes by validating thoughts. The main idea inspiring this research is that emotion can affect thought confidence. This possibility follows directly from the finding that emotional states can relate to confidence, with happy people being more certain and confident than sad individuals (e.g., Smith & Ellsworth, 1985). If emotion influences thought confidence, then people in a happy state should be more reliant on their thoughts than people in a sad state. Consistent with this idea, Briñol et al. (2007) found that when people were placed in a happy state following message processing, attitudes and behavioral intentions were more influenced by the recipients' thoughts about the arguments than when they were placed in a sad state following the message.

Subsequent research has replicated these effects by inducing emotions through facial expressions, which validated self-relevant thoughts rather than thoughts in response to persuasive messages. For example, in one study, Briñol, Stavraki, Paredes, & Petty (2011) asked participants to think about and write down their good or bad qualities as job candidates while they were smiling or frowning. In line with our previous studies, it was predicted and found that the thoughts participants generated only affected self-evaluations among those in the happy face condition. Not only happiness but also other emotions related to confidence can influence evaluations by self-validation, such as anger (Briñol, Petty, Stavraki, & Wagner, 2009) and disgust (Wagner, Briñol, & Petty, 2009).

Bodily Responses Can Validate Emotional Thoughts

We have already explained how facial expressions related to emotions can validate thoughts about the self and about persuasive messages. We argue here that embodied manipulations can also validate (or invalidate) thoughts about current emotional states. Specifically, we postulate that one's emotion-relevant thoughts can be validated or invalidated by embodied manipulations, thereby affecting the person's emotional experience. In a test of this idea, Rucker, Briñol, and Petty (2011) asked participants to write about happy or sad experiences with either their dominant or nondominant hand. As noted earlier, writing emotional experiences with the dominant hand should lead to greater confidence in the emotional experiences and, consequently, stronger emotions than should writing with the nondominant hand. In line with this assumption, writing about emotional experiences with the dominant hand led to a larger biasing impact of the activated emotion on subsequent judgments of the likelihood of irrelevant emotional events than did writing about emotional experiences with the nondominant hand. This research revealed that emotion-relevant thoughts can be affected by metacognitive confidence, thereby influencing the emotion that is experienced.

Bodily Responses Can Validate Even Confidence-Related Thoughts

We have described how the thought confidence induced by bodily movements and facial expressions can influence evaluative judgments by affecting metacognitive processes. Our review on the effects of self-validation processes has also examined some cases in which these bodily responses influenced not only thoughts in response to a persuasive proposal, but also other kinds of cognitions, such as self-related thoughts and emotional thoughts. As mentioned earlier, research on self-validation suggests that the confidence that emerges from the body can also be applied to any primary cognition.

Given that metacognitive confidence can be applied to any cognition, an interesting case to examine would be that in which people have confidence in (or doubt about) their own confidence or doubt. Especially interesting would be the case in which people doubt their own doubts. In one study about doubting one's own doubt due to bodily responses (Wichman et al., 2010), participants were first primed with doubt or certainty and then exposed to a head movement manipulation.

Specifically, the initial writing task used to prime uncertainty asked participants to write about a time when they were uncertain and doubtful or about a time when they were certain and confident. Following this task, participants completed a head movement induction, which was described as a study on "motor–eye coordination." For a few minutes, participants followed, with their heads, a ball moving either vertically (i.e., nodding condition) or horizontally (i.e., shaking condition) on a computer screen. Supporting the idea that people can either trust or doubt their own doubts, head nodding (vs. shaking) accentuated (vs. attenuated) the impact of the initial doubt (vs. certainty) manipulation. This study demonstrated that a secondary, embodied manipulation of certainty or uncertainty can interact with an initial induction in the manner specified by the self-validation hypothesis rather than in the additive way that would be expected from prior work on sequential inductions of constructs.

Bodily Responses Can Validate Any Primed Thoughts

Regardless of whether people were asked to think about persuasive messages or to generate self- or emotion-relevant thoughts, all studies described thus far specifically asked participants to think about the object, issue, idea, or proposal under consideration. Although the original research applied confidence to intentionally generated mental contents relevant for persuasion, the research described in this section examines whether people validate whatever thoughts they have in mind, including subtly primed constructs. We argue that the self-validation framework can be applied to domains other than persuasion, such as priming, because metacognitive confidence should apply to whatever the salient or available mental contents are at a given moment. Thoughts caused by primes are also interesting to examine because, unlike the thoughts that participants explicitly generate in response to a persuasive message or request, prime-induced thoughts may occur even though participants do not have a conscious goal to generate them.

Although it is clear that people can be unaware of the source of validation (e.g., they are unaware that their head nodding is the cause of perceived validity), we were interested in examining whether it is possible to validate cognitions that stem from unknown origins rather than being generated with conscious intention. Indeed, it is unclear if there is a role for thought validation when participants do not have an explicit goal to generate thoughts. If people do not have an explicit goal to generate thoughts, then they might also lack a goal to evaluate their thoughts.

We examined these issues by testing whether head nodding would moderate the impact of subtle primes on participants' judgments. Specifically, in one of the studies of this series, DeMarree, Briñol, and Petty (2011) subliminally primed participants with words related to the Black (vs. White) stereotype. Prior research has shown that such primes can affect what people think of themselves (see Wheeler, DeMarree, & Petty, 2007, for a review). Following this induction, participants were instructed to use their heads to follow a ball moving vertically or horizontally on the screen. Consistent with the self-validation logic for vertical versus horizontal head movements, we found that the direction of the prime affected participants' felt aggression on an implicit measure as well as their deliberative ratings of closeness to African Americans in the head nodding but not in the head shaking condition. Thus, as was the case with head nodding affecting confidence in thoughts to a persuasive message, so too did head nodding appear to affect the validity and use of mental contents that were subtly activated via priming.

In another experiment of this series, participants subliminally primed with the concept of resistance (vs. persuasion) showed more resistance to subsequent persuasive proposals. However, this only occurred when participants were nodding (compared with shaking) their heads immediately following the priming induction. In still other studies on priming, a goal was activated, followed by a validation manipulation; in each case, the behavioral effects of the goal were more evident when the goal priming was followed by a confidence (head nodding) than a doubtful (head shaking) behavioral induction (DeMarree et al., 2011). In comparison with our studies exploring the embodied validation of several types of intentionally generated thoughts, our studies on priming extended the range of mental contents that are subject to metacognitive influence.

MODERATING FACTORS OF EMBODIED SELF-VALIDATION

In addition to proposing thought confidence as a general mediator of the impact of bodily responses on judgment, self-validation research also points to unique moderators for this metacognitive process. Thus, another contribution of our research on embodied validation has been to specify the circumstances under which thought confidence is likely to influence judgments. Next, we describe the two moderating conditions about which the most research has been conducted so far.

Elaboration

Petty and colleagues (2002) demonstrated that self-validation is more likely to take place when people have the motivation and ability to attend to and interpret their own cognitive experiences (e.g., if participants are high in need for cognition, Cacioppo & Petty, 1982, or when there is high personal relevance of the persuasion topic, Petty & Cacioppo, 1979). There are at least two reasons for this. First, for validation processes to matter, people need to have some thoughts to validate. Second, people need substantial motivation and ability not only to think at the primary level of cognition but also to think and care about their own thoughts. Thus, the self-validation processes we document have some boundary conditions, including the requirement that people are engaging in relatively high levels of thinking.[1]

As an illustration of the moderating role of elaboration, consider the research on arm movements described earlier. Cacioppo and his colleagues (1993) found that arm flexion was associated with more positive evaluations of neutral stimuli than was arm extension, and that these body influences were more likely to occur under relatively low-elaboration conditions. More recently, Centerbar and Clore (2006) found that arm flexion (vs. extension) only led to more positive evaluations when the stimuli evaluated were already considered positive. Interestingly, arm flexion (vs. extension) was associated with *less* favorable evaluations for previously *negative* stimuli. If one assumes that participants generated either positive or negative thoughts in response to the valenced material, then arm flexion (vs. extension) could have affected attitudes by influencing the confidence with which those thoughts were held. Taken together, these two lines of research imply that, similarly to other behaviors, arm flexion can influence attitude change by serving as a simple cue (i.e., when elaboration is low) or by affecting thought confidence (i.e., when elaboration is high).

In a formal test of this possibility, Wagner, Briñol, Petty, and Cacioppo (2009) conducted a series of studies in which elaboration likelihood was varied along with arm movements and thought direction. Specifically, they assigned participants to the cells of a 2 (stimulus valence: positive vs. negative) × 2 (arm posture: flexion vs. extension) × 2 (elaboration: cognitive load vs. no load) between-subjects factorial design. They predicted and found that individuals engaging in arm flexion were more likely to use their thoughts in evaluating novel objects than were individuals engaging in arm extension. One explanation for this finding is that participants in the flexion condition were "approaching" (i.e., using) their thoughts about valenced stimuli, whereas participants in the extension condition were "avoiding" (i.e., not using) their thoughts about the same stimuli.

Further, they found that this effect was observed primarily among individuals who were engaged in much rather than little thought, given that thought validation is a fairly complex cognitive process, unlike classical conditioning. These findings demonstrated that arm posture can affect the extent to which individuals use their own thoughts in evaluating novel objects, provided that the individuals are thinking relatively deeply. In contrast, those who were in low thinking tended to show more favorable evaluation in the arm flexion than in the arm extension condition. Taking together high- and low-thinking conditions, these findings are consistent with the idea that the same bodily response (i.e., arm movement) can influence attitudes by different mechanisms (e.g., as a peripheral cue, by validating thoughts) as a function of elaboration likelihood. Viewed differently, this research suggests that the same behavior can lead to the same outcome (e.g., arm flexion increasing persuasion) by very different underlying processes (e.g., thought validation, classical conditioning).

In another illustration relevant to the role of elaboration likelihood in determining the mechanism by which embodied manipulations affect attitude change, Briñol and Petty (2011) manipulated the "openness" of participants' body postures. In one study, participants received a persuasive message containing either strong or weak arguments. While reading this message, participants were instructed to keep their knees separated with their legs spread apart (i.e., open posture) or to keep their knees touching with their legs and feet together (i.e., closed posture; McGinley, LeFevre, & McGinley, 1975). Amount of thinking was assessed in this experiment by asking participants to report how much they thought about the message. For participants reporting low thinking about the proposal, a main effect of body posture was found, such that open displays led to more favorable attitudes than closed displays. This finding is consistent with research described earlier showing that body postures and movements can have a direct impact on attitudes when elaboration is low (e.g., Priester, Cacioppo, & Petty, 1996; Taylor, 1975). For participants reporting high thinking, however, an interaction between argument quality and body posture was found, demonstrating that the same body postures can influence attitudes through self-validation processes.

Timing

Subsequent research has identified another limiting condition on the influence of the body on attitudes via thought validation. That is, the confidence that emerges from the body should be salient *following* (or at least, during) thought generation rather than prior to thought generation. For example, Briñol, Petty, Valle, Rucker, and Becerra (2007) conducted a study in which the order in which the validating variable (power) and message processing took place was varied. Specifically, they manipulated the timing of the power induction to demonstrate the consequences of two different psychological processes: high power decreasing information processing when preceding the message and increasing the use of thoughts compared to low power when following the message.

In this study, participants received a strong message in favor of a new cell phone. The message was presented either immediately before or after participants engaged in a power manipulation (for a review of bodily responses related to power, see Schubert, Waldzus, & Seibt, 2008). Compared to the low-power groups, it was expected and found that the high-power (vs. low-power) conditions reduced persuasion when the power induction came *prior to* the presentation of the message. This is because high-power individuals processed the strong arguments less than did the low-power individuals. However, it was found that high—compared to low—power enhanced persuasion when manipulated *after* processing of the proposal. Presumably, this is because high-power individuals were more reliant on their positive thoughts about the strong arguments than were low-power individuals. These findings suggest that the same power-relevant behaviors can have different (and opposite) effects in persuasive settings depending on when the power manipulations are introduced.

THE UNIQUENESS OF SELF-VALIDATION

New Mediation and Moderation for Ease of Retrieval Effects

Now that the self-validation approach has been described, it is important to note that the self-validation framework shares features with some other metacognitive theories in social psychology, but also has notable differences from these theories. Most relevant to the present review, the self-validation approach agrees with other recent theories on the importance of secondary cognition. However, previous approaches have generally examined and attempted to explain one single source of metacognitive influence. For example, Kruglanski's (1989) lay epistemic theory (LET) has been applied to causal attributions and argues that validation processes are affected by the number of causal explanations generated—the more alternative explanations that are generated for any given event, the less confidence a person has in any one causal explanation. Generating few explanations, then, leads to greater confidence in each explanation.

Another well-known metacognitive theory involves the role of ease-of-retrieval in social judgment (Schwarz et al., 1991; for a review, see Sanna & Lundberg, this volume). In their classic studies, Schwarz and colleagues demonstrated that when thoughts come to mind easily, those thoughts have more of an impact on judgment than if those same thoughts come to mind less easily. Specifically, these researchers asked participants to generate either two (i.e., easy to generate) or eight (i.e., difficult to generate) occasions on which they had behaved assertively. Somewhat paradoxically, participants judged themselves to be more assertive after listing two—as opposed to eight—instances of assertive behavior. That is, if the number of behaviors listed were the chief determinant of participants' self-judgments (i.e., primary cognition), then participants should have reported being more assertive in the condition in which they listed eight assertive behaviors. However, participants used the ease with which they could generate their thoughts to judge how assertive they were. The original interpretation of this effect is that ease worked in a heuristic fashion, indicating the availability (or prevalence) of assertive behaviors in their entire lives (see also Kahneman & Tversky, 1972).

Meta-cognitive ease could also operate through other mechanisms, depending on specific characteristics of the situation (for a review on ease and persuasion, see Briñol, Tormala, & Petty, in press). For instance, as indicated above, ease-of-retrieval has been assumed to influence judgment through the operation of a relatively simple judgment heuristic linking ease with prevalence, likelihood, and availability. If this is the case, then ease-of-retrieval effects should be particularly pronounced among people who are not thinking very much (e.g., for a low importance topic; see Rothman & Schwarz, 1998). Consistent with the self-validation perspective, however, people can also infer that thoughts that are generated easily are particularly valid, at least in contrast to thoughts that are generated with relatively more difficulty (Tormala, Petty, Briñol, 2002). In this case, the validating (or invalidating) effects of ease (or difficulty) should be most pronounced when people are likely to be thinking carefully about the topic or issue at hand. This is because metacognitive judgments regarding ease (and difficulty) require that individuals be motivated and able to consider not only the primary cognitions that they have generated but, also, the metacognitive experiences accompanying the generation of those primary cognitions. Clearly, such a process involves careful and deliberative thinking, and would not be expected under low-thinking conditions.

Indeed, across a series of studies designed to explore this possibility (Tormala, et al. 2002; Tormala, Briñol, Falces, & Petty, 2007), we found evidence that ease-of-retrieval effects can operate through self-validation processes. Moreover, it was also found that such effects were strongest in high-thinking situations. This is not to say, of course, that ease-of-retrieval cannot affect judgment via the operation of a simple heuristic process. In fact, such a finding seems likely under low-thinking conditions. What is critical, here, is that the self-validation perspective provided both a boundary condition (i.e., moderator: amount of thinking) for ease-of-retrieval effects and a new mechanism (i.e., mediator: validation/invalidation of primary cognitions) through which ease-of-retrieval can operate. We believe that the novel predictions (and findings) provided by the self-validation perspective reflects the fact that this perspective can be understood as a general account of how meta-cognitive processes can influence social judgments. As such, the self-validation perspective can highlight—or uncover—the possibility that well-studied variables, such as ease-of-retrieval, can operate by validating thoughts. Specifically, because many researchers focus on the study of particular variables, they may not consider the possibility that other, seemingly-unrelated variables, might operate according to similar fundamental processes. The self-validation perspective, as general approach, integrates the operation of different variables (e.g., source credibility, recipient's power, social consensus, message matching; see Briñol & Petty, 2009a) through the same underlying mechanism.

The Self-Validation Perspective and Emotion

As a final example of the utility of the self-validation perspective in providing novel predictions for well-studied social judgment variables, let us consider the case of emotion. As noted earlier, research inspired by the ELM has shown that incidental emotions can influence persuasion through multiple processes (Petty, Fabrigar, & Wegener, 2003). When elaboration is constrained to be low, emotions affect attitudes through the operation of simple cues or heuristics (e.g., "if I am happy, I must be satisfied with my life"; Schwarz & Clore, 1983; Petty, Schumann, Richman, & Strathman, 1993). When elaboration is unconstrained by individual or contextual factors, then emotions can change how much people think about the message or issue under consideration. For example, people may think more when they are sad because sadness can serve as a cue that they are not progressing satisfactorily toward their goals (Carver & Scheier, 1990) and need to engage in problem-solving to eliminate, or at least deal with, the source of the sadness (Bless, Bohner, Schwarz, & Strack, 1991). Conversely, people may think less when they are happy because happiness makes them feel especially certain (Tiedens & Linton, 2001) or because happiness interferes with individuals' ability to engage in care-ful, deliberate information processing (Mackie & Worth, 1989). When elaboration is constrained at a high level, emotions can bias the content of the thoughts that people generate. For instance, people who are placed in a happy state estimate that positive outcomes are more likely to occur than do people who are placed in a sad state and this can lead them to be more influenced by positive than negative arguments (Wegener, Petty, & Klein, 1994; see also, DeSteno, Petty, Wegener, & Rucker, 2000).

To this set of mechanisms by which incidental emotions can impact persuasion, the self-validation perspective adds one more. Specifically, the self-validation per-spective notes that emotions can affect people's general feelings of confidence and doubt (Tiedens & Linton, 2001) and, as such, should also be able to influence the confidence with which people hold their thoughts. In one relevant study, Briñol, Petty, & Barden (2007) exposed undergraduate participants to a persuasive mes-sage varying in argument quality. Strong arguments elicited predominantly favor-able thoughts toward the proposal (i.e., the adoption of personal identification cards at the participants' university), whereas weak arguments elicited predominantly unfavorable thoughts. After reading the message, participants were asked to write about a time when they felt either happy or sad. Then, attitudes toward the proposal were measured. Results showed that the direction of participants' thoughts mattered more among participants in the happiness condition than among participants in the sadness condition. Viewed differently, participants who had read the strong message—and who had generated generally favorable thoughts about it—reported more favorable attitudes when they were feeling happy than when they were feeling sad. However, an opposite pattern emerged among participants who had read the weak message. These participants reported more favorable attitudes when they were feeling sad than when they were feeling happy. Mediational analysis indicated that these persuasion effects reflected the impact of emotions on thought confidence, as happy participants reported greater thought confidence than did sad participants. This research illustrates that the self-validation perspective offers novel predictions regarding not only ease but also another well-studied variable such as emotion. Importantly, though, it should be noted that self-validation effects for emotion were anticipated (and found) only in specific situations, namely when emotions were induced *after* message processing and when elaboration likelihood was *high*. As such, the self-validation perspective identified both a new *mediator* (i.e., validating primary thoughts) through which emotion can operate as well as a new *moderator* (i.e., timing of the emotion manipulation) of the effects of emotion on attitudes and judgments (For a review of the role of positive emotions in increasing the use of primary cognitions, see also, Huntsinger & Clore, this volume.)

CONCLUSIONS AND FUTURE DIRECTIONS IN EMBODIED PERSUASION AND VALIDATION

This review has described the various ways in which bodily movements and overt behaviors not only can affect the number and valence of thoughts, but also can validate a person's own thoughts. Thus, self-validation provides a completely new, metacognitive mechanism by which a large number of traditional (e.g., head movements, facial expressions) and more recent (e.g., handwriting, body postures) bodily variables can impact attitudes and judgments. Importantly, the conditions necessary for metacognitive processes to operate have been clearly specified. As described throughout, specifying these moderating conditions is important because our body can influence social judgments through multiple processes relevant to primary and secondary cognition.

Probably due to the very physical nature of these variables (i.e., bodily responses), researchers have usually speculated that the underlying mechanism for embodied persuasion effects has to be a relatively simple, rudimentary, primitive one. Indeed, this "matching assumption" between variables and processes is partially correct because bodily responses can affect attitudes by processes that require very little thinking (e.g., classical conditioning, self-perception). However, bodily responses are capable of affecting attitudes via not only low-thinking processes but also more deliberative ones (e.g., by affecting the direction of the thoughts that come to mind). Importantly, the most recent research described in this chapter has revealed that behaviors such as head nodding or smiling can validate (rather than merely change) what we are thinking.

Identifying Critical Aspects of the Behavior

The studies we have reviewed examined behaviors ranging from relatively simple bodily movements to more complex behaviors. Indeed, future research might benefit from exploration of new behaviors other than the ones covered in this review (Lakoff & Johnson, 1999). We argue, however, that in addition to identifying new behaviors, it is critical to determine which dimensions of already studied behaviors are responsible for the effects they produce. Potential dimensions of interest are *valence* (i.e., whether the behavior is positive or negative), *certainty* (i.e., whether the behavior is associated with confidence or doubt), *motivation orientation* (i.e., approach–avoidance), *intensity and effort* (i.e., arousing or relaxing), *movement* (i.e., motor action or static pose), and *perceptions of agency* (i.e., self or other, deliberative or involuntary).

The Meaning of Behavior

Most of the behaviors used in the experiments described in this review have very clear meanings attached to them. For instance, nodding is often associated with agreement and validation, whereas arm flexion tends to be associated with approaching objects. However, the meaning of these behaviors can vary across individuals and situations. For example, nodding can be associated with disagreement in certain contexts (e.g., yea–yea responding), and arm extension can be seen as approaching in other settings (e.g., extending the arm to reach a desired object). We argue that if the meaning associated with a behavior changes, the effect of that behavior on subsequent attitudes could also change, at least under high-elaboration conditions and when attitudes are assessed with explicit measures (see, for example, Briñol, Petty, & Tormala, 2006). Indeed, it would be interesting to study whether there is a default meaning for certain behaviors tapped in low-thinking conditions or on measures of automatic evaluation that are then modified in high-thinking situations or on deliberative measures. Thus, as has been the case with the attitude domain in general (Petty, Fazio, & Briñol, 2009), future research on embodied persuasion would likely benefit from the inclusion of measures involving automatic rather than deliberative attitudes.

Future research should also explore the conditions and processes by which the meaning of behavior and that of the context interact. Literature on placebo effects can be particularly informative in this domain. Studies on placebo effects often involve participants performing a behavior (e.g., taking pills, using a lotion) for which a particular meaning is "artificially" provided. Extensive research has documented subsequent internal changes consistent with these ascribed meanings (for reviews, see Kirsch, 1999; Moerman, 2002). Also interesting is the fact that this literature has shown that the more extreme the behavior is, the stronger are the placebo effects that result (e.g., taking two pills is better than taking just one, an injection is better than pills, and placebo surgery is better than other treatments; e.g., Guess, Kleinman, Kusek, & Engel, 2004).

Performing the Behavior

There is substantial evidence suggesting that it might not be necessary to act physically for behavior to produce attitude change. That is, simply imagining behavior might be sufficient for the "behavior" to affect attitudes (e.g., feedback about behavior, Valins, 1966; visual illusions suggesting that we acted, Neumann & Strack, 2000; computer-controlled digital representations of the person acting in a virtual environment, Bailenson & Yee, 2005). Similarly, there is plenty of evidence suggesting that simply imagining or retrieving instances of behavior activates the same areas of the brain as actual behavior, and thus embodiment can have similar effects regardless of whether a given action is performed or a simulation of that experience occurs in the brain (e.g., Anderson, 1983). Recent research has also revealed that the perception of agency can be even more important than the actual agency of the behavior in producing attitude change effects (Taylor, Lord, & Bond, 2009).

Among other things, this notion brings the question of whether physical motor performance adds anything above and beyond the mere activation of the mental representation of behavior. Also important is that it is not entirely clear whether a given behavior has to be perceived as one's own for it to influence attitudes. That is, merely observing the behaviors of others might produce effects similar to performing the behavior oneself, perhaps by the action of mirror neurons in automatic imitation. For example, consistent with classic studies revealing that people change their behavior to conform to others (Asch, 1955; Sherif, 1936), it has been repeatedly shown that people tend to imitate and mimic the behaviors they observe in others in order to facilitate social interaction (e.g., Byrne, 1971). Also, others' behavior can function as a prime to activate our own behavior automatically (Chartrand & Bargh, 1999).[3] We argue that future research should explore whether the different means by which the mental representations of behavior are activated (e.g., performing vs. observing the behavior) are consequential for persuasion and social judgment.

NOTES

1. It is important to note that this does not mean that it is necessary to ask people explicitly to evaluate their thought confidence in order to observe self-validation effects. In fact, our research has clearly shown that self-validation processes occur regardless of *whether* (or not), *when* (before or after reporting attitudes), and *how* (individually or globally) thought confidence is assessed (for a review, see, Briñol & Petty, 2009a). In other words, the notion that people might not be constantly aware of their confidence in their thoughts does not make it less impactful or any less metacognitive in nature. Indeed, metacognition (like regular, primary cognition) can sometimes have implicit bases and implicit effects. People might not even be able consciously to verbalize or explain the basis of their metacognition when asked to do so (just as they cannot verbalize the basis of their primary cognition). Yet, such cognition could still have an

impact. We have found that when asked to do so, people are capable of reporting their confidence in their thoughts and that this confidence maps onto predictable and potentially important outcomes. However, people are unlikely to have much conscious recognition of the *origins* of this confidence.

2. Although self-validation focuses on confidence as the main metacognitive dimension, it is important to note that other metacognitive factors can also be explored in relation to primary cognitions. For example, it is well established that thoughts and mental constructs that are highly accessible are more consequential in terms of durability and subsequent impact than are less accessible thoughts (e.g., DeMarree, Petty, & Briñol, 2007). Although accessibility and other features of thoughts (e.g., importance) are often related to confidence, these are relatively independent features of cognition (for a review, see Petty et al., 2007). Furthermore, our research on self-validation has also distinguished, on both conceptual and operational levels, between confidence and other previously studied dimensions, such as desirability and likelihood (Briñol, Petty, & Tormala, 2004). We have distinguished thought confidence not only from other dimensions at the primary level of cognition, but also from other approaches to confidence that have focused exclusively on one aspect of confidence, such as confidence in the *likelihood* component of a belief. Thought confidence is a broader concept that incorporates this as well as other sources of confidence (e.g., confidence in desirability, confidence that stems from ease of retrieval of the thought, etc.).

3. Niedenthal, Brauer, Halberstadt, and Innes-Ker (2001) found that when participants were prevented from mimicking others, it took them longer to detect changes in emotional material relative to a group that was free to mimic. This suggests that mimicking might be related to very basic forms of social perception and categorization (see Briñol, DeMarree, & Smith, 2010, for a discussion).

REFERENCES

Anderson, C. A. (1983). Imagination and expectation: The effect of imagining behavioral scripts on personal intentions. *Psychological Bulletin, 93,* 30–56.

Asch, S. E. (1955). Opinions and social pressure. *Scientific American, 11,* 31–35.

Bailenson, J., & Yee, N. (2005). Digital chameleons: Automatic assimilation of nonverbal gestures in immersive virtual environments. *Psychological Science, 16,* 814–819.

Baron, R. S. (2000). Arousal, capacity, and intense indoctrination. *Personality and Social Psychology Review, 4,* 238–254.

Bem, D. J. (1972). Self-perception theory. In L. Berkowitz (Ed.), *Advances in experimental social psychology* (Vol. 6, pp. 1–62). New York, NY: Academic Press.

Briñol, P., DeMarree, K. G., & Petty, R. E. (2010). Processes by which confidence (vs. doubt) influences the self. In R. M. Arkin, K. C. Oleson, & P. J. Carroll (Eds.), *Handbook of the uncertain self* (pp. 13–35). New York, NY: Psychology Press.

Briñol, P., DeMarree, K. G., & Smith, K. R. (2010). The role of embodied change in perceiving and processing facial expressions of others. *Behavioral and Brain Sciences, 33,* 437–438.

Briñol, P., & Petty, R. E. (2003). Overt head movements and persuasion: A self-validation analysis. *Journal of Personality and Social Psychology, 84,* 1123–1139.

Briñol, P., & Petty, R. E. (2008). Embodied persuasion: Fundamental processes by which bodily responses can impact attitudes. In G. R. Semin & E. R. Smith (Eds.), *Embodiment grounding: Social, cognitive, affective, and neuroscientific approaches* (pp. 184–207). Cambridge, England: Cambridge University Press.

Briñol, P., & Petty, R. E. (2009a). Persuasion: Insights from the self-validation hypothesis. In M. P. Zanna (Ed.), *Advances in experimental social psychology* (pp. 69–118). New York, NY: Elsevier.

Briñol, P., & Petty, R. E. (2009b). *Smiling as embodied persuasion: A self-validation analysis*. Unpublished manuscript.

Briñol, P., & Petty, R. E. (2009c). Source factors in persuasion: A self-validation approach. *European Review of Social Psychology, 20*, 49–96.

Briñol, P., & Petty, R. E. (2011). *The influence of a recipient's body position on persuasion: An information processing approach*. Unpublished Manuscript.

Briñol, P., Petty, R. E., & Barden, J. (2007). Happiness versus sadness as determinants of thought confidence in persuasion: A self-validation analysis. *Journal of Personality and Social Psychology, 93*, 711–727.

Briñol, P., Petty, R. E., & Tormala, Z. L. (2004). The self-validation of cognitive responses to advertisements. *Journal of Consumer Research, 30*, 559–573.

Briñol, P., Petty, R. E., & Tormala, Z. L. (2006). The meaning of ease and its malleability. *Psychological Science, 17*, 200–206.

Briñol, P., Petty, R. E., Stavraki, M., & Wagner, B. C. (2009). *Anger: A self-validation analysis*. Unpublished manuscript.

Briñol, P., Petty, R. E., Valle, C., Rucker, D. D., & Becerra, A. (2007). The effects of message recipients' power before and after persuasion: A self-validation analysis. *Journal of Personality and Social Psychology, 93*, 1040–1053.

Briñol, P., Petty, R. E., & Wagner, B. C. (2009). Body posture effects on self-evaluation: A self-validation approach. *European Journal of Social Psychology, 39*, 1053–1064.

Briñol, P., Stavraki, M., Paredes, B., & Petty, R. E. (2011). *Smiling validates positive and negative thoughts: A self-validation analysis*. Unpublished Manuscript.

Byrne, D. (1971). *The attraction paradigm*. New York, NY: Academic Press.

Cacioppo, J. T., Marshall-Goodell, B. S., Tassinary, L. G., & Petty, R. E. (1992). Rudimentary determinants of attitudes: Classical conditioning is more effective when prior knowledge about the attitude stimulus is low than high. *Journal of Experimental Social Psychology, 28*, 207–233.

Cacioppo, J. T., & Petty, R. E. (1982). The need for cognition. *Journal of Personality and Social Psychology, 42*, 116–131.

Cacioppo, J. T., Priester, J. R., & Berntson, G. G. (1993). Rudimentary determinants of attitudes II: Arm flexion and extension have differential effects on attitudes. *Journal of Personality and Social Psychology, 65*, 5–17.

Carver, C. S., & Scheier, M. F. (1990). Origins and functions of positive and negative affect: A control-process view. *Psychological Review, 97*, 19–35.

Centerbar, D. B., & Clore, G. L. (2006). Do approach-avoidance actions create attitudes? *Psychological Science, 17*, 22–29.

Chartrand, T. L., & Bargh, J. A. (1999). The chameleon effect: The perception behavior link and social interaction. *Journal of Personality and Social Psychology, 76*, 893–910.

Clore, G. L., & Huntsinger, J. R. (2007). How emotions inform judgment and regulate thought. *Trends in Cognitive Science, 11*, 393–399.

DeMarree, K. G., Briñol, P., & Petty, R. E. (2011). *Implicit self-validation: The effects of overt behavior on subliminally primed constructs*. Unpublished manuscript.

DeMarree, K. G., Petty, R. E., & Briñol, P. (2007). Self and attitude strength parallels: Focus on accessibility. *Social and Personality Psychology Compass, 1*, 441–468.

DeSteno, D., Petty, R. E., Wegener, D. T., & Rucker, D. D. (2000). Beyond valence in the perception of likelihodd: The role of emotion specificity. *Journal of Personality and Social Psychology, 78*, 397–416.

Förster, J., & Stepper, S. (2000). Compatibility between approach/avoidance simulation and valenced information determines residual attention during the process of encoding. *European Journal of Social Psychology, 30,* 853–871.

Förster, J., & Strack, F. (1996). Influence of overt head movements on memory for valence words: A case of conceptual-motor compatibility. *Journal of Personality and Social Psychology, 71,* 421–430.

Guess, H. A., Kleinman, A., Kusek, J. W., & Engel, L. W. (2004). *The science of the placebo: Toward an interdisciplinary research agenda.* London, England: BMJ Books.

Jostmann, N. B., Lakens, D., & Schubert, T. W. (2009). Weight as an embodiment of importance. *Psychological Science, 20,* 1169–1174.

Kellerman, J., Lewis, J., & Laird, J. D. (1989). Looking and loving: The effects of mutual gaze on feelings of romantic love. *Journal of Research in Personality, 23,* 145–161.

Kirsch, I. (1999). *How expectancies shape experience.* Washington, DC: American Psychological Association.

Kruglanski, A. W. (1989). *Lay epistemics and human knowledge: Cognitive and motivational bases.* New York, NY: Plenum Press.

Lakoff, G., & Johnson, M. (1999). *Philosophy in the flesh: The embodied mind and its challenge to Western thought.* New York, NY: Basic Books.

McGinley, H., LeFevre, R., & McGinley, P. (1975). The influence of a communicator's body position on opinion change in others. *Journal of Personality and Social Psychology, 31,* 686–690.

Moerman, D. (2002). *Meaning, medicine, and the "placebo effect."* Cambridge, England: Cambridge University Press.

Neumann, R., Förster, J., & Strack, F. (2003). Motor compatibility: The bidirectional link between behavior and evaluation. In J. Musch & K. C. Klauer (Eds.), *The psychology of evaluation: Affective processes in cognition and emotion* (pp. 371–391). Mahwah, NJ: Lawrence Erlbaum Associates.

Neumann, R., & Strack, F. (2000). Approach and avoidance: the influence of proprioceptive and exteroceptive cues on encoding of affective information. *Journal of Personality and Social Psychology, 79,* 39–48.

Niedenthal, P. M., Brauer, M., Halberstadt, J. B., & Innes-Ker, A. H. (2001). When did her smile drop? Facial mimicry and the influences of emotional state on the detection of change in emotional expression. *Cognition and Emotion, 15,* 853–864.

Petty, R. E., Briñol, P., & Tormala, Z. L. (2002). Thought confidence as a determinant of persuasion: The self-validation hypothesis. *Journal of Personality and Social Psychology, 82,* 722–741.

Petty, R. E., Briñol, P., Tormala, Z. L., & Wegener, D. T. (2007). The role of meta-cognition in social judgment. In E. T. Higgins & A. W. Kruglanski, (Eds.) *Social psychology: A handbook of basic principles* (2nd ed., pp. 254–284). New York, NY: Guilford Press.

Petty, R. E., & Cacioppo, J. T. (1979). Issue-involvement can increase or decrease persuasion by enhancing message-relevant cognitive responses. *Journal of Personality and Social Psychology, 37,* 1915–1926.

Petty, R. E., & Cacioppo, J. T. (1986). *Communication and persuasion: Central and peripheral routes to attitude change.* New York, NY: Springer-Verlag.

Petty, R. E., Fabrigar, L. R., & Wegener, D. T. (2003). Emotional factors in attitudes and persuasion. In R. J. Davidson, K. R. Scherer, & H. H. Goldsmith (Eds.), *Handbook of affective sciences* (pp. 752–772). Oxford, England: Oxford University Press.

Petty, R. E., Fazio, R. H., & Briñol, P. (Eds.) (2009). *Attitudes: Insights from the new implicit measures.* New York: Psychology Press.

Petty, R. E., Schumann, D. W., Richman, S. A., & Strathman, A. J. (1993). Positive mood and persuasion: Different roles for affect under high and low elaboration conditions. *Journal of Personality and Social Psychology, 64,* 5–20.

Petty, R. E., Wells, G. L., Heesacker, M., Brock, T. C., & Cacioppo, J. T. (1983). The effects of recipient posture on persuasion: A cognitive response analysis *Personality and Social Psychology Bulletin, 9,* 209–222.

Priester, J. M., Cacioppo, J. T., & Petty, R.E. (1996). The influence of motor processes on attitudes toward novel versus familiar semantic stimuli. *Personality and Social Psychology Bulletin, 22,* 442–447.

Rothman, A. J., & Schwarz, N. (1998). Constructing perceptions of vulnerability: Personal relevance and the use of experiential information in health judgments. *Personality and Social Psychology Bulletin, 24,* 1053–1064.

Rucker, D. D., Briñol, P., & Petty, R. E. (2006). *The role of metacognition in relying on one's emotions.* Unpublished manuscript.

Schubert, T. W., Waldzus, S., & Seibt, B. (2008). The embodiment of power and communalism in space and bodily contact. In G. R. Semin & E. R. Smith (Eds.), *Embodiment grounding: Social, cognitive, affective, and neuroscientific approaches* (pp. 160–183). Cambridge, England: Cambridge University Press.

Schwarz, N., Bless, H., Strack, F., Klumpp, G., Rittenauer-Schatka, H., & Simons, A. (1991). Ease of retrieval as information: Another look at the availability heuristic. *Journal of Personality and Social Psychology, 61,* 195–202.

Sherif, M. (1936). *The psychology of social norms.* New York, NY: Harper & Row.

Smith, C. A., & Ellsworth, P. C. (1985). Patterns of cognitive appraisal in emotion. *Journal of Personality and Social Psychology, 48,* 813–838.

Stepper, S., & Strack, F. (1993). Proprioceptive determinants of emotional and nonemotional feelings. *Journal of Personality and Social Psychology, 64,* 211–220.

Strack, F., Martin, L., & Stepper, S. (1988). Inhibiting and facilitating conditions of the human smile: A nonobtrusive test of the facial feedback hypothesis. *Journal of Personality and Social Psychology, 54,* 768–777.

Taylor, C. A., Lord, C. G., & Bond, C. F., Jr. (2009). Embodiment, agency, and attitude change. *Journal of Personality and Social Psychology, 97,* 946–962.

Taylor, S. E. (1975). On inferring one's attitude from one's behavior: Some delimiting condition. *Journal of Personality and Social Psychology, 31,* 126–131.

Tiedens, L. Z., & Linton, S. (2001). Judgment under emotional certainty and uncertainty: The effects of specific emotions on information processing. *Journal of Personality and Social Psychology, 81,* 973–988.

Tormala, Z. L., Falces, C., Briñol, P., & Petty, R. E. (2007). Ease of retrieval effects in social judgment: The role of unrequested cognitions. *Journal of Personality and Social Psychology, 93,* 143–157.

Tormala, Z. L., Petty, R. E., & Briñol, P. (2002). Ease of retrieval effects in persuasion: A self-validation analysis. *Personality and Social Psychology Bulletin, 28,* 1700–1712.

Valins, S. (1966). Cognitive effects of false heart-rate feedback. *Journal of Personality and Social Psychology, 4,* 400–408.

Wagner, B. C., Briñol, P., & Petty, R. E. (2009). *Disgust: A self-validation analysis.* Unpublished manuscript.

Wagner, B. C., Briñol, P., Petty, R. E., & Cacioppo, J. T. (2009). *Arm movements: A self-validation analysis.* Unpublished manuscript.

Wegener, D. T., & Petty, R. E. (1997). The flexible correction model: The role of naive theories of bias in bias correction. In M. P. Zanna (Ed.), *Advances in experimental social psychology* (Vol. 29, pp. 141–208). San Diego, CA: Academic Press.

Wegener, D. T., Petty, R. E., & Klein, D. J. (1994). Effects of mood on high elaboration attitude change: The mediating role of likelihood judgments. *European Journal of Social Psychology, 23*, 25–44.

Wells, G. L., & Petty, R. E. (1980). The effects of overt head movements on persuasion: Compatibility and incompatibility of responses. *Basic and Applied Social Psychology, 1*, 219–230.

Wheeler, S. C., Briñol, P., & Hermann, A. (2007). Resistance to persuasion as self-regulation: Ego-depletion and its consequences for attitude change processes. *Journal of Experimental Social Psychology, 43*, 150–156.

Wheeler, S. C., DeMarree, K. G., & Petty, R. E. (2007). Understanding the role of the self in prime-to-behavior effects: The active self account. *Personality and Social Psychology Review, 11*, 234–261.

Wichman, A. L., Briñol, P., Petty, R. E., Rucker, D. D., Tormala, Z. L., & Weary, G. (2010). Doubting one's doubt: A formula for confidence? *Journal of Experimental Social Psychology, 46*, 350–355.

Section *IV*

Interpersonal Metacognition

13

Metacognition in Stereotypes and Prejudice

VINCENT Y. YZERBYT and STÉPHANIE DEMOULIN

INTRODUCTION

Stereotypes have huge interpersonal and intergroup consequences (for a review, see Yzerbyt & Demoulin, 2010). Social psychologists view stereotypes as the cognitive component of a triad that also comprises prejudice, corresponding to the emotional side, and discrimination, which refers to the behavioral facet. Modern wisdom on intergroup relations suggests that stereotypes are best seen as the antecedent of prejudice and discrimination: Because people think of group members or the entire group as having certain features, emotional reactions ensue and behavioral tendencies materialize. As is the case with other primary cognitions (i.e., initial associations of some object with some attribute; Petty, Briñol, Tormala, & Wegener, 2007), people can think about their stereotypic beliefs along a number of dimensions. In particular, the evaluation of and confidence about stereotypes play a role in how these beliefs shape subsequent dealings with group members. The present chapter examines several lines of research that deal with those secondary cognitions.

The first section starts by examining perceivers' secondary cognitions about their stereotypic judgments (i.e., various aspects that people pay attention to when in position to be using stereotypes as a basis for social judgment). This includes social desirability and presentational concerns as well as the (naïve) theories of judgments that people rely upon when judging others in stereotypic terms. The section then turns to implicit theories about groups that likely boost perceivers' confidence in their stereotypic beliefs.

The second section focuses on the growing literature on metastereotypes. Admittedly, metastereotypes are perhaps not to be seen as "standard" metacognitions because they do not concern people's thoughts about their *own* thoughts.

Rather, metastereotypes deal with people's thoughts about *other people*'s stereotypic beliefs. After focusing on the content of these metastereotypes, a series of moderating factors are considered. Finally, the section dwells on the consequences of people paying attention to metastereotypes.

METACOGNITIONS

A variety of factors leads perceivers to appraise social targets in terms of social categories and, as a consequence, to activate the associated network of stereotypic beliefs (Fiske, 1998; Kunda, 1999). Whether these stereotypes end up shaping judgments is an entirely different question. Oftentimes, perceivers are not in a condition that alerts them about the possible intrusion of stereotypes in their judgment (Devine, 1989; Gilbert & Hixon, 1991). There is then little that can prevent stereotypes from influencing emotional and behavioral reactions. However, when a minimal degree of cognitive control is available and when there is awareness that stereotypes could interfere, perceivers are likely to gauge whether their judgment rests on firm ground and forms a strong foundation for future (re)actions.

The applicability of a stereotypic judgment has much to do with what can be considered its subjective acceptability. Because stereotypes are widely taken to be an improper basis for judgment, perceivers need to cross-check the validity and appropriateness of their judgment both in their own eyes and in the eyes of others. If successful, this check leads to the application of the stereotypes, along with its consequences.

Appropriateness and Validity of Stereotypic Judgments

Few consider that relying on stereotypic beliefs is a decent way to come up with a verdict about a target person (but see Leyens, Yzerbyt, & Schadron, 1994; Oakes, Haslam, & Turner, 1994; Park & Judd, 2005; Yzerbyt, 2010). Indeed, most of the literature builds around the idea that stereotypic beliefs ought to be seen with suspicion and that their constant interference in social judgment should be fought against with the greatest energy (Fiske & Neuberg, 1990).

Several research efforts illustrate that people vary in how they avoid expressing their stereotypes. Constructs such as modern racism (McConahay, 1986) or aversive racism (Dovidio & Gaertner, 2004) address the various ways by which perceivers handle the simultaneous presence of an egalitarian value system and of their negative thoughts and feelings about minorities. These measures tap people's willingness to rely on or stay away from stereotypes in a rather direct way (i.e., primary cognitions). Several individual difference measures also assess people's secondary cognitions about stereotyping, gauging their motivation to control and suppress prejudice and preconceptions.

Plant and Devine (1998) propose that the desire to respond without prejudice stems from two sources: personal beliefs and social pressure. Violations against internal motivations (i.e., personal beliefs) should produce feelings of guilt, whereas failure to conform to social pressures (i.e., external motivation) results in reactions of anger and threat regarding other people's reactions. Interestingly, people high in internal motivation but low in external motivation respond in more positive ways than those high in both. Dunton and Fazio (1997) speak of a general concern with acting against prejudice that finds its roots in a proegalitarian upbringing and positive experiences with stigmatized people. These authors point to people's restraint to avoid disputes that stem from a prejudiced background and negative experiences with stigmatized members, which involves staying away from trouble and arguments with targets of the prejudice.

Because avoiding bias in judgment is a prime goal on people's agendas, they are prone to evaluate the appropriateness and the validity of their judgments, and several theoretical and empirical efforts have examined how people correct their judgments when they perceive them to be inappropriate or incorrect. Martin's (1986) set–reset model and Schwarz and Bless's (1992) inclusion–exclusion model, as well as the flexible correction model (Petty & Wegener, 1993; Wegener & Petty, 1995, 1997), posit that people may recognize the fact that their judgment is likely to be biased and needs to be corrected.

Whereas the first two models point to subtraction of (assumed) unwanted influences as the key process (e.g., people suspect the undue impact of primes and correct in their judgment), the third model stresses the role of specific naïve theories of bias (e.g., people believe that gender should not come into play when assessing leadership and overcorrect for this aspect). These various correction models are decidedly concerned with secondary cognitions (see Petty et al., 2007). They differ from a number of judgment models in which correction, considered as a final step in judgment construction, remains at the level of primary cognitions (Gilbert, 1998; Trope, 1986).

A nice illustration of the role of naïve theories in stereotypical judgment can be found in the social judgeability theory (SJT) of Leyens, Yzerbyt, and Schadron (1992) and Yzerbyt, Schadron, Leyens, and Rocher (1994). These authors wanted to address the fact that people may sometimes feel free to judge others, even in stereotypical ways, provided that certain conditions are fulfilled. They argued that people rely on a number of assumptions embodied in rules about making social judgments. They hold theories concerning the conditions that are sufficient and/or necessary to make a decision. For example, there is wide consensus that a decision about an individual is precluded when no relevant individuating information is available (Darley & Gross, 1983). According to SJT, a conclusion that is potentially seen as being tainted by stereotypes could still be promoted as long as it appears to be based on sound evidence or to result from a process that is beyond any doubt.

Yzerbyt and colleagues (1994) conducted a series of studies to test this idea. The first experiment purportedly concerned the impact of daily activities on social judgment processes. Participants were confronted with minimal category information about a target person. One half of the participants received category information related to introversion (i.e., the target was an archivist) and the other half to extraversion (i.e., the target was a comedian). Next, participants performed a vigilance task (i.e., a dichotic listening task). Half of the participants then immediately proceeded to the third part of the experiment. The other participants learned that, during the vigilance task, they had received information about the target in the unattended ear. Actually, participants had received no information at all. Finally, all participants conveyed their impressions of the target by filling out a series of questionnaires. As expected, participants who did not hear about the alleged sub-liminal individuating information refrained from judging the target. In sharp contrast, participants who thought that they had received individuating information felt entitled to judge and produced stereotypical answers.

A second experiment (Yzerbyt et al., 1994, Exp. 2) replicated this pattern and confirmed that the nature of the information allegedly provided to participants was a key aspect of the rule. Specifically, when participants thought that they had received information about the social category of the target rather than about the specific target, they refrained from using their stereotypes and their answers no longer differed from a no-information condition. In sum, perceivers are likely to make a stereotypical judgment to the extent that they can convince themselves that stereotypes are not their main source of information. Any factor promoting the awareness that individuating information is not informative or that social categorization forms the basis for judgment will lead to a *less biased* evaluation, presumably because it decreases the subjective validity of this judgment.

Closely related to the ideas of SJT, Crandall and Eshleman (2003) developed their suppression–justification model and suggested that social perceivers often feel (or know) that they should not rely on their stereotypes when evaluating other people. Social norms exist in this domain pointing to the stereotypic views that are less problematic and may be expressed (e.g., stereotypes of child abusers) as opposed to those that need to be silenced (e.g., stereotypes of African Americans) (Crandall, Eshleman, & O'Brien, 2002). For those stereotypic thoughts that are condemned by public sanction, perceivers will try to suppress their influence. This force of suppression involves the thwarting of a motivational state and creates tension and reactance. As a result, people become motivated to relieve this tension and to seek ways to express the suppressed prejudice. This is where a second force comes into play—one that refers to any kind of justification that can serve as an opportunity to express genuine prejudice without suffering external or internal sanction. Only when some justification presents itself do perceivers fall back on their spontaneous inclination.

Several illustrations of this suppression–justification mechanism can be found in the literature (Esses, Dietz, & Bhardwaj, 2006; Norton, Vandello, & Darley, 2004). In a classic study, Snyder, Kleck, Strenta, and Mentzer (1979) had non-disabled participants choose whether they wanted to watch a movie alongside a disabled individual or next to a nondisabled individual (both were confederates). When participants thought that the exact same (versus a different) movie was being played, they chose to watch the movie slightly more often (versus almost never) in the company of the disabled individual. There is an even more radical way to avoid the impact of bias in general and stereotypes in particular: keep these thoughts from coming to mind altogether. Unfortunately, inhibition of stereotypes is not always effective and comes with a cost (Macrae, Bodenhausen, Milne, & Jetten, 1994; for a review, see Yzerbyt & Demoulin, 2010).

Although the contempt for stereotypes as potential bases for judgment seems to be shared by perceivers and researchers alike, some voices have taken issue with the idea that stereotypes would necessarily be despicable sources of information. Indeed, stereotypes serve a series of important goals in the context of interpersonal and intergroup relations (Park & Judd, 2005; Yzerbyt, 2010; Yzerbyt & Corneille, 2005). As such, they may thus be of immense benefit from the perspective of the individual as well as the group (see, for instance, Brown & Hewstone, 2005; Wolsko, Park, Judd, & Wittenbrink, 2000).

Still, a great deal of work suggests that perceivers are generally prone to suspicion when they come to realize that stereotypes may influence their judgment. This is mainly because perceivers have internalized, but also feel pressured by, the fact that they should avoid relying on preconceptions to judge others. These secondary cognitions regarding appropriateness may trigger a number of corrective attempts or initiate a consideration for criteria thought to lead to correct judgment. When the (subjective) validity of the conclusions increases, stereotypes are quick to sneak in again and to influence social judgment.

Structural Properties and Implicit Theories in the Perception of Groups

Although stereotypes may possibly concern all sorts of group aspects, the association between personality traits and certain groups constitutes the example par excellence of what a stereotype is all about. But whereas traits are hardly disputed as providing valid ways to describe specific individuals, it is widely understood that a trait should normally not be associated with a group in any strict sense. In line with this reasoning, the strength of a stereotype has been defined as the extent to which people perceive variability among group members for a given trait (Judd & Park, 1988). Two classes of factors lead perceivers to consider that the members of a given group can be defined by a given trait: factors associated with the target group and factors associated with perceivers (Yzerbyt, Corneille, & Estrada, 2001; Yzerbyt, Rocher, & Schadron, 1997).

As far as the target factors are concerned, a number of variables increase perceivers' confidence that their stereotypic views are legitimate. These variables are all related to what is known as "entitativity," a term coined by Campbell (1958) to refer to the extent to which a social aggregate is or is not perceived as a coherent, unified, and meaningful entity (Hamilton, 2007; Lickel et al., 2000). The recent revival of interest for this concept stemmed from the observation that individuals and groups triggered qualitatively different information processes. Hamilton and Sherman (1996) proposed that online processes are initiated for entitative targets such as individuals, whereas memory-based processes dominate for less entitative targets, such as a group. When high unity is expected, however, online processes are initiated for both individual and group targets (McConnell, Sherman, & Hamilton, 1997). That is, entitative groups trigger the same information processes that individuals do.

Several researchers examined the impact of various group properties on the emergence of entitativity (Gaertner & Schopler, 1998; Lickel et al., 2000; Wilder & Simon, 1998). Their work suggests the existence of two clusters of group attributes: the similarity cluster (homogeneity, similarity, size, proximity, etc.) and the organization cluster (organization, interdependence, interaction, goals, etc.). In isolation or in combination, these properties encourage the perception of groups as entitative

(Brewer & Harasty, 1996; Castano, Yzerbyt, & Bourguignon, 2003; Dasgupta, Banaji, & Abelson, 1999; McGarty, Haslam, Hutchinson, & Grace, 1995).

The perception of entitativity, in turn, increases the likelihood that people feel comfortable at characterizing groups in terms of personality traits. For instance, Yzerbyt, Rogier, and Fiske (1998) showed that perceived entitativity promotes perceivers' readiness to rely on traits in dealing with a group. That is, entitativity triggers higher levels of (unwarranted) dispositional inference and a disregard for the impact of the situation on people's behavior.

Turning to factors associated with the perceivers, research suggests that holding an *essentialistic* view of groups is a prime determinant of the willingness to rely on stereotypes in judgments. As an implicit theory, essentialism refers to the fact that some categories are represented as having deep, hidden, unchanging properties that make their members what they are (see, for instance, Haslam, Rothschild, & Ernst, 2000; Rothbart & Taylor, 1992; Yzerbyt et al., 1997; see also Rangel & Keller, 2011). Empirical evidence suggests that essentialist beliefs increase people's tendency to see similarity among group members (Miller & Prentice, 1999; Yzerbyt et al., 2001) and favor the emergence of stereotypic judgments (Bastian & Haslam, 2006; Hoffman & Hurst, 1990; Martin & Parker, 1995; Williams & Eberhardt, 2008; Yzerbyt et al., 2001). For instance, Williams and Eberhardt (2008) found that individuals who endorsed a biological conception of race were more likely to endorse African American stereotypes than were individuals who endorsed a social conception of race. Also, psychological essentialism was found to reduce people's motivation to eliminate disparities between groups and to cross category boundaries.

Essentialist and nonessentialist perception in the intergroup domain bears striking resemblance to the distinction between entitativity and incrementalism that Dweck and her colleagues introduced in the area of developmental and personality psychology (Chiu, Hong, & Dweck, 1997; Dweck, Hong, & Chiu, 1993). Whereas entity theorists believe that personal attributes are fixed, incremental theorists are convinced that traits are malleable. Several studies found that entity theorists make stronger trait inferences from behavior and use traits or trait-relevant information to make stronger future behavioral predictions than incrementalists. The same pattern has been observed when implicit beliefs are manipulated.

More relevant to the present discussion, peoples' implicit theories about the fixedness versus malleability of human attributes predict differences in social stereotyping (Levy, Stroessner, & Dweck, 1998). Relative to those holding an incremental theory, people holding an entity theory make more stereotypical trait judgments of ethnic and occupational groups, and they form more extreme trait judgments of novel groups.

Implicit theories also influence the degree to which people attribute stereotyped traits to inborn group qualities versus environmental forces. Along similar lines, Plaks, Stroessner, Dweck, and Sherman (2001) found that people holding an entity (versus incrementalist) theory display greater attention to and recognition of stereotype-consistent (-inconsistent) information. Thus, in general, entity theorists are more prone than their incrementalist counterparts to lay dispositionism—that is, the tendency to use traits as the basic unit of analysis in social perception (Ross & Nisbett, 1991).

Although the concepts of entitativity and essentialism need to be distinguished, they also go hand in hand (Demoulin, Leyens, & Yzerbyt, 2006; Martin & Parker, 1995; Prentice & Miller, 2007; Yzerbyt, Judd, & Corneille, 2004). One way to formalize the respective roles of entitativity and essentialism is to distinguish two aspects of social perception: Whereas entitativity stands for the more ecological side of group perception, essentialism refers to its inferential facet. What Yzerbyt et al. (2001) have called the *phenotypic* and the *genotypic* levels of social perception both contribute to make people members of a real unitary social entity. This means that the (assumed) structural properties of the groups and the implicit theories of the perceivers about the group combine to give way to a strong sense that the group can be described in stereotypic terms. In other words, the nature of perceivers' primary cognitions about a given group (e.g., Italians are creative and they are so "naturally") may greatly constrain their secondary cognitions with respect to using stereotypic beliefs about the group or one of its members (e.g., it is appropriate and valid to say that this specific Italian is creative).

Summary

Although stereotypes are quick to intrude social judgment, people tend to make sure that their judgment does not come across as manifestations of bigotry and prejudice. In general, most perceivers would try to avoid making stereotyped judgments unless they have the feeling that some good rationale underlies their seemingly partisan decision. With a few notable exceptions, a priori expectations about groups are thus banned from judgments. In contrast, naïve rules of judgment and rationalizations, as well as perceptions and implicit theories relating to groups, may strengthen stereotypic beliefs and color social judgment.

INTERGROUP METABELIEFS

Aside from the work on people's justifications, heuristics, and other implicit theories, a growing area of research in the field of intergroup relations relates to metaperceptions. For decades, scholars have devoted a great deal of energy to documenting people's stereotypes—that is, their beliefs about their own and other groups. Recently, however, some scholars have called attention to the study of intergroup metabeliefs and their consequences on intergroup relations.

Intergroup metabeliefs have sometimes been referred to as "reflected ingroup stereotypes" (Bond, 1986; Horenczyk & Bekerman, 1997), but most authors now rely on the more common label of "metastereotypes" introduced by Sigelman and Tuch in 1997. Metastereotypes are people's beliefs about (out)group members' stereotypes concerning their ingroup. As such, metastereotypes are but one specific kind of primary cognition in a larger constellation of attributed beliefs. Judd, Park, Yzerbyt, Gordijn, and Muller (2005) proposed a typology that aptly characterizes beliefs in terms of the people to whom the beliefs are attributed (oneself, ingroup members, outgroup members) and in terms of the target group that is the object of these beliefs (endobeliefs for the ingroup and exobeliefs for the outgroup of the perceiver). In Judd and colleagues' (2005) terminology, metastereotypes are known as *outgroup attributed exobeliefs*—that is, outgroup members' beliefs about *their* outgroup (i.e., the ingroup of the perceiver).

The Content of Metastereotypes

What do metastereotypes look like? A first possibility is that they are unpredictable and correspond to a combination of traits and features that vary as a function of the specific groups in presence. Indeed, a number of studies have examined metastereotypes using ad hoc characteristics (Kamans, Gordijn, Oldenhuis, & Otten, 2009). In contrast to a complete lack of specification, some scholars have argued that metastereotypes are uniformly negative in valence (Sigelman & Tuch, 1997). Others have nuanced this proposal and suggested that negativity of metastereotypes is a function of perceivers' level of prejudice (Vorauer, Main, & O'Connell, 1999). Specifically, low-prejudice individuals would be holding more negative metastereotypes than high-prejudice persons.

Yet others have hypothesized that the valence of metastereotypes depends on the specific motivation of the perceiver (Lammers, Gordijn, & Otten, 2008). To the extent that self-enhancement motivation prevails, people should use only positive metastereotypes to repair or favor their self-worth. When comprehension goals are at stake, however, both positive and negative information should be useful in predicting and comprehending how others think about one's group (van den Bos & Stapel, 2009).

A study by Lammers and colleagues (2008) confirms the importance of both positive and negative metastereotypes in intergroup contexts. These authors investigated the activation and application of metastereotypes as a function of group status. They found that all groups tended to activate and apply both positive and negative metastereotypes but that members of low-status, low-power groups tended to do so to a larger extent. In addition, the increased tendency for low-status groups to activate and apply positive and negative metastereotypes is partly explained by their motivation to take the other group's perspective into account.

To the extent that metastereotypes can be considered as intergroup beliefs just as stereotypes are, it is also plausible to assume that the content of metastereotypes would vary in some systematic ways (just like stereotypes do). Recent research on the content of stereotypes demonstrated that only a limited number of "themes" account for people's characterization of social groups. According to the stereotype content model (SCM; Fiske, Cuddy, Glick, & Xu, 2002; for a review, see Cuddy, Fiske, & Glick, 2008), groups are perceived along two fundamental dimensions: warmth and competence (see also Judd, James-Hawkins, Yzerbyt, & Kashima, 2005). Whereas the relations of cooperation versus competition between groups give rise to high versus low evaluations on the warmth dimension, the groups' respective statuses determine competence ascription, with high-status groups being granted higher levels of competence.

By analogy, it could be argued that the content of people's metastereotypes is organized in terms of the two fundamental dimensions of warmth and competence, and that these evaluations depend on group members' representation of the intergroup structure. Interestingly, this approach predicts that people's metastereotypes should very much resemble their endostereotypes (i.e., people's beliefs about their own ingroup). For instance, if perceivers see their group as being dominant and expect outgroup members to make the same analysis, they should reach the conclusion that they are competent and conclude that outgroup members see them as such. Empirical evidence, however, fails to support this simplistic view that metastereotypes are in line with people's own stereotypes.

There are at least three reasons explaining the discrepancy between people's metastereotypes and their endostereotypes. First, according to social identity theory, group members are motivated to distinguish their ingroup positively from other groups in the social environment (Tajfel & Turner, 1979). As a consequence, people's stereotypes about their ingroup should largely be biased toward positivity. Consistent with this prediction, SCM theorists have argued that the quadrant where groups are assigned both high competence and high warmth is usually reserved to ingroups or aspirational groups. In contrast, the two ambivalent and the negative quadrants are largely populated by outgroups (Cuddy et al., 2008). In a similar vein, van den Bos and Stapel (2009) have shown that self-enhancement goals led to high levels of negative but not positive stereotypes about the outgroup.

Second, it has been argued that people rely on their own perceptions in order to gain insights on how outgroup members might think of their ingroup (Ames, 2004; Frey & Tropp, 2006). Because intergroup relations are generally characterized as distrustful and because stereotypes about outgroups are often negative, people should thus expect outgroup members to evaluate them negatively. That is, people expect to be treated badly by bad persons. This hypothesis is put forth by Frey and Tropp (2006), who propose that negative prototypical characteristics of the ingroup are the bases of intergroup metaperceptions but that positive prototypical features are prevalent in intragroup metaperceptions (see also Krueger, 1998). Similarly, Judd, Park, et al. (2005) report a series of studies showing that people attribute to others (both ingroup and outgroup members but especially the latter) more evaluative biases than they themselves espouse.

A third reason that may explain a lack of correlation between metastereotypes and people's stereotypes about their ingroup is related to their antecedents. As stated before, perceptions of groups' warmth and competence depend on participants' representations of the social structure (Fiske, Xu, Cuddy, & Glick, 1999). It could be that dissimilarity expectations that usually characterize intergroup relations prevent people from directly projecting their own views and representations of the social structure onto outgroup members (Ames, 2004).

This idea is supported by Robbins and Krueger's (2005) meta-analysis on social projection showing that projection is much weaker with outgroup members than it is with ingroup members. Thus, if people believe outgroup members perceive the social structure differently, they make different inferences concerning the stereotype that ingroup and outgroup members associate with the ingroup. In addition, people might also be tempted to believe that outgroup members do not share their views concerning the perceived legitimacy of a given social arrangement. If this is the case, they may infer that metastereotypes will likely be different from their endobeliefs. For instance, metaperceptions that the group's high status is illegitimate should give rise to the perception of high-status groups' arrogance rather than competence.

In addition to the issue of the valence, Judd, Park, et al. (2005) also tackled structural aspects of stereotypic beliefs—namely, stereotypes' and metastereo-types' perceived variability in terms of stereotypicality and judgment's dispersion. Stereotypicality refers to the perceived difference *between groups* on stereotypical attributes. Dispersion speaks to the perceived degree of *within-group* variation. Their studies revealed that, on top of assuming more evaluative biases on the part of others, people also believe that others are more biased in their evaluation of perceived variability between and within groups. Specifically, individuals expect others to display larger between-groups and smaller within-group differences in their social judgments.

Moderators of Metastereotypic Beliefs

Before delineating the various consequences of metastereotypes, it is necessary to understand the circumstances under which these beliefs will be activated and applied in a given social environment. A first element that moderates metaste-reotype activation is the groups' relative position within the social structure. Lammers and colleagues (2008) investigated the role of membership in high- ver-sus low-status groups on metastereotype activation and application. They reasoned that powerless people should be especially motivated to predict and ascertain how powerful outgroup members see them because of their general orientation to pre-vent losses and threats (Keltner, Gruenfeld, & Anderson, 2003), their tendencies to see themselves as tools in the attainment of the goals of others (Keltner et al., 2003), and their greater likelihood to take the perspective of others spontaneously (Galinsky, Magee, Inesi, & Gruenfeld, 2006).

In four experiments using a variety of methods to manipulate power, these authors showed that powerless people indeed activate and make more use of metastereotypes than their powerful counterparts. Metastereotype activation was made independently of traits' valence and the effects were partially mediated by participants' tendency to take the outgroup's perspective into account. These three factors notwithstanding, it is also likely that members of low-status groups are generally more uncertain about their views than members of high-status groups. Evidence from the persuasion domain supports the idea that, compared to high-status group members, low-status group members need to think more about their environment, including how others see them (Briñol, Petty, Valle, Rucker, & Becerra, 2007).

Social status alone may not be sufficient to predict the activation of metastereo-types. In her information search model of evaluative concerns, Vorauer (2006) pro-poses that the importance that an individual attaches to another person's opinion depends on the perceived diagnosticity of that person's evaluation. Perceived diag-nosticity is a function of the person's control over resources (contingency) and/or this person's ability to provide accurate assessments (expertise). Clearly, Lammers and colleagues' (2008) findings (reported earlier) speak to the contingency part of the model, with high-status group members controlling larger shares of resources and therefore triggering strong activation and use of metastereotypes among low-status group members.

According to the information search model, reliance on metastereotyping also depends on people's perception that the outgroup has special expertise to provide valid evaluations in a given domain. In line with this conjecture, Vorauer and Sakamoto (2008) report evidence that concerns about an outgroup member's opinion increase with the perception that the outgroup has expertise in a particular domain (i.e., the competence domain for high-status groups under legitimate status differences and the moral domain for low-status groups under illegitimate status differences). In short, it is plausible to assume that the activation (and application) of metastereotypes is not only a function of group members' standing in the social environment but also a matter of other contextual variables, such as the outgroup's expertise, the goals pursued in the intergroup interaction, and the like.

Consequences of Metastereotypic Beliefs

Given that metastereotypic beliefs are predominantly negative in tone, it is most likely the case that they will induce negative feelings of anxiety and threat in individuals. The very first reaction to metastereotypic beliefs should thus be one of avoidance. As a matter of fact, an impressive number of studies reveal that intergroup encounters are anxiety-arousing (Cunningham et al., 2004; Phelps, Cannistraci, & Cunningham, 2003; see also Hart et al., 2000) and that people are prompt to avoid outgroup members. The intergroup anxiety model (Stephan & Stephan, 1985) proposes that anxiety arises because of the negative expectations people hold concerning the intergroup interaction. These negative expectations derive to a large extent from people's primary cognitions concerning the outgroup (i.e., their stereotypes) but most definitely also because of their cognitions concerning the way in which outgroup members perceive their ingroup (i.e., their metastereotypes).

Disconfirmatory Behaviors   To the extent that intergroup encounters are inevitable, the anxiety caused by the prospect of intergroup encounters is likely to represent a serious threat for the individual. As people fear the association between the negative metastereotype they hold and their personal self, they will be motivated to overcome or disconfirm it.

High- and low-status group members likely face very different types of threats. Specifically, dominant group members are mainly concerned with the fact that they come across as being prejudiced (Vorauer & Kumhyr, 2001). In contrast, members of stigmatized groups are more often afraid of meeting with a negative evaluation of their performance (e.g., Schmader, Johns, & Forbes, 2008; Steele, 1997; Steele & Aronson, 1995; Steele, Spencer, & Aronson, 2002). In other words, members of high-status groups face a threat on the social dimension of social judgment, whereas low-status groups deal with a difficulty on the competence dimension of social judgment. This rationale is at the heart of a fascinating series of studies conducted by Bergsieker, Shelton, and Richeson (2010).

These authors theorized that the pervasive stereotypes associated with racial groups led their members to pursue divergent impression management strategies during interracial interactions. They proposed that because Blacks and Latinos are often stereotyped as incompetent and lazy and because (in)competence is closely related to (dis)respect (Cuddy et al., 2008), members of those groups should primarily be concerned with seeking respect (rather than liking) in mixed-race (as compared to same-race) interactions where stereotype activation is prevalent. In contrast, White people face the threat of being seen as bigots and amoral people. Because morality is related to liking (Cuddy et al., 2008), they should thus primarily seek likeable (rather than respectful) evaluations in interracial interactions. Results confirmed the divergent goal hypothesis with divergent goals translating into specific impression management behaviors displaying self-promotion, respect-seeking behaviors, or ingratiation, liking-seeking behaviors as a function of the type of group under scrutiny (Jones & Pittman, 1982).

Stereotype activation was never explicit in Bergsieker and colleagues' (2010) studies, suggesting that category membership of the interaction partner is the sole determinant for the observed effect. It is unclear at this stage whether divergent impression management goals result from the activation of exostereotypes (i.e., "I believe that members of this group usually treat members of my group disrespectfully and I want to avoid that."), from the activation of endostereotypes (i.e., "I believe that members of my group are incompetent and I want to avoid being assimilated with them."), or from the activation of metastereotypes (i.e., "I believe that members of this group usually think that members of my group are incompetent, and I want to avoid being perceived as such.").

A partial response to this question can be found in the work of Vorauer, Hunter, Main, and Roy (2000). These authors proposed and found that when people find themselves in intergroup contexts and when the potential for evaluation is high, they "spontaneously frame the interaction in terms of how they are perceived by outgroup members" (p. 691). That is, metastereotypes rather than stereotypes are automatically activated in such an intergroup context and become the focus of evaluative concerns. Still, because the activation of endostereotypes was not measured in these studies, it remains difficult to conclude that metastereotypes constitute the unique determinant of impression management goals in intergroup interactions.

Trying to disconfirm a negative social reputation comes at a cost for the individual. People often perform less well in domains that are related to a negative stereotype about their group (Steele & Aronson, 1995). The motivation to prevent failure and to avoid being assimilated to the stigmatized group creates an additional burden that interferes with the successful completion of the task (e.g., Schmader, 2010). For stereotypes to produce their threatening effect, targets of these stereotypes first need to be made aware of the possibility that a negative belief can be applied to them (Wout, Shih, Jackson, & Sellers, 2009). Second, they need to assess the probability that the perceiver will apply this negative belief to them (Wout et al., 2009).

Stereotype threat impairs performance only to the extent that the stereotyped targets believe that their evaluators hold such stereotypic expectations about them. Supporting this idea, Wout and colleagues (2009) showed that, in the absence of individuating information about the evaluator, targets rely on the evaluator's group membership to determine the probability of being negatively stereotyped (see also

Sloan et al., 2008). Because stereotyping is more probable in intergroup than intra-group settings, performance impairment only occurred under conditions in which targets thought that they would be evaluated by an outgroup member. These latter results suggest that the phenomenon is less a matter of the targets' own beliefs (i.e., exo- and endostereotypes) than a question of their beliefs concerning other people's stereotypes about the ingroup (i.e., metastereotypes).

On top of the various consequences observed at the individual level, meta-stereotyping and the motivation to disconfirm the negative reputation also trigger interpersonal consequences in the interaction (Richeson & Shelton, 2007). Indeed, self-regulation efforts are sometimes praised, leading to the paradoxical consequence that those who need the most to disconfirm the negative reputation (e.g., high-prejudice individuals) make more efforts at controlling their behaviors, appear more engaged in the interaction, and therefore are better appreciated by their outgroup partner than those whose implicit attitudes are less in line with the negative metastereotype (e.g., low-prejudice individuals) (Shelton, Richeson, Salvatore, & Trawalter, 2005). In addition, dominant and dominated group members' tendency to focus on different aspects of judgment (liking versus respect, respectively; see Bergsieker et al., 2010) increases the probability for intergroup misunderstandings (for a review, see Demoulin, Leyens, & Dovidio, 2009) and disliking in intergroup interactions.

Metastereotype Confirmation   The studies reported in the previous sub-section suggest that perceivers facing negative metastereotypes are largely moti-vated to try to disconfirm their negative reputations. Still, there are cases in which confirmation rather than disconfirmation is the strategy that group members pur-sue. In a recent series of studies, Gordijn, Oldenhuis, and Otten (2009) investi-gated the conditions under which assimilation to the negative metastereotype is preferred over disconfirmation. These authors reasoned that under intergroup conflict conditions, people are motivated to distance themselves from the out-group (Spears, Gordijn, Dijksterhuis, & Stapel, 2004) and as a result assimilate their behaviors to the negative metastereotype. Because high-prejudice people are more likely than low-prejudice individuals to frame the intergroup context in conflictual terms, they should also be more inclined to assimilate to the negative metastereotype of their ingroup.

Indeed, survey data among Dutch Moroccan teenagers confirmed that those who expected indigenous Dutch people to perceive Moroccans as fundamentalists and who were also high in prejudice acted in line with the negative metastereo-type by legitimizing criminality, aggression, and Muslim extremism (Kamans et al., 2009). Similarly, high-prejudice Christians who thought they would be evalu-ated by a non-Christian outgroup displayed higher levels of conservative behaviors (a stereotype strongly associated with Christianity) than low-prejudice individu-als and individuals that did not anticipate outgroup evaluations (Gordijn et al., 2009; see also Oldenhuis, Gordijn, & Otten, 2009). Interestingly, when positive rather than negative metastereotypes are at stake, low-prejudice rather than high-prejudice people were the ones to assimilate to the metastereotype, presumably because of low-prejudice people's inclination to search for positive intergroup relations and smaller intergroup distancing.

According to these studies, the activation of the metastereotype leads to confirmatory behaviors for individuals who are highly vested in intergroup conflict (e.g., high-prejudice people), searching for intergroup distancing, and anticipating outgroup evaluations. Further research is needed in order to understand better the exact conditions under which confirmation versus disconfirmation behaviors occur. For instance, one could examine whether assimilation or contrast to the metastereotypes varies as a function of social structural factors. That is, does group status moderate the direction of behavioral responses to the metastereotype?

Similarly, intergroup interdependence could be an important factor. As suggested by the research of Gordijn and colleagues (2009), intergroup competition might indeed be an important determinant of behavioral confirmation of negative metastereotypes, whereas intergroup cooperation triggers the confirmation of positive metastereotypes. In addition, although interdependence direction between groups might influence behavioral responses on the sociability dimension of judgment, it is plausible to assume that group status might moderate behavioral responses on the competence dimension (see Bergsieker et al., 2010).

Summary

Intergroup metabeliefs have recently become the focus of extensive research. Most studies in this domain investigated the content, moderators, and consequences of metastereotypes—that is, people's beliefs concerning the stereotypes held by outgroup members about their ingroup. Clearly, research efforts addressing other types of intergroup metabeliefs are much needed.

CONCLUSIONS

Metacognitions are a key aspect of people's cognitive life. As is the case for other psychological constructs such as attitudes, the self, and the like, people have perceptions, knowledge, and additional judgments about stereotypes or stereotype-relevant judgments. The present chapter reviewed the work on people's secondary cognitions about their own stereotype-relevant beliefs (e.g., appropriateness, justifiability, social judgeability) and on implicit theories about groups (entitativity, essentialism). Another important facet of stereotypes and prejudice studies concerns what is commonly referred to as metastereotypes. As was made clear, in all these cases, because they determine the extent to which perceivers go along with the stereotyped judgment, metacognitions related to stereotypes are likely to be quite consequential and to determine the shape of intergroup interactions.

REFERENCES

Ames, D. (2004). Strategies for social inference: A similarity contingency model of projection and stereotyping in attribute prevalence estimates. *Journal of Personality and Social Psychology, 87*, 573–585.

Bastian, B., & Haslam, N. (2006). Psychological essentialism and stereotype endorsement. *Journal of Experimental Social Psychology, 42*, 228–235.

Bergsieker, H. B., Shelton, J. N., & Richeson, J. A. (2010). To be liked versus respected: Divergent goals in interracial interaction. *Journal of Personality and Social Psychology, 99*, 248–264.

Bond, M. H. (1986). Mutual stereotypes and the facilitation of interaction across cultural lines. *International Journal of Intercultural Relations, 10*, 259–276.

Brewer, M. B., & Harasty, A. S. (1996). Seeing groups as entities: The role of perceiver motivation. In R. M. Sorrentino & E. T. Higgins (Eds.), *Handbook of motivation and cognition* (Vol. 3, pp. 347–370). New York, NY: Guilford.

Briñol, P., Petty, R. E., Valle, C., Rucker, D. D., & Becerra, A. (2007). The effects of message recipients' power before and after persuasion: A self-validation analysis. *Journal of Personality and Social Psychology, 93*, 1040–1053.

Brown, R. J., & Hewstone, M. (2005). An integrative theory of intergroup contact. *Advances in Experimental Social Psychology, 37*, 255–343.

Campbell, D. T. (1958). Common fate, similarity, and other indices of the status of aggregates of persons as social entities. *Behavioral Sciences, 3*, 14–25.

Castano, E., Yzerbyt, V. Y., & Bourguignon, D. (2003). We are one and I like it: The impact of group entitativity on group identification. *European Journal of Social Psychology, 33*, 735–754.

Chiu, C., Hong, Y., & Dweck, C. S. (1997). Lay dispositionism and implicit theories of personality. *Journal of Personality and Social Psychology, 73*, 19–30.

Crandall, C. S., & Eshleman, A. (2003). A justification–suppression model of the expression and experience of prejudice. *Psychological Bulletin, 129*, 414–446.

Crandall, C. S., Eshleman, A., & O'Brien, L. (2002). Social norms and suppression of prejudice: The struggle for internalization. *Journal of Personality and Social Psychology, 82*, 359–378.

Cuddy, A. J. C., Fiske, S. T., & Glick, P. (2008). Warmth and competence as universal dimensions of social perception: The stereotype content model and the BIAS map. *Advances in Experimental Social Psychology, 40*, 61–149.

Cunningham, W. A., Johnson, M. A., Raye, C. L., Gatenby, J. C., Gore, J. C., & Banaji, M. R. (2004). Separable neural components in the processing of Black and White faces. *Psychological Science, 15*, 806–813.

Darley, J. M., & Gross, P. H. (1983). A hypothesis-confirming bias in labeling effects. *Journal of Personality and Social Psychology, 44*, 20–33.

Dasgupta, N., Banaji, M. R., & Abelson, R. P. (1999). Group entitativity and group perception: Associations between physical features and psychological judgment. *Journal of Personality and Social Psychology, 77*, 991–1003.

Demoulin, S., Leyens, J.-Ph., & Dovidio, J. F. (2009). *Intergroup misunderstandings: Impact of divergent social realities.* New York, NY: Psychology Press.

Demoulin, S., Leyens, J.-Ph., & Yzerbyt, V. Y. (2006). Lay theories of essentialism. *Group Processes and Intergroup Relations, 9*, 25–42.

Devine, P. G. (1989). Stereotypes and prejudice: Their automatic and controlled components. *Journal of Personality and Social Psychology, 56*, 5–18.

Dovidio, J. F., & Gaertner, S. L. (2004). Aversive racism. In M. P. Zanna (Ed.), *Advances in experimental social psychology* (Vol. 36, pp. 1–52). Thousand Oaks, CA: Sage.

Dunton, B. C., & Fazio, R. H. (1997). An individual difference measure of motivation to control prejudiced reactions. *Personality and Social Psychology Bulletin, 23*, 316–326.

Dweck, C. S., Hong, Y., & Chiu, C. (1993). Implicit theories: Individual differences in the likelihood and meaning of dispositional inference. *Personality and Social Psychology Bulletin, 19*, 644–656.

Esses, V. M., Dietz, J., & Bhardwaj, A. (2006). The role of prejudice in the discounting of immigrant skills. In R. Mahalingam (Ed.), *The cultural psychology of immigrants* (pp. 113–130). Mahwah, NJ: Lawrence Erlbaum Associates.

Fiske, S. T. (1998). Stereotyping, prejudice, and discrimination. In D. T. Gilbert, S. T. Fiske, & G. Lindzey (Eds.), *The handbook of social psychology* (4th ed. Vol. 2, pp. 357–411). New York, NY: McGraw-Hill.

Fiske, S. T., Cuddy, A. J. C., Glick, P., & Xu, J. (2002). A model of (often mixed) stereotype content: Competence and warmth respectively follow from the perceived status and competition. *Journal of Personality and Social Psychology, 82,* 878–902.

Fiske, S. T., & Neuberg, S. L. (1990). A continuum of impression formation from category-based to individuating processes: Influences of information and motivation on attention and interpretation. In M. P. Zanna (Ed.), *Advances in experimental social psychology* (Vol. 23, pp. 1–74). New York, NY: Academic Press.

Fiske, S. T., Xu, J., Cuddy, A. J. C., & Glick, P. (1999). (Dis)respecting versus (dis)liking: Status and interdependence predict ambivalent stereotypes of competence and warmth. *Journal of Social Issues, 55,* 473–489.

Frey, F. E., & Tropp, L. R. (2006). Being seen as individuals versus as group members: Extending research on metaperception to intergroup contexts. *Personality and Social Psychology Review, 10,* 265–280.

Gaertner, L., & Schopler, H. (1998). Perceived ingroup entitativity and intergroup bias: An interconnection of self and others. *European Journal of Social Psychology, 28,* 963–980.

Galinsky, A. D., Magee, J. C., Inesi, M. E., & Gruenfeld, D. H. (2006). Power and perspectives not taken. *Psychological Science, 17,* 1068–1074.

Gilbert, D. T. (1998). Ordinary personology. In D. T. Gilbert, S. T. Fiske, & G. Lindzey (Eds.), *The handbook of social psychology* (4th ed., Vol. 2, pp. 89–150). New York, NY: McGraw-Hill.

Gilbert, D. T., & Hixon, J. G. (1991). The trouble of thinking: Activation and application of stereotypic beliefs. *Journal of Personality and Social Psychology, 60,* 509–517.

Gordijn, E., Oldenhuis, H., & Otten, S. (2009). *"If that is what you think about us…": Reacting to others' perceived stereotypes as a function of prejudice.* University of Groningen. Unpublished manuscript.

Hamilton, D. L. (2007). Understanding the complexities of group perception: Broadening the domain. *European Journal of Social Psychology, 37,* 1077–1101.

Hamilton, D. L., & Sherman, S. J. (1996). Perceiving persons and groups. *Psychological Review, 103,* 336–355.

Hart, A. J., Whalen, P. J., Shin, L. M., McInerney, S. C., Fischer, H., & Rauch, S. L. (2000). Differential responses in the human amygdala to racial outgroup vs. ingroup face stimuli. *Neuroreport: For Rapid Communication of Neuroscience Research, 11,* 2351–2355.

Haslam, N., Rothschild, L., & Ernst, D. (2000). Essentialist beliefs about social categories. *British Journal of Social Psychology, 39,* 113–127.

Hoffman, C., & Hurst, N. (1990). Gender stereotypes: Perception or rationalization? *Journal of Personality and Social Psychology, 58,* 197–208.

Horenczyk, G., & Bekerman, Z. (1997). The effects of intercultural acquaintance and structured intergroup interaction on ingroup, outgroup, and reflected ingroup stereotypes. *International Journal of Intercultural Relations, 21,* 71–83.

Jones, E. E., & Pittman, T. S. (1982). Toward a general theory of strategic self-presentation. In J. Suls (Ed.), *Psychological perspectives on the self* (pp. 231–262). Hillsdale, NJ: Lawrence Erlbaum Associates.

Judd, C. M., James-Hawkins, L., Yzerbyt, V. Y., & Kashima, Y. (2005). Fundamental dimensions of social judgment: Understanding the relations between competence and warmth. *Journal of Personality and Social Psychology, 89,* 899–913.

Judd, C. M., & Park, B. (1988). Outgroup homogeneity: Judgments of variability at the individual and group levels. *Journal of Personality and Social Psychology, 54,* 778–788.

Judd, C. M., Park, B., Yzerbyt, V. Y., Gordijn, E., & Muller, D. (2005). They show more intergroup bias and have stronger stereotypes than do I: Evidence from ethnic, gender, and nationality intergroup contexts. *European Journal of Social Psychology, 35,* 677–704.

Kamans, E., Gordijn, E., Oldenhuis, H., & Otten, S. (2009). What I think you see is what you get: Influence of prejudice on assimilation to negative metastereotypes among Dutch Moroccan teenagers. *European Journal of Social Psychology, 39,* 842–851.

Keltner, D., Gruenfeld, D. H., & Anderson, C. (2003). Power, approach, and inhibition. *Psychological Review, 110,* 265–284.

Krueger, J. (1998). On the perception of social consensus. *Advances in experimental social psychology, 30,* 163–240

Kunda, Z. (1999). *Social cognition: Making sense of people.* Cambridge, MA: MIT Press.

Lammers, J., Gordijn, E. H., & Otten, S. (2008). Looking through the eyes of the powerful: Power (or lack thereof) and metastereotyping. *Journal of Experimental Social Psychology, 44,* 1229–1238.

Levy, S. R., Stroessner, S. J., & Dweck, C. S. (1998). Stereotype formation and endorsement: The role of implicit theories. *Journal of Personality and Social Psychology, 74,* 1421–1436.

Leyens, J.-Ph., Yzerbyt, V. Y., & Schadron, G. (1992). The social judgeability approach to stereotypes. In W. Stroebe & M. Hewstone (Eds.), *European review of social psychology* (Vol. 3, pp. 91–120). Chichester, UK: Wiley.

Leyens, J.-Ph., Yzerbyt, V. Y., & Schadron, G. (1994). *Stereotypes and social cognition.* London, England: Sage.

Lickel, B., Hamilton, D. L., Wieczorkowska, G., Lewis, A., Sherman, S. J., & Uhles, A. N. (2000). Varieties of groups and the perception of group entitativity. *Journal of Personality and Social Psychology, 78,* 223–246.

Macrae, C. N., Bodenhausen, G. V., Milne, A. B., & Jetten, J. (1994). Out of mind but back in sight: Stereotypes on the rebound. *Journal of Personality and Social Psychology, 67,* 808–817.

Martin, C. L., & Parker, S. (1995). Folk theories about sex and race differences. *Personality and Social Psychology Bulletin, 21,* 45–57.

Martin, L. L. (1986). Set/reset: The use and disuse of concepts in impression formation. *Journal of Personality and Social Psychology, 51,* 493–504.

McConahay, J. B. (1986). Modern racism, ambivalence, and the modern racism scale. In J. F. Dovidio & S. L. Gaertner (Eds), *Prejudice, discrimination, and racism* (pp. 91–125). Orlando, FL: Academic Press.

McConnell, A. R., Sherman, S. J., & Hamilton, D. L. (1997). Target entitativity: Implications for information processing about individual and group targets. *Journal of Personality and Social Psychology, 72,* 750–762.

McGarty, C., Haslam, S. A., Hutchinson, K. J., & Grace, D. M. (1995). Determinants of perceived consistency: The relationship between group entitativity and the meaningfulness of categories. *British Journal of Social Psychology, 34,* 237–256.

Miller, D. T., & Prentice, D. A. (1999). Some consequences of a belief in group essence: The category divide hypothesis. In D. A. Prentice & D. T. Miller (Eds.), *Cultural divides: Understanding and overcoming group conflict* (pp. 213–238). New York, NY: Russell Sage Foundation.

Norton, M. I., Vandello, J. A., & Darley, J. M. (2004). Casuistry and social category bias. *Journal of Personality and Social Psychology, 87,* 817–831.

Oakes, P. J., Haslam, S. A., & Turner, J. C. (1994). *Stereotyping and social reality.* Oxford, England: Basil Blackwell.

Oldenhuis, H., Gordijn, E., & Otten, S. (2009). *If you don't like us, we won't be likeable: The influence of metastereotype activation on behavior and attitudes.* University of Groningen, the Netherlands. Unpublished manuscript.

Park, B., & Judd, C. M. (2005). Rethinking the link between categorization and prejudice within the social cognition perspective. *Personality and Social Psychology Review, 9,* 108–130.

Petty, R. E., Briñol, P., Tormala, Z. L., & Wegener, D. T. (2007). The role of metacognition in social judgment. In E. T. Higgins & A. W. Kruglanski (Eds.), *Social psychology: A handbook of basic principles* (2nd ed., pp. 254–284). New York, NY: Guilford Press.

Petty, R. E., & Wegener, D. T. (1993). Flexible correction processes in social judgment: Correcting for context-induced contrast. *Journal of Experimental Social Psychology, 29,* 137–165.

Phelps, E. A., Cannaistraci, C. J., & Cunningham, W. A. (2003). Intact performance on an indirect measure of race bias following amygdala damage. *Neuropsychologia, 41,* 203–208.

Plaks, J. E., Stroessner, S. J., Dweck, C. S., & Sherman, J. (2001). Person theories and attention allocation: Preferences for stereotypic vs. counterstereotypic information. *Journal of Personality and Social Personality, 80,* 876–893.

Plant, E. A., & Devine, P. G. (1998). Internal and external motivation to respond without prejudice. *Journal of Personality and Social Psychology, 75,* 811–832.

Prentice, D. A., & Miller, D. T. (2007). Psychological essentialism of human categories. *Current Directions in Psychological Science, 16,* 202–206.

Rangel, U., & Keller, J. (2011). Essentialism goes social: Belief in social determinism as a component of psychological essentialism. *Journal of Personality and Social Psychology, 100,* 1056–1078.

Richeson, J. A., & Shelton, J. N. (2007). Negotiating interracial interactions: Costs, consequences, and possibilities. *Current Directions in Psychological Science, 16,* 316–320.

Robbins, J. M., & Krueger, J. I. (2005). Social projection to ingroups and outgroups: A review and meta-analysis. *Personality and Social Psychology Review, 9,* 32–47.

Ross, L., & Nisbett, R. E. (1991). *The person and the situation: Perspectives of social psychology.* New York, NY: McGraw-Hill.

Rothbart, M., & Taylor, M. (1992). Category labels and social reality: Do we view social categories as natural kinds? In G. R. Semin & K. Fiedler (Eds.), *Language, interaction and social cognition* (pp. 11–36). London, UK: Sage.

Schmader, T. (2010). Stereotype threat deconstructed. *Current Directions in Psychological Science, 19,* 14–18.

Schmader, T., Johns, M., & Forbes, C. (2008). An integrated process model of stereotype threat effects on performance. *Psychological Review, 115,* 336–356.

Schwarz, N., & Bless, H. (1992). Constructing reality and its alternatives: An inclusion/exclusion model of assimilation and contrast effects in social judgment. In L. Martin & A. Tesser (Eds.), *The construction of social judgment.* Hillsdale, NJ: Lawrence Erlbaum Associates.

Shelton, J. N., Richeson, J. A., Salvatore, J., & Trawalter, S. (2005). Ironic effects of racial bias during interracial interactions. *Psychological Science, 16,* 397–402.

Sigelman, L., & Tuch, L. A. (1997). Metastereotypes—Blacks' perceptions of Whites' stereotypes of Blacks. *Public Opinion Quarterly, 61,* 87–101.

Sloan, L., Wilburn, G., Van Camp, D., Barden, J., Glover, C., & Martin, D. (2008). Stereotype threat impacts in uniformly minority contexts may require both majority presence and majority-involved evaluation. *International Journal of Psychology, 43,* 809–810.

Snyder, M. L., Kleck, R. E., Strenta, A., & Mentzer, S. J. (1979). Avoidance of the handicapped: An attributional ambiguity analysis. *Journal of Personality and Social Psychology, 37,* 2297–2306.

Spears, R., Gordijn, E. H., Dijksterhuis, A., & Stapel, D. A. (2004). Reaction in action: Intergroup contrast in automatic behavior. *Personality and Social Psychology Bulletin, 30,* 605–616.

Steele, C. M. (1997). A threat in the air: How stereotypes shape intellectual identity and performance. *American Psychologist, 52,* 613–629.

Steele, C. M., & Aronson, J. (1995). Stereotype threat and the intellectual test performance of African Americans. *Journal of Personality and Social Psychology, 69,* 797–811.

Steele, C. M., Spencer, S. J., & Aronson, J. (2002). Contending with bias: The psychology of stereotype and social identity threat. In M. P. Zanna (Ed.), *Advances in experimental social psychology* (Vol. 34, pp. 277–341). San Diego, CA: Academic Press.

Stephan, W. G., & Stephan, C. W. (1985). Intergroup anxiety. *Journal of Social Issues, 41,* 157–175.

Tajfel, H., & Turner, J. C. (1979). An integrative theory of intergroup conflict: The social identity theory of intergroup behavior. In W. G. Austin, & S. Worchel (Eds.), *The social psychology of intergroup relations* (pp. 33–47). Monterey, CA: Brooks/Cole.

Trope, Y. (1986). Identification and inferential processes in dispositional attribution. *Psychological Review, 93,* 239–257.

van den Bos, A., & Stapel, D. A. (2009). Why people stereotype affect how they stereotype: The differential influence of comprehension goals and self-enhancement goals on stereotyping. *Personality and Social Psychology Bulletin, 35,* 101–113.

Vorauer, J. D. (2006). An information search model of evaluative concerns in intergroup interaction. *Psychological Review, 113,* 862–886.

Vorauer, J. D., Hunter, A. J., Main, K. J., & Roy, S. A. (2000). Metastereotype activation: Evidence from indirect measures for specific evaluative concerns experienced by members of dominant groups in intergroup interaction. *Journal of Personality and Social Psychology, 78,* 690–707.

Vorauer, J. D., & Kumhyr, S. M. (2001). Is this about you or me? Self- versus other-directed judgments and feelings in response to intergroup interaction. *Personality and Social Psychology Bulletin, 27,* 706–719.

Vorauer, J. D., Main, K. J., & O'Connell, G. B. (1999). How do individuals expect to be viewed by members of lower status groups? Content and implications of metastereotypes. *Journal of Personality and Social Psychology, 75,* 917–937.

Vorauer, J. D., & Sakamoto, Y. (2008). Who cares what the outgroup thinks? Testing an information search model of the importance individuals accord to an outgroup members' view of them during intergroup interaction. *Journal of Personality and Social Psychology, 95,* 1467–1480.

Wegener, D. T., & Petty, R. E. (1995). Flexible correction processes in social judgment: Correcting for context-induced contrast. *Journal of Experimental Social Psychology, 29,* 137–165.

Wegener, D. T., & Petty, R. E. (1997). The flexible correction model: The role of naïve theories of bias in bias correction. In M.P. Zanna (Ed.), *Advances in experimental social psychology* (Vol. 29, pp. 141–208). Mahwah, NJ: Lawrence Erlbaum Associates.

Wilder, D. A., & Simon, A. (1998). The group as a category and an interactive entity: Implications for social perception and intergroup behavior. In C. Sedikides, J. Schopler, & C. A. Insko (Eds.), *Intergroup cognition and intergroup behavior* (pp. 27–44). Hillsdale, NJ: Lawrence Erlbaum Associates.

Williams, M. J., & Eberhardt, J. L. (2008). Biological conceptions of race and the motivation to cross racial boundaries. *Journal of Personality and Social Psychology, 94,* 1033–1047.

Wolsko, C., Park, B., Judd, C. M., & Wittenbrink, B. (2000). Framing interethnic ideology: Effects of multicultural and color-blind perspectives on judgments of groups and individuals. *Journal of Personality and Social Psychology, 78,* 635–654.

Wout, D. A., Shih, M. J., Jackson, J. S., & Sellers, R. M. (2009). Targets as perceivers: How people determine when they will be negatively stereotyped. *Journal of Personality and Social Psychology, 96,* 349–362.

Yzerbyt, V. Y. (2010). Motivational—Processes in prejudice, stereotyping, and discrimination. In J. Dovidio, M. Hewstone, & P. Glick (Eds.), *Handbook of prejudice, stereotyping, and discrimination* (pp. 146–162). Thousand Oaks, CA: Sage.

Yzerbyt, V. Y., & Corneille, O. (2005). Cognitive process: Reality constraints and integrity concerns in social perception. In J. F. Dovidio, P. Glick, & L. Rudman (Eds.), *On the nature of prejudice: 50 years after Allport.* London, UK: Blackwell.

Yzerbyt, V. Y., Corneille, O., & Estrada, C. (2001). The interplay of subjective essentialism and entitativity in the formation of stereotypes. *Personality and Social Psychology Review, 5,* 141–155.

Yzerbyt, V. Y., & Demoulin, S. (2010). Intergroup relations. In S. T. Fiske, D. T. Gilbert, & G. Lindzey (Eds.), *Handbook of social psychology* (Vol. 2, 5th ed., pp. 1024–1083). Hoboken, NJ: Wiley.

Yzerbyt, V. Y., Judd, C. M., & Corneille, O. (2004). *The psychology of group perception: Perceived variability, entitativity, and essentialism.* London, England: Psychology Press.

Yzerbyt, V. Y., Rocher, S. J., & Schadron, G. (1997). Stereotypes as explanations: A subjective essentialistic view of group perception. In R. Spears, P. Oakes, N. Ellemers, & A. Haslam (Eds.), *The psychology of stereotyping and group life* (pp. 20–50). Oxford, England: Basil Blackwell.

Yzerbyt, V. Y., Rogier, A., & Fiske, S. (1998). Group entitativity and social attribution: On translating situational constraints into stereotypes. *Personality and Social Psychology Bulletin, 24,* 1090–1104.

Yzerbyt, V. Y., Schadron, G., Leyens, J.-Ph., & Rocher, S. (1994). Social judgeability: The impact of meta-informational cues on the use of stereotypes. *Journal of Personality and Social Psychology, 66,* 48–55.

14

Do You See What I See? Antecedents, Consequences, and Remedies for Biased Metacognition in Close Relationships

JACQUIE D. VORAUER

INTRODUCTION

Few subjects rival close relationships in the sheer amount and intensity of analysis they prompt. Indeed, individuals' ongoing preoccupation and fascination with the nature and progress of their personal relationships are reflected in the themes of popular music and movies, as well as in the proliferation of relationship-focused advice columns and self-help books. In many—if not most—cases, the reflection and rumination center on trying to understand the thoughts and feelings of a current or potential relationship partner. This makes sense from an information search perspective because, although individuals are highly invested in knowing what a partner is thinking and feeling by virtue of being outcome dependent on him or her, they are also necessarily uncertain by virtue of limited access to the inner workings of their partner's mind (see, for example, Vorauer, 2006).

Notably, individuals' preoccupation with discerning and predicting a partner's thoughts and feelings applies across the full span of possible relationship stages, from initiation to breakup. For example, at the very beginning, the desire to avoid the embarrassment of rejection fuels a need to gauge the potential partner's likely response to any overtures (see, for example, Vorauer, Cameron, Holmes, & Pearce, 2003). Once a relationship is established, the need to regulate dependence on a partner to minimize risk to self prompts efforts to understand the extent of his or her positive regard (Murray, Holmes, & Collins, 2006). Among other things, an individual needs to know if he or she can trust a partner to be responsive to his or her needs and whether the partner's commitment to the relationship is similar to his or her own. Often, then, an individual's analysis of a partner's inner thoughts and feelings centers on trying to determine how they themselves are perceived.

In line with the types of issues that tend to preoccupy individuals in the relationships domain, this chapter will focus on judgments about a romantic partner's thoughts and feelings. Sometimes individuals' desire to make such judgments and the recruitment of potentially relevant information such as self-knowledge arise in a top-down manner, driven by factors such as the general need to know what the partner is thinking for prediction and planning purposes or an ongoing need to know their standing with the partner (see, for example, Murray et al., 2006). At other times, the process is more from the bottom up, driven by events or experiences that raise questions about the partner's reactions. In particular, individuals' own perceptions may often prompt questions about the implications of those perceptions for their partner's thoughts and feelings. For example, a woman may wonder whether doubts that she is having about her relationship with her partner are obvious to or shared by her partner.

In either the top-down or bottom-up case (perhaps especially the latter because personal reactions are more likely to be the starting point), judgments about the partner tend to involve *metacognition*—that is, individuals' thoughts about their own thoughts or thought processes (see, for example, Dunlosky & Metcalfe, 2009; Petty, Briñol, Tormala, & Wegener, 2007). Using the terminology adopted in work on metacognition, the negative relationship perceptions held by the woman in the earlier example are primary cognitions, involving initial associations of some object with some attribute; her thoughts about whether her partner detects or shares her perceptions are secondary cognitions, involving reflections on the first-level thoughts. Indeed, whenever individuals try to determine the extent to which information that they possess about themselves is relevant to understanding another person's thoughts, feelings, and traits, they are engaged in a fundamentally metacognitive process. Questions regarding the connection between their own and others' judgments represent metacognitions, as do qualities of and reactions to their own cognitions that may guide the extent to which a connection is perceived, such as the confidence with which their own cognitions are held or the desire to conceal them.

This chapter examines the important role played by metacognition in close relationships, with a particular focus on the egocentric bias that tends to characterize individuals' secondary cognitions regarding the extent to which their own perceptions are relevant to judging a partner's thoughts and feelings. Individuals tend to perceive greater relevance of self to other than is warranted, especially when their self is the starting point for the judgment. This egocentric bias arises for a variety of reasons, including eagerness to reduce uncertainty and ready availability of self-relevant information. Although on some level individuals may appreciate the possibility of egocentrism and the potential need for correction (Wegener & Petty, 1995), any resultant adjustments are often insufficient (Epley, Keysar, Van Boven, & Gilovich, 2004).

OVERVIEW

I begin by examining factors that increase the extent to which individuals judge their own perceptions to be relevant to their inferences about another person and thus enhance egocentric bias. Specifically, I review research indicating that the magnitude of egocentric bias that individuals exhibit can depend on the salience of their self-concept or its relevance to the judgment in question, individuals' closeness to the person being judged, and individuals' motivation to perceive similarity and understanding between themselves and the other person. Notably, these factors can combine to create a "perfect storm" for fostering high egocentrism when individuals' judgments involve a romantic partner's thoughts about and feelings toward them. Next, I consider the potential benefits and costs of different forms of egocentric bias within a romantic relationship.

Finally, I examine the likely effectiveness of different strategies for reducing egocentrism—that is, for limiting the extent to which individuals judge their own perceptions to be relevant to their inferences about another person. The role of individual differences in self-esteem is considered throughout because self-esteem is a key potential predictor at each stage of analysis, likely guiding the extent of egocentric bias, the consequences of the bias, and the efficacy of bias-reducing strategies. Although the emphasis will be on romantic relationships, many aspects of the analysis apply to friendships and close family relations as well.

EGOCENTRIC BIAS

Individuals are well practiced—and, in many respects, adept—at estimating what is going on in another person's mind (see, for example, Epley & Waytz, 2010; Funder, 1995). Indeed, they are even attuned to the extent to which a close relationship partner views them more positively than is warranted (Boyes & Fletcher, 2007). At the same time, however, they exhibit a number of systematic judgmental biases. For example, a wealth of research documents that individuals tend to judge close others in an overly positive light (Murray, Holmes, & Griffin, 1996a), much as they do themselves (Taylor & Brown, 1988).

Egocentrism, the propensity to rely too much on self-knowledge, is one bias that is uniquely relevant to making judgments about others. For example, people exhibit a false consensus effect, exaggerating the degree to which others share their own beliefs, values, and opinions (Marks & Miller, 1987). They use themselves as a standard and guide when judging others (Markus, Smith, & Moreland, 1985; Murray et al., 1996a) and base their implicit theories of personality—that is, their beliefs about the traits that do and do not "go together" in others—on how traits are configured in their own personality (Crichter & Dunning, 2009).

In another vein, individuals overestimate the extent to which their actions and appearance are noted by others (Gilovich, Medvec, & Savitsky, 2000) and exaggerate the extent to which others' behavior is caused by and directed at them (Fenigstein, 1984; Zuckerman et al., 1983). That is, individuals tend to assume that their beliefs about the significance of their own actions and remarks are shared by others.

What's on Your Mind? Salience and Relevance of the Self

Sharing the cognitive focus of another person is key to making accurate judgments about his or her thoughts and feelings (Thomas, Fletcher, & Lange, 1997). Yet, even at fairly low levels, individuals' focus on themselves is unlikely to be matched by an interaction partner, who is instead apt to be focused on himself or herself. Thus, any factor that enhances self-focus is apt to increase egocentrism: The more prominent the self is in an individual's mind, the more difficult it is for the individual to suppress it and avoid relying on it too much in judgments of others' thoughts and feelings (see, for example, Fenigstein & Abrams, 1993; Vorauer & Ross, 1999; Ward, 1965). Generally speaking, then, although egocentric bias is quite ubiquitous, it is more likely to arise when self-relevant information is salient. For example, self-focus increases the likelihood that individuals will answer "yes" to questions such as "Can the store clerk tell how impatient I am feeling with her?" or "Does my date think this movie is as offensive as I do?"

By extension, it seems likely that judgments about others that directly implicate the self, such as metaperceptions regarding how the self is viewed, should be especially prone to egocentric bias. Along these lines, ample research indicates a robust tendency for individuals to perceive much greater correspondence between their self-views and others' views of them than actually exists (Gilovich, Savitsky, & Medvec, 1998; Kenny & DePaulo, 1993; Vorauer & Ross, 1999). Thus, answers to questions such as "Can she tell how nervous I am?" (in contrast to "Does she think that this wine is as awful as I do?") are particularly likely to be affirmative. Moreover, because confidence may serve as a cue to probable consensus and also heighten perceived relevance, egocentrism seems more likely to arise for beliefs and perceptions that individuals hold with greater certainty. Further along these lines, individuals who exhibit higher levels of self-concept clarity (Campbell, 1990), possessing more clearly articulated notions of who and what they are, should generally be more likely to exaggerate their transparency to others than those with lower levels of self-concept clarity.

The idea that greater certainty of self-beliefs leads to greater influence of those beliefs is consistent with recent work on metacognition indicating that the confidence with which individuals hold a particular self-evaluation predicts its impact on judgment and behavior (Briñol, Demarree, & Petty, 2010; DeMarree, Petty, & Briñol, 2007). As well, long-standing work on self-verification shows that individuals who hold self-beliefs with greater confidence are more likely to convince others of those beliefs (e.g., Pelham & Swann, 1994; Swann & Ely, 1984). Notably, however, the specific prediction of a link between self-certainty and egocentric bias hinges on the assumption that the effect of self-certainty on metaperceptions regarding how the self is viewed exceeds the effect of self-certainty on behavior. Previous research indicating, albeit indirectly, that individuals' feelings of transparency increase more readily than their actual transparency (see Cameron & Vorauer, 2008; Vorauer & Cameron, 2002) suggest that this assumption is valid, although it awaits empirical testing.

Getting to Know You: Interpersonal Closeness

Ironically, another factor that increases the likelihood of egocentric bias is interpersonal closeness. Simply put, individuals should be especially inclined to use their self when judging another person's thoughts and feelings to the extent that they perceive themselves and that person to be "one." The distance between their own and the other person's perceptions will seem especially short and the applicability of self-judgments to other-judgments will seem especially high when self and other are merged together this way in people's minds.

Along these lines, in a series of studies, Vorauer and Cameron (2002) found that individuals were more likely to exaggerate the transparency of their traits, values, and preferences to a close other if they were high in horizontal collectivism, an orientation that involves seeing oneself as similar to others and emphasizing interdependence and sociability (Triandis & Gelfand, 1998); this effect was mediated by self–other merging. Notably, parallel results were obtained in a study in which individuals' felt bond with a friend was experimentally manipulated: Feeling closer to the friend was associated with greater feelings of transparency but not greater actual transparency to the friend. The results of this study further indicated that the degree of transparency overestimation that individuals exhibited depended on the length of their friendship, which was correlated with the extent to which they felt a bond with the friend. To be sure, individuals do gain more insight into others with increasing time spent together and acquaintanceship (Funder & Colvin, 1988; Thomas & Fletcher, 2003). However, increases in felt transparency appear to outpace increases in actual transparency (see Cameron & Vorauer, 2008).

Notably, because the underlying psychological mechanism is the same, the effect of closeness on egocentrism should apply to any type of egocentric bias. The fact that individuals are more likely to show a false consensus bias when estimating the opinions of ingroup as compared to outgroup members (see Marks & Miller, 1987) is consistent with this possibility.

Hopes or Fears Fulfilled? The Role of Motivation

Of course, individuals are not necessarily dispassionate when gauging how much they should rely on self-knowledge in estimating another person's thoughts and feelings. For example, research and theory regarding the motive for self-verification (see, for example, Swann, 1987) suggest that individuals' desire to perceive congruence between their own and others' judgments is considerable with respect to metaperceptions. Believing that others' views of them match their own self-views validates individuals' perceptions and provides existential security. Thus, the pursuit of self-verification should fuel transparency overestimation and possibly other egocentric biases, such as self-as-targeting, as well. Motivated perception should result in a pattern whereby the more that individuals wish for their inner self to be readily apparent to others, the more they perceive that it is.

Interestingly, however, transparency overestimation has also been documented in contexts where individuals are trying to *conceal* some aspect of themselves—that is, when they are engaged in deception. For example, in one study by Gilovich et al. (1998), individuals overestimated their transparency to observers when they were trying to hide that they were sampling a foul- rather than a pleasant-tasting drink: They exaggerated the observers' ability to detect which drink they were actually tasting. How might such a countermotivational bias arise? Conceivably, a strong desire to conceal a particular self-aspect, whether it be an impatient nature or dislike of a friend's cooking or boyfriend, could fuel transparency overestimation via a type of ironic monitoring metacognitive process: The more that individuals seek to hide a given thought, feeling, or inclination, the more prominent it may become in their mind and thus the more difficult it may be to suppress.

In scanning their behavior to ensure that the thought, feeling, or inclination does not leak out, individuals are apt to set a low threshold for identifying cues—one that they inappropriately assume is shared by their audience. The mechanism here would seem somewhat akin to that described in the preoccupation model of secrecy, whereby efforts to keep a secret or conceal an aspect of self lead to obsessive preoccupation with the secret (see, for example, Lane & Wegner, 1995; Wegner, 1994), with the added egocentric dimension of assuming preoccupation-driven perceptions to be shared by others. (See Chapter 5, this volume, for an extended discussion of thought suppression.)

There has been no direct comparison to date of the magnitude of transparency overestimation bias that individuals exhibit when trying to convey versus conceal some aspect of themselves, so the impact of motivation on this bias is currently unclear. It is possible that strong motivation either way similarly enhances bias by virtue of the heightened salience of the self-aspect in question. Alternatively, either motivated perception or ironic monitoring could exert a more powerful influence, such that individuals are more likely to exaggerate the transparency of self-aspects they wish to convey or of self-aspects they wish to conceal.

Self-Esteem and Egocentric Bias

The question of how motivation affects transparency judgments appears to be quite amenable to experimental investigation. It also seems, however, that this question could be profitably examined via testing the influence of individual differences in self-esteem, defined here as the overall valence of individuals' general evaluations of themselves. To the extent that individuals fundamentally wish to be loved and viewed in a positive light by their partners (Murray et al., 1996a, 2006), individuals' desire for their true selves to be readily apparent to their relationship partners should be positively correlated with their levels of self-esteem. Individuals with more favorable self-evaluations should hope that their partners can fully perceive and appreciate their personal qualities, whereas those with less favorable self-evaluations should be less anxious for their partners to see what they are "really" like.

Thus, examining the extent to which individuals lower versus higher in self-esteem exaggerate how accurately their partners can judge self-aspects such as their personal qualities, values, and preferences (as well as temporary affective states and current thoughts) should speak to the role of motivation in transparency judgments. Specifically, if individuals higher in self-esteem evidence greater egocentrism, this would suggest that motivated perception exerts a more powerful influence. If individuals lower in self-esteem evidence greater egocentrism, this would suggest instead that ironic monitoring exerts a more powerful influence.

However, other factors aside from motivation could account for self-esteem effects on transparency overestimation. For example, to the extent that lower self-esteem individuals are more inclined than higher self-esteem individuals to perceive another person's reactions to them as contingent on their behavior and personal qualities (see, for example, Baldwin & Sinclair, 1996), lower self-esteem individuals may feel more transparent by virtue of the heightened self-awareness—and thus self-salience—that accompanies the feeling that one is being evaluated (see Vorauer & Ross, 1999).

Alternatively, higher self-esteem individuals might feel more transparent by virtue of feeling closer to others in general and romantic partners in particular (Murray, Rose, Bellavia, Holmes, & Kusche, 2002) via the aforementioned self–other merging mechanism or by virtue of the greater clarity of their self-concept (Campbell, 1990). That is, the stronger connection they perceive between self and other or the greater confidence with which they hold their self-beliefs might increase the extent to which they assume that primary cognitions, such as "I feel upset," can be used to understand other people's perceptions of them. Along these lines, research by Harber (1995) suggests that because individuals higher in self-esteem consider their own reactions to be more valid sources of information, they rely on them more when judging others' reactions.

Although indirect, experimental evidence to date pertaining to the connection between self-esteem and transparency overestimation suggests a positive relation whereby individuals with higher self-esteem are more egocentric (see Campbell & Fehr, 1990; Swann, Stein-Seroussi, & McNulty, 1992). Interestingly, this pattern clashes with the results of correlational self-report studies suggesting that higher self-esteem is connected to greater perspective-taking and empathic concern (Davis, 1983). Conceivably, the fact that individuals higher in self-esteem report higher levels of perspective-taking and empathic concern reflects these individuals' tendency to experience stronger feelings of closeness with relationship partners, which, ironically, fosters elevated egocentrism in their actual judgments. A clear and direct test of the relation between self-esteem and egocentric biases such as transparency overestimation and false consensus would be useful for identifying the types of problems that different types of individuals are most apt to encounter in their relationships. Of course, any intervention efforts need to take into account the fact that, in some cases, egocentric biases are beneficial for rather than detrimental to relationships.

CONSEQUENCES OF BIAS

In many cases, egocentric biases have negative consequences for individuals and their relationships. When individuals exaggerate the extent to which feelings such as embarrassment or nervousness are obvious to others, the perceived transparency of these states can itself make them more intense, resulting in a self-exacerbating syndrome that detracts from performance and communication effectiveness (see Gilovich, Kruger, & Savitsky, 1999). More relationally, exaggerating the transparency of negative states such as anger or sadness to relationship partners can lead to conflict when individuals await social support that is not forthcoming because the need for it has not been adequately conveyed (Cameron & Vorauer, 2008).

Perceiving positive feelings such as romantic interest or concern for another person to be more readily apparent than they actually are is also apt to be problematic because here transparency overestimation can reduce communication efforts (why try to convey a feeling that is already obvious?), resulting in behavior that is difficult to read and less positive than intended (Vorauer, 2005; Vorauer et al., 2003; Vorauer, Martens, & Sasaki, 2009). When positive feelings and social inclinations fail to get across, both current and potential relationship partners may assume indifference—or worse—and disengage. For example, Vorauer and Sakamoto (2006) found that individuals' unwarranted tendency to assume that their interest in forming a relationship was obvious to a potential partner enhanced their propensity to interpret an apparent lack of reciprocation as personal rejection and ultimately led them to distance themselves defensively from the potential partner. That is, they decided that they were not interested after all.

Other egocentric biases can be similarly problematic. For example, exaggerating personal contributions to joint products can foster resentment toward relationship partners who may seem to be trying to take advantage (Ross & Sicoly, 1979). Assuming that a partner's preferences are the same as one's own when they are not can lead to insensitive social behavior and interpersonal conflict.

Nonetheless, it is also true that egocentrism can be beneficial for individuals and their relationships, as when exaggerating congruence between their own and others' opinions provides a sense of existential security (Swann, 1987) and enhances satisfaction within close relationships by promoting a sense of having found a "kindred spirit" in their partner (Murray, Holmes, Bellavia, Griffin, & Dolderman, 2002; see also Thomas et al., 1997). How can the seemingly contradictory ideas that egocentrism is problematic and beneficial be reconciled? As others have suggested (e.g., Murray, Holmes, et al., 2002), the extent to which the judgment in question is specific or general may be one deciding factor.

For example, it may be beneficial for individuals to exaggerate how much their partner shares general values and attitudes such as love of nature. Because these perceptions are broad and abstract, they can enhance feelings of closeness and of being "one" without too much risk of fostering behavior that comes across as insensitive or selfish to their partner. In contrast, with respect to more specific judgments, such as enthusiasm about camping, the risk is greater. If individuals erroneously assume that their partner shares a love of sleeping outdoors, they may suggest a trip that is highly unappealing to their partner and seems selfishly motivated. Similarly, it seems apt to be more beneficial for individuals to exaggerate the extent to which their partner shares their love for children in general than for them to exaggerate agreement regarding the specific number of children they and their partner should have.

A parallel analysis applies to metaperceptual judgments regarding how the self is viewed. Exaggerating the transparency of their general values, beliefs, and traits may fuel individuals' feelings of being understood and loved by their partner and ultimately enhance relationship satisfaction. On the other hand, exaggerating the transparency of specific preferences (e.g., enthusiasm for surprise parties) may hinder the communication of important information and set the stage for conflict.

Here, however, egocentrism can be detrimental even at the general level if the self-views that individuals are projecting are negative. When individuals who are lower in self-esteem assume that their partner views them as harshly as they view themselves, their lower levels of perceived regard lead them defensively to distance from their partner and ultimately to be less satisfied with their relationship (Murray, Holmes, & Griffin, 2000). In the face of seemingly impending rejection, these individuals are disinclined to let themselves trust and depend on their partners.

Not surprisingly, then, lower self-esteem individuals' propensity to underestimate their partners' positive regard for them has been shown to have a wide range of negative consequences (see Murray et al., 2006). For example, these unwarranted negative metaperceptions can lead individuals to be suspicious of their partner's authenticity and to feel powerless within the relationship (Lemay & Dudley, 2009), to suffer rather than benefit from disclosing negative experiences to their partner (Cameron, Holmes, & Vorauer, 2009), and to be particularly vulnerable to the negative consequences of miscommunication within the relationship (Cameron & Robinson, 2010). In sum, when the self is the target of the judgment in question, the valence of the self that is being projected needs to be taken into account when considering the costs and benefits of egocentrism.

Thus, from an intervention perspective, reducing egocentrism in any kind of specific judgment should be broadly beneficial, and reducing egocentrism in general judgments regarding how the self is viewed should be beneficial for lower self-esteem individuals. That is, it may be fruitful to try to cut or weaken the link from lower self-esteem individuals' self-concepts to their beliefs about how their partner views them.

REMEDIES FOR BIAS

How might egocentrism be reduced? That is, how can individuals be discouraged from relying on self-knowledge when judging others? Perhaps the most obvious potential remedy is to encourage individuals to try to take their partner's perspective and appreciate how it might well be different from their own—that is, to prompt them to question the applicability of self-knowledge to judgments about their partner.

Perspective-Taking

At first blush, a strategy such as perspective-taking would seem quite promising, particularly for lower self-esteem individuals' metaperceptual judgments. Orienting these individuals toward their partner's more positive view of them might not only reduce egocentric bias in their judgments but also pave the way for their partner's more positive appraisals of them to affect their self-views. That is, if these individuals could be discouraged from relying on their negative self-concepts when forming metaperceptions about how their partner views them and instead encouraged to become more attuned to their partner's actual impressions, the negative self-concepts that cause them to experience difficulties in their relationships might be at least partially mitigated via reflected appraisal processes (see Shrauger & Schoeneman, 1979).

Moreover, individuals at any self-esteem level would seem apt to benefit from trying to take their partner's perspective regarding many specific everyday preferences, feelings, and inclinations by virtue of decreasing the likelihood of misunderstanding and conflict. Consistent with this possibility, the findings of numerous correlational studies suggest an association between individuals' reports of trying to take their partners' perspectives and positive relationship outcomes (e.g., Davis & Oathout, 1987; Franzoi, Davis, & Young, 1985; Long & Andrews, 1990).

Yet the problem here is more complex than it might originally seem to be because experimental research suggests that one key effect of perspective-taking effort is the activation of self-relevant information (Davis et al., 2004) and cognitive merging of self and other (Davis, Conklin, Smith, & Luce, 1996). When, as is often the case, the goal is to lead individuals who feel more positively about themselves than they do about another person to be more favorable toward the other person and to feel a greater bond with him or her, increasing the accessibility of the self-concept and the extent to which it is projected onto the other should clearly be beneficial. Indeed, the literature on intergroup relations contains numerous experimental demonstrations of the advantages of encouraging individuals to try to adopt an outgroup member's perspective (see, for example, Galinsky & Moskowitz, 2000).

However, in view of the aforementioned relations of self-salience and self–other merging to egocentrism (Vorauer & Cameron, 2002), the activation and projection of self involved in these beneficial effects of perspective-taking also seem apt to increase egocentric biases such as exaggerated perceptions of transparency and similarity. For example, in making plans with a close relationship partner, individuals who try to take their partner's perspective might be especially likely to exaggerate the extent to which he or she understands their disinclination to attend a large party. If the unlucky partner happens to suggest that the couple attend such an event, he or she may be the target of some vexation by virtue of seeming to have done so despite the individual's ostensibly obvious preference to have a more romantic evening.

Moreover, even just with respect to the positivity of individuals' feelings toward the person whose perspective they are trying to adopt, research and theory in the context of intergroup relations have revealed that the benefits of perspective-taking depend on individuals' levels of self-esteem. The self that is being projected onto outgroup members needs to be favorable if reactions to outgroup members are to be improved (Galinsky & Ku, 2004). These findings raise the question as to whether, in a relationship context, the perspective-taking efforts of individuals lower in self-esteem might sometimes result in more negative than more positive partner perceptions. For example, perspective-taking efforts might lead individuals who are lower in self-esteem to perceive that their partner shares negative traits such as selfishness or impatience that they believe themselves to possess.

Research on intergroup relations has further revealed that in the context of actual intergroup interactions, where there is the potential for evaluation, efforts to take an outgroup member's perspective can quickly evolve into concerns about how the self is evaluated: When individuals try to look at the world through an outgroup interaction partner's eyes, one of the first things that they are apt to see is themselves. They then become focused on trying to deduce the outgroup member's impression of them and activate (largely negative) metastereotypes regarding the outgroup's view of their ingroup, so as to gain some insight into how they are being evaluated (Vorauer et al., 2009; Vorauer & Sasaki, 2009). It seems possible that a somewhat parallel dynamic arises in the context of close relationships for individuals lower in self-esteem. When these individuals try to take a relationship partner's perspective, perhaps even on an issue in which they are not directly involved, they might become focused on imagining their partner's likely negative evaluations of them. That is, their negative self-perceptions may contaminate their metaperceptions and lead them to be more preoccupied with their partner's possible criticisms of them than they already were.

Several of these potential pitfalls of perspective-taking are suggested by studies focused on intergroup relations; thus, the extent to which they extend to the domain of close relationships is currently unclear. Possibly, because individuals typically possess a considerable amount of information about their romantic partner, perspective-taking efforts are less likely to turn problematic in the context of greater intimacy. For example, by virtue of the richer other-representations that characterize close as compared with intergroup relations, self–other merging that occurs with respect to romantic partners may be more apt to involve some projection of other onto self (see Galinsky, Wang, & Ku, 2008), which could be particularly beneficial for individuals lower in self-esteem.

Alternatively or in addition, as a function of the close preexisting connection, projecting even negative self-aspects onto a relationship partner could foster a sense of having a "kindred spirit" and deepen an individual's felt bond with him or her (see, for example, Murray, Holmes, et al., 2002). Finally, perspective-taking might not lead so quickly to evaluative concerns and egocentrism when individuals have clear preexisting beliefs about how they are regarded, based on extensive experience with a particular relationship partner.

Given the current lack of clarity on the implications of directly prompting perspective-taking efforts in the context of close relationships, the issue seems ripe for investigation. The extent to which perspective-taking generally prompts individuals to evidence greater egocentric bias (i.e., overestimation of transparency and similarity) and the extent to which it prompts individuals with lower self-esteem to evidence more negative partner perceptions and metaperceptions would be of particular interest.

One principal advantage of an experimental approach would be to avoid confounds potentially involved in relying on self-reported perspective-taking. In particular, it is possible that the correlational studies that have used such measures and found positive effects of perspective-taking have missed negative outcomes such as more egocentric judgments or problems specific to individuals with more negative self-views. Although self-reported perspective-taking has been connected to more accurate social judgments, at least with respect to deducing strangers' traits (Bernstein & Davis, 1982), in ongoing relationships it may also be connected to a charitable and positive motivational stance toward self, partner, and the relationship that is broadly adaptive and that contributes to relationship satisfaction and longevity more so than does the act of perspective-taking per se. Alternatively, negative consequences of perspective-taking might not arise at all in the context of close relationships by virtue of individuals' felt bond with and extensive information about their partner, or any negative outcomes that do occur might be dwarfed by the positive outcomes stimulated by perspective-taking.

Imagine-Self Versus Imagine-Other Perspective-Taking

Of course, any effort to encourage perspective-taking would need to consider carefully the specific type of perspective-taking that is promoted. One approach would be to advise individuals to put themselves in their partner's shoes and imagine how they would feel in his or her position. Although this strategy does suggest using the self as a starting point or anchor for judgment, it also suggests potential differences between individuals' own and their partners' points of view and thus might serve as a cue to potential bias and the need for correction. However, given that adjustments from initial anchors tend to be insufficient (Epley et al., 2004), the resultant judgments might still be biased, and overcorrection is also possible (Wegener & Petty, 1995).

Another, more seemingly promising approach would be to advise individuals to try to get inside their partner's head and imagine what they would think and feel if they were their partner and possessed his or her traits and inclinations. Notably, this strategy essentially involves changing the starting point of the judgment from self to other, such that self is no longer the anchor. Rather than beginning with an aspect of self-knowledge such as "I feel angry" or "I want to see a romantic comedy tonight" and then making decisions about its applicability to judgments about another person's thoughts and feelings, the inference would begin with an effort to get inside the other person's head. In metacognitive terms, individuals' judgments about another person's thoughts and feelings would then be primary rather than secondary cognitions.

These two types of perspective-taking have sometimes been referred to as situational versus individual perspective-taking (see Higgins, 1981) and more often as imagine-self versus imagine-other perspective-taking (e.g., Batson, Early, & Salvarani, 1997; Davis et al., 2004; Stotland, 1969). Because imagine-other perspective-taking does not invoke the self-concept as explicitly as does imagine-self perspective-taking, imagine-other perspective-taking could be less likely to trigger self-activation and egocentric projection. Indeed, research suggests that fewer thoughts about self and more thoughts about other are triggered by imagine-other as compared with imagine-self instructions (Batson, Polycarpou, et al., 1997; Davis et al., 2004). Notably, however, recent research demonstrating that an impression formation mind-set best helps individuals deal with potentially stressful social interactions (Sasaki & Vorauer, 2010) suggests that direct encouragement to try to learn about a relationship partner's thoughts and feelings might be particularly helpful for reducing egocentric bias.

Because only some forms of egocentrism seem apt to be detrimental for relationships (namely, egocentrism in any kind of specific concrete judgment and egocentrism in lower self-esteem individuals' general judgments regarding how they are viewed), it would be of interest to examine the effects of different kinds of perspective-taking on a range of judgment types and whether perspective-taking can be tailored to focus on the forms of egocentrism that are most likely to be problematic. Notably, any decrease in egocentrism seems apt to be greatest for issues where information about the partner's actual thoughts and feelings is most available.

Enhanced Communication: Self-Disclosure and Feedback

Indeed, if individuals are to be less egocentric in their judgments, it is obviously critical that information from and about their partner is available to them: Limiting reliance on self-knowledge to "fill in the blanks" depends on having alternatives. Efforts to encourage clearer and more direct communication should be beneficial, then, whether implemented on their own or together with prompts to engage in perspective-taking. Along these lines, recent research confirms that although direct communication may initially be negatively received, it predicts positive outcomes over the longer term regardless of its valence (Overall, Fletcher, Simpson, & Sibley, 2009).

Increasing direct communication is a straightforward recommendation. Yet there are possible drawbacks to be considered. In particular, if the communication is overly focused on individuals' own self-evaluative needs (e.g., sensitivity about appearance), it can backfire by leading their partner to "walk on eggshells" and fostering attributional ambiguity that leads individuals to doubt their partner's authenticity (Lemay & Clark, 2008). For example, a woman who explains that she is concerned about a recent weight gain may subsequently be suspicious that compliments from her partner are designed to be reassuring rather than convey accurate information.

Other potential problems are especially relevant for individuals lower in self-esteem. For example, recent experimental research reveals that disclosing information about personal failures activates concerns about evaluation for these individuals and that these secondary cognitions about how their disclosure will be received prevent them from deriving the same benefits from self-disclosure as individuals higher in self-esteem (see Cameron et al., 2009). By extension, it would seem that individuals lower in self-esteem might well be disinclined to communicate directly with their partner on any seemingly risky topic (e.g., personal needs or differences of opinion) and may become focused on the possibility of negative evaluation if prompted to do so (see also Murray et al., 2006).

Individuals lower in self-esteem may also be apt to attach negative interpretations to communications they receive from their partner, even if these communications are not explicitly evaluative in nature or are intended to convey positive feelings and inclinations. For example, these individuals might be inclined somehow to find criticism in their partner's words if he or she reports feeling anxious about an upcoming social event, as reflected by the secondary cognition: "Is my partner worried that I will embarrass him or her?" Although the overall tendency to take others' behavior more personally than is warranted (i.e., self-as-targeting) is, if anything, greater for individuals higher rather than lower in self-esteem (Zuckerman et al., 1983), the bias is generally substantial and self-as-target inferences of a negative nature are apt to be more common for lower self-esteem individuals by virtue of self-fulfilling prophecy processes (see, for example, Murray, Holmes, & Griffin, 1996b; Shrauger & Schoeneman, 1979). Further along these lines, recent research suggests that even explicitly positive self-affirmations can backfire for individuals lower in self-esteem by leading them to focus on how they fall short of personal standards (Wood, Perunovic, & Lee, 2009).

In sum, then, individuals lower in self-esteem may be hesitant to communicate their thoughts, feelings, and preferences directly to their partner, and doing so may exacerbate their concerns with evaluation. They may also tend to put a negative spin on communications they receive from their partner. Thus, encouraging communications that are as detailed and nonevaluative as possible would seem advisable for circumventing possible negative secondary cognitions, as would coupling enhanced communication with other-focused mind-sets such as efforts to learn more about a partner. Indeed, because explicitly evaluative communications are generally counternormative even in close relationships (Blumberg, 1972), they might exert a stronger effect on individuals higher in self-esteem by suggesting the possibility of evaluation to those whose thoughts would not otherwise have run in that direction. Thus, in addition to providing the best chance for individuals lower in self-esteem to get beyond their negative preconceptions, enhanced nonevaluative communication with greater other-focus might also be most broadly beneficial for reducing egocentrism.

SUMMARY AND CONCLUSIONS

Overall, the present analysis highlights the critical role played by metacognitive processes in the context of close relationships. Although individuals are generally too ready to extrapolate from their own primary cognitions about themselves and the world to make judgments about others' thoughts and feelings, egocentrism is, ironically, especially evident in their perceptions of relationship partners. In the relationship context, a "perfect storm" of closeness, heightened motivation, and—for metaperceptions—self-salience is apt to result in the hyperinsinuation of self into judgments pertaining to others. When individuals ask themselves whether a current reaction, such as "I feel angry," is evident to or shared by their partner, their secondary cognitions are likely to involve unwarranted affirmative answers.

Notably, heightened motivation in a relationship context could conceivably involve a strong desire to perceive understanding or to conceal the self, either of which might enhance egocentrism. Further, the hyperinsinuation of self into judgments of a partner might be elevated for individuals higher in self-esteem by virtue of their propensities to perceive a closer connection between self and other and/or to hold their self-beliefs with greater confidence than individuals lower in self-esteem. Both of these could lead individuals higher in self-esteem to perceive their own reactions as more relevant to their partners' reactions.

When individuals extrapolate from knowledge about self to fill in the blanks and answer general questions about a relationship partner, these egocentric secondary cognitions are often beneficial for deepening feelings of intimacy and connection.

However, for secondary cognitions of a metaperceptual nature, the benefits of egocentrism only apply to individuals higher in self-esteem. For individuals lower in self-esteem, egocentric secondary cognitions here involve perceiving more negative evaluations than is warranted and a host of concomitant relationship problems. Egocentrism in specific judgments has the potential to lead to miscommunications that result in conflict and reduced satisfaction—costs that may be borne by all.

At first blush, encouraging perspective-taking would seem to be an obvious route to reduced egocentrism and more accurate judgments about a partner's thoughts and feelings. However, at least with respect to egocentrism, this strategy has the potential to backfire and instead exacerbate bias by virtue of rendering the self more accessible and increasing projection. Of course, this cost might often be outweighed by the benefits of self–other merging for closeness and positive feelings toward a partner, although these benefits are most apt to be enjoyed by individuals higher in self-esteem, who have more positive perceptions to project. Possibly, perspective-taking is most helpful, both for reducing egocentrism and for limiting negative projection by individuals lower in self-esteem, when it is combined with enhanced (direct but nonevaluative) communication and efforts to learn more about the partner's thoughts and feelings.

REFERENCES

Baldwin, M. W., & Sinclair, L. (1996). Self-esteem and "if…then" contingencies of interpersonal acceptance. *Journal of Personality and Social Psychology, 71,* 1130–1141.

Batson, C. D., Early, S., & Salvarani, G. (1997). Perspective taking: Imagining how another feels versus imagining how you would feel. *Personality and Social Psychology Bulletin, 23,* 751–758.

Batson. C. D., Polycarpou, M. P., Harmon-Jones, E., Imhoff, H. J., Mitchener, E. C., Bednar, L. L., Klein, T. R., & Highberger, L. (1997). Empathy and attitudes: Can feeling for a member of a stigmatized group improve feelings toward the group? *Journal of Personality and Social Psychology, 72,* 105–118.

Bernstein, W. M., & Davis, M. H. (1982). Perspective-taking, self-consciousness, and accuracy in person perception. *Basic and Applied Social Psychology, 3,* 1–19.

Blumberg, H. H. (1972). Communication of interpersonal evaluations. *Journal of Personality and Social Psychology, 23,* 157–162.

Boyes, A. D., & Fletcher, G. J. O. (2007). Metaperceptions of bias in intimate relationships. *Journal of Personality and Social Psychology, 92,* 286–306.

Briñol, P., Demarree, K. G., & Petty, R. E. (2010). Processes by which confidence (vs. doubt) influences the self. In R. M. Arkin, K. C. Oleson, & P. J. Carroll (Eds.), *Handbook of the uncertain self* (pp. 13–35). New York, NY: Psychology Press.

Cameron, J. J., Holmes, J. G., & Vorauer, J. D. (2009). When self-disclosure goes awry: Negative consequences of revealing personal failures for low self-esteem individuals. *Journal of Experimental Social Psychology, 45,* 217–222.

Cameron, J. J., & Robinson, K. J. (2010). Don't you know how much I need you? Consequences of miscommunication vary by self-esteem. *Social Psychological and Personality Science, 1,* 136–142.

Cameron, J. J., & Vorauer, J. D. (2008). Feeling transparent: On metaperceptions and miscommunications. *Social and Personality Psychology Compass, 2,* 1098–1108.

Campbell, J. D. (1990). Self-esteem and clarity of the self-concept. *Journal of Personality and Social Psychology, 59*, 538–549.

Campbell, J. D., & Fehr, B. (1990). Self-esteem and perceptions of conveyed impressions: Is negative affectivity associated with greater realism? *Journal of Personality and Social Psychology, 58*, 122–133.

Crichter, C. R., & Dunning, D. (2009). Egocentric pattern projection: How implicit personality theories recapitulate the geography of the self. *Journal of Personality and Social Psychology, 97*, 1–16.

Davis, M. H. (1983). Individual differences in empathy: Evidence for a multidimensional approach. *Journal of Personality and Social Psychology, 44*, 113–126.

Davis, M. H., Conklin, L., Smith, A., & Luce, C. (1996). Effect of perspective-taking on the cognitive representation of persons: A merging of self and other. *Journal of Personality and Social Psychology, 70*, 713–726.

Davis, M. H., & Oathout, H. A. (1987). Maintenance of satisfaction in romantic relationships: Empathy and relational competence. *Journal of Personality and Social Psychology, 53*, 397–410.

Davis, M. H., Soderlund, T. A., Cole, J., Gadol, E., Kute, M., Myers, M., & Weihing, J. (2004). Cognitions associated with attempts to empathize: How *do* we imagine the perspective of another? *Personality and Social Psychology Bulletin, 30*, 1625–1635.

Demarree, K. G., Petty, R. E., & Briñol, P. (2007). Self-certainty: Parallels to attitude certainty. *International Journal of Psychology and Psychotherapy, 7*, 159–188.

Dunlosky, J., & Metcalfe, J. (2009). *Metacognition.* Thousand Oaks, CA: Sage Publications, Inc.

Epley, N., Keysar, B., Van Boven, L., & Gilovich, T. (2004). Perspective taking as egocentric anchoring and adjustment. *Journal of Personality and Social Psychology, 87*, 327–339.

Epley, N., & Waytz, A. (2010). Mind perception. In S. T. Fiske, D. T. Gilbert, & G. Lindsay (Eds.), *The handbook of social psychology* (5th ed.). New York, NY: John Wiley & Sons.

Fenigstein, A. (1984). Self-consciousness and the overperception of self as a target. *Journal of Personality and Social Psychology, 47*, 860–870.

Fenigstein, A., & Abrams, D. (1993). Self-attention and the egocentric assumption of shared perspectives. *Journal of Experimental Social Psychology, 29*, 287–303.

Franzoi, S. L., Davis, M. H., & Young, R. D. (1985). The effects of private self-consciousness and perspective taking on satisfaction in close relationships. *Journal of Personality and Social Psychology, 48*, 1584–1594.

Funder, D. C. (1995). On the accuracy of personality judgment: A realistic approach. *Psychological Review, 102*, 652–670.

Funder, D. C., & Colvin, C. R. (1988). Friends and strangers: Acquaintanceship, agreement, and the accuracy of personality judgment. *Journal of Personality and Social Psychology, 55*, 149–158.

Galinsky, A. D., & Ku, G. (2004). The effects of perspective-taking on prejudice: The moderating role of self-evaluation. *Personality and Social Psychology Bulletin, 30*, 594–604.

Galinsky, A. D., & Moskowitz, G. B. (2000). Perspective-taking: Decreasing stereotype expression, stereotype accessibility, and ingroup favoritism. *Journal of Personality and Social Psychology, 78*, 708–724.

Galinsky, A. D., Wang, C. S., & Ku, G. (2008). Perspective-takers behave more stereotypically. *Journal of Personality and Social Psychology, 95*, 404–419.

Gilovich, T., Kruger, J., & Savitsky, K. (1999). Everyday egocentrism and everyday interpersonal problems. In R. M. Kowalski & M. R. Leary (Eds.), *The social psychology of emotional and behavioral problems: Interfaces of social and clinical psychology* (pp. 69–95). Washington, DC: American Psychological Association.

Gilovich, T., Medvec, V. H., & Savitsky, K. (2000). The spotlight effect in social judgment: An egocentric bias in estimates of the salience of one's own actions and appearances. *Journal of Personality and Social Psychology, 78*, 211–222.

Gilovich, T., Savitsky, K., & Medvec, V. H. (1998). The illusion of transparency: Biased assessments of others' ability to read one's emotional states. *Journal of Personality and Social Psychology, 75*, 332–346.

Harber, K. D. (2005). Self-esteem and affect as information. *Personality and Social Psychology Bulletin, 31*, 276–288.

Higgins, E. T. (1981). Role taking and social judgment: Alternative developmental perspectives and processes. In J. H. Flavell & L. Ross (Eds.), *Social cognitive development: Frontiers and possible futures* (pp. 119–153). Cambridge, England: Cambridge University Press.

Kenny, D. A., & DePaulo, B. M. (1993). Do people know how others view them? An empirical and theoretical account. *Psychological Bulletin, 114*, 145–161.

Lane, J. D., & Wegner, D. M. (1995). The cognitive consequences of secrecy. *Journal of Personality and Social Psychology, 69*, 237–253.

Lemay, E., & Dudley, K. (2009). Implications of reflected appraisals of interpersonal insecurity for suspicion and power. *Personality and Social Psychology Bulletin, 35*, 1672–1686.

Lemay, E. P., & Clark, M. S. (2008). "Walking on eggshells." How expressing relationship insecurities perpetuates them. *Journal of Personality and Social Psychology, 95*, 420–441.

Long, E. C. J., & Andrews, D. W. (1990). Perspective taking as a predictor of marital adjustment. *Journal of Personality and Social Psychology, 59*, 126–131.

Marks, G., & Miller, N. (1987). Ten years of research on the false-consensus effect: An empirical and theoretical review. *Psychological Bulletin, 102*, 72–90.

Markus, H., Smith, J., & Moreland, R. L. (1985). Role of the self-concept in the perception of others. *Journal of Personality and Social Psychology, 49*, 1494–1512.

Murray, S. L., Holmes, J. G., Bellavia, G., Griffin, D. W., & Dolderman, D. (2002). Kindred spirits? The benefits of egocentrism in close relationships. *Journal of Personality and Social Psychology, 96*, 620–639.

Murray, S. L., Holmes, J. G., & Collins, N. L. (2006). Optimizing assurance: The risk regulation system in relationships. *Psychological Bulletin, 132*, 641–666.

Murray, S. L., Holmes, J. G., & Griffin, D. W. (1996a). The benefits of positive illusions: Idealization and the construction of satisfaction in close relationships. *Journal of Personality and Social Psychology, 70*, 79–98.

Murray, S. L., Holmes, J. G., & Griffin, D. W. (1996b). The self-fulfilling nature of positive illusions in romantic relationships: Love is not blind, but prescient. *Journal of Personality and Social Psychology, 71*, 1155–1180.

Murray, S. L., Holmes, J. G., & Griffin, D. W. (2000). Self-esteem and the quest for felt security: How perceived regard regulates attachment processes. *Journal of Personality and Social Psychology, 78*, 478–498.

Murray, S. L., Rose, P., Bellavia, G., Holmes, J. G., & Kusche, A. (2002). When rejection stings: How self-esteem constrains relationship-enhancement processes. *Journal of Personality and Social Psychology, 83*, 556–573.

Overall, N. C., Fletcher, G. J. O., Simpson, J. A., & Sibley, C. G. (2009). Regulating partners in intimate relationships: The costs and benefits of different communication strategies. *Journal of Personality and Social Psychology, 96*, 620–639.

Pelham, B. W., & Swann, W. B. Jr. (1994). The juncture of intrapersonal and interpersonal knowledge: Self-certainty and interpersonal congruence. *Personality and Social Psychology Bulletin, 20*, 349–357.

Petty, R. E., Briñol, P., Tormala, Z. L., & Wegener, D. (2007). The role of metacognition in social judgment. In A. W. Kruglanski & E. T. Higgins (Eds.), *Social psychology: Handbook of basic principles* (2nd ed., pp. 254–284). New York, NY: Guilford Press.

Ross, M., & Sicoly, F. (1979). Egocentric biases in availability and attribution. *Journal of Personality and Social Psychology, 37,* 322–336.

Sasaki, S. J., & Vorauer, J. D. (2010). Contagious resource depletion and anxiety? Spreading effects of evaluative concern and impression formation in dyadic social interaction. *Journal of Experimental Social Psychology, 46,* 1011–1016.

Shrauger, J. S., & Schoeneman, T. J. (1979). Symbolic interactionist view of self-concept: Through the looking glass darkly. *Psychological Bulletin, 86,* 549–573.

Stotland, E. (1969). Exploratory investigations of empathy. In L. Berkowitz (Ed.), *Advances in experimental social psychology* (Vol. 4, pp. 271–314). New York, NY: Academic Press.

Swann, W. B., Jr. (1987). Identity negotiation: Where two roads meet. *Journal of Personality and Social Psychology, 53,* 1038–1051.

Swann, W. B., Jr., & Ely, R. W. (1984). A battle of wills: Self-verification versus behavioral confirmation. *Journal of Personality and Social Psychology, 46,* 1287–1302.

Swann, W. B., Jr., Stein-Seroussi, A., & McNulty, S. (1992). Outcasts in a white lie society: The enigmatic worlds of people with negative self-conceptions. *Journal of Personality and Social Psychology, 62,* 618–624.

Taylor, S. E., & Brown, J. D. (1988). Illusion and well-being: A social psychological perspective on mental health. *Psychological Bulletin, 103,* 193–210.

Thomas, G., & Fletcher, G. J. O. (2003). Mind-reading accuracy in intimate relationships: Assessing the roles of the relationship, the target, and the judge. *Journal of Personality and Social Psychology, 85,* 1079–1094.

Thomas, G., Fletcher, G. J. O., & Lange, C. (1997). Online empathic accuracy in marital interaction. *Journal of Personality and Social Psychology, 72,* 839–850.

Triandis, H., & Gelfand, M. J. (1998). Converging measurement of horizontal and vertical individualism and collectivism. *Journal of Personality and Social Psychology, 74,* 118–128.

Vorauer, J. D. (2005). Miscommunications surrounding efforts to reach out across group boundaries. *Personality and Social Psychology Bulletin, 31,* 1653–1664.

Vorauer, J. D. (2006). An information search model of evaluative concerns in intergroup interaction. *Psychological Review, 113,* 862–886.

Vorauer, J. D., & Cameron, J. J. (2002). So close, and yet so far: Does collectivism foster transparency overestimation? *Journal of Personality and Social Psychology, 83,* 1344–1352.

Vorauer, J. D., Cameron, J. J., Holmes, J. G., & Pearce, D. G. (2003). Invisible overtures: Fears of rejection and the signal amplification bias. *Journal of Personality and Social Psychology, 84,* 793–812.

Vorauer, J. D., Martens, V., & Sasaki, S. J. (2009). When trying to understand detracts from trying to behave: Effects of perspective-taking in intergroup interaction. *Journal of Personality and Social Psychology, 96,* 811–827.

Vorauer, J. D., & Ross, M. (1999). Self-awareness and transparency overestimation: Failing to suppress one's self. *Journal of Experimental Social Psychology, 35,* 415–440.

Vorauer, J. D., & Sakamoto, Y. (2006). I thought we could be friends, but...Systematic miscommunication and defensive distancing as obstacles to cross-group friendship formation. *Psychological Science, 17,* 326–331.

Vorauer, J. D., & Sasaki, S. J. (2009). Helpful only in the abstract? Ironic effects of empathy in intergroup interaction. *Psychological Science, 20,* 191–197.

Ward, C. D. (1965). Ego involvement and the absolute judgment of attitude statements. *Journal of Personality and Social Psychology, 2,* 202–208.

Wegener, D. T., & Petty, R. E. (1995). Flexible correction processes in social judgment: The role of naïve theories in correction for bias. *Journal of Personality and Social Psychology, 68*, 36–51.

Wegner, D. M. (1994). Ironic processes of mental control. *Psychological Review, 101*, 34–52.

Wood, J. V., Perunovic, W. Q. E., & Lee, J. W. (2009). Positive self-statements: Power for some, peril for others. *Psychological Science, 20*, 860–866.

Zuckerman, M., Kernis, M. H., Guarnera, S. M., Murphy, J. F., & Rappoport, L. (1983). The egocentric bias: Seeing oneself as cause and target of others' behavior. *Journal of Personality, 51*, 621–630.

15

Metacognition in Teams and Organizations

LEIGH THOMPSON and TAYA R. COHEN

INTRODUCTION

*M*etacognition is cognition about cognition, thinking about thinking, knowing about knowing, and feeling about thinking (Alter & Oppenheimer, 2009; Petty, Briñol, Tormala, & Wegener, 2007; Schwarz, Sanna, Skurnik, & Yoon, 2007). In the case of teams and groups, metacognition is team members thinking about how their team processes information, works on problems, and feels about the team process (Hinsz, 2004; Hinsz, Tindale, & Vollrath, 1997). Similarly, in the case of organizations, metacognition is members of organizations thinking about how their organization functions and feels about the way their organization functions. We use the distinction between primary and secondary cognition to guide our review (Petty et al., 2007). Primary thoughts are those that occur at a direct level of cognition and involve people's initial associations. Following a primary thought, people can also generate secondary thoughts (i.e., metacognitions) that occur as reflections on the first-level thoughts or the processes that generated the primary thoughts.

In this review, we focus on people's cognitions and feelings about groups, teams, and their organizations. We situate our review with regard to people as they interact with and work in teams and business organizations, as opposed to people cognizing about crowds or aggregates with whom they have no social or organizational relationship. Unfortunately, literature searches using the phrases "metacognition and organizations," "metacognition and teams," and "metacognition and groups" yielded very little (see Hinsz, 2004, for an exception). Yet, organizational behavior (OB) researchers resonate to the idea that managers, leaders, and their teams contemplate their thinking, behavior, and each other. Our thesis is that metacognition is alive and well in OB; it simply operates under a variety of banners (including transactive memory, shared mental models, group reflexivity, and so on) that paradoxically do not recognize one another.

Throughout our review, we explore the following questions:

- Does metacognition help or hurt teams?
- Do metacognitive processes naturally emerge and develop or are they something that can be taught, leveraged, and trained?

AWARENESS OF TEAM MEMBERS' SKILLS, ATTRIBUTES, AND ABILITIES

A key issue in metacognition as it pertains to organizational behavior is group members' thinking about who has what skills and competencies. The notion that members of groups develop concepts of who-knows-what is reflected in research on group mental models, distributed cognition, and teamwork.

Group Mental Models

Klimoski and Mohammed (1997) describe group mental models as the degree of correspondence between group members' mental models. A *group mental model* is a group's understanding of a system in terms of cause-and-effect relationships. Group mental models reflect the expectations members have about what they should do in a given situation and also what they think other members will do (or should do). They are built naturally and without much cognitive awareness or deliberate thought (Klimoski & Mohammed, 1997). There are two key considerations in terms of the effectiveness of group mental models: correspondence and accuracy.

Correspondence refers to the degree of overlap or commonality among group members' mental models. For example, if group members have different understandings of a process or how their group works, this reflects a lack of correspondence. Team member schema similarity (TMSS) refers to the degree to which team members have similar or compatible knowledge structures for organizing and understanding team-related phenomena (Rentsch & Woehr, 2004). Correspondence among team members' schemas facilitates smooth interpersonal interactions and constructive task behaviors. For example, a team member who intends to collaborate constructively may offer corrective feedback to others and offer alternative opinions. Teammates who interpret these behaviors similarly (i.e., as being constructive) are likely to engage in constructive conflict; however, teammates who interpret these behaviors as personal attacks may instigate conflict.

Accuracy refers to whether group mental models are correct with respect to a system. Accurate group mental models can be a matter of life and death in high-stress situations. Perrow's (1984) recounting of the tragic sinking of the *Cuyahoga* illustrates the dangers of inaccurate group mental models. In this situation, the first mate saw lights of another vessel approaching the ship. However, the captain falsely assumed the vessel was heading in the same direction (which it was not). The first mate did not verbalize his concerns when he realized his captain was not taking evasive action because he (falsely) assumed the captain had a shared mental model of the vessel. Eleven coastguardsmen died in the collision.

Orasanu and Salas (1993) posited that teams must dynamically form shared mental models of their situation and appropriate strategies for coping with task demands (referred to as shared problem models). Whereas shared mental models are preexisting knowledge structures developed over time and generalized to a variety of situations, shared problem models are skills that team members develop that enable them to apply task and team knowledge to form a concerted response.

Overall, research on group mental models suggests that metacognition facilitates group functioning and shared understanding. For example, negotiators who reach optimal settlements have greater mental model similarity about the negotiation (Van Boven & Thompson, 2003). There is widespread consistency across different research programs that common cognitions among team members are associated with team effectiveness. It is likely that the mere experience of working on a task together leads to the development of shared mental models (accurate or not); it is also likely that structured interaction among team members enhances the development of shared mental models.

Distributed Cognition

Distributed cognition is the idea that it is difficult for individual group members to each represent an entire system, so the knowledge is distributed or spread among others in the group or organization (Hutchins, 1991). Hutchins analyzed the confirmation bias to address the question of distributed information in teams. If a community is composed of people who possess similar mental models about a situation or a problem, members of the community are likely to arrive at a similar conclusion. However, if there is diversity in the mental models, then there are likely to be different interpretations, which can be an asset or a liability depending on the context. On the one hand, members of aircraft crews must coordinate their actions with each other and hold a single interpretation of the environment. However, if this precludes other reasonable hypotheses, the aircraft crew's performance may suffer. Hutchins (1991) terms this dilemma a "fundamental trade-off for organizations." Thus, although metacognition in the form of shared mental models is often advantageous for teams, overly similar cognitions can magnify biases, such as the confirmation bias.

Effective Teamwork

Metacognition in teams can promote effective teamwork. For example, McIntyre and Salas (1995) studied teamwork in naval gunfire-support teams, anti-submarine warfare teams, and guided missile teams. They identified two tracks in the maturation period of a team, both of which involve metacognition about team functioning. The *taskwork track* involves the operations-related activities to be performed by the team members. The *teamwork track* includes interactions, relationships, cooperation, communication, and coordination among team members. Through their study of these tracks, McIntyre and Salas identified four essential principles of effective teamwork that reflect metacognitive principles:

- Performance monitoring
- Feedback
- Closed-loop communication
- Willingness to back up team members during operations

Likewise, Cannon-Bowers, Tannenbaum, Salas, and Volpe (1995) investigated several types of teams in high-stress environments and found that a core set of skill dimensions characterized the most effective teams: adaptability, shared situational awareness, performance monitoring and feedback, leadership/team management, interpersonal skills, coordination skills, communication skills, and decision-making skills. Performance monitoring is particularly relevant to metacognition because it relates to the classic distinction between metacognitive monitoring and control (Koriat & Goldsmith, 1996; Nelson & Narens, 1994). Just as individuals monitor and control their mental functioning, teams monitor and control their team functioning.

In summary, various research programs on teamwork highlight the importance of metacognitive processes for enhancing team performance. These processes include monitoring team performance, discussing team processes and outcomes, and having shared mental models and situational awareness. According to this research, metacognition is critical for fostering productive teamwork. We speculate that in some teams these processes occur naturally, but in others, conscious efforts must be made to enact them.

AWARENESS OF ORGANIZATIONAL KNOWLEDGE AND NETWORKS

People in organizations not only define and situate themselves in small groups and teams, but also situate themselves in larger networks composed of multiple teams and others. In this section, we consider people's awareness of organizational knowledge and networks.

Structural Holes and Closed-Loop Networks

In an organizational network, some members are more connected to others than are other members (Granovetter, 1973). Moreover, some people connect individuals, dyads, and groups who would otherwise not be directly connected. Under the brokerage principle in network theory, there is a competitive advantage to building certain relationships because resources flow disproportionately to people who provide indirect connections between otherwise disconnected groups (Burt, 1992). However, *structural holes* can form when members of the network are unaware of the benefits they could offer to one another. A structural hole indicates that there is a lack of relationship between certain network members. The structural hole between two clusters (e.g., teams of people) does not necessarily mean that people in the two clusters are unaware of each other. Rather, it means that people are so focused on their own activities that they have little time to consider the activities of people in the other cluster cognitively.

Structural holes imply that people on either side of the hole circulate in different flows of information, much like what occurs in closed-loop networks. People in closed-loop or clique networks are more exposed to consistent third-party gossip and more peer pressure to conform to the gossip (Burt, 1992). Managers in these networks have less experience in making sense of inconsistent interpretations of events and are more accustomed to relying on third-party interpretations (Burt, 1992). In contrast, people who span structural holes and operate in open networks are exposed to more diverse views and fewer shared mental models. They are forced to synthesize and weigh disparate information, which helps buttress them from the negative effects of high agreement in groups (e.g., the confirmation bias).

Research on structural holes and closed-loop networks highlights the importance of metacognition for organizational functioning. Without accurate or sufficient metacognitive awareness of others in the network, organizations are unlikely to realize the benefits that highly connected actors in an open network could provide to one another. Moreover, structural holes and closed-loop networks can foster shared mental models that are too similar, thus making network members vulnerable to the confirmation bias. The lack of congruence in mental models that is fostered by open networks might facilitate better organizational decision making and effectiveness by buffering network members against judgmental biases resulting from a lack of cognitive diversity.

Accuracy of Network Perceptions

According to network theory, it is more important for organizational actors to hold accurate perceptions about the network of relationships than to possess actual power or status (Krackhardt, 1990). Cognitive accuracy of one's own informal network is a base of power and influence in organizations. Specifically, Krackhardt (1990) examined two types of networks in a small entrepreneurial firm: *friendship networks* (largely communal relationships that provide socioemotional support) and *advice networks* (largely exchange-based relationships that provide information, advice, and opportunities). Centrality in friendship networks was a key factor in reputational power, but cognitive accuracy in advice networks strongly predicted reputational power.

Accurate network perceptions are important for achieving power and status (Krackhardt, 1990). Inaccurate perceptions, however, are quite common in organizations, and these erroneous perceptions have important implications for organizational behavior. Menon and Thompson (2007) examined the erroneous perceptions people have about how others in their organization view them—a type of faulty mental model. Organizational actors often falsely believe that others are more threatened by their own talent, beauty, and achievements than is actually the case. Menon and Thompson found that organizational actors believed that others were envious of them when, in fact, others were not. This faulty perception led to several dysfunctional organizational outcomes, including a tendency for people to downplay their own accomplishments for fear that others might overreact with defensiveness. Moreover, people who believed that they threatened others were less likely to share relevant organizational knowledge. This research corroborates Krackhardt's (1990) assertion that accurate knowledge about one's own network relationships enhances organizational effectiveness. This research is related to work on metastereotypes—the views that members of one group believe that members of another group hold about them (Vorauer, Main, & O'Connell, 1998; Yzerbyt, Judd, & Muller, 2008).

Some organizational actors are more motivated than others to think about their social networks. Moreover, some situational conditions may provoke organizational actors to be highly vigilant in terms of analyzing their organizational environment. Specifically, Kramer's (1999) work suggests that there is an inverse relationship between organizational power and the motivation to attend to and think about one's own social network. For example, Kramer (1999) found that organizational actors low in power (i.e., graduate students not yet admitted to candidacy) were more keenly aware of their organizational environment than those in positions of power (i.e., dissertation chairpersons).

To return to the two questions raised in the introduction, research on networks clearly indicates that accurate metacognition helps organizational actors. Accurate metacognitive knowledge about one's network is an important source of power in organizations (Krackhardt, 1990) and faulty metacognitive knowledge is detrimental for organizational functioning (Menon & Thompson, 2007). With regard to whether metacognition develops naturally, Kramer's (1999) research suggests that metacognitive knowledge is likely to develop naturally among low-power organizational actors, but may require additional motivation and effort for its development among high-power actors. Indeed, people with lower power process information more carefully because they lack certainty and confidence in their own views (Briñol, Petty, Valle, Rucker, & Becerra, 2007).

BEHAVIOR, PERFORMANCE, AND LEARNING IN TEAMS AND ORGANIZATIONS

In this section, we take up the question of how metacognition influences the ways in which members of teams and organizations behave, act, process information, and learn from one another.

Group Potency

Group potency is the collective belief of group members that their group can be effective (Shea & Guzzo, 1987). It is similar to the concept of *collective efficacy*, which refers to a group member's belief that a team can perform successfully (Guzzo, Yost, Campbell, & Shea, 1993). Jung and Sosik (2003) found that groups who see themselves as powerful and able to effect change are more successful than those that do not and that group members develop more similar perceptions of their efficacy over time.

Group potency is an important predictor of group performance above and beyond actual ability. For example, in one investigation, 143 officer cadets working in 51 groups with higher group potency outperformed those with lower group potency, controlling for ability (Hecht, Allen, Klammer, & Kelly, 2002). Similarly, Jordan, Field, and Armenakis (2002) examined 648 military officers working in 50 self-managed teams over a 5-week period and found that group potency had more predictive power in explaining team performance than did group cohesion.

Group Planning Fallacy

Groups underestimate the time it will take for projects to be completed—a bias that Sanna, Parks, Chang, and Carter (2005) refer to as the *group planning fallacy*. Noteworthy examples of this fallacy include the Sydney Opera House (10 years late), Boston's Central Artery/Tunnel project (8 years late), and Boeing's 787 dreamliner, which (at the time this chapter was written) was 2 years late. Sanna and colleagues' research indicates that temporal framing influences the group planning fallacy. In one study, students had to estimate when they would complete a semester-long group project. The researchers varied how far away the deadline seemed with a clever (and subtle) manipulation: Students were informed that "you still have 12 weeks remaining" or that "you only have 12 weeks remaining." The group planning fallacy was attenuated in the latter condition. Groups in the little-time-remaining condition were more accurate in their estimates of when they would complete the project.

Sanna et al. (2005) also included a control condition with no temporal frame. Interestingly, the estimates in the control condition were similar to those in the lots-of-time condition, suggesting that groups naturally assume they have lots of time to complete a project, which can lead them to underestimate severely the amount of time it will take to complete the project. This research suggests that faulty metacognitive beliefs about time are prevalent in group planning and can negatively impact team performance. Thus, groups and organizations that wish to reduce the group planning fallacy should frame deadlines as near rather than far in the future.

Metamemory

Metamemory in groups refers to what group members know about how they remember in groups (Hinsz, 2004). It is possible for members of a team to be in complete agreement with regard to a particular perception or mental model of their group; however, it is also possible that this perception is inaccurate. In an experiment that investigated metamemory in groups, Hinsz (2004) studied the accuracy of group members' assessments of how divergent beliefs within the group would affect group decisions. Participants watched a recording of a job interview and were randomly assigned to groups to complete an individual recognition memory test, followed by a group recognition test. They were asked to indicate the likelihood that groups would choose true or false responses in the group recognition task under all possible distributions of members' beliefs. Group member metamemory was only partially accurate with respect to how different beliefs within the group affected group decisions. Groups consistently underestimated the influence of majorities and overestimated the influence of minorities, particularly if the minority belief was incorrect.

Transactive Memory and Communication Overhead

Transactive memory was introduced by Wegner (1986) in his research on couples to refer to the idea that the combined memory of two people is more efficient than the memory of either person alone. Liang, Moreland, and Argote (1995) extended the provocative findings and theorizing of Wegner (1986) to the domain of groups and teams (see Moreland, 1999, for a review). As described by Gino, Argote, Miron-Spektor, and Todorova (2010), transactive memory is "the cooperative division of labor for learning, remembering and communicating team knowledge" (p. 103). Transactive memory is a secondary cognition that involves knowing what other members of the group know and knowing which group members are good at which tasks. Transactive memory facilitates the smooth exchange of ideas and enhances team performance in a variety of domains, including product production (Liang et al., 1995; Moreland, 1999) and team creativity (Gino et al., 2010).

One of the most well-known and compelling studies of transactive memory examined groups' ability to assemble transistor radios (Liang et al., 1995). In this investigation, participants were assigned to three-person work groups and given training on how to assemble radios. The key manipulation was whether participants received training individually or in their work groups. The critical question was how well people would be able to perform (i.e., assemble transistor radios) a week later without any instruction. Groups who trained together outperformed groups who trained individually; they recalled more information about the procedure and made fewer assembly errors. In related studies, the researchers measured the number of errors in groups' assembly of the transistor radios, how many times members "corrected" one another, how many pieces they dropped on the floor, and so on (see Moreland, 1999, for a review). Groups who trained and practiced together developed distributed information processing systems (largely unconsciously); assembled radios faster, with fewer errors; dropped fewer pieces on the floor; and questioned each other less. In short, their performance was superior compared to groups whose members had received the same quality and amount of training, but had not previously performed as a group.

Research on transactive memory suggests that group member's secondary cognitions of who-knows-what facilitate team performance by fostering coordination among team members. A seemingly paradoxical phenomenon known as *communication overhead* suggests that too much explicit communication of secondary cognitions can hinder (not help) team performance (MacMillan, Entin, & Serfaty, 2004). The issue of communicating metacognitions is a uniquely group issue because it is only in a social context that people can articulate their secondary thoughts to others. "Overhead" refers to the fact that communication among team members requires both time and resources. Explicit communication of secondary cognitions requires conscious articulation of plans, actions, and responsibilities.

In some contexts, this communication can hurt team performance by disrupting coordination among team members.

In one investigation of communication overhead, military team performance was compared under two different team structures: one optimized for an air- and sea-based mission (which involved less communication among members) and one that involved a more traditional organizational structure (MacMillan et al., 2004). The traditional organizational structure was developed by subject matter experts in which similar resources were controlled by the same node without consideration of the need to coordinate their use in the mission. The optimized team structure, on the other hand, was based on two objectives: simultaneously minimizing the communication required to accomplish the mission and balancing workload across the team. This structure allocated the team's resources so that team members could act more independently, thus reducing the need for explicit communication about the team process. A lower communication rate was associated with better performance. Team members in the optimized structure condition experienced a lower workload and were able to devote more effort to understanding the roles and actions of other team members; they communicated less, but more efficiently.

The fateful story of the sinking of the *Cuyahoga* (Perrow, 1984) described earlier points to the importance of explicit communication for avoiding tragic mistakes. Simply stated, had the first mate articulated his thoughts to the captain about the approaching ship, the fateful accident might have been avoided. The transistor radio (Liang et al., 1995; Moreland, 1999) and military team (MacMillan et al., 2004) studies, on the other hand, point to the advantages of implicit coordination for team performance. As evidenced by the studies of military teams (MacMillan et al., 2004), too much explicit communication can be problematic in situations in which team members need greater control over their own resources to optimize performance. Collectively, these investigations suggest that greater metacognition about team members and the team's process can facilitate performance. However, the question of whether metacognitions should be explicitly discussed remains somewhat an open one. We speculate that it likely depends on the nature of the task and might change over time as team members become more familiar with one another.

Articulating and Representing Shared Knowledge

Part of learning involves the articulation of knowledge or the verbal transmission of ideas. *Cognitive tuning* refers to the fact that people often tailor their message to take the listener's opinion into account when communicating (Higgins, King, & Mavin, 1982; Krauss & Fussell, 1996). Such "audience tuning" not only changes the attitudes and cognition of the communicators, but also alters their judgments and knowledge. Higgins (1999) paradoxically argues that the mere act of sharing knowledge leads to distortion of messages. The speaker naturally takes what she assumes to be the audience's point of view into consideration when formulating the message. Such tuning not only is common, but also is considered to be a principle of good communication (Krauss & Fussell, 1996).

Unfortunately, speakers do not realize that they have tuned (adjusted) their message to suit the audience and a bias is introduced when they later attempt to use the knowledge they communicated. This problem is compounded when the message is experienced as a shared reality between the speaker and the audience because this makes the message seem objective and accurate. These findings regarding audience tuning are compatible with Wegener and colleagues' work on bias correction (e.g., Petty et al., 2007; Wegener & Petty, 1995). Whereas Higgins (1999) shows that audience tuning can unknowingly create biases, Wegener and colleagues show that correcting for biases that do not exist can also unknowingly create biases.

A small body of research has taken a more structured approach to the question of how groups can best represent shared knowledge. In one investigation, Sycara and Lewis (2004) tested the efficacy of four different "team aids" for articulating and representing knowledge in teams: individual clipboards, team checklists, team clipboards, and a control condition that contained no clipboards or checklists. Teams were challenged with a complex task regarding target identification in terms of a military operation in which a target could be peaceful or hostile, military or civilian, and approach by air, surface, or submarine. Team aids (i.e., team checklists and team clipboards) enhanced team performance more than individual aids (i.e., individual clipboards), even though individual aids reduced memory load and increased individual accessibility.

Membership Change

One situation that leads members to articulate and represent knowledge is the entry and exit of new members in a group. Levine and Moreland (1999) argue that when newcomers enter a group, this instigates a type of metacognitive process in which old members feel obliged to talk about how the group works. This is part of a larger process, called *group socialization,* in which members of the team mutually shape each other's cognitions and behaviors (Moreland & Levine, 2000). Studies of newcomers' transition into groups of "old-timers" reveal a tendency for the entry of newcomers to prompt old-timers to engage in reflective accounting of how their groups operate.

According to Swann, Milton, and Polzer (2000), new group members can engage in either self-verification or appraisal. Self-verification occurs when group members persuade others in the team to see them as they see themselves; in contrast, appraisal occurs when groups persuade members to see themselves as the group sees them. Self-verification is more prevalent than appraisal, and this leads to greater feelings of connection to the team and improves performance on creative tasks. Research on confidence (Briñol, DeMarree, & Petty, 2010) and self-certainty (DeMarree, Petty, & Briñol, 2007) suggests that when a person is more confident or certain about himself or herself, verification is more likely than appraisal.

How do old-timers react when newcomers enter a group? Existing members often expect newcomers to be anxious, passive, dependent, and conforming. Gruenfeld and Fan (1999) explored the discontinuity between *what old-timers say and what newcomers see* by examining groups over a significant amount of time and analyzing essays written by team members. Often, the entrance of a newcomer prompts old-timers to explain how the group works and attempt to educate the newcomer. Yet, there is often a disconnect between the explanations provided and the behaviors that old-timers display. When groups were changed (by exchanging a single group member) and recomposed after 10 weeks, those who became newcomers displayed greater integrative complexity in their essays about group functioning than they did prior to their "experience" (Gruenfeld & Fan, 1999). Moreover, newcomers often displayed greater integrative complexity than did old-timers (people who did not change groups). Although newcomers experienced cognitive growth spurred by sense-making motivations, they were distinctly less influential in groups because old-timers used a greater number of their own ideas after newcomers arrived than beforehand.

Other research on membership change has focused on team creativity (Choi & Thompson, 2005; Gino et al., 2010). Choi and Thompson (2005) examined whether teams would be more creative if they remained intact (i.e., did not experience any membership change) or if they were reorganized (i.e., experienced membership change). Presumably, intact teams develop implicit shared cognition and transactive memory in innovative performance exercises (Gino et al., 2010). This would argue that intact teams would have an advantage on subsequent exercises. However Choi and Thompson theorized that in the case of divergent thinking, too many shared-knowledge processes might hinder the ability of teams to generate novel solutions. Teams that underwent membership change generated more ideas and displayed greater cognitive flexibility than did teams that remained intact. The presence of newcomers in teams had profound effects on old-timers (i.e., members who had the longest history in the team)—the presence of newcomers prompted them to generate more ideas. Shared cognition may not be ideal for divergent thinking tasks, which are qualitatively different from convergent thinking tasks, such as radio assembly and flight operations.

Learning in Organizations

Ancona and Bresman's (2006) investigation of successful teams in organizations revealed that the most successful teams were those that were uninhibited in terms of "begging, borrowing, and stealing" great ideas from their own organizations. According to Ancona, Henrik, and Katrin (2002), X-teams engage in five behaviors that make them particularly effective in the organization. At least of two of these five behaviors are related to metacognition: *scouting* and *task coordination*. Scouting activities are behaviors that involve lateral and downward searches through the organization to understand who has knowledge and expertise. Task coordination is much more focused than scouting. When team members coordinate, they negotiate with other groups in terms of information exchange, trade their services, and get feedback on how well their work is meeting expectations. Task coordination involves a metaknowledge of which teams are working on which activities and then optimizing the work.

One of the keys to success when using extensive network relationships is the ability to engage in vicarious learning. According to Ancona and Bresman (2006), vicarious learning is a specialized form of scouting in which team members learn processes in the absence of critical experience inside their own team. This is possible through strategies such as *bypass application,* in which, for example, one team uses data from an experiment that another team had run in the past so that the team does not have to learn how to conduct the particular experiment. *Imitative application* involves copying a practice from the outside but simultaneously adapting it to the present context.

Hargadon's (2006) constructs of bridging and building are similar to Ancona and Bresman's (2006) constructs of scouting and task coordination. Hargadon proposes two organizational-level processes—building and bridging—to examine the creative process of teams embedded in organizations. Bridging and building require team members to develop representations of their organizations that shape understanding and action. Hargadon uses network theory to predict bridging and building efforts and prescriptively argues that individuals need to have a combination of "weak ties" that enable them to bridge old worlds and "strong ties" within their organization and team.

A final question related to learning in organizations concerns how members of intact teams and organizations value knowledge offered by their team members. Whereas the ingroup bias literature would suggest that team members show an ingroup bias and devalue the contributions of outgroup members, this may not be true in organizational settings in which members of ingroups compete for status and influence. Menon, Thompson, and Choi (2006) found that people are much more reluctant to use knowledge of insiders (in their own network) than that of outsiders. Specifically, organizational actors were more likely to feel threatened when a good idea emanated from an insider (versus an outsider). This threat triggered a pattern of organizational distancing in which team members devalued the contributions of "brilliant insiders" and refused to adopt best practices.

MEMBERS' FEELINGS ABOUT TEAM AND ORGANIZATIONAL STRUCTURE AND PROCESS

In this section, we review the reflective aspects of teamwork and organizational behavior. We focus on members' motivations, emotions, and feelings about their teams and organizations.

Processing Fluency

Processing fluency refers to the subjective ease or difficulty with which people process information and is a metacognitive cue with important implications for groups and teams (for reviews of processing fluency, see Alter & Oppenheimer, 2009; Schwarz et al., 2007). Processing difficulty can be instantiated visually via unclear fonts, linguistically via difficult- versus easy-to-pronounce names, physically via activation of the corrugator muscle (i.e., frowning), and cognitively via priming (Alter & Oppenheimer, 2009). Schwarz and colleagues (1991) generated fluency via a memory recall task in which participants were instructed to recall few versus many examples of a particular event. Generating many examples is difficult and thus paradoxically diminishes the impact of the thought content.

Alter and Oppenheimer (2009) "united the tribes of fluency" to show that despite the breadth and diversity of techniques for manipulating processing fluency, these techniques show strikingly similar effects in a vast array of domains, such as truth, liking, confidence, familiarity, and intelligence, among others. Notably absent from Alter and Oppenheimer's "metacognitive nation," however, was the domain of groups and teams. We introduce the term *group-process fluency* to fill this gap and define it as the subjective ease or difficulty of the group process—how easy or difficult it is for the group or team to work together. Research in the areas of creativity and task conflict highlight the impact of group-process fluency on team outcomes.

People report enjoying group brainstorming sessions and they believe that groups are more creative than individuals. However, groups do not brainstorm as many ideas as aggregated individuals (see Brown & Paulus, 2002; Paulus & Brown, 2007, for reviews). On average, group members only generate half as many ideas as individuals working alone (Paulus & Brown, 2007). Why then do people believe that brainstorming is effective? One possibility is that brainstorming fosters positive metacognitions that lead people to believe erroneously that groups are more useful for stimulating ideas than is actually the case. Specifically, enjoyment of brainstorming in groups may lead people to believe that it is effective and, accordingly, they choose to brainstorm as a group rather than to "brainwrite" individually (Brown & Paulus, 2002). Thus, the positive emotional experience of generating ideas in groups (secondary cognitions) may lead people to adopt suboptimal strategies for increasing creativity.

Jehn (1994) proposed that task conflict improves team performance on complex, nonroutine tasks. However, a meta-analysis by De Dreu and Weingart (2003) revealed that oftentimes task conflict has negative effects on team performance. One reason that task conflict might hinder team performance is that disagreement can create negative emotional experiences (secondary cognitions) that are detrimental for team functioning. The negative metacognitions associated with conflict and disagreement might lead teams to focus their discussions solely on shared opinions and areas of agreement and thus suffer detriments in team performance as a result (cf. Janis, 1972; Stasser & Titus, 1985).

An interesting question related to processing fluency in organizations concerns how organizations gauge their employees' and customers' opinions. Consider the following example. A manager consistently gets requests from one employee that a company policy be changed. From those requests, the manager must decide how the other people in the organization feel about the issue in question. Will the vocal employee's frequent requests bias the manager's sense of how the rest of the people in the organization feel about the policy? Research by Weaver, Garcia, Schwartz, and Miller (2007) suggests the answer is yes. In a series of six experiments, they demonstrated that people have a tendency to infer that a familiar opinion is a prevalent one, even if the perceived familiarity is the result of one particularly vocal group member. Thus, this research indicates that opinions that feel familiar are believed to be representative of the group's opinion, even when the source of the familiarity is irrelevant.

Team Reflexivity

Team reflexivity is the "extent to which team members collectively reflect upon the team's objectives, strategies, and processes, as well as their wider organizations and environments, and adapt them accordingly" (West, 1996, p. 559). There are three central elements to the concept of team reflexivity: reflection, planning, and action (or adaptation). *Reflection* consists of attention, awareness, monitoring, and evaluation of the object of reflection. High reflexivity exists when reflection is characterized by heightened awareness and monitoring of the team's process. *Planning* refers to the contemplation of action, formation of intentions, development of plans, and assessment of potential for carrying actions out; planning creates a conceptual readiness for action and innovation. High reflexivity exists when team planning is characterized by more detailed planning, including the identification of potential problems, hierarchical ordering of plans, and plans for long- and short-range goals. Finally, *action* refers to goal directed behaviors relevant to achieving the desired changes in team objectives, strategies, processes, organization, or environments. Empirically, reflexivity is linked to innovation and team effectiveness (Carter & West, 1998; West, Patterson, & Dawson, 1999).

Psychological Safety

According to Edmondson (1999), people in teams evaluate how "safe" they feel bringing up certain subjects and seeking assistance from their team. Psychological safety reflects the extent to which people feel that they can raise issues and questions without fear of being rebuffed. Psychological safety describes taken-for-granted beliefs that others will respond positively when one exposes one's thoughts, such as by asking a question, seeking feedback, reporting a mistake, or proposing a new idea (Edmondson, 1999). In this sense, a higher degree of psychological safety increases the likelihood that a given group member will express a secondary cognition. Psychological safety in teams is related to individual confidence, such that people are more likely to speak up with questions and concerns about understanding. Empirical research indicates that psychological safety leads to better group outcomes; teams in a hospital with higher measured psychological safety were more likely to engage in learning about how to use a new technological procedure and, subsequently, were more successful in implementing change in the neonatal intensive care unit (Tucker, Nembhard, & Edmondson, 2006).

Group Identification

Group identity refers to how people think about themselves in relation to others or collectives (Roccas, Sagiv, Schwartz, Halevy, & Eidelson, 2008). As discussed by Roccas et al., group identification is a multifaceted construct that includes the importance of a group to one's self (importance), one's commitment to helping a group (commitment), the degree to which one views a group as superior to other groups (superiority), and the degree to which one honors, reveres, and submits to the group's norms and leaders (deference). Group identification is a secondary cognition about a group that reflects the importance of the group to the group member, just as attitude strength is a secondary cognition about an attitude that reflects the importance of the attitude to the individual (Petty & Krosnick, 1995). Happiness felt about one's own group (or collective anger about a rival group) increases the identification that people feel with their group (Kessler & Hollbach, 2005). Identification also increases when group members think about their identity (i.e., what they stand for) and what they have in common (Prentice, Miller & Lightdale, 1994).

Group identification affects employees' experiences in their organizations as well. One field investigation examined how remoteness affected newly hired employees' experiences in their organizations (Bartel, Wrzesniewski, & Wiesenfeld, 2007). Remoteness was operationalized as the (a) percentage of time that participants were away from coworkers with whom they worked interdependently and interacted socially, (b) percentage of time that participants were away from supervisors who established their goals and evaluated them; and (c) total time spent in an isolated setting, away from the symbolic representations of the organization. Remoteness was negatively correlated with both membership claiming (i.e., desire and effort on the part of the employee to be on the team) and membership granting (a reciprocal response to when someone makes an attempt to assert his or her sense of belonging and inclusion in the organization). Remote employees often felt insecure about their organizational membership: They felt out of the loop and not respected as a group member.

Cognition about one's identity also influences behavior at the broader level of organizational networks. Spataro and Chatman (2007) examined feelings of identity in eight firms that comprised 91% of the public accounting market. They focused on how competition among firms affected employees' normative commitment—a person's identification with what the organization stands for as well as internalization of the organization's norms and values (Caldwell, Chatman, & O'Reilly, 1990). Employees were more likely to base their attachment to their organization on normative commitment when companies were engaged in low to moderate levels of interorganizational competition, as opposed to high levels of competition.

CONCLUSION

Throughout our review we considered whether metacognition is helpful for teams and organizations (e.g., does it enhance team performance?). The cognitive awareness of who-knows-what and who-knows-whom seems to facilitate group functioning, and this assertion was unambiguously supported in several empirical investigations, such as Moreland and colleagues' studies of transistor radio production teams (Liang et al., 1995; Moreland, 1999). Hutchins's (1991) and Cannon-Bowers and colleagues' (1995) intensive examinations of high-stakes naval and combat teams certainly suggest that shared mental models are paramount for safety and performance.

However, our research review yielded some cautionary notes. Higgins's (1999) studies of cognitive tuning revealed that sharing knowledge can lead to the development of bias and distortion in both sender and receiver. Similarly, knowledge sharing can create a false sense of group efficiency and confidence. Team communication overhead, or the volume of communication necessary for teams to understand one another, actually was linked to worse team performance (MacMillan et al., 2004). Similarly, research investigations on creativity and innovation clearly indicate that closed-loop networks and intact teams experience less divergent thinking than teams that undergo membership change and reorganization (cf. Ancona & Bresman, 2006; Choi & Thompson, 2005; Gino et al., 2010; Hargadon, 2006).

We also raised the question of whether metacognition is something that naturally occurs in groups and organizations or whether it needs to be facilitated consciously. Most of the research we reviewed suggests that metacognition is a natural process that develops in teams and organizations. Indeed, this viewpoint was advanced directly by Wegner, Giuliano, and Hertel (1995) in their study of married couples. The idea that metacognition develops naturally in teams is also implied in the work on transactive memory (e.g., Liang et al., 1995; Moreland, 1999). However, research on metamemory (Hinsz, 2004) and judgmental biases (e.g., the group planning fallacy; Sanna et al., 2005) suggests that *accurate* metacognition may need to be prompted explicitly in many circumstances. Left to their own devices, teams might not engage in sufficient explicit communication, which could have devastating consequences when communication is required to avoid a disaster, like the sinking of a ship (e.g., Perrow, 1984).

The study of metacognition in teams and organizations is alive and well and borrows richly from three domains: social psychology, human performance (e.g., studies of military crews), and organizational sociology. These three literature streams are often unaware of one another's existence; in this review, we have attempted to increase awareness of the common threads among them.

REFERENCES

Alter, A. L., & Oppenheimer, D. M. (2009). Uniting the tribes of fluency to form a metacognitive nation. *Personality and Social Psychology Review, 13,* 219–235.

Ancona, D., & Bresman, H. (2006). Begging, borrowing, and building on ideas from the outside to create pulsed innovation inside teams. In L. Thompson & H. S. Choi (Eds.), *Creativity and innovation in organizational teams* (pp. 183–198). Mahwah, NJ: Lawrence Erlbaum Associates.

Ancona, D., Henrik B., & Katrin, K. (2002). The comparative advantage of X-teams. *Sloan Management Review, 43*(3), 33–39.

Bartel, C. A., Wrzesniewski, A., & Wiesenfeld, B. (2007). The struggle to establish organizational membership and identification in remote work contexts. In C. A. Bartel, S. Blader, & A. Wrzesniewski (Eds.), *Identity and the modern organization* (pp. 119–133). Mahwah, NJ: Lawrence Erlbaum Associates.

Briñol, P., DeMarree, K. G., & Petty, R. E. (2010). Processes by which confidence (vs. doubt) influences the self. In R. M. Arkin, K. C. Oleson, & P. J. Carroll (Eds.), *Handbook of the uncertain self* (pp. 13–35). New York, NY: Psychology Press.

Briñol, P., Petty, R. E., Valle, C., Rucker, D. D., & Becerra, A. (2007). The effects of message recipients' power before and after persuasion: A self-validation analysis. *Journal of Personality and Social Psychology, 93,* 1040–1053.

Brown, V. R., & Paulus, P. B. (2002). Making group brainstorming more effective: Recommendations from an associative memory perspective. *Current Directions in Psychological Science, 11,* 208–212.

Burt, R. S. (1992). *Structural holes.* Cambridge, MA: Harvard University Press.

Caldwell, D. F., Chatman, J. A., & O'Reilly, C. A. (1990). Building organizational commitment: A multiform study. *Journal of Occupational Psychology, 61,* 245–261.

Cannon-Bowers, J. A., Tannenbaum, S. I., Salas, E., & Volpe, C. E. (1995). Defining team competencies and establishing team training requirements. In R. Guzzo & E. Salas (Eds.), *Team effectiveness and decision making in organizations* (pp. 333–380). San Francisco, CA: Jossey-Bass.

Carter, S. M., & West, M. A. (1998). Reflexivity, effectiveness, and mental health in BBC-TV production teams. *Small Group Research, 29*(5), 583–601.

Choi, H. S., & Thompson, L. (2005). Old wine in a new bottle: Impact of membership change on group creativity. *Organizational Behavior and Human Decision Processes, 98,* 121–132.

De Dreu, C. K. W., & Weingart, L. R. (2003). Task versus relationship conflict, team performance, and team member satisfaction: A meta-analysis. *Journal of Applied Psychology, 88,* 741–749.

DeMarree, K. G., Petty, R. E., & Briñol, P. (2007). Self-certainty: Parallels to attitude certainty. *International Journal of Psychology and Psychological Therapy, 7,* 159–188.

Edmondson, A. (1999). Psychological safety and learning behavior in work teams. *Administrative Science Quarterly, 44,* 350–383.

Gino, F., Argote, L., Miron-Spektor, E., & Todorova, G. (2010). First, get your feet wet: The effects of learning from direct and indirect experience on team creativity. *Organizational Behavior and Human Decision Processes, 111*(2), 102–115.

Granovetter, M. S. (1973). The strength of weak ties. *American Journal of Sociology, 78,* 1360–1380.

Gruenfeld, D. H., & Fan, E. T. (1999). What newcomers see and what old-timers say: Discontinuities in knowledge exchange. In L. Thompson, J. Levine, & D. Messick (Eds.), *Shared cognition in organizations: The management of knowledge* (pp. 245–266). Mahwah, NJ: Lawrence Erlbaum Associates.

Guzzo, R. A., Yost, P. R., Campbell, R. J., & Shea, G. P. (1993). Potency in groups: Articulating a construct. *British Journal of Social Psychology, 32,* 87–106.

Hargadon, A. B. (2006). Bridging and building: Towards a microsociology of creativity. In L. Thompson & H. S. Choi (Eds.), *Creativity and innovation in groups and organizations* (pp. 199–216). Mahwah, NJ: Lawrence Erlbaum Associates, Inc.

Hecht, T. D., Allen N. J., Klammer, J. D., & Kelly, E. C. (2002). Group beliefs, ability and performance: The potency of group potency. *Group dynamics: Theory, research and practice, 6*(2), 143–152.

Higgins, E. T. (1999). "Saying is believing" effects: When sharing reality about something biases knowledge and evaluations. In L. Thompson, J. M. Levine, & D. M. Messick (Eds.), *Shared cognition in organizations: The management of knowledge* (pp. 33–48). Mahwah, NJ: Lawrence Erlbaum Associates.

Higgins, E. T., King, G. A., & Mavin, G. H. (1982). Individual construct accessibility and subjective impressions and recall. *Journal of Personality and Social Psychology, 43,* 35–47.

Hinsz, V. B. (2004). Metacognition and mental models in groups: An illustration with metamemory of group recognition memory. In E. Salas & S. M. Fiore (Eds.), *Team cognition: Understanding the factors that drive process and performance* (pp. 33–58). Washington, DC: American Psycological Association.

Hinsz, V. B., Tindale, R. S., & Vollrath, D. A. (1997). The emerging conceptualization of groups as information processors. *Psychological Bulletin, 121,* 43–64.

Hutchins, E. (1991). The social organization of distributed cognition. In L. B. Resnick, J. M. Levine, & S. D. Teasley (Eds.), *Perspectives on socially shared cognition* (pp. 283–307). Washington, DC: American Psychological Association.

Janis, I. (1972). *Victims of groupthink*. Boston, MA: Houghton Mifflin.

Jehn, K. (1994). Enhancing effectiveness: An investigation of advantages and disadvantages of value-based intragroup conflict. *International Journal of Conflict Management, 5,* 223–228.

Jordan, M. H., Field, H. S., & Armenakis, A. A. (2002). The relationship of group process variables and team performance. *Small Group Research, 33*(1), 121–150.

Jung, D. I., & Sosik, J. J. (2003). Group potency and collective efficacy: Examining their predictive validity, level of analysis, and effects of performance feedback on future group performance. *Group and Organization Management, 28,* 366–391.

Kessler, T., & Hollbach, S. (2005). Group-based emotions as determinants of ingroup identification. *Journal of Experimental Social Psychology, 41,* 677–685.

Klimoski, R., & Mohammed, S. (1997). Team mental model: Construct or metaphor? *Journal of Management, 20,* 403–437.

Koriat, A., & Goldsmith, M. (1996). Monitoring and control processes in the strategic regulation of memory accuracy. *Psychological Review, 103,* 490–517.

Krackhardt, D. (1990). Assessing the political landscape: Structure, cognition and power in organizations. *Administrative Science Quarterly, 35,* 342–369.

Kramer, R. M. (1999). Trust and distrust in organizations: Emerging perspectives, enduring questions. *Annual Review of Psychology, 50,* 569–598.

Krauss, R. M., & Fussell, S. R. (1996). Social psychological models of interpersonal communication. In E. T. Higgins & A. Kruglanski (Eds.), *Social psychology: A handbook of basic principles* (pp. 655–701). New York, NY: Guilford.

Levine, J. M., & Moreland, R. L. (1999). Knowledge transmission in work groups: Helping newcomers to succeed. In L. L. Thompson, J. M. Levine, & D. M. Messick (Eds.), *Shared cognition in organizations: The management of knowledge* (pp. 267–296). Mahwah, NJ: Lawrence Erlbaum Associates.

Liang, D. W., Moreland, R., & Argote, L. (1995). Group versus individual training and group performance: The mediating factor of transactive memory. *Personality and Social Psychology Bulletin, 21,* 384–393.

MacMillan, J., Entin, E. E., & Serfaty, D. (2004). Communication overhead: The hidden cost of team cognition. In E. Salas, S. M. Fiore, & J. A. Cannon-Bowers (Eds.), *Team cognition: Process and performance at the inter- and intraindividual level.* Washington, DC: American Psychological Association.

McIntyre, R. M., & Salas, E. (1995). Team performance in complex environments: What we have learned so far. In R. Guzzo & E. Salas (Eds.), *Team effectiveness and decision making in organizations* (pp. 9–45). San Francisco, CA: Josey-Bass.

Menon, T., & Thompson, L. L. (2007). Don't hate me because I'm beautiful: Self-enhancing biases in threat appraisal. *Organizational Behavior and Human Decision Processes, 104,* 45–60.

Menon, T., Thompson, L. L. & Choi, H. (2006). Tainted knowledge versus tempting knowledge: People avoid knowledge from internal rivals and seek knowledge from external rivals. *Management Science, 52*(8), 1129–1144.

Moreland, R. L. (1999). Transactive memory: Learning who knows what in work groups and organizations. In L. Thompson, D. Messick, & J. Levine (Eds.), *Shared cognition in organizations: The management of knowledge* (pp. 3–31). Mahwah, NJ: Lawrence Erlbaum Associates.

Moreland, R. L., & Levine J. M. (2000). Socialization in organizations and work groups. In M. Turner (Ed.), *Groups at work: Theory and research* (pp. 69–112). Mahwah, NJ: Lawrence Erlbaum Associates.

Nelson, T. O., & Narens, L. (1994). Why investigate metacognition? In J. Metcalfe & A. Shimamura (Eds.), *Metacognition: Knowing about knowing* (pp. 1–25). Cambridge, MA: MIT Press.

Orasanu, J., & Salas, E. (1993). Team decision making in complex environments. In G. Klein, J. Orasanu, R. Calderwood, & C. E. Zsambok (Eds.), *Decision making in action: Models and methods* (pp. 327–345). Norwood, NJ: Ablex.

Paulus, P. B., & Brown, V. R. (2007). Toward more creative and innovative group idea generation: A cognitive-social-motivational perspective of brainstorming. *Social and Personality Psychology Compass, 1,* 248–265.

Perrow, C. (1984). *Normal accidents: Living with high-risk technologies.* New York, NY: Basic Books.

Petty, R. E., Briñol, P., Tormala, Z. L., & Wegener, D. T. (2007). The role of metacognition in social judgment. In A. W. Kruglanski & E. T. Higgins (Eds.), *Social psychology: A handbook of basic principles* (Vol. 2, pp. 254–284). New York, NY: Guilford.

Petty, R. E., & Krosnick, J. A. (1995). *Attitude strength: Antecedents and consequences.* Hillsdale, NJ: Lawrence Erlbaum Associates.

Prentice, D. A., Miller, D. T., & Lightdale, J. R. (1994). Asymmetries in attachments to groups and to their members: Distinguishing between common-identity and common-bond groups. *Personality and Social Psychology Bulletin, 20,* 484–493.

Rentsch, J. R., & Woehr, D. J. (2004). Quantifying congruence in cognition: Social relations modeling and team member schema similarity. In E. Salas & S. M. Fiore (Eds.), *Team cognition: Understanding the factors that drive process and performance* (pp. 11–31). Washington, DC: American Psychological Association.

Roccas, S., Sagiv, L., Schwartz, S., Halevy, N., & Eidelson, R. (2008). Toward a unifying model of identification with groups: Integrating theoretical perspectives. *Personality and Social Psychology Review, 12,* 280–306.

Sanna, L. J., Parks, C. D., Chang, E. C., & Carter, S. E. (2005). The hourglass is half full or half empty: Temporal framing and the group planning fallacy. *Group Dynamics: Theory, Research, and Practice, 9,* 173–188.

Schwarz, N., Bless, H., Strack, F., Klumpp, G., Rittenauer, Schatka, H., & Simons, A. (1991). Ease of retrieval as information: Another look at the availability heuristic. *Journal of Personality and Social Psychology, 61,* 195–202.

Schwarz, N., Sanna, L. J., Skurnik, I., & Yoon, C. (2007). Metacognitive experiences and the intricacies of setting people straight: Implications for debiasing and public information campaigns. *Advances in Experimental Social Psychology, 39,* 127–161.

Shea, G. P., & Guzzo, R. A. (1987). Group effectiveness: What really matters? *Sloan Management Review, 28*(3), 25–31.

Spataro, S., & Chatman, J. (2007). The effects of interorganizational competition on individual commitment: A cross-level investigation. In C. Bartel, S. Blader, & A. Wrzesniewski (Eds.), *Identity and the modern organization.* Mahwah, NJ: Lawrence Erlbaum Associates.

Stasser, G., & Titus, W. 1985. Pooling of unshared information in group decision making: Biased information sampling during discussion. *Journal of Personality and Social Psychology, 48,* 1467–1478.

Swann, W. B., Milton, L. P., & Polzer, J. T. (2000). Should we create a niche or fall in line? Identity negotiation and small group effectiveness. *Journal of Personality and Social Psychology, 79*(2), 238–250.

Sycara, K., & Lewis, M. (2004). Integrating intelligent agents into human teams. In E. Salas & S. Fiore (Eds.), *Team cognition: Understanding the factors that drive process and performance.* Washington, DC: American Psychological Association.

Tucker, A. L., Nembhard, I. M., & Edmondson, A. (2006). Implementing new practices: An empirical study of organizational learning in hospital intensive care units. *Management Science, 53,* 894–907.

Van Boven, L., & Thompson, L. (2003). A look into the mind of the negotiator: Mental models in negotiation. *Group Processes & Intergroup Relations, 6,* 387–404.

Vorauer, J. D., Main, K. J., & O'Connell, G. B. (1998). How do individuals expect to be viewed by members of lower status groups? Content and implications of meta-stereotypes. *Journal of Personality and Social Psychology, 75,* 917–937.

Weaver, K., Garcia, S. M., Schwarz, N., & Miller, D. T. (2007). Inferring the popularity of an opinion from its familiarity: A repetitive voice can sound like a chorus. *Journal of Personality and Social Psychology, 92,* 821–833.

Wegener, D. T., & Petty, R. E. (1995). Flexible correction processes in social judgment: The role of naïve theories in corrections for perceived bias. *Journal of Personality and Social Psychology, 68,* 36–51.

Wegner, D. M. (1986). Transactive memory: A contemporary analysis of the group mind. In B. Mullen & G. R. Goethals (Eds.), *Theories of group behavior* (pp. 185–208). New York, NY: Springer-Verlag.

Wegner, D. M., Giuliano, T., & Hertel, P. (1995). Cognitive interdependence in close relationships. In W. J. Ickes (Ed.), *Compatible and incompatible relationships* (pp. 253–276). New York: Springer-Verlag.

West, M. A. (Ed.) (1996). *The handbook of work group psychology.* Chichester, England: John Wiley & Sons.

West, M. A., Patterson, M. G., & Dawson, J. F. (1999). A path to profit? Teamwork at the top. *CentrePiece, 4*(3), 6–11.

Yzerbyt, V. Y., Judd, C. M., & Muller, D. (2008). How do they see us? The vicissitudes of metaperception in intergroup relations. In S. Demoulin, J.-P. Leyens, & J. F. Dovidio (Eds.), *Intergroup misunderstandings: Impact of divergent social realities* (pp. 63–83). New York, NY: Psychology Press.

16

Metacognitive Theory in Consumer Research

DEREK D. RUCKER and ZAKARY L. TORMALA

INTRODUCTION

*I*magine the following scenario: Two consumers, Suzy and Carrie, are both looking to buy a new car. They have identical demographic and socioeconomic profiles, go to the same dealer, interact with the same salesperson, and ultimately arrive at the same price after negotiating. Furthermore, imagine that it is possible to open up the "black box" of their minds and observe their thought processes. As it turns out, they have identical thoughts about the features of the car, from their preference for the leather interior to their appreciation for the modern-shaped arch of the back fender. But a curious thing happens. Despite having identical thoughts about the car, Suzy purchases the car and Carrie decides to pass.

At first glance, this scenario appears to present a conundrum. How could two consumers—who have identical backgrounds, interact with the same salesperson, and ultimately generate the same profile of thoughts about the product—exhibit such different behaviors when it comes to making a purchase decision? Decades of prior research investigating the role of accessible thought content in consumer choice and behavior might find it challenging to explain this outcome. Based on recent advances in metacognitive theory in marketing and consumer behavior, however, this situation can be explained by considering consumers' thoughts about their own thoughts in the sales context. In other words, by moving from cognitive to metacognitive approaches, consumer research has expanded its ability to explain consumers' decisions and choices in the marketplace.

METACOGNITION: PRIMARY VERSUS SECONDARY THOUGHT

Early research taking a psychological approach to consumer behavior focused on perceptual and cognitive influences on consumers' responses to products and advertising. Perceptual variables of interest have included elements of advertising or products related to color, iconography, or brand name, whereas cognitive variables of interest have included consumers' thoughts or associations with a brand (for reviews, see Rucker & Sternthal, 2010; Sternthal & Rucker, 2009). For instance, in the opening scenario, Suzy and Carrie's evaluations of the car might be positively affected by colors they perceive as pleasing (e.g., cherry red) and negatively affected by colors they perceive as displeasing (e.g., burnt orange). Similarly, their decisions might be affected by thoughts and associations they have with respect to the brand. Both Suzy and Carrie might view the specific car in question as very reliable because this benefit has been portrayed in the brand's advertising, presented by the salesperson, or obtained via word-of-mouth communications from other consumers.

While perceptual and cognitive factors remain important topics in consumer research, a growing literature has turned to examine how *metacognitive* processes can further elucidate consumers decision making (e.g., Briñol, Petty, & Tormala, 2004; Lee & Aaker, 2004; Pham, 2004; Pham & Muthukrishnan, 2002; Rucker, Petty, & Briñol, 2008; Schwarz, 2004; Tormala, Petty, & Briñol, 2002). By metacognitive processes, we mean processes that involve an assessment or reflection at a secondary level of thinking or thoughts that occur at a primary level. For example, one might have a thought at a primary level that "this car is reliable" and simultaneously form an assessment of this thought (e.g., "I believe this thought is correct."). Thus, metacognitive processes involve at least two levels of thinking: one at the cognitive level, which we call primary, and one at the metacognitive level, which we call secondary (see Petty, Briñol, Tormala, & Wegener, 2007). Importantly, these terms reflect the relationship between the thoughts and not their respective importance. As the previous chapters in this book attest, secondary metacognitive processes can be as important in shaping behavior as primary cognitive processes.

CHAPTER OVERVIEW

In this chapter, we discuss frameworks that have been developed to examine consumer behavior through a metacognitive lens. Rather than provide an exhaustive review of all of the literature related to metacognition in consumer research, we focus our attention on a few major models and frameworks that have been applied specifically to consumer behavior. In particular, we review the persuasion knowledge model, the accessibility–diagnosticity model, and the multiple pathway anchoring and adjustment model, and we explore recent perspectives on how consumers appraise their own certainty and how the subjective experiences of fluency and fit can dictate consumer thought and action. Our goal is to familiarize the reader with each perspective or framework, provide a summary of the most relevant literature, and highlight opportunities for future research to understand further the role of metacognition in consumer behavior.

THE PERSUASION KNOWLEDGE MODEL

The persuasion knowledge model (Friestad & Wright, 1994, 1995) proposes that people hold lay theories about persuasion and how it operates. This involves knowledge about the agent of persuasion, the target of persuasion, and their interactions. These lay theories are known as *persuasion knowledge.* Through the accumulation of experiences over time, people draw upon their persuasion knowledge and utilize it when they are exposed to a variety of marketing efforts ranging from one-on-one sales pitches to mass media communications. Furthermore, because of the activation and use of persuasion knowledge, persuasive outcomes are not solely a function of what an advertiser or salesperson does. Rather, they depend on lay theories that are brought to bear by the recipient of the marketing effort and the conclusions drawn from these theories (Campbell & Kirmani, 2000; Kirmani & Campbell, 2004; Wright, Friestad, & Boush, 2005).

The persuasion knowledge model offers several observations about the role of metacognition in consumer behavior. First, consistent with the concept of primary and secondary cognition, the model suggests that people have not only primary thoughts in response to a marketing appeal (e.g., "This message source has gorgeous eyes and a beautiful face."), but also secondary thoughts about the implications of those primary thoughts (e.g., "I know I like this product because of the attractive source, but I don't think that's a valid input or something I should be persuaded by."). Viewed differently, consumers' lay theories reside at the primary level of thinking, but the fact that consumers react to and use these lay theories to guide how they respond to marketing appeals reflects a secondary level of thinking.

In one study, Campbell and Kirmani (2000) asked participants to imagine themselves as a shopper interacting with a salesperson while considering a purchase. In one condition, participants were asked to imagine receiving a compliment from the salesperson *prior* to making the purchase. In another condition, participants were asked to imagine receiving the compliment *after* making the purchase. Results indicated that the salesperson was more likely to be viewed as insincere when the flattering comment came before as opposed to after the consumer had made the purchase. The explanation for this, according to a persuasion knowledge model, is that consumers believe that flattery is a frequently used form of coercion. This belief is especially accessible when flattery comes prior to a purchase, but less so when it arrives after a purchase, even though a similar motive for flattery might operate after purchase (i.e., hoping the consumer will return for repeat purchase). From a metacognitive perspective, people identify the flattery (primary cognition), but view this as an insincere and thus invalid attitudinal input (secondary cognition) because of their persuasion knowledge.

Persuasion knowledge is more likely to have an effect when it is both accessible and people have the ability to utilize it. As evidence for this, Campbell and Kirmani (2000) tested how flattery by a salesperson affected perceived sincerity as a function of (a) the accessibility of the relevant persuasion knowledge, and (b) cognitive load. They found that participants judged the salesperson to be the most insincere when they had activated beliefs about insincerity and were under low cognitive load. These findings suggest that both accessibility and cognitive capacity are critical in the application of persuasion knowledge.

A final observation from the model is that because people have different knowledge and prior experience with persuasion, they develop different lay theories about it. Friestad and Wright (1995) demonstrated that lay people (e.g., people holding administrative positions, clerical positions, students) and researchers (i.e., members of the Association for Consumer Research) held different beliefs with regard to various aspects of persuasion. For example, compared to lay people, researchers reported that attention was less necessary for persuasion and that it was easier to elicit emotions. Indeed, when one thinks about the history of research demonstrating the power of incidental emotions (e.g., Petty, DeSteno, & Rucker, 2001; Schwarz & Clore, 2003) and persuasion heuristics even when attention is low (see Petty & Wegener, 1998), it is easy to understand how those trained in the area might come to hold different beliefs than lay people. The general point is that lay theories about persuasion can vary from person to person, with important implications for persuasion, and that expertise is only one determinant of such variance (see also Petty & Wegener, 1993; Chapter 5, this volume).

THE ACCESSIBILITY–DIAGNOSTICITY MODEL

Developed by Lynch and colleagues (Feldman & Lynch, 1988; Lynch, 2006; Lynch, Marmorstein, & Weigold, 1988), the accessibility–diagnosticity model seeks to explain when consumers' beliefs, such as attitudes, influence their behavior. According to this model, whether a belief serves as an input into a consumer's behavior depends on whether that belief is accessible and viewed as diagnostic. That is, the model recognizes that there are both cognitive (primary) and metacognitive (secondary) components linking beliefs to behavior.

At the cognitive or primary level, the belief has to be accessible in the appropriate consumer context. For example, even if one holds the belief that "Godiva is expensive chocolate," that belief might or might not influence behavior depending on whether it is accessible when one is making a decision to purchase chocolate. At the metacognitive or secondary level, the belief also has to be viewed as diagnostic for behavior. For example, one might reason, "Godiva is expensive chocolate, and I am trying to impress my date" or "Godiva is expensive chocolate, and I am trying to save money." In either case, the belief that "Godiva is expensive chocolate" might be viewed as diagnostic or relevant to the goal at hand, though the particular implications for purchasing would be different—favorable in the former context but unfavorable in the latter.

A core emphasis of the accessibility–diagnosticity model is that diagnosticity is context dependent. That is, beliefs are seen as diagnostic (or not) for a particular behavior in a particular situation. Thus, the belief that Godiva is expensive chocolate might be viewed as extremely diagnostic in the context of picking out a gift to impress a date or in the context of saving money. However, the same belief might be viewed as nondiagnostic when one is attempting to lose weight. In this context, the belief that Godiva is expensive might be viewed as nondiagnostic in assessing whether one should buy the chocolate because it is irrelevant to weight loss. Under these circumstances, even if the belief that Godiva is expensive is highly accessible, it might be discounted and exert little influence on purchasing compared to other beliefs (e.g., that Godiva is high in calories).

In addition, according to the accessibility–diagnosticity model, the likelihood that any cognition about an object, such as a product, will be used as input into decision making is a function not only of the accessibility and diagnosticity of that cognition, but also of the accessibility and diagnosticity of alternative cognitions. For example, in deciding whether to buy Godiva for one's date, the influence of the belief that "Godiva is expensive chocolate" might be mitigated if an individual also has an accessible belief that "Fannie May is impressive and it's more aligned to my budget." That is, the accessibility and diagnosticity of this second belief might lead one to avoid purchasing Godiva despite the fact that the cognition about Godiva's cost is accessible and viewed as diagnostic. Thus, the core contribution of the accessibility–diagnosticity model is that it delineates how consumer behavior is influenced by multiple available inputs to a decision, as well as the accessibility and perceived diagnosticity of those inputs.

In a test of the accessibility–diagnosticity framework, Lynch and colleagues (1988) found that when consumers made decisions about products (e.g., whether to purchase them), they relied more heavily on recalled attribute evaluations when those evaluations were accessible rather than inaccessible in memory, providing support for the cognitive layer of their model. Then, in a follow-up experiment, Lynch et al. demonstrated that reliance on accessible evaluations depended on the consistency of those evaluations.

Specifically, the authors argued that if a consumer's accessible evaluations suggested that brand A was consistently superior to brand B on the dimensions of interest, then these evaluations would be used to determine behavior (i.e., purchase brand A). However, if there were inconsistencies in these evaluations (i.e., some attributes favored brand A, whereas others favored brand B), additional cognitive work would be required to resolve the discrepancy (e.g., considering and integrating new attribute information). In this case, the recalled evaluations, in and of themselves, would not be viewed as diagnostic for behavior because they were contradictory. Indeed, consistent with the authors' argument, evaluations of brand attributes were used when they were consistent (i.e., diagnostic), but not when they were inconsistent (nondiagnostic). Thus, both cognitive (accessibility) and metacognitive (diagnosticity) elements were important in guiding consumers' decisions.

Since these early findings, the accessibility–diagnosticity framework has been used to understand a variety of additional consumer-relevant behaviors such as responses to brand names (Ahluwalia & Gurhan-Canli, 2000), word-of-mouth communications (Herr, Kardes, & Kim, 1991), and people's estimates of the frequency with which they engage in specific behaviors (Menon, Raghubir, & Schwarz, 1995).

THE MULTIPLE PATHWAY ANCHORING
AND ADJUSTMENT MODEL

Cohen and Reed (2006) proposed a multiple pathway anchoring and adjustment (MPAA) model. Although there are various similarities between the MPAA and the accessibility–diagnosticity model (see Lynch, 2006, for a discussion), the MPAA focuses specifically on attitudes and predicting when individuals' attitudes will guide their behavior. For instance, it posits that attitudes are derived from both "inside-out" factors (e.g., internal reflections) and "outside-in" factors (e.g., external reflections) and that this distinction can lead to the formation of dual or multiple attitudes, which in turn influences the attitude–behavior relation.

According to the MPAA, people ask themselves two questions in assessing their own attitude and deciding whether it should be used as a guide for behavior. First, they ask if they have a clear and well-formed position with respect to the attitude object (e.g., "Do I know what my attitude toward this product is?"). Second, after establishing that they do have a well-formed position, consumers ask themselves whether this attitude provides adequate basis to proceed or engage in a behavior (e.g., "Is my attitude based on enough information?"). The authors describe these questions as assessments of *representational sufficiency* and *functional sufficiency,* respectively. Cohen and Reed (2006) suggest that a given behavior will be influenced by an individual's attitude when that attitude meets the individual's requirements for both representational and functional sufficiency. Thus, consumers' metacognitive assessments of their own attitudes are thought to be core drivers of the attitude–behavior relationship.

Although Cohen and Reed (2006) did not focus their framework on attitude certainty—the degree of conviction associated with one's attitude (Rucker & Petty, 2006; Tormala & Rucker, 2007)—as a moderator of attitude–behavior consistency, recent work on attitude certainty resonates with their distinction between representational and functional sufficiency. In particular, Petrocelli, Tormala, and Rucker (2007) proposed that attitude certainty can be decomposed into two core features: attitude clarity and attitude correctness. Attitude clarity refers to the subjective sense that one's attitude is clear in one's mind, whereas attitude correctness refers to the subjective sense that one's attitude is correct, or valid. Thus, clarity and correctness bear some resemblance to representational and functional sufficiency, respectively.

Furthermore, underlining Cohen and Reed's emphasis on the importance of inside-out and outside-in factors, Petrocelli et al. (2007) found that attitude clarity was derived from metacognitive activity focused on confirming what one personally thinks (e.g., repeatedly expressing the same attitude), whereas attitude correctness was determined by metacognitive activity aimed at confirming what other people think (e.g., receiving social consensus feedback). Moreover, both of these forms of certainty predicted resistance to a persuasive appeal. That is, feeling greater clarity and feeling greater correctness independently contributed to making one's attitude more resistant to a counterattitudinal attack. Thus, assuming some overlap between clarity/correctness and representational/functional sufficiency, the Petrocelli et al. findings suggest that these distinct metacognitive assessments can influence not only consumers' use of their attitudes as guides to behavior, but also their defense of those attitudes against attack (e.g., competitive advertising, counterattitudinal word of mouth, etc.).

A CERTAINTY APPRAISALS FRAMEWORK

As the previous section highlights, one important metacognitive judgment of interest to consumer psychologists is attitude certainty, which is defined as the confidence or conviction one has about one's attitude (e.g., Gross, Holtz, & Miller, 1995). Attitude certainty reflects a metacognitive assessment of an attitude in that it is a secondary cognition attached to a primary cognition. For instance, just as one can have a primary belief about a product (e.g., "This MacBook Air seems very durable.") and then assess the certainty with which that belief is held (e.g., "I'm pretty sure because I've dropped it several times and it still works!"), so too can one have a general attitude toward a product ("I like this laptop.") and then assess the certainty with which that attitude is held ("I'm certain of my opinion because I've tried it out several times.").

A large body of research attests to the fact that as the certainty associated with attitudes increases, attitudes are generally more stable and influential (for reviews, see Gross et al., 1995; Tormala & Rucker, 2007; cf. Clarkson, Tormala, & Rucker, 2008). Specifically, compared to attitudes held with uncertainty, attitudes held with certainty tend to influence behavior (Fazio & Zanna, 1978; Rucker & Petty, 2004; Tormala & Petty, 2004a; Wan, Rucker, Tormala, & Clarkson, 2010), persist over time (Bassili, 1996; Bizer, Tormala, Rucker, & Petty, 2006), resist persuasive attempts (Clarkson et al., 2008; Tormala & Petty, 2002), and decrease the need to acquire or process new information (Briñol, Petty, Valle, Rucker, & Becerra, 2007; Maheswaran & Chaiken, 1991).

Given the consequences of attitude certainty, a certainty appraisals framework (Petty, Tormala, & Rucker, 2004; Tormala & Petty, 2004b; Tormala & Rucker, 2007) has been developed to understand the processes by which consumers come to hold attitudes with certainty or uncertainty. This framework essentially postulates that when people encounter a persuasion attempt (e.g., an advertisement or sales pitch), they can

- assess whether they succumbed to (changed) or resisted (no change) the attempt
- appraise the underlying reason for succumbing or resisting
- form attributional inferences about their attitudes that affect their attitude certainty and, thus, subsequent behavior

In other words, following an interaction with an advertisement or salesperson, people's appraisals of their responses can engender an attribution-like process whereby people reflect on their resistance or yielding in the situation and then form specifiable inferences about their attitudes. In this framework, the mental action of resisting or succumbing to persuasion resides at the primary level of cognition, whereas people's perceptions of or inferences about their own resisting or succumbing reflect the secondary level of cognition. Moreover, depending on the specific appraisals people form, they can become more or less certain of their original or changed attitudes and thus more or less likely to act on and defend those attitudes in the future.

Resistance Appraisals

First consider the case in which an individual successfully resists persuasion. How does resisting a persuasive attempt affect attitude certainty? It depends on the appraisals or attributions people make for the resistance. If individuals attribute resistance to having generated compelling arguments against a strong attack they might reason, "I successfully resisted a credible attack; my attitude must be correct!"—producing an increase in attitude certainty. However, if individuals attribute resistance to a poor message, they might instead reason, "I successfully resisted a pathetic attack; this is not very informative about the correctness of my attitude," rendering attitude certainty unchanged.

Indeed, research has shown that individuals who successfully resist a persuasive attack become more certain of their original attitudes when they believe the attack contains strong as opposed to weak arguments (Tormala & Petty, 2002) or comes from a credible versus noncredible source (Tormala & Petty, 2004a). For example, Tormala and Petty (2004a) exposed undergraduates to identical arguments in an advertisement for a controversial new pain relief product. However, half of the participants were told that the arguments came from an expert source, whereas the other half were told that the arguments came from a nonexpert source. All participants were instructed to think of counterarguments while reading the ad. Results indicated that although participants were equally successful in resisting the ad (i.e., no attitude change toward the product occurred in either condition), participants became more certain of their initial negative attitudes when the ad they resisted was believed to contain arguments from an expert as opposed to a nonexpert. When participants resisted an expert, they interpreted their successful resistance as an indicator that their initial attitude was valid. When they resisted a nonexpert, however, participants appeared to attribute resistance to the weak source rather than the validity of their attitude.

Of course, this does not mean that resisting a nonexpert source inevitably has zero impact on one's attitude certainty. In fact, if individuals struggle in their resistance efforts against a nonexpert, this struggle can leave them feeling *less* certain of their attitudes because the attribution for having difficulty resisting a weak source might be that the support for one's attitude is questionable (Tormala, Clarkson, & Petty, 2006). For example, an individual might reason, "I resisted that message, but I just barely did so and the source was not even an expert in this area. Maybe my position isn't correct after all." Evidence supports precisely this type of metacognitive reasoning.

Persuasion Appraisals

Now consider the case in which an individual succumbs to an advertisement or salesperson. How certain will this person be of his or her attitude? Again, it depends on the appraisals made for succumbing. For example, if people believe that they succumbed because they made a thorough effort to examine the available information (e.g., in a product review online) and the available information was persuasive, they are more likely to be certain of their (new) attitude than if they succumbed but were not as thorough as they could have been. Indeed, in the former case, a person might reason, "I gave in after carefully considering all of the information in the product review, so I am not missing anything now." In the latter case, a person might reason, "I gave in, but only after a cursory consideration of the information. Perhaps a more exhaustive search would have led me to resist." Indeed, past research on omission neglect has found that individuals are less certain when they believe important information has not been conveyed (see also Sanbonmatsu, Kardes, & Herr, 1992). Thus, the more people attribute their succumbing to considering relevant information fully, the more certain they should be of their new attitude.

To test this notion, Rucker and Petty (2004) presented participants with an advertisement for a pain reliever that was pretested to be highly persuasive. They found that, after reading it, participants were more certain of their newly changed attitudes when they changed after a concentrated effort to consider potential weaknesses in the ad compared to when they made an effort only to consider potential strengths. The authors explained this result as stemming from the fact that making a concentrated effort to consider the drawbacks led people to infer that they were knowledgeable of both the strengths and potential weaknesses as opposed to only the strengths (see also Rucker et al., 2008).

Similarly, Wan and colleagues (2010) presented consumers with persuasive advertisements for a new snack product and found that those who were more cognitively depleted were more certain of their post-ad attitudes than were non-depleted individuals. The authors found that this occurred because, although all participants in the study were given ample motivation and ability to process the ad regardless of depletion condition, depleted participants misattributed their depletion to even more thorough processing, which led them to infer that they could be more certain of their newly changed attitudes.

It is also important that, consistent with the notion that these resistance and persuasion appraisals are metacognitive in nature, some degree of cognitive effort is required to observe the effects. For example, both Rucker et al. (2008) and Tormala and Petty (2004a) found that attitude certainty adjustments following resistance and persuasion only occurred among individuals who were naturally or situationally disposed to think carefully (i.e., those high in need for cognition [Cacioppo & Petty, 1982] or under low cognitive load). These findings are consistent with the general theme that metacognition requires a high degree of thought to operate.

Taken together, the certainty appraisals framework suggests that, following resistance or yielding to a persuasion attempt, people form appraisals about their attitudes that play an important role in shaping attitude certainty. Because certainty can be viewed as one input into perceived diagnosticity (Lynch, 2006)—that is, high attitude certainty makes an attitude seem more diagnostic of one's true thoughts and feelings or of the correct thoughts and feelings—this framework also provides insight into the factors that modulate perceived diagnosticity and thus serve as a basis for subsequent behavior.

FLUENCY AND FIT PERSPECTIVES

A final domain within metacognitive consumer research that has received considerable attention relates to fluency and fit. These constructs refer to subjective feelings or experiences related to information processing. Whereas the actual information processed resides at the cognitive level, people's subjective experience of information processing resides at the metacognitive level. Fluency is used to describe the perceived ease of processing or generating information, whereas fit reflects a general sense of "feeling right" that stems from correspondence between a person's goal orientation and means of goal pursuit. Both tie into metacognition in that they relate to people's thoughts about the subjective experience of thinking or evaluating. We focus our attention on how each of the constructs has been linked to outcomes of interest to consumer behavior researchers.

Fluency Experiences

The subjective feeling of ease of processing has sparked a great deal of attention in consumer research following the demonstration of the *ease of retrieval effect* by Schwarz and colleagues (1991). The basic idea behind this effect is that when thinking of reasons supporting an idea or attitude, individuals consider not only the reasons generated (i.e., the cognitive level), but also how easy or difficult it is to retrieve those reasons (i.e., the metacognitive level). For example, consider a situation in which a consumer is asked to retrieve one reason versus 10 reasons that a BMW is a good car. How might this manipulation affect consumers' attitudes? From a pure cognitive perspective, retrieving 10 reasons why BMW is good should be far more compelling, or persuasive, than generating just one reason. From a metacognitive point of view, however, generating one reason is considerably easier than generating 10 reasons. If people rely on the experienced ease of generating reasons, rather than solely on the content of those reasons, then they might show more favorable attitudes after generating one as opposed to 10 supportive reasons, or more negative attitudes after generating one as opposed to 10 counterarguments.

In a study exploring this possibility in an advertising context, Wänke, Bohner, and Jurkowitsch (1997) presented participants with an ad for a BMW that was accompanied by the copy "There are many reasons to choose a BMW. Can you name one?" or "There are many reasons to choose a BMW. Can you name 10?" Participants had more favorable attitudes toward BMW when they received the ad asking for one as opposed to 10 reasons. Thus, although asking for 10 reasons might be expected to anchor consumers at a higher number and offer a more compelling case than asking for just one reason, people instead appeared to rely on the experienced or imagined ease of completing the task.

Although some scholars have argued that the ease of retrieval effect is a heuristic that operates under relatively low thinking conditions (Schwarz, 2004), work by Tormala et al. (2002) suggests that, like other metacognitive processes, the ease of retrieval effect is more likely to emerge when motivation and ability to think are high. To test this hypothesis, Tormala et al. asked undergraduate participants to generate two or 10 arguments in support of instituting senior comprehensive exams as a college graduation requirement. In addition, they manipulated participants' motivation to think about this issue by varying its personal relevance. Tormala et al. found that under low relevance (i.e., low thinking) conditions, participants were more supportive of the policy when they generated 10 rather than two arguments in favor of it. That is, they used the content or number of arguments generated to determine their attitudes.

Under high relevance (i.e., high thinking) conditions, however, participants were more supportive of the policy when they generated two rather than 10 arguments in favor of it. Here, participants appeared to focus on the ease associated with argument generation. When it was easier to complete the task (i.e., the two-arguments condition), participants felt more confident about the arguments they generated and thus based their attitudes on those arguments to a greater degree. This reflected a *self-validation* process under high thinking conditions (see Petty, Chapter 3, this volume, for further discussion of the self-validation hypothesis). In short, Tormala and colleagues' (2002) findings elucidated the conditions under which cognitive and metacognitive processes can differentially contribute to attitude change and persuasion (see also Tormala, Falces, Briñol, & Petty, 2007; Tybout, Sternthal, Malaviya, Bakamitsos, & Park, 2005).

Of importance, however, processing fluency can be derived from many other sources beyond the perceived ease or difficulty of generating arguments on a topic (see Alter & Oppenheimer, 2009, for a review) that affect consumer judgment and behavior. For example, both fluency and liking can be induced through prior exposure to an ad, brand, or product (e.g., Janiszewski & Meyvis, 2001; Lee, 2001). Lee and Labroo (2004) expanded on these mere exposure findings and demonstrated that fluency (and liking) can be increased by presenting target brands or products in conceptually relevant contexts (e.g., an ad featuring a bottle of beer in a bar setting) or following conceptually relevant primes (e.g., showing an image of ketchup immediately after an ad for a particular mayonnaise; see also Labroo, Dhar, & Schwarz, 2008).

Other examples abound. For instance, fluency has been manipulated by presenting ads or other messages in font or color combinations that are easy versus difficult to read (e.g., Briñol, Petty, & Tormala, 2006; Novemsky, Dhar, Schwarz, & Simonson, 2007). Thomas and Morwitz (2009) found that when consumers estimated price differences between two items, easy-to-compute differences (e.g., $5.00 – $4.00) were perceived to be greater than more difficult-to-compute differences (e.g., $4.97 – $3.96), even when objectively the opposite was true. Mayer and Tormala (2010) recently showed that when consumers receive ads framed in ways that match rather than mismatch their cognitive or affective orientations, those ads feel subjectively easier to process. Furthermore, in each of these contexts, fluency was revealed to have an important and typically positive effect on consumers' attitudes, preferences, and choices (but see Briñol et al., 2006, for moderation of this effect by naïve theories). In fact, Alter and Oppenheimer (2006) recently demonstrated that the effects of fluency can be so powerful that they even dictate stock fluctuations. Specifically, easy-to-pronounce stocks and ticker symbols are expected to and actually do outperform stocks with names and symbols that are more difficult to pronounce.

Fit Experiences

Whereas fluency has been defined with respect to ease of processing, fit experiences have been defined as a "feeling right" that stems from the correspondence between one's goal orientation and means of goal pursuit. Experiences of fit might sometimes affect evaluations through fluency (e.g., Lee & Aaker, 2004), but the key feature of fit is that it involves a match between goal orientation and goal pursuit. In particular, work in this area has focused on regulatory goals associated with promotion versus prevention.

The idea of differential regulatory goals has its origin in regulatory focus theory (Higgins, 1987), which posits two distinct self-regulation strategies. The first involves the pursuit of hopes and aspirations toward ideals and has been termed *promotion*. The second strategy involves the pursuit of safety, security, and the fulfillment of obligations and has been termed *prevention*. These two orientations have been shown to lead to distinct strategic foci on eagerness versus vigilance such that promotion-focused individuals prefer pursuing their goals in an eager fashion and prevention-focused individuals prefer pursuing their goals in a vigilant fashion (for reviews, see Cesario, Higgins, & Scholer, 2008; Higgins, 2000). The subjective experience of fit, which occurs when one's regulatory focus matches one's means of goal pursuit, is psychologically consequential.

Of primary interest to consumer psychologists, it has been shown that people typically evaluate products and brands more favorably when they are promoted by messages framed in ways that match, or fit, their higher order regulatory goals (Cesario, Grant, & Higgins, 2004; Lee & Aaker, 2004; see Cesario et al., 2008). For example, Lee and Aaker (2004) examined the interaction between consumers' regulatory orientation and advertisement framing on persuasive outcomes. Participants were randomly assigned to receive an advertisement that first activated a promotion or prevention orientation followed by a tagline designed to appeal to promotion or prevention. Lee and Aaker hypothesized that a tagline framed in terms of gains would appeal more to promotion-focused participants, whereas a tagline framed in terms of losses would appeal more to prevention-focused participants (see also Labroo & Lee, 2006).

Specifically, all participants received an advertisement for grape juice. After receiving some basic information about the product, participants in the promotion focus condition received arguments emphasizing gains obtained from consuming the product, such as more vitamin C and higher energy levels. In contrast, participants in the prevention focus condition received arguments emphasizing losses avoided by using the product, such as reducing the likelihood of cancer and heart disease. Following this information, the advertisement ended with a tagline designed to match or mismatch the orientation induced.

In the promotion focus condition, the tagline was framed in terms of a gain—"Get Energized!" (fit)—or a loss—"Don't Miss Out on Getting Energized!" (nonfit). In the prevention focus condition, the gain frame tagline was "Prevent Clogged Arteries!" (nonfit), whereas the loss frame tagline was "Don't Miss Out on Preventing Clogged Arteries!" (fit). Results indicated that individuals had more favorable attitudes toward the advertised product under fit compared to nonfit conditions. Furthermore, the effects were not mediated by differences in the content of participants' thoughts, but rather by the experience of fluency accompanying fit. That is, the experience of fit translated into greater processing fluency, which enhanced persuasion (see also Cesario et al., 2004). Of course, this does not mean that fit is always beneficial to persuasion; for example, if individuals primarily have negative thoughts in response to a message, fit might decrease persuasion (Cesario et al., 2004).

Finally, it is important to note that although fluency and fit are metacognitive experiences in that they refer to feelings associated with one's thoughts or reactions, they can also affect consumer behavior through cognitive processes. As but one example, Tormala and colleagues (2007) demonstrated that ease of retrieval effects in persuasion can be co-mediated by metacognitive assessments, such as thought confidence, and more strictly cognitive processes, such as the presence of unrequested cognitions.

PAST RESEARCH AND EMERGING PERSPECTIVES

In summary, considerable research attention has been devoted to understanding the role of metacognitive factors in consumer behavior. This research has facilitated the development of several frameworks and perspectives designed to explain (1) how people arrive at and assess their own attitudes, beliefs, and thoughts, and (2) how these constructs link to behavior. As the current review suggests, these different perspectives converge in highlighting the importance of secondary cognition in driving consumer thought and action. In addition, they appear to support a general conclusion that metacognitive processes are more likely to operate under high rather than low levels of thinking (e.g., Briñol et al., 2004; Campbell & Kirmani, 2000; Rucker et al., 2008; Tormala et al. 2002; Tormala & Petty, 2004a).

Although research on metacognition in consumer behavior has deepened our insight into these processes, a number of exciting and important questions about consumer behavior remain understudied from a metacognitive perspective. For example, the perspectives outlined in this chapter largely, though not exclusively, revolve around attitudes and persuasion. This emphasis in the literature might simply stem from the rich history of attitudes and persuasion research in marketing-relevant contexts more generally. Nevertheless, we submit that consumer research in many other areas could benefit from a more explicit consideration of metacognitive influences.

Decision Making

As but one possible direction for future research on metacognition in consumer behavior, consider work in behavioral decision theory or decision heuristics (e.g.,

Kahneman, Knetsch, & Thaler, 1990; Simonson, 1993). Researchers in this area might gain new insight into consumer decision making and the consequences of that decision making by considering both the heuristics people use to guide their decisions and their perceptions of those heuristics and/or their reliance on them. For instance, perhaps people lose certainty about a decision when they perceive that they have made it by following a heuristic or cognitive shortcut, which implies that they have not been as thoughtful as possible (e.g., Wan et al., 2010). Alternatively, people might sometimes feel quite certain of decisions based on heuristics or shortcuts to the extent that those decisions feel intuitive or easy to generate (e.g., Simmons & Nelson, 2006).

Recent research by Tormala, Clarkson, and Henderson (2011) hints at the possibility that perceived reliance on quick decision heuristics can have a malleable effect on attitude certainty. Across several studies, Tormala et al. manipulated the perceived speed with which people evaluated objects and assessed their subsequent certainty in their evaluations. For example, in one experiment, they asked participants to evaluate an abstract painting, gave them feedback on how quickly they evaluated, and then measured attitude certainty. They found that the effect of perceiving fast versus slow evaluation depended on the familiarity of the painting. When participants evaluated an unfamiliar painting, they felt more certain when they believed they took their time and evaluated thoughtfully. In contrast, when participants evaluated a familiar painting, they felt more certain when they believed they went with their gut and evaluated quickly. Extending this finding to the current concerns, there might be a dynamic effect of perceived reliance on decisions heuristics or other cognitive shortcuts on the certainty with which consumers hold their attitudes or judgments.

Compensatory Consumption

Recent research on compensatory consumption suggests that consumers purchase products to compensate for psychological deficits or threats (e.g., Gao, Wheeler, & Shiv, 2009; Rucker, 2009). For instance, Rucker and Galinsky (2008, 2009) found that consumers who feel powerless are more likely to purchase high-status objects than low-status objects, presumably to compensate and restore a feeling of power. There are a number of ways that work on compensatory consumption might be informed by metacognitive theory. For example, from an accessibility–diagnosticity perspective, psychological need states, such as the need for power, might affect what product attributes are accessible, viewed as diagnostic for need fulfillment, and, ultimately, seen as desirable for consumption.

It is also relevant, when one is facing a threat to one's power, to ask what the implications are of recognizing and observing that one is engaging in compensatory consumption. Whereas some consumers might view compensatory consumption as a legitimate means to resolve threat, others might view it as illegitimate. For example, perhaps when two individuals feel besieged by a threat to power from an overbearing boss, one believes that buying himself status-conveying products is an appropriate means to restore power, whereas the other believes the threat can only be adequately addressed by standing up to the boss. From an accessibility-diagnosticity perspective, these two individuals might differ when considering buying a status-implying "power tie." Only the individual who believes status is an appropriate means to restore power would view the status signaled by a tie as diagnostic. In this scenario, the primary cognition related to the product would be the tie's ability to garner respect (e.g., "I think owning this would give me respect and esteem in the eyes of others."), and the secondary cognition would be the diagnosticity of that input (e.g., "I think the status-implying aspect of the tie is a valid input into deciding to buy it.").

Marketplace Confidence

Consumers vary in their perceptions of and perceived ability to defend against marketplace deception (Boush, Friestad, & Wright, 2009; see also Darke & Ritchie, 2007; Vohs, Baumeister, & Chin, 2007). Boush et al. (2009) argue that this variance is partly dictated by consumers' self-efficacy, which manifests as confidence in their ability to navigate through and withstand deceptive advertising and other marketing actions. The research we reviewed on certainty appraisals, highlighting how attitude certainty can be shaped by people's exchanges with persuasion attempts, might be relevant to understanding when and by what means consumers develop high versus low confidence in this arena. We see this as an intriguing and potentially important direction for future research.

In short, there are exciting opportunities to test metacognitive theory in new domains of consumer research. The research noted here represents just a few areas that might be enriched through consideration of metacognitive factors. Many other important topics of consumer research—for example, research exploring consumers' reliance on their emotions (Pham, 2004)—are beginning to be explored from a metacognitive perspective as well. Looking forward, it seems likely that these domains will benefit from the application of metacognitive theories and also help provide new insight into basic metacognitive processes.

FINAL THOUGHTS

Recall the scenario presented at the outset of this chapter involving Suzy and Carrie. The metacognitive perspectives reviewed in this chapter provide several possible solutions as to why Suzy and Carrie, despite having similar thoughts, might have made such different decisions with regard to buying the car. From a persuasion knowledge perspective, Carrie might have been more likely to have an accessible theory regarding the salesperson's intent to persuade, which led her to question his or her sincerity and thus resist the purchase. From an accessibility–diagnosticity perspective, perhaps Carrie viewed her accessible favorable thoughts and beliefs about the car as less diagnostic, which led her to discount those thoughts in making her purchase decision. From a certainty appraisals perspective, although both might have been persuaded by the salesperson's description of the car's features, Suzy might have viewed the arguments fostering persuasion as more balanced than did Carrie (even if they were not), thus enhancing Suzy's attitude certainty to the point that she was willing to make the purchase. Or, perhaps Suzy's favorable thoughts and resulting attitude came to mind more easily and thus were held with greater confidence.

These are but a handful of means by which metacognitive perspectives might be directed at explaining the scenario we presented. Indeed, by considering the role of metacognition, we gain deeper insight into why two consumers with the exact same thoughts and attitudes might differ dramatically in their behavior. Thus, metacognitive theory offers a crucial lever for understanding, predicting, and ultimately shaping consumers' attitudes, preferences, choices, and behaviors. Our hope is that this chapter will provide some direction to researchers interested in applying metacognitive perspectives to consumer-relevant questions and that it will help open the door to new questions and further research in this area.

REFERENCES

Ahluwalia, R., & Gurhan-Canli, Z. (2000). The effects of extensions on the family brand name: An accessibility–diagnosticity perspective. *Journal of Consumer Research, 27,* 371–381.

Alter, A. L., & Oppenheimer, D. M. (2006). Predicting short-term stock fluctuations by using processing fluency. *Proceedings of the National Academy of Sciences, 103,* 9369–9372.

Alter, A. L., & Oppenheimer, D. M. (2009). Uniting the tribes of fluency to form a metacognitive nation. *Personality and Social Psychology Review, 13,* 219–235.

Bassili, J. N. (1996). Meta-judgmental versus operative indexes of psychological attributes: The case of measures of attitude strength. *Journal of Personality and Social Psychology, 71,* 637–653.

Bizer, G. Y., Tormala, Z. L., Rucker, D. D., & Petty, R. E. (2006). Memory-based versus online processing: Implications for attitude strength. *Journal of Experimental Social Psychology, 42,* 646–653.

Boush, D. M., Friestad, M., & Wright, P. (2009). *Deception in the marketplace.* New York, NY: Routledge.

Briñol, P., Petty, R. E., & Tormala, Z. L. (2004). The self-validation of cognitive responses to advertisements. *Journal of Consumer Research, 30,* 559–573.

Briñol, P., Petty, R. E., & Tormala, Z. L. (2006). The malleable meaning of subjective ease. *Psychological Science, 17,* 200–206.

Briñol, P., Petty, R. E., Valle, C., Rucker, D. D., & Becerra, A. (2007). The effects of message recipients' power before and after persuasion: A self-validation analysis. *Journal of Personality and Social Psychology, 93,* 1040–1053.

Cacioppo, J. T., & Petty, R. E. (1982). The need for cognition. *Journal of Personality and Social Psychology, 42,* 116–131.

Campbell, M. C., & Kirmani, A. (2000). Consumers' use of persuasion knowledge: The effects of accessibility and cognitive capacity on perceptions of an influence agent. *Journal of Consumer Research, 27,* 69–83.

Cesario, J., Grant, H., & Higgins, E. T. (2004). Regulatory fit and persuasion: Transfer from "feeling right." *Journal of Personality and Social Psychology, 86,* 388–404.

Cesario, J., Higgins, E. T., & Scholer, A. A. (2008). Regulatory fit and persuasion: Basic principles and remaining questions. *Social and Personality Psychology Compass, 2,* 444–463.

Clarkson, J. J., Tormala, Z. L., & Rucker, D. D. (2008). A new look at the consequences of attitude certainty: The amplification hypothesis. *Journal of Personality and Social Psychology, 95,* 810–825.

Cohen, J. B., & Reed, A. (2006). A multiple pathway anchoring and adjustment (MPAA) model of attitude generation and recruitment. *Journal of Consumer Research, 33,* 1–15.

Darke, P. R., & Ritchie, R. J. B. (2007). The defensive consumer: Advertising deception, defensive processing, and distrust. *Journal of Marketing Research, 44,* 114–127.

Fazio, R. H., & Zanna, M. P. (1978). Attitudinal qualities relating to the strength of the attitude–behavior relationship. *Journal of Experimental Social Psychology, 14,* 398–408.

Feldman, J. M., & Lynch, J. G., Jr. (1988). Self-generated validity and other effects of measurement on belief, attitude, intention, and behavior. *Journal of Applied Psychology, 73,* 421–435.

Friestad, M., & Wright, P. (1994). The persuasion knowledge model: How people cope with persuasion attempts. *Journal of Consumer Research, 21,* 1–31.

Friestad, M., & Wright, P. (1995). Persuasion knowledge: Lay peoples and researchers beliefs about the psychology of advertising. *Journal of Consumer Research, 22,* 62–74.

Gao, L., Wheeler, S. C., & Shiv, B. (2009). The "shaken self": Product choices as a means of restoring self-view confidence. *Journal of Consumer Research, 36,* 29–38.

Gross, S. R., Holtz, R., & Miller, N. (1995). Attitude certainty. In R.E. Petty & J. A.Krosnick (Eds.), *Attitude strength: Antecedents and consequences* (pp. 215–246). Mahwah, NJ: Lawrence Erlbaum Associates.

Herr, P. M., Kardes, F. R., & Kim, J. (1991). Effects of word-of-mouth and product-attribute information on persuasion—An accessibility–diagnosticity perspective. *Journal of Consumer Research, 17,* 454–462.

Higgins, E. T. (1987). Self-discrepancy—A theory relating self and affect. *Psychological Review, 94,* 319–340.

Higgins, E. T. (2000). Making a good decision: Value from fit. *American Psychologist, 55,* 1217–1230.

Janiszewski, C., & Meyvis, T. (2001). Effects of brand logo complexity, repetition, and spacing on processing fluency and judgment. *Journal of Consumer Research, 27,* 18–32.

Kahneman, D., Knetsch, J., & Thaler, R. (1990). Experimental test of the endowment effect and the Coase theorem. *Journal of Political Economy, 98,* 1325–1348.

Kirmani, A., & Campbell, M. C. (2004). Goal seeker and persuasion sentry: How consumer targets respond to interpersonal marketing persuasion. *Journal of Consumer Research, 31,* 573–582.

Labroo, A. A., Dhar, R., & Schwarz, N. (2008). Of frowning watches and frog wines: Semantic priming, perceptual fluency, and brand evaluation. *Journal of Consumer Research, 34,* 819–831.

Labroo, A. A., & Lee, A. Y. (2006). Between two brands: A goal fluency account of brand evaluation. *Journal of Marketing Research, 43,* 374–385.

Lee, A. Y. (2001). The mere exposure effect: An uncertainty reduction explanation revisited. *Personality and Social Psychology Bulletin, 27,* 1255–1266.

Lee, A. Y., & Aaker, J. L. (2004). Bringing the frame into focus: The influence of regulatory fit on processing fluency and persuasion. *Journal of Personality and Social Psychology, 86,* 205–218.

Lee, A. Y., & Labroo, A. A. (2004). The effect of conceptual and perceptual fluency on brand evaluation. *Journal of Marketing Research, 41,* 151–165.

Lynch, J. G. (2006). Accessibility–diagnosticity and the multiple pathway anchoring and adjustment model. *Journal of Consumer Research, 33,* 25–27.

Lynch, J. G., Marmorstein, H., & Weigold, M. F. (1988). Choices from sets including rememberd brands: Use of recalled attributes and prior overall evaluations. *Journal of Consumer Research, 15,* 169–184.

Maheswaran, D., & Chaiken, S. (1991). Promoting systematic processing in low-motivation settings—Effect of incongruent information on processing and judgment. *Journal of Personality and Social Psychology, 61,* 13–25.

Mayer, N. D., & Tormala, Z. L. (2010). "Think" versus "feel" framing effects in persuasion. *Personality and Social Psychology Bulletin, 36,* 443–454.

Menon, G., Raghubir, P., & Schwarz, N. (1995). Behavioral frequency judgments—An accessibility diagnosticity framework. *Journal of Consumer Research, 22,* 212–228.

Novemsky, N., Dhar, R., Schwarz, N., & Simonson, I. (2007). Preference fluency in consumer choice. *Journal of Marketing Research, 44,* 347–356.

Petrocelli, J. V., Tormala, Z. L., & Rucker, D. D. (2007). Unpacking attitude certainty: Attitude clarity and attitude correctness. *Journal of Personality and Social Psychology, 92,* 30–41.

Petty, R. E., Briñol, P., Tormala, Z. L., & Wegener, D. T. (2007). The role of metacognition in social judgment. In A. W. Kruglanski & E. T. Higgins (Eds.), *Social psychology: Handbook of basic principles* (2nd ed., pp. 254–284). New York, NY: Guilford Publishers.

Petty, R. E., DeSteno, D., & Rucker, D. (2001). The role of affect in persuasion and attitude change. In J. Forgas (Ed.), *Handbook of affect and social cognition* (pp. 212–233). Mahwah, NJ: Lawrence Erlbaum Associates.

Petty, R. E., Tormala, Z. L., & Rucker, D. D. (2004). Resistance to persuasion: An attitude strength perspective. In J. T. Jost, M. R. Banaji, & D. A. Prentice (Eds.), *Perspectivism in social psychology: The yin and yang of scientific progress* (pp. 37–51). Washington, DC: American Psychological Association.

Petty, R. E., & Wegener, D. T. (1993). Flexible correction processes in social judgment: Correcting for context-induced contrast. *Journal of Experimental Social Psychology, 29,* 137–165.

Petty, R. E., & Wegener, D. T. (1998). Attitude change: Multiple roles for persuasion variables. In D. Gilbert, S. Fiske, & G. Lindzey (Eds.), *The handbook of social psychology* (4th ed., Vol. 1, pp. 323–390). New York, NY: McGraw-Hill.

Pham, M. (2004). The logic of feeling. *Journal of Consumer Psychology, 14,* 360–369.

Pham, M. T., & Muthukrishnan, A. V. (2002). Search and alignment in judgment revision: Implications for brand positioning. *Journal of Marketing Research, 39,* 18–30.

Rucker, D. D. (2009). Compensatory consumption: How threat directs consumers' product preferences. *Advances in Consumer Research, 36,* 131–134.

Rucker, D. D., & Galinsky, A. (2008). Desire to acquire: Powerlessness and compensatory consumption. *Journal of Consumer Research, 35,* 257–267.

Rucker, D. D., & Galinsky, A. D. (2009). Conspicuous consumption versus utilitarian ideals: How different levels of power shape consumer behavior. *Journal of Experimental Social Psychology, 45,* 549–555.

Rucker, D. D., & Petty, R. E. (2004). When resistance is futile: Consequences of failed counterarguing for attitude certainty. *Journal of Personality and Social Psychology, 86,* 219–235.

Rucker, D. D., & Petty, R. E. (2006). Increasing the effectiveness of communications to consumers: Recommendations based on elaboration likelihood and attitude certainty perspectives. *Journal of Public Policy & Marketing, 25,* 39–52.

Rucker, D. D., Petty, R. E., & Briñol, P. (2008). What's in a frame anyway? A metacognitive analysis of the impact of one- versus two-sided message framing on attitude certainty. *Journal of Consumer Psychology, 18,* 137–149.

Rucker, D. D., & Sternthal, B. (2011). Advertising strategy. In A. M. Tybout & B. Calder (Eds.), *Kellogg on marketing* (pp. 209–231). Hoboken, NJ: John Wiley & Sons, Inc.

Sanbonmatsu, D. M., Kardes, F. R., & Herr, P. (1992). The role of prior knowledge and missing information in multi-attribute evaluation. *Organizational Behavior and Human Decision Processes, 51,* 76–91.

Schwarz, N. (2004). Metacognitive experiences in consumer judgment and decision making. *Journal of Consumer Psychology, 14,* 332–348.

Schwarz, N., Bless, H., Strack, F., Klumpp, G., Rittenauerschatka, H., & Simons, A. (1991). Ease of retrieval as information—Another look at the availability heuristic. *Journal of Personality and Social Psychology, 61,* 195–202.

Schwarz, N., & Clore, G. L. (2003). Mood as information: 20 years later. *Psychological Inquiry, 14,* 296–303.

Simmons, J. P., & Nelson, L. D. (2006). Intuitive confidence: Choosing between intuitive and nonintuitive alternatives. *Journal of Experimental Psychology: General, 135,* 409–428.

Simonson, I. (1993). Get closer to your customers by understanding how they make choices. *California Management Review, 35,* 68–84.

Sternthal, B., & Rucker, D. D. (2009). *Advertising strategy.* Acton, MA: Copley Custom Textbooks.

Thomas, M., & Morwitz, V. G. (2009). The ease of computation effect: The interplay of metacognitive experiences and naïve theories in judgments of price difference. *Journal of Marketing Research, 46,* 81–91.

Tormala, Z. L., Clarkson, J. J., & Petty, R. E. (2006). Resisting persuasion by the skin of one's teeth: The hidden success of resisted persuasive messages. *Journal of Personality and Social Psychology, 91,* 423–435.

Tormala, Z. L., Falces, C., Briñol, P., & Petty, R. E. (2007). Ease of retrieval effects in social judgment: The role of unrequested cognitions. *Journal of Personality and Social Psychology, 93,* 143–157.

Tormala, Z. L., Henderson, M. D., & Clarkson, J. J. (2010). It's not just the speed that counts: Perceived evaluation duration and attitude certainty. In M. C. Campbell, J. Inman, & R. Pieters (Eds.), *Advances in Consumer Research,* 188–189.

Tormala, Z. L., & Petty, R. E. (2002). What doesn't kill me makes me stronger: The effects of resisting persuasion on attitude certainty. *Journal of Personality and Social Psychology, 83,* 1298–1313.

Tormala, Z. L., & Petty, R. E. (2004a). Source credibility and attitude certainty: A metacognitive analysis of resistance to persuasion. *Journal of Consumer Psychology, 14,* 427–442.

Tormala, Z. L., & Petty, R. E. (2004b). Resistance to persuasion and attitude certainty: A metacognitive analysis. In E. S. Knowles & J. A. Linn (Eds.), *Resistance and persuasion* (pp. 65–82). Mahwah, NJ: Lawrence Erlbaum Associates.

Tormala, Z. L., Petty, R. E., & Briñol, P. (2002). Ease of retrieval effects in persuasion: A self-validation analysis. *Personality and Social Psychology Bulletin, 28,* 1700–1712.

Tormala, Z. L., & Rucker, D. D. (2007). Attitude certainty: A review of past findings and emerging perspectives. *Social and Personality Psychology Compass, 1,* 469–492.

Tybout, A. M., Sternthal, B., Malaviya, P., Bakamitsos, G. A., & Park, S. B. (2005). Information accessibility as a moderator of judgments: The role of content versus retrieval ease. *Journal of Consumer Research, 32,* 76–85.

Vohs, K. D., Baumeister, R. F., & Chin, J. (2007). Feeling duped: Emotional, motivational, and cognitive aspects of being exploited by others. *Review of General Psychology, 11,* 127–141.

Wan, E. W., Rucker, D. D., Tormala, Z. L., & Clarkson, J. J. (2010). The effects of regulatory depletion on attitude certainty. *Journal of Marketing Research, 47,* 531–541.

Wänke, M., Bohner, G., & Jurkowitsch, A. (1997). There are many reasons to drive a BMW: Does imagined ease of argument generation influence attitudes? *Journal of Consumer Research, 24,* 170–177.

Wright, P., Friestad, M., & Boush, D. M. (2005). The development of marketplace persuasion knowledge in children, adolescents, and young adults. *Journal of Public Policy & Marketing, 24,* 222–233.

17

Metacognition and Psychological Therapy

ADRIAN WELLS

INTRODUCTION

*P*sychological disorder is characterized by perseveration of negative thoughts and a sense of diminished control of these experiences. It seems crucial, therefore that we should aim to understand the factors that underlie mental control and the cessation or continuation of some but not all thoughts.

Until recently, the cognitive revolution in psychological therapies has focused on the content of negative thoughts rather than the regulation of thinking. Beck (1976) and Ellis (1962) in their respective cognitive and rational emotive therapies located psychological disorder at the level of the content of schemas or irrational beliefs about the social and physical self and the world. These should be challenged and reality tested during the course of treatment. The idea is that such beliefs are rigid, containing absolutistic rules and standards that cannot be achieved or giving rise to biased interpretations.

However, most individuals have negative thoughts and beliefs and yet they do not develop long-term psychological problems. A basic premise of metacognitive therapy theory is that emotional and psychological recovery from the experience of negative thoughts and beliefs is normal and common. These experiences become abnormal and meet the criteria of psychological disorder when they are repetitive and persistent (Wells & Matthews, 1994, 1996).

If we assume that negative thoughts and beliefs are usually transient, then we must begin to address a fundamental question: What is it that causes mental persistence? Cognitive theories suggest a crucial role of behaviors. In anxiety, for instance, avoidance of situations may prevent the habituation of anxiety or the challenging of erroneous beliefs. But this does not acknowledge that negative beliefs and thoughts can be reasonably accurate and there remain ways of avoiding psychological disorder—for instance, by changing the way we relate to these inner experiences.

A conundrum presented by content-based models is that they crucially depend on general beliefs about the self and world (e.g., "I'm a failure"), generating persistent negative thinking. This level of explanation does not account for how people may have different reactions to such a belief. One person may dismiss the belief as being overly self-critical but another may spend days analyzing why he is a failure. The point I am making is that the control of cognition and action is separate from the content of ordinary beliefs and thoughts. It is the control of sustained negative thinking that is a more direct source of disorder.

Elsewhere in this volume, cognition has been labeled *primary cognition* and metacognition labeled *secondary cognition*. However, the metacognitive model described in this chapter views metacognition as both primary and secondary. Metacognition is secondary when it focuses on appraising a thought, but it is primary when it is a control process that initiates a new train of thoughts and when it becomes the focus of change.

The separation of content of "primary cognition" from the control of cognition (secondary cognition) is important because it redirects the emphasis of treatment. It moves away from reality-testing negative beliefs about the self and world to modifying the knowledge and strategies that are responsible for controlling and monitoring thinking. In other words, as I have argued for some time, we should turn our attention to metacognition.

Both cognitive therapy and metacognitive therapy involve teaching patients to think about their thoughts. On this level, they both involve instruction in metacognition. However, there are crucial differences. Cognitive therapy aims to change the content of primary cognition while metacognitive therapy aims to change the content of secondary cognition (metacognition). Furthermore, metacognitive therapy (Wells, 2000) explicitly enhances metacognitive control skills but cognitive–behavior therapy (CBT) does not. Metacognitive therapy (MCT) focuses on reducing thinking so that clients do not "overthink" while CBT maintains thinking as the individual reality-tests negative thoughts, identifies errors in his or her thinking, or attempts problem solving.

In this chapter, I describe the metacognitive model of disorder and for illustrative purposes briefly show how it is applied in the treatment of traumatic stress reactions. The data supporting the proposed role of metacognition in psychological disorder and its treatment are briefly reviewed.

THE METACOGNITIVE MODEL OF PSYCHOLOGICAL DISORDER

A basic premise of the metacognitive approach (Wells, 2009; Wells & Matthews, 1994) is that psychological disorder is closely associated with a specific form of extended thinking that maintains a sense of threat to the physical, social, or psychological self. This extended thinking is called the cognitive attentional syndrome (CAS; Wells & Matthews, 1994). It comprises chains of conceptual activity in the form of worry and rumination, a fixation of attention on threat, a preoccupation with memory, and coping behaviors that have ironic effects of interfering with more appropriate metacognitive control and metacognitive belief change.

For instance, the person suffering from generalized anxiety disorder reacts to the negative thought, "What if my partner has had an accident?" by trying to work out how she would cope with this and similar events. This extended negative thinking process, called worry, prolongs and strengthens negative ideas and the sense of threat. To take another example, the person with a history of depression responds to feelings of low motivation with the thought, "I must work out if this is my illness returning." This thought marks a metacognitive directive of focusing on and trying to think about symptoms and conveys the implicit message that symptoms are a sign of danger. Thus, negative feelings and the sense of threat (from emotion itself) are maintained.

As we have seen earlier, psychological disorder results from the thinking pattern that is activated in response to a negative thought or emotion. Those patterns that extend negative thinking and/or lead to a greater awareness of threat are the direct cause of psychological disorder.

Anatomy of the CAS

The CAS consists of chains of perseverative conceptual activity in the form of worry and rumination. Worry focuses on possible future threats and planning of avoidance and ways of coping; it features chains of "what if…" questions. Rumination focuses on the past and analyzes the meaning of and reasons for events. It largely consists of questions such as "Why?" and "What does it mean?" and statements such as "if only…." In disorders such as posttraumatic stress disorder (PTSD), perseveration can take the form of dwelling on the memory of events and trying to fill gaps in memory. This process has been termed "gap filling" (Wells, 2009).

In addition to this, the CAS comprises fixation of attention on threat. In emotional disorder, threat is often internal, such as the occurrence of certain unwanted thoughts in obsessive–compulsive disorder, bodily sensations in health anxiety, or memories in trauma. Threats can be external, such as the presence of stains that could be feared contaminants in obsessive–compulsive disorder, or people who could be potential assailants in someone recovering from PTSD following an assault.

There are other coping behaviors that form components of the CAS; these are the ones that backfire because they contribute to the maintenance of negative beliefs and failures to terminate extended thinking—for example, strategies that consist of trying to avoid or suppress certain kinds of thoughts. Suppression can be associated with ironic effects of increasing intrusions or awareness of the target material. When coping strategies are appraised as effectively preventing threat, the person may fail to revise erroneous beliefs. For example, the patient with obsessional thoughts responds to an intrusion of thoughts of harming someone by locking away all knives in the home. Thus, the person fails to discover that intrusive thoughts do not lead to the commission of unwanted acts, and erroneous beliefs about thoughts and fear of them persist.

The consequence of activation of the CAS is that it maintains a sense of threat. Worry and rumination focus processing on negative information and threat monitoring increases the perception of danger. Coping behaviors prevent disconfirmation of erroneous beliefs and disrupt the self-regulation of cognition.

Metacognition and the CAS

The CAS is a manifestation of the control that metacognition exerts on processing. The model identifies two broad domains of metacognitive beliefs that influence choice of cognitive style in response to negative thoughts and emotions. These two domains are (1) positive metacognitions and (2) negative metacognitions. The former are beliefs about the advantages of worry, rumination, gap filling, and threat monitoring. For example, the person with generalized anxiety believes: "Worrying will help me avoid problems in the future." The hypochondriacal patient believes: "Thinking the worst about my symptoms means I won't miss something important." In traumatic stress there are similar positive beliefs about worry and rumination and also beliefs about the need for a complete memory (e.g., "Remembering everything that happened will help me avoid similar threats in the future."). Metacognitions concerning attention focus on the usefulness of monitoring for potential threats. Some examples include the following: "Focusing on symptoms of sadness will help me know when I'm getting better" and "Being alert to threats in the street will help me avoid problems."

Negative metacognitions concern the uncontrollability, danger, and importance of thoughts. Examples include:

"Worrying is uncontrollable."
"Some thoughts could make me lose control."
"Thoughts of harming someone will make me do it."
"Thinking bad thoughts means I'm a bad person."
"Worrying too much could damage my body."

Negative metacognitions lead to the appraisal of thoughts as dangerous, thus contributing to worry, perseveration, and a sense of threat. The belief that thoughts are uncontrollable leads to a failure to interrupt chains of worry and rumination. In each instance, metacognition leads to the persistence of thinking that maintains psychological disturbance.

Metacognitive beliefs as described here have been represented as propositional knowledge, but they may be better conceptualized as programs or procedural knowledge involved in the monitoring and control of cognition in pursuit of goals. Closely associated with each of these propositions is a generic program for monitoring and controlling cognition. Thus, metacognitive therapy should be viewed not simply as changing the content of metacognitive knowledge, but rather as modifying monitoring and control processes, effectively giving rise to new and alternative plans for processing. This may be equated with enhancing flexible executive control over processing and modifying the way in which individuals experience inner mental events.

Modes and the Nature of Direct Mental Experience

Absence of a clear distinction between cognition and metacognition in earlier psychological therapies has meant that the focus of CBT has been on reality-testing negative thoughts or training problem solving or emotional coping strategies. A focus on the validity of thoughts is only one means of responding to cognition, and additional possibilities emerge from the metacognitive analysis. Rather than testing the validity of individual negative thoughts, such as the thought that "I'm foolish," the metacognitive approach tests metacognitive beliefs and enables individuals to develop a new perspective in relation to thoughts more directly. It does so by altering the nature of metacognitive awareness and changing the type of response made to thinking.

Conscious mental experience may be usefully divided into modes that represent a default "object mode" or an alternative "metacognitive mode" of processing (Wells, 2000). In object mode, thoughts are experienced as facts and are indistinct from direct perception of reality. In metacognitive mode, thoughts are seen as separate from the individual as perceiver and separate from external events. In this latter mode, thoughts are objectified and can be more readily seen as passing events in the mind. For example, when asked to give a presentation, a person with public speaking anxiety turns attention inward onto an image of the self appearing foolish and anxious. This person is in object mode and fails to recognize that processing is dominated by an inner image of the self rather than processing the external environment. In metacognitive mode, the same person can see the inner image as a thought within a broader landscape and choose to redirect attention onto the reactions of others and the task at hand.

When individuals can step back from the negative thoughts, they can apply control over extended thinking. One of the goals of metacognitive therapy is to help the individual develop the metacognitive knowledge and skills to enable such a shift in modes and to interrupt the CAS.

An implication of the metacognitive approach is that, in order to be effective, all treatments, whether they focus on cognitive content or use exposure methods, will depend on metacognitive change to realize their effects. However, in these therapies, such changes occur fortuitously rather than by direct intention.

EVIDENCE FOR THE METACOGNITIVE MODEL OF DISORDER

Having introduced the central features of the metacognitive theory, in this section the empirical evidence is summarized. Later in the chapter, treatment is described and evidence of its effectiveness presented.

The CAS: Worry and Rumination

It is now reasonably well established that worry and rumination have deleterious consequences for emotional and cognitive regulation, thus supporting the hypothesized impact of specific forms of perseverative thinking on psychological disorder.

Brief periods of induced worry lead to an increase in subsequent intrusive thoughts (Borkovec, Robinson, Pruzinsky, & DePree, 1983; York, Borkovec, Vasey, & Stern, 1987). Instructing participants to worry after exposure to a stressful stimulus is associated with an increase in intrusive thoughts over the following 3 days (Butler, Wells, & Dewick, 1995; Wells & Papageorgiou, 1995).

Studies of rumination have explored the effects of induced rumination and of individual differences in rumination cross-sectionally and longitudinally. Rumination leads to prolonged and more severe periods of depression than distraction and it predicts future depressive episodes (see Lyubomirsky & Tkach, 2004, for a review).

Rumination affects cognition, motivation, and problem solving behavior in stressful situations (Nolen-Hoeksema & Morrow, 1991). It reduces motivation to engage in pleasant activities (Lyubomirsky & Nolen-Hoeksema, 1993) and impairs cognitive performance (Hertel, 1998).

In a community study of more than 1,100 adults, those who showed clinical depression and a ruminative style at initial assessment had more severe and longer lasting depression 1 year later, were less likely to enter remission, and were more likely to show anxiety (Nolen-Hoeksema, 2000).

Metacognitive Control Strategies

A central concept in metacognitive therapy theory is that vulnerable individuals use ineffective or inappropriate forms of mental control. They are ineffective because they backfire and lead to ironic effects of lower levels of subjective control of cognition, they prevent disconfirmation of negative beliefs about thoughts, and some extend negative thinking rather than terminating it. Worry and rumination are seen as part of the individual's strategy for dealing with negative thoughts and emotions rather than being viewed simply as symptoms of emotional disorder.

Evidence from studies of the effects of attempts to suppress a target thought such as the thought of a "white bear" have demonstrated that this can have immediate effects of enhancing the thought or a delayed effect of increasing intrusions (Purdon, 1999; Wegner, Schnedier, Carter, & White, 1987). However, the immediate or delayed effect is not entirely consistent across studies. More consistent findings have emerged from self-report of metacognitive control strategies.

Wells and Davies (1994) developed the thought control questionnaire (TCQ) to assess the maladaptive strategies postulated in the metacognitive model. The TCQ has five subscales, each assessing different sets of strategies for dealing with unpleasant and/or unwanted thoughts. The subscales are worry, punishment, social control, reappraisal, and distraction. Two of these strategies—worry and punishment—are considered problematic in the metacognitive model.

A large number of studies examining relationships between different symptoms or disorders and the TCQ subscales have been published. It has been consistently demonstrated that worry and punishment are elevated in patient samples and that one or both of these dimensions correlate positively with symptoms of anxiety (Amir, Cashman, & Foa, 1997; Coles & Hiemberg, 2005), traumatic stress (Warda & Bryant, 1998), depression (Wells & Carter, 2009), hallucination proneness, and personality pathology (Rosenthal, Cukrowicz, Cheavens, & Lynch, 2006). Other studies have shown that individuals with schizophrenia use greater worry and punishment and fewer distraction strategies than nonpatient controls (Morrison & Wells, 2000).

These studies demonstrate reliable associations between psychological disorder and specific patterns of metacognitive control characterized by extended negative thinking in the form of worry and self-punitive ideation and behavior.

Metacognitive Knowledge/Beliefs

The metacognitive model proposes that positive and negative metacognitive beliefs should be positively associated with the CAS and psychological disorder. The predominant measure of metacognitive beliefs tapping these domains is the metacognitions questionnaire (MCQ; Cartwright-Hatton & Wells, 1997; Wells & Cartwright-Hatton, 2004).

As predicted, the MCQ subscales show significant positive correlations with measures of psychological vulnerability such as trait anxiety (Cartwright-Hatton & Wells, 1997) and worry (Wells & Papageorgiou, 1998). Reliable links between metacognitive beliefs and monitoring and obsessive–compulsive symptoms have been demonstrated by several groups (Hermans, Martens, De Cort, Pieters, & Eelen, 2003; Janeck, Calamari, Riemann, & Heffelfinger, 2003).

In the area of vulnerability to psychotic symptoms, positive relationships with metacognitive beliefs have been found (Morrison, Wells, & Nothard, 2000; Stirling, Barkus, & Lewis, 2007). Lobban, Haddock, Kinderman, and Wells (2002) investigated differences between schizophrenic patients who were currently experiencing hallucinations and those who had never experienced them. The control groups were patients with anxiety disorders and nonpatients. Current hallucinators had higher scores on beliefs about the uncontrollability and danger of thoughts than the anxiety group and higher scores on cognitive self-consciousness than nonpatients.

Different disorders appear to be characterized by different metacognitions within the broad positive and negative domains. For example, obsessive–compulsive symptoms are associated with beliefs about the power and importance of thoughts (e.g., "My thoughts alone have the power to change the course of events."). In posttraumatic stress, beliefs concern the nature of memory (e.g., "If I remember everything, I'll be able to move on.") and in depression they focus on rumination (e.g., "If I analyze why I feel like this, I'll find a solution to my depression."). There are also common metacognitions, and in each disorder there is the belief that thinking is uncontrollable. Metacognitive beliefs (secondary cognition) appear to be a better correlate of symptoms than primary cognition (e.g., Bennett & Wells, 2010).

Causal Status of Metacognition

It is evident from the preceding summary of studies that metacognitive control strategies and metacognitive beliefs are reliably and meaningfully associated with psychological disorder and symptoms of emotional distress. While this is important data, it does not address the direct and indirect causal effects linked with metacognition. In order to examine this question, we now turn attention to studies that have used longitudinal designs or have manipulated metacognition.

Prospective studies have investigated the temporal precedence of metacognitive beliefs or metacognitive coping strategies. In these studies, beliefs about the uncontrollability and danger of worry predicted the development of generalized anxiety several weeks later (Nassif, 1999). Similarly, negative beliefs about thoughts predicted the development of depression over 12 weeks (Papageorgiou & Wells, 2009) and the subsequent development of obsessive–compulsive symptoms (Myers, Fisher, & Wells, 2009; Sica, Steketee, Ghisi, Chiri, & Franceschini, 2007). Apart from beliefs, metacognitive control strategies have been shown to predict later PTSD symptoms (Roussis & Wells, 2008) and the development of PTSD after motor vehicle accidents (Holeva, Tarrier, & Wells, 2001).

Rassin, Merckelbach, Muris, and Spaan (1999) manipulated metacognitive beliefs about thought suppression and tested the effects on intrusive thoughts and discomfort. Some participants were led to believe that an EEG apparatus could detect the thought "apple" and that, on doing so, an electric shock would be delivered to another participant. Other participants were told that the apparatus could detect the thought but no information about electric shocks was given. Those subjects were led to believe that thoughts that had significance showed greater discomfort, more internally directed anger, and greater efforts to avoid thinking.

Reuven-Magril, Rosenman, Liberman, and Dar (2009) manipulated metacognitive beliefs about the ease of suppressing scratching. Participants were asked to suppress scratching while working on a questionnaire that presented scratching-related situations. Some participants were told that suppressing scratching is quite easy for everyone; other subjects were told that suppressing scratching is very difficult for everybody. The "easy for everybody" group scratched more than the "difficult for everybody" group. Thus, a manipulation of beliefs had effects on post-suppression rebound of suppressed behavior (scratching); however, it is not entirely clear that the beliefs manipulated were purely metacognitive.

The Effects of Recovery and Treatment on Metacognition

A small number of studies have begun to explore the impact of recovery or psychological treatments on metacognition. These studies show that (1) improvement in symptoms is correlated with metacognitive change, (2) metacognition predicts relapse following treatment, and (3) change in metacognition is a better predictor of symptom improvement than change in cognition.

Reynolds and Wells (1999) tested patients with depression and/or PTSD on two occasions. Recovered subjects used distraction more than unrecovered subjects, and distraction increased with recovery while it remained the same in those who were unrecovered. The use of punishment to deal with intrusive thoughts decreased with recovery. A main effect was obtained for worry with those who recovered using less worry. Bryant, Moulds, and Guthrie (2001) examined changes in thought control strategies following treatment for acute stress disorder. Treatment led to reductions in worry and punishment and increases in the use of social control and reappraisal.

Spada, Caselli, and Wells (2009) investigated the role of emotion and metacognition in predicting drinking status among problem drinkers 3, 6, and 12 months following a course of cognitive–behavior therapy. Beliefs about the need to control thoughts measured before treatment predicted drinking status at 3 and 6 months and level of weekly alcohol use at 3, 6, and 12 months. These relationships were independent of negative emotion and initial severity of alcohol use.

Solem, Haland, Vogel, Hansen, and Wells (2009) examined belief change in 83 outpatients with obsessive–compulsive disorder undergoing treatment using exposure and response prevention. Metacognitive beliefs (secondary cognition) and "ordinary" beliefs (i.e., primary cognition—responsibility, perfectionism) changed during treatment. Changes in metacognitive beliefs explained 22% of the variance in symptoms at posttreatment when controlling for pretreatment symptoms and mood. Only decreases in metacognitive beliefs, but not change in primary cognition, predicted posttreatment symptom levels when the overlap between them was controlled.

METACOGNITIVE THERAPY

The aim of MCT is removal of the CAS and modification of negative and positive metacognitive beliefs. This depends on strategies used to detect and interrupt the CAS, which can be construed as building new metacognitive regulation routines and skills. Experiential change strategies are also used; they are aimed at challenging the content of metacognitive beliefs. Detailed treatment manuals describing the implementation of this treatment have been published (Wells, 2000, 2009).

Treatment is typically implemented in a series of 12 sessions and proceeds on the basis of disorder-specific metacognitive models. One might ask why individual models are required when a universal process, the CAS, has been linked to disorder. Indeed, one of the implications of this approach is that a generic treatment can be used across most types of psychological disturbance. However, there is specificity in the content of negative and positive metacognitive beliefs in individual disorders and some variability in features of the CAS.

Metacognitive treatment follows a series of stages. In the first, the therapist works with the client to generate a case conceptualization based on the model being used. This is followed by socializing to the model. Here the therapist helps the patient to see how negative emotions are maintained by worry, rumination, and coping behaviors such as thought suppression.

Socialization

Socialization involves sharing the case conceptualization and using guided discovery to illustrate the effects depicted in the model. In particular, the therapist may ask the patient what happens to anxiety or mood when he or she continues to worry or ruminate and then presents the question: "What would happen if you could do this less?" Other questions that might be used include: "What would happen to your anxiety if you discovered that you could control your worrying?" or "If you discovered that your intrusive thoughts were meaningless, how much of a problem would you have left?"

The socialization process begins to shift the patient out of the "object mode" of processing and toward the "metacognitive mode" in which new knowledge about thoughts and ways of experiencing them can be achieved.

Once initial socialization is accomplished, the therapist proceeds by challenging beliefs about the uncontrollability of worry/rumination. This is achieved through verbal methods such as questioning the patient to help him or her discover that he or she has, at times, been distracted from worrying and also asking how the process stops if it is truly out of control. This is a prerequisite to the introduction of direct experiential techniques that involve learning to relate to the thoughts that trigger worry and rumination in a new way. This is through detached mindfulness and worry/rumination postponement.

Detached Mindfulness

In the context of metacognitive modes of processing, a particular style of relating to inner mental events has been identified as advantageous for emotional recovery. This metacognitive style is called detached mindfulness (DM; Wells & Matthews, 1994). Detached mindfulness is the antithesis of the cognitive attentional syndrome. As the name implies, it consists of mindfulness and detachment.

Mindfulness refers to becoming aware of a thought (meta-awareness) and learning to discriminate an initial negative thought that normally acts as a trigger for the CAS from subsequent responses to it. It also comprises detachment, which refers to stopping any response to the thought and also seeing oneself as an observer separate from the thought. DM is introduced and achieved through the use of metaphors and a series of exercises in treatment. The goal of these exercises is to develop metacognitive modes of experiencing, to interrupt the CAS in response to thoughts, and to develop flexibility and choice in the implementation of metacognitive control.

An example of a task used to build knowledge and DM skills is the "free association task." Here, the therapist instructs the patient to listen passively to a series of words and watch the flow of consciousness without influencing or controlling thinking in any way. Between six and 10 words are then slowly articulated (e.g., apple, bicycle, birthday, seaside, friend, tree). At the end of the exercise, the therapist asks if the patient succeeded in passively observing mental events and determines that any thoughts that occurred were spontaneous experiences as intended. The therapist also asks, "What happened to the first thought by the end?" In this way, the patient is helped to see how detaching from thoughts, from the process of mental control, and active sustained thinking permit the spontaneous decay of ideas. This can be contrasted with the strategies that the patient normally uses in response to negative thoughts.

The concept of detached mindfulness resonates somewhat with the inclusion of mindfulness-based meditation practices in recent cognitive therapies as a means of reducing depressive relapse (e.g., Teasdale et al., 2000). However, there are differences in the origins and nature of these techniques. Meditation is diverse, incorporating many more components than DM, such as focusing on present-moment experience, using the breath as an anchor to bring attention back to the present, concepts of acceptance, and cultivating a "beginner's mind" (e.g., Kabat-Zinn, 1994). The complexity and diverse nature of these concepts means that it is difficult to interpret or predict the impact of such practices on metacognition and sustained processing. It is likely that meditation will increase facets such as metacognitive awareness, but the effects on executive control and metacognitive beliefs remain to be explored. The more specific features of DM include discriminating triggering thoughts and subsequent worry- or rumination-based responses, and directing the individual to suspend any further conceptual processing.

Worry/Rumination Postponement

Following the introduction of detached mindfulness, the therapist continues to work on interrupting worry and rumination processes. The patient is instructed to disengage worry and rumination in response to negative thoughts or beliefs when they are activated. The therapist introduces the idea that they should be postponed until a specified time later in the day. This designated "worry time" can be used to think through problems, but it is emphasized that it is not necessary to use the worry time. The whole postponement procedure is usually presented in the form of an explicit experiment to begin challenging metacognitive beliefs that worry/rumination are uncontrollable. During this process, the therapist monitors the level of belief in uncontrollability with the aim of decreasing it to 0%. This usually requires refinements of the postponement experiment and additional procedures as outlined in the next section.

Treatment proceeds with monitoring the frequency and duration of subsequent worry and rumination episodes, and use of DM and postponement is strengthened and generalized. In the treatment of obsessive–compulsive disorder, the postponement strategy is also applied to overt and covert rituals that are normally used in response to intrusions.

Challenging Negative and Positive Metabeliefs

The next step involves more intensive challenging of negative beliefs about thoughts. This is done using verbal restructuring methods such as questioning the evidence supporting such beliefs, reviewing counterevidence, and questioning and challenging the mechanism by which thoughts are important or dangerous.

Behavioral experiments are used to demonstrate that thoughts are unimportant or harmless. For example, the person who believes that worrying could lead to mental breakdown or loss of control is asked to worry intensely to see if he or she can lose control of the activity or induce hallucinations. The patient with obsessions who believes that thoughts have the power to cause unwanted acts is invited to test this by having thoughts, such as thoughts of hitting the therapist, to see if this actually happens.

Once negative beliefs are effectively challenged, the therapist works on positive metacognitive beliefs about the need to worry, ruminate, engage in threat monitoring, and suppress or control thoughts. These beliefs are modified in a way similar to modification of negative beliefs by using verbal reattribution and a range of behavioral experiments that have been devised for this purpose. For example, the therapist questions the mechanism by which worry or rumination can have positive outcomes and helps the patient to see how these processes are biased and therefore unlikely to be helpful. Experiments include the "worry-modulation experiment," in which a person is asked to predict outcomes if he or she worries more or worries less. The individual can be asked to increase his or her worry and then decrease worry while performing a daily task to determine if outcomes really change for the better when worry occurs.

New Plans for Processing and Relapse Prevention

Toward the end of treatment, relapse prevention strategies are implemented. This consists of reviewing metacognitive belief levels and working on any residual beliefs. Disorder-specific or generic scales are used to assess the level of beliefs and intensity of the CAS during the course of treatment and can reveal residual issues that require attention. If necessary, the therapist works more to reduce negative and positive metacognitive beliefs and abandonment of unhelpful coping strategies.

Relapse prevention also consists of writing out a "therapy blueprint" summarizing what has been learned in therapy and a copy of a "new plan for processing." The new plan consists of a summary of the old way of dealing with negative ideas, which describes features of the CAS. The new plan is a summary of new and alternative responses to thoughts. It involves viewing thoughts as separate from the sense of self, remaining detached from them, postponing or banning worry/rumination, increasing activities in the presence of self-defeating thoughts, and banning other unhelpful coping strategies such as threat monitoring and avoidance.

A BRIEF ILLUSTRATION: TREATMENT OF PTSD

The metacognitive model of PTSD (Wells, 2000, 2009) is presented in Figure 17.1. Following a traumatic event, the majority of individuals recover over a period of days or weeks. However, the activation of the CAS resulting from biases in metacognitive knowledge or features of the environment (e.g., repeated and uncontrollable stresses) interferes with this process. As a result, the sense of threat persists and arousal is maintained, contributing to the formation of PTSD.

After a traumatic event, the person who develops PTSD responds to intrusive thoughts or memories with worry about danger in the future, rumination about the causes or meaning of the event, focusing attention on future sources of threat, and a preoccupation with memory. For instance, individuals often engage in "gap filling" consisting of going over memories and trying to make them complete. The metacognitive beliefs behind this behavior include positive beliefs, such as "Filling in all the gaps will help me understand how to prevent this from happening again," and negative beliefs, "Unless I have a complete memory I will never get over it." There are similar positive and negative beliefs about worry and rumination and about "threat monitoring" (e.g., "If I'm vigilant for potential danger I'll be safe."). This constellation of metacognitions and the CAS lead to a persistence of a sense

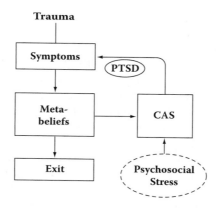

Figure 17.1   The metacognitive model of PTSD. (From Wells, A. 2009. *Metacognitive therapy for anxiety and depression*, p. 129. New York, NY: Guilford Press.)

of threat. In addition, the individual often holds negative beliefs about the significance of thoughts about the trauma, leading to a further sense of threat from the symptoms themselves.

In treatment, the therapist helps the patient to see how the CAS maintains anxiety with the aid of a personalized case formulation based on the model in Figure 17.1. To engage the client, the therapist explains how recovery from trauma can occur spontaneously, but that it has been blocked by the person's thinking style. This spontaneous psychological healing process is likened to the body's inbuilt capacity for healing itself. The therapist explains how this might be impaired by trying to make healing happen rather than allowing it to occur in the background in its own way. The patient is guided toward discovering that responding to intrusive thoughts, memories, and emotions with worry and thought suppression is like constantly working on a wound and that these processes prevent the individual from moving on from the trauma.

In the next step, the patient is helped to distinguish between spontaneously occurring intrusive thoughts and the subsequent worry/rumination or gap-filling response connected with them. This is followed by introducing alternative responses of detached mindfulness and worry/rumination postponement and the banning of gap filling. In order to achieve this, erroneous beliefs about the uncontrollability of worry and rumination are challenged and work on positive beliefs about the need to engage these styles, such as the advantages/disadvantages analysis, is undertaken. The following dialogue illustrates the nature of this guided discovery focusing on metacognitive level change:

Therapist: In the past week, how much time have you spent in going over the trauma?
Patient: I think about it most of the time.
T: Do you think there are any advantages to doing that?
P: It will help to remember exactly what happened so I can avoid similar situations in the future. I try to remember how I turned the wheel when the car was skidding and whether I could have braked earlier.

T: Do you think there are any disadvantages with going over things and trying to fill gaps in your memory?

P: Well, I suppose I can't forget about it, but I don't want it to happen again.

T: How long have you been going over it like this?

P: Since the accident, about 9 months.

T: Have you found an answer yet that will help you avoid this in the future?

P: No. I can't remember what happened just before the accident; I just remember some of the time being awake afterward.

T: So how much longer will it take before you can find the answer in this way?

P: Maybe I can't. But it would be hard for me to stop thinking about it.

T: Perhaps it isn't so black and white. It's not a matter of not thinking about it. Could you try to postpone going over the event the next time you have a thought about what happened?

P: I'm not sure; if I don't work it through, I'll never get it out of my mind.

T: Do you have any evidence that the thought will remain if you don't do this?

P: Not really. I haven't tried just to leave it alone.

T: Let's explore some ways that you can do just that. Then we can see what happens?

P: Okay, I'm willing to try.

T: When you notice a thought about the accident, I want you to be aware of that thought but choose to put aside any analysis or trying to fill the gaps in what happened until a time between 7 p.m. and 7:15 p.m. When that time arrives, you may engage in your analysis and gap filling, but this is not compulsory and hopefully you will decide it is not necessary.

P: But I'm not sure I can just leave the thought alone. When I think of it, I feel scared—like I'm going to be hurt again, so I try not to think it or I go over what I could do to avoid accidents in the future.

T: Let's look at what it's like to leave the thought alone. We can practice a technique called detached mindfulness so you can develop that ability.

P: Okay.

T: What don't you like to think about?

P: I don't like to think about the car and driving.

P: Okay, I'm going to draw an outline of a car on the glass window over there. Now, I'd like you to look at that outline. How does that make you feel?

P: Not too bad. I know it's only a drawing

T: Can you look through that image at the scene outside? What do you see?

P: I can see the clouds in the sky and the trees.

T: The next time you have a thought, can you react to it in that way—just look through it and do nothing about it? Don't try to remove the thought and postpone any response.

P: I'll try.

Detached mindfulness and worry and rumination postponement experiments like this are used to contain the effects of perseveration and also to act as experiments to test beliefs about uncontrollability. Unhelpful coping strategies such as thought suppression and using alcohol to block out cognitions are also removed.

Later in treatment, once the individual is able to respond to the majority of intrusions with DM and a lack of sustained processing, the therapist works on threat monitoring. Here, positive beliefs about the process are challenged and the patient is asked to ban threat monitoring or to engage in alternative attentional strategies such as focusing on neutral and safety signals in the environment instead.

The final sessions consist of developing the therapy blueprint and working to reverse any residual avoidance of situations. Typically, the treatment of PTSD and other emotional disorders is implemented in eight to 12 sessions.

EFFECTIVENESS OF METACOGNITIVE THERAPY AND TECHNIQUES

Studies have set out to evaluate the effects of the full MCT treatment package and also the effects of individual techniques. One technique, attention training, was developed to increase flexible control over attention so that patients are better able to suspend conceptual processing. This technique has been tested in single-case experimental studies (Wells, 1990), case-replication series (Papageorgiou & Wells, 1998, 2000; Wells, White, & Carter, 1997), and in a controlled treatment study (Cavanagh & Franklin, 2000). Siegle, Ghinassi, and Thase (2007) used a modified version of the technique and found it to be superior to their treatment as usual (medication) in depressed patients. Analysis of a small subgroup of their patients revealed significant changes associated with attention training in neurobiological responses under exposure to emotional material.

Wells and Papageorgiou (1998) used a different form of attentional control during exposure of socially anxious patients to feared social situations. The attention regulation condition was superior to the equivalent length of exposure in reducing anxiety and negative beliefs. Fisher and Wells (2005) asked patients with obsessive–compulsive disorder to listen to a loop tape of their obsessional thoughts under a control (habituation) condition (exposure and response prevention) or a metacognitive condition. In the metacognitive condition, patients were asked to stop neutralizing to test specific metacognitive beliefs about the importance and power of their thoughts. The metacognitive condition was superior in reducing anxiety, negative beliefs, and the urge to neutralize.

Several studies have tested the effectiveness of the full MCT treatment protocol across disorders including generalized anxiety (Wells & King, 2006; Wells et al., 2010), major depression (Wells et al., 2009), social phobia (Wells & Papageorgiou, 2001), obsessive–compulsive disorder (Fisher & Wells, 2008; Simons, Schneider, & Herpertz-Dahlman, 2006), and posttraumatic stress disorder (Wells & Sembi, 2004; Wells et al., 2008). In each of these cases, MCT was associated with large treatment effects, and high standardized recovery rates of 60%–80% were achieved.

In three studies, MCT has been compared against cognitive–behavior therapy. Wells et al. (2010) showed that MCT was superior to applied relaxation in the treatment of generalized anxiety disorder.

Proctor, Walton, Lovell, and Wells (submitted) compared MCT with exposure therapy in the treatment of chronic PTSD. MCT was superior to exposure in measures of psychological distress and heart rate in response to reminders of the trauma. Nordahl (2009) examined the effects of a transdiagnostic version of MCT when compared with CBT in a naturalistic outpatient setting. The results showed that MCT was superior in reducing anxiety and worry and that both treatments were associated with similar improvements in depression.

In summary, these preliminary studies of metacognitive therapy suggest that it is a highly effective treatment for a range of psychological disorders. The intervention can be delivered in a small number of sessions (typically eight to 12) and the treatment effects appear stable over follow-up.

CONCLUSION

This chapter has described how metacognition has been applied and developed into a comprehensive approach to understanding and treating psychological disorder. This approach changes the focus of clinical intervention, moving it away from the predominant CBT emphasis on challenging the content of cognition to controlling styles of thinking and challenging the content of metacognition.

The development and testing of the metacognitive approach described here has been a 25-year journey and has depended on the development of new measures of metacognitive belief domains and metacognitive strategies. A large number of studies have affirmed important relationships between metacognition and symptoms of disorder. Moreover, elevated or biased metacognition is not simply a symptom of disorder but appears to be a causal factor, although further investigation into its causal status is required.

The metacognitive theory identifies specific domains of metacognitive beliefs and thought control strategies in the development of disorder. Dysfunction is linked closely with the control of thinking and choice of cognitive processing style. Perseveration of negative thinking and of threat-related processing is the primary cause of failures to down-regulate distressing emotions.

Metacognitive therapy has several optimistic features. First, initial indications are that treatment effects are large and consistent across a range of disorders, including those, such as GAD, that have been considered hard to treat. Second, treatment is proving to be efficient. In most cases, complete implementation is achieved in no more than 12 sessions (hours). Third, metacognitive therapy focuses on transdiagnostic processes and belief domains that can be identified in most and probably all psychological disorders. It therefore provides a potentially universal set of treatment techniques that can be applied across a range of disorders with less need to choose a treatment that is closely matched to a specific diagnosis. This might have benefits in treating complex comorbid presentations and problems that do not meet specific diagnostic criteria.

A large evidence base supports central aspects of the metacognitive theory and the next step is a continuation of treatment outcome trials to determine the effects of this treatment. Although CBT and MCT principally aim to produce changes at different levels, change in metacognition also appears to change primary level beliefs. Similarly, exposure methods, such as exposing patients to memories of trauma or obsessional thoughts, appear to change both metacognition and cognition. However, exciting initial findings suggest that it may be change at the metacognitive level that is the stronger overall predictor of symptom improvement and recovery.

REFERENCES

Amir, N., Cashman, L., & Foa, E. B. (1997). Strategies of thought control in obsessive–compulsive disorder. *Behavior Research and Therapy, 35,* 775–777.

Beck, A. T. (1976). *Cognitive therapy and the emotional disorders.* New York, NY: International Universities Press.

Bennett, H., & Wells, A. (2010). Metacognition, memory disorganization, and rumination in posttraumatic stress symptoms. *Journal of Anxiety Disorders, 24,* 318–325.

Borkovec, T. D., Robinson, E., Pruzinsky, T., & DePree, J. A. (1983). Preliminary exploration of worry: Some characteristics and processes. *Behavior Research and Therapy, 21,* 9–16.

Bryant, R., Moulds, M., & Guthrie, R. M. (2001). Cognitive strategies and the resolution of acute stress disorder. *Journal of Traumatic Stress, 14,* 213-219.

Butler, G., Wells, A., & Dewick, H. (1995). Differential effects of worry and imagery after exposure to a stressful stimulus: A pilot study. *Behavioral and Cognitive Psychotherapy, 23,* 45–56.

Cartwright-Hatton, S., & Wells, A. (1997). Beliefs about worry and intrusions: The metacognitions questionnaire and its correlates. *Journal of Anxiety Disorders, 11,* 279–296.

Cavanagh, M. J., & Franklin, J. (2000). *Attention training and hypochondriasis: Preliminary results of a controlled treatment trial.* Paper presented at the World Congress of Behavioral and Cognitive Therapies, Vancouver.

Coles, M. E., & Heimberg, R. G. (2005). Thought control strategies in generalized anxiety disorder. *Cognitive Therapy and Research, 29,* 47–56.

Ellis, A. (1962). *Reason and emotion in psychotherapy.* New York, NY: Lyle Stuart.

Fisher, P. L., & Wells, A. (2005). Experimental modification of beliefs in obsessive–compulsive disorder: A test of the metacognitive model. *Behavior Research and Therapy, 43,* 821–829.

Fisher, P. L., & Wells, A. (2008). Metacognitive therapy for obsessive–compulsive disorder: A case series. *Journal of Behavior Therapy and Experimental Psychiatry, 39,* 117–132.

Hermans, D., Martens, K., De Cort, K., Pieters, G., & Eelen, P. (2003). Reality monitoring and metacognitive beliefs related to cognitive confidence in obsessive–compulsive disorder. *Behavior Research and Therapy, 41,* 383–401.

Hertel, P. T. (1998). Relation between rumination and impaired memory in dysphoric moods. *Journal of Abnormal Psychology, 107,* 166–172.

Holeva, V., Tarrier, N., & Wells, A. (2001). Prevalence and predictors of acute PTSD following road traffic accidents: Thought control strategies and social support. *Behavior Therapy, 32,* 65–83.

Janeck, A. S., Calamari, J. E., Riemann, B. C., & Heffelfinger, S. K. (2003). Too much thinking about thinking? Metacognitive differences in obsessive–compulsive disorder. *Journal of Anxiety Disorders, 17,* 181–195.

Kabat-Zinn, J. (1994). *Mindfulness meditation for everyday life.* New York, NY: Hyperion.

Lobban, F., Haddock, G., Kinderman, P., & Wells, A. (2002). The role of metacognitive beliefs in auditory hallucinations. *Personality and Individual Differences, 32,* 1351–1363.

Lyubomirsky, S., & Nolen-Hoeksema, S. (1993). Self-perputuating properties of dysphoric rumination. *Journal of Personality and Social Psychology, 65,* 339–349.

Lyubomirsky, S., & Tkach, C. (2004). The consequences of dysphoric rumination. In C. Papageorgiou & A. Wells (Eds.). *Depressive rumination: Nature, theory and treatment* (pp. 21–41). Chichester, UK: John Wiley & Sons.

Morrison, A. P., & Wells, A. (2000). Thought control strategies in schizophrenia: A comparison with nonpatients. *Behavior Research and Therapy, 38,* 1205–1209.

Morrison, A. P., Wells, A., & Nothard, S. (2000). Cognitive factors in predisposition to auditory and visual hallucinations. *British Journal of Clinical Psychology, 39,* 67–78.

Myers, S., Fisher, P. L., & Wells, A. (2009). An empirical test of the metacognitive model of obsessive–compulsive symptoms: Fusion beliefs, beliefs about rituals and stop signals. *Journal of Anxiety Disorders, 23,* 436–442.

Nassif, Y. (1999). *Predictors of pathological worry.* Unpublished M.Phil. thesis, University of Manchester, UK.

Nolen-Hoeksema, S. (2000). The role of rumination in depressive disorders and mixed anxiety/depressive symptoms. *Journal of Abnormal Psychology, 109,* 504–511.

Nolen-Hoeksema, S., & Morrow, J. (1991). A prospective study of depression and posttraumatic stress symptoms after a natural disaster: The 1989 Loma Prieta earthquake. *Journal of Personality and Social Psychology, 61,* 115–121.

Nordahl, H. M. (2009). Effectiveness of brief metacognitive therapy versus cognitive–behavioral therapy in a general outpatient setting. *International Journal of Cognitive Therapy, 2,* 152–159.

Papageorgiou, C., & Wells, A. (1998). Effects of attention training in hypochondriasis: An experimental case series. *Psychological Medicine, 28,* 193–200.

Papageorgiou, C., & Wells, A. (2000). Treatment of recurrent major depression with attention training. *Cognitive and Behavioral Practice, 7,* 407–413.

Papageorgiou, C., & Wells, A. (2009). A prospective test of the metacognitive model of depression. *International Journal of Cognitive Therapy, 2,* 123–131.

Proctor, D., Walton, D. L., Lovell, K., & Wells, A. *A randomized trial of metacognitive therapy versus exposure therapy for posttraumatic stress disorder.* Manuscript submitted for publication.

Purdon, C. (1999). Thought suppression and psychopathology. *Behavior Research and Therapy, 37,* 1029–1054.

Rassin, E., Merckelbach, H., Muris, P., & Spaan, V. (1999). Thought–action fusion as a causal factor in the development of intrusions. *Behavior Research and Therapy, 37,* 231–237.

Reuven-Magril, O., Rosenman, M., Liberman, N., & Dar, R. (2009). Manipulating metacognitive beliefs about the difficulty to suppress scratching: Implications for obsessive–compulsive disorder. *International Journal of Cognitive Therapy, 2,* 143–151.

Reynolds, M., & Wells, A. (1999). The thought control questionnaire—Psychometric properties in a clinical sample, and relationships with PTSD and depression. *Psychological Medicine, 29,* 1089–1099.

Rosenthal, M. Z., Cukrowicz, K. C., Cheavens, J. S., & Lynch, T. R. (2006). Self-punishment as a regulation strategy in borderline personality disorder. *Journal of Personality Disorders, 20,* 232–246.

Roussis, P., & Wells, A. (2008). Psychological factors predicting stress symptoms: Metacognition, thought control and varieties of worry. *Anxiety, Stress and Coping, 21,* 213–225.

Sica, C., Steketee, G., Ghisi, M., Chiri, L. R., & Franceschini, S. (2007). Metacognitive beliefs and strategies predict worry, obsessive–compulsive symptoms and coping styles: A preliminary prospective study on an Italian nonclinical sample. *Clinical Psychology and Psychotherapy, 14,* 258–268.

Siegle, G. J., Ghinassi, F., & Thase, M. E. (2007). Neurobehavioral therapies in the 21st century: Summary of an emerging field and an extended example of cognitive control training for depression. *Cognitive Therapy and Research, 31,* 235–262.

Simons, M., Schneider, S., & Herpertz-Dahlmann, B. (2006). Metacognitive therapy versus exposure and response prevention for pediatric obsessive–compulsive disorder. *Psychotherapy and Psychosomatics, 75,* 257–264.

Solem, S., Haland, A. T., Vogel, P. A., Hansen, B., & Wells, A. (2009). Change in metacognitions predicts outcome in obsessive–compulsive disorder patients undergoing treatment with exposure and response prevention. *Behavior Research and Therapy, 47,* 301–307.

Spada, M., Caselli, G., & Wells, A. (2009). Metacognitions as a predictor of drinking status and level of alcohol use following CBT in problem drinkers: A prospective study. *Behavior Research and Therapy, 47,* 882–886.

Stirling, J., Barkus, E., & Lewis, S. (2007). Hallucination proneness, schizotypy and metacognition. *Behavior Research and Therapy, 45,* 1401–1408.

Teasdale, J. D., Segal, Z. V., Williams, J. M. G., Ridgeway, V. A., Soulsby, J. M., & Lau, M. A. (2000). Prevention of relapse/recurrence in major depression by mindfulness-based cognitive therapy. *Journal of Consulting and Clinical Psychology, 68,* 615–623.

Warda, G., & Bryant, R. A. (1998). Thought control strategies in acute stress disorder. *Behavior Research and Therapy, 36,* 1171–1175.

Wegner, D. M., Schneider, D. J., Carter, S. R., III, & White, T. L. (1987). Paradoxical effects of thought suppression. *Journal of Personality and Social Psychology, 53,* 5–13.

Wells, A. (1990). Panic disorder in association with relaxation induced anxiety: An attention training approach to treatment. *Behavior Therapy, 21,* 273–280.

Wells, A. (2000). *Emotional disorders and metacognition: Innovative cognitive therapy.* Chichester, UK: John Wiley & Sons.

Wells, A. (2009). *Metacognitive therapy for anxiety and depression.* New York, NY: Guilford Press.

Wells, A., & Carter, K. (2009). Maladaptive thought control strategies in generalized anxiety disorder, major depressive disorder, and nonpatient groups and relationships with trait anxiety. *International Journal of Cognitive Therapy, 2,* 224–234.

Wells, A., & Cartwright-Hatton, S. (2004). A short form of the metacognitions questionnaire: Properties of the MCQ 30. *Behavior Research and Therapy, 42,* 385–396.

Wells, A., & Davies, M. (1994). The thought control questionnaire: A measure of individual differences in the control of unwanted thought. *Behavior Research and Therapy, 32,* 871–878.

Wells, A., Fisher, P. L., Myers, S., Wheatley, J., Patel, T., & Brewin, C. (2009). Metacognitive therapy in recurrent and persistent depression: A multiple-baseline study of a new treatment. *Cognitive Therapy and Research, 33,* 291–300.

Wells, A., & King, P. (2006). Metacognitive therapy for generalized anxiety disorder: An open trial. *Journal of Behavior Therapy and Experimental Psychiatry, 37,* 206–212.

Wells, A., & Matthews, G. (1994). *Attention and emotion: A clinical perspective.* Hove, UK: Lawrence Erlbaum Associates.

Wells, A., & Matthews, G. (1996). Modeling cognition in emotional disorder: The S-REF model. *Behavior Research and Therapy, 32,* 867–870.

Wells, A., & Papageorgiou, C. (1995). Worry and the incubation of intrusive images following stress. *Behavior Research and Therapy, 33,* 579–583.

Wells, A., & Papageorgiou, C. (1998). Relationships between worry, obsessive–compulsive symptoms, and metacognitive beliefs. *Behavior Research and Therapy, 39,* 899–913.

Wells, A., & Papageorgiou, C. (2001). Brief cognitive therapy for social phobia: A case series. *Behavior Research and Therapy, 39,* 713–720.

Wells, A., & Sembi, S. (2004). Metacognitive therapy for PTSD: A preliminary investigation of a new brief treatment. *Journal of Behavior Therapy and Experimental Psychiatry, 35*, 307–318.

Wells, A., Welford, M., Fraser, J., King, P., Mendel, E., Wisely, J., Knight, A., & Rees, D. (2008). Chronic PTSD treated with metacognitive therapy: An open trial. *Cognitive and Behavioral Practice, 15*, 85–92.

Wells, A., Welford, M., King, P., Papageorgiou, C., Wisely, J., & Mendel, E. (2010). A pilot randomized trial of metacognitive therapy vs. applied relaxation in the treatment of adults with generalized anxiety disorder. *Behavior Research and Therapy, 48*, 429–434.

Wells, A., White, J., & Carter, K. (1997). Attention training: Effects on anxiety and beliefs in panic and social phobia. *Clinical Psychology and Psychotherapy, 4*, 226–232.

York, D., Borkovec, T. D., Vasey, M., & Stern, R. (1987). Effects of worry and somatic anxiety induction on thoughts, emotion and physiological activity. *Behavior Research and Therapy, 25*, 523–526.

Author Index

Chai, A.L., 131
Chaiken, S., 33, 44, 48, 114, 309
Chang, E.C., 186, 189, 190, 191, 289, 298
Chapin, J., 150
Chaponis, D.M., 162
Charman, S.D., 8
Chartrand, T., 130
Chartrand, T.L., 206, 235
Chase, S.K., 111
Chatman, J.A., 297
Cheavens, J.S., 329
Cheung, T.-S., 109
Chin, J., 317
Chiri, L.R., 330
Chiu, C.-Y., 107, 110, 248
Cho, H., 189
Choi, H., 294
Choi, H.S., 293, 298
Choi, I., 110
Christensen, C.J., 165
Christensen-Szalanski, J.J.J., 182
Christiansen, S., 129
Chuang, Y.C., 28, 29
Cialdini, R.B., 149
Clark, J.K., 33, 85, 86
Clark, L.F., 133
Clark, M.S., 275
Clarkson, J., 88, 311
Clarkson, J.J., 26, 35, 53, 54, 309, 310, 316
Claypool, H.M., 93
Clore, G.L., 48, 90, 186, 189, 190, 192, 194, 200,
    201, 202, 203, 206, 207, 208, 209,
    210, 211, 213, 228, 232, 306, C12
Coats, S., 83
Cohen, J.B., 308
Cole, J., 272, 274
Coles, M.E., 328
Collins, N.L., 263, 264, 268, 271, 275
Colvin, C.R., 267
Conklin, L., 272
Conner, M., 33
Conway, M., 142, 144
Cooley, C.H., 165
Cooper, J., 48
Cooper, M.L., 111
Corneille, O., 88, 89, 247, 248, 249
Corson, Y., 200
Cosmides, L., 166
Costermans, J., 7, 70
Cowey, A., 163, 164
Crandall, C.S., 246
Crelia, R.A., 83
Crichter, C.R., 265
Critcher, C.R., 73
Crites, S.L., Jr., 25, 30
Crocker, J., 111, 112
Cross, D., 169
Cuddy, A.J.C., 250, 251, 254

Cukrowicz, K.C., 329
Cunningham, W.A., 253

D

D'Agostino, P.R., 191, 192
Dahme, B., 129
Damasio, A., 200
Damisch, L., 91
Dar, R., 330
Dardenne, B., 8
Darke, P.R., 317
Darley, J.M., 245, 246
Dasgupta, N., 248
Davidson, A.R., 29
Davies, M., 328
Davis, M.H., 269, 272, 273, 274
Dawson, J.F., 296
De Cort, K., 329
De Dreu, C.K.W., 208, 295
de Ridder, D., 128
de Waal, F.B.M., 165, 167
de Wit, J., 128
DeHart, T., 106
deLiver, Y., 33
DeMarree, K.G., 15, 24, 51, 54, 85, 94, 103,
    104, 105, 106, 107, 108, 109, 113,
    190, 225, 227, 228, 236, 266, 292
Demoulin, S., 243, 246, 249, 255
DePaulo, B.M., 266
DePree, J.A., 328
Derryberry, D., 200
DeSensi, V.L., 33
DeSteno, D., 85, 94, 232, 306
Deutsch, R., 92
Devine, P.G., 29, 82, 88, 90, 93, 112, 244
Dewick, H., 328
Dhar, R., 313
Díaz, D., 52
Dibble, T., 127
Dickinson, E., 142
Dienes, B., 194
Dierselhuis, J., 112, 113
Dietz, J., 246
Dijksterhuis, A., 78, 108, 186, 206, 255
Dodge, T., 31
Dolan, R.J., 15
Dolderman, D., 270, 273
Dove, N., 91
Dovidio, J.F., 244, 255
Dubow, E.F., 132, 133
Duckworth, A.L., 121
Dudley, K., 271
Duff, K., 86
Dumont, M., 88, 89
Dunlosky, J., 2, 3, 7, 103, 141, 159, 170, 264
Dunn, D.S., 31, 56
Dunn, E., 207

Subject Index

A

Ability to think, ease and, 193
Academic contingencies, self-worth and, 111–112
Accessibility, 236
  attitude certainty and, 25
  attitude importance and, 29
  attitude strength and, 23
  declarative information and, 193
  influence of affective coherence on the value of, 211–212
  influence of on consumer behavior, 306–307
  judgments and, 181–184
  self-strength and, 106–107
Accessibility–diagnosticity model, 306–307
Accessible attitudes, signaling the value of, 202–203
Accuracy
  assessments of confidence and, 74
  discrimination and, 65
  experiential inputs and, 70–71
  group mental models and, 284–285
  overconfidence and, 65–66
Action, team reflexivity and, 296
Actional phase of goal pursuit, 124
Actual attitude-relevant knowledge, attitude certainty and, 25
Actual prior elaboration, attitude certainty and, 25
Adjustment of responses, 90–91
Advertisement framing, 314
Advice networks, 287
Affect
  effect of on creativity, 208–209
  effect of on implicit–explicit attitude relations, 204
  effect of on perceptual styles, 207–208
  effect of on processing styles vs. message relevant thoughts, 205
  effect of on stereotyping, 205–207
  effect on metacognitive judgments about goals, 204–205
  impact of on metacognition, 4, 12
  value conferred on accessible thoughts by, 202–203
Affective coherence
  epistemic consequences of, 210–211
  influence of on the value of accessible mental content, 211–212
  vs. affective incoherence, 201–202
Affective feedback, cognition and, 199–200

Affective reactions
  attitude importance and, 29
  mere exposure effect and, 191–192
Aggregate performances, 64
Altruism, comparisons between human and nonhuman primates, 167
Ambivalence
  antecedents of, 31–32
  attitude strength and, 23
  implicit attitudinal, 55
  objective vs. metacognitive indices of, 33–34
Analytical processes vs. heuristics, 164
Anger, impact of on judgment, 51–52
Animal psychology, metacognition and, 11
Animals
  consciousness and metacognition in, 163–164
  directed forgetting in, 161–162
  knowledge of others in, 165–167
  self- and other-awareness in, 165
Arguments, bodily responses serving as, 223
Arm posture
  affective coherence and, 211
  as cue to persuasion, 221
  elaboration likelihood and, 228–229
Arousal, cognitive processing and, 200
Assessments of confidence. See Confidence
Attitude certainty, 309–310
  antecedents of, 24–26
  consequences of, 27
  persuasion appraisals and, 310–312
  regulatory depletion and, 53–54
  resistance appraisals and, 310
Attitude change, 142–143
  impact of on attitude representation, 54–55
  perceived target of primary thoughts and, 47–48
  perceptions of secondary cognitions and, 52–53
Attitude clarity, 308
Attitude confidence, 5, 8
Attitude correctness, 308
Attitude expression, attitude importance and, 28
Attitude importance
  antecedents, 27–28
  consequences of, 28–29
  object importance and, 36–37
  self-worth and, 111–112
Attitude judgments, metacognitive dimensionality and, 35–36
Attitude representation, impact of attitude change on, 54–55